Crimes against Nature

Crimes against Nature

Squatters, Poachers, Thieves, and the Hidden History of American Conservation

Karl Jacoby

UNIVERSITY OF CALIFORNIA PRESS
Berkeley · Los Angeles · London

University of California Press
Berkeley and Los Angeles, California

University of California Press, Ltd.
London, England

© 2001 by Karl Jacoby

Library of Congress Cataloging-in-Publication Data
Jacoby, Karl, 1965–
    Crimes against nature : squatters, poachers,
    thieves, and the hidden history of American
    conservation / Karl Jacoby.
        p.   cm.
    Includes bibliographical references and index.
    ISBN 0-520-22027-7 (cloth : alk. paper)
    1. National parks and reserves—Social as-
pects—United States.   2. Nature conservation—Social aspects—United States.   3. National parks and
reserves—History—United States.   I. Title.

SB486.S65 J34 2001
333.78'0973—dc21

                                00-061521

Manufactured in the United States of America

08   07   06   05   04   03   02   01

10   9   8   7   6   5   4   3   2   1

The paper used in this publication meets the minimum requirements of ANSI/NISO Z39 0.48-1992
(R 1997) (Permanence of Paper).

To my father and in memory of my mother

In this actual world there is then not much point in counter-posing or restating the great abstractions of Man and Nature. We have mixed our labour with the earth, our forces with its forces too deeply to be able to draw back and separate either out.
Raymond Williams, 1980

The people of this country, as a rule, do not and will not look upon a man who violates the game and fish laws…as they would upon any other criminal.
Ohio Fish Commission, 1881

The forest history of our most valuable woodlands would be a record of the doings of timber-thieves.
Franklin B. Hough, 1878

Contents

Illustrations

Tables

Preface

The volume that you hold in your hands is not the book I planned to write when I began this project some eight years ago. Initially, I set out to describe the rise of a peculiar American enthusiasm: the wilderness cult that, beginning in the latter half of the nineteenth century, propelled growing numbers of America's new urban classes into the United States countryside. What better way to approach this subject, I reasoned, than to focus on the history of American parks, which in the closing decades of the nineteenth century underwent an abrupt transformation from obscure locales to popular tourist destinations?

No sooner did I venture into the archives, however, than this tidy research project began to fall apart. Instead of encountering accounts of proper bourgeois tourists communing with nature, I found myself stumbling over documents about poachers, squatters, arsonists, and other outlaws. At first, I tried to ignore these materials. After all, most of the histories of the American conservation movement I had consulted suggested that, unlike in modern-day parks in Africa, Asia, or Latin America, where confrontations between conservation officials and local inhabitants remain commonplace, such conflicts have been rare in the United States. They supposedly occurred only in distant Third World countries, not in a developed nation like the United States.[1]

Yet the more familiar I became with the documents produced during the early years of American conservation, the harder it became for me to maintain the view that poaching, squatting, timber theft, and other crimes had been minor phenomena in the United States. The violations were too widespread, those arrested too broad a cross section of rural society. All my initial evidence from the archives suggested that in the late nineteenth century, American conservationists considered controlling those they viewed as criminals to be one of the most pressing issues their movement faced.

Unsettled by these findings, I abandoned my previous focus and redirected my efforts toward the struggles over law enforcement that surrounded conservation's early years. With little other research to guide me, I was unsure of what I might find. But as I assembled the available shards of evidence, it quickly became apparent that what had at first seemed like a few isolated and minor rural crimes had in fact posed a considerable challenge to the nascent American conservation movement.

Revising the history of conservation to include this new perspective would eventually thrust me into some of the murkiest, least-explored nooks and crannies of American rural life—terrain that social historians and environmental historians alike had long avoided. Even though social history has long emphasized the import of revisioning the past "from below," its chief focus has remained the development of the urban working class. The result has been a lopsided understanding of the past, one rich in studies of unions, workplaces, saloons, streets, and tenements, but considerably thinner on rural life during this same time. As the historian Hal Barron once observed, "The majority of people in nineteenth-century America lived in rural communities, but most of the social history of nineteenth-century America is not about them."[2]

In contrast, environmental history—like social history, one of the "new histories" that emerged amid the ferment of the 1960s—has remained rooted in the American countryside. The field's practitioners, however, have often found it difficult to step outside the "man/nature" dichotomy prevalent in much of environmental thinking and analyze the complexity within each of these categories. As a result, they have frequently overlooked crimes such as poaching, timber stealing, and arson, which speak not only to the human relationship with nature but also to the distribution of power within human society—of the ability of some groups of humans to legitimize certain environmental practices and to criminalize others.[3]

Because of such lacunas, one of my ultimate goals for this study is for it to help erase the current boundaries between social and environmental history. We need a social history that is attuned to rural life and the ecological relationships that shape and sustain it. And we need an environmental history that takes into account social difference and the distribution of power within human society. We need, in short, a history that regards humans and nature not as two distinct entities but as interlocking parts of a single, dynamic whole.

I never would have completed this project without the help of many other people. My first thanks go to the two individuals who codirected the dissertation on which this manuscript was based, Howard Lamar and Bill Cronon. Howard oversaw my study with the good humor and enthusiasm that are his trademarks. I could not have hoped for a more supportive or open-minded mentor; indeed, Howard is the model of everything I hope to become as a historian. This book started as a research paper that I wrote in Bill's environmental history seminar during my first semester in graduate school. Through the intervening years and the intervening miles, Bill has helped me to refine my thinking and to express myself more gracefully. I am truly grateful for his patience, perseverance, and countless insights into the historian's craft. I was never fortunate enough to take a class with John Faragher, but I am very glad that he agreed to join my dissertation committee upon his arrival at Yale. Johnny has proven to be an exceptionally acute reader, and he and his wife, Michelle, have grown to be dear friends. Ann Fabian, Robert Johnston, and Karen Merrill did me the favor of reading large portions of my work, and I have benefited enormously from their trenchant comments. Lastly, special thanks to James Scott, who not only provided an invaluable intellectual resource through his Agrarian Studies Program but generously read my entire manuscript, providing many key connections drawn from his encyclopedic knowledge of rural life.

One of the best things about studying at Yale is coming into contact with a wonderfully talented group of fellow graduate students. I learned a great deal from everyone I met in New Haven, but there are a few people who deserve special mention for their help and inspiration: Sam Truett, Ben Johnson, Aaron Frith, Leslie Butler, Bob Bonner, Rob Campbell, Ray Craib, Greg Grandin, Patricia Mathews, J. C. Mutchler, Michelle Nickerson, Jenny Price, Jackie Robinson, Dave Saunders, K. Sivaramakrishnan, and Steven Stoll. All have become good friends as well as intellectual companions.

My colleagues at Oberlin College and at Brown University provided me with the stimulation and support necessary to turn a raw dissertation into a finished book manuscript. Clayton Koppes and Lynda Payne at

Oberlin were particularly generous with their insights into environmental history and the history of science, while Barbara Blodgett, Geoffrey Blodgett, Antoinette Charfauros McDaniel, Marcia Colish, Ron Di-Cenzo, Mike Fisher, Leigh Gibson, Gary Kornblith, Wendy Kozol, Carol Lasser, Len Smith, Bob Soucy, Benson Tong, Steve Volk, and Jim Walsh all made small-town Ohio a much more enjoyable place to be. At Brown, Howard Chudacoff served as my sage guide to the federal manuscript census, while Nancy Jacobs and Jack Thomas were useful sounding boards for all matters relating to environmental history. I owe another, deeper debt of thanks to Howard and Jack, who, along with Jim Patterson, first inspired me to pursue advanced research in American history. Thanks, too, to my new colleagues at Brown, who have made my return to campus a most pleasant one: Engin Akarli, Phil Benedict, Mari Jo Buhle, Doug Cope, Richard Davis, Carolyn Dean, Tom Gleason, Mary Gluck, Jerry Grieder, Sumit Guha, Tim Harris, Pat Herlihy, Carl Kaestle, David Kertzer, Jim McClain, Charles Neu, Amy Remensnyder, Joan Richards, Ken Sacks, Tom Skidmore, Kerry Smith, and Gordon Wood.

As a fledgling academic, I had the good fortune to be introduced to Monica McCormick at the University of California Press. Monica not only has endured all my questions and delays with considerable goodwill, she even has been generous enough to pretend that I still understand the publishing process despite having left it almost a decade ago. My readers at the University of California Press, Steve Aron and Louis Warren, both aided me tremendously during the rewriting process, saving me from far more errors of judgment than I care to recall. This is not the first time that Louis has helped me out. Much of what I know about environmental history I learned when I was his teaching assistant at Yale, and his path-breaking work on poaching, *The Hunter's Game,* was the first to identify many of the issues that I grapple with in these pages. Dear friend and big-city agent Gordon Kato deciphered my contract for me and, through his timely phone calls and care packages, helped keep me tethered to the world outside academia. Portions of chapter 3 appeared previously in *Environmental History.* I am grateful to Hal Rothman, the journal's editor, for the permission to reprint this material here.

Research can be a trying experience, but during my adventures in the archives I was fortunate enough to meet many supportive librarians and scholars. I offer special notes of appreciation to Jim Meehan and Gerry Pepper of the Adirondack Museum; Charles Brumley, who knows more about Adirondack guides than anyone; the friendly staffs at the Hamilton, Essex, and Franklin County courthouses; James Folts at the New

York State Archives; John Keating of the New York State Department of Environmental Conservation; Lee Whittlesey and Bev Whitman of Yellowstone National Park; the staff at the Grand Canyon National Park museum; Jim Muhn, who took time from his position at the Bureau of Land Management to guide me through the intricacies of federal record keeping; and George Miles of Yale's Beinecke Library. I also want to thank Mark Spence, David Godshalk, and Ray Rast, all of whom were generous enough to share their excellent studies of Yellowstone National Park with me.

Financial support as well as emotional support is vital to the completion of any manuscript. I am grateful to Richard Franke, the MacKinnon family, the Mellon Foundation, and Yale's Agrarian Studies Program for their timely grants.

My mother, to whom I have dedicated this book, passed away shortly after I completed the dissertation on which *Crimes against Nature* is based, but not before we were able to take a memorable trip together to upstate New York. I was researching the Adirondacks, she our family's genealogy, and to our mutual surprise, our projects converged. One branch of my mother's family, the McFarlands, came from a village on the southern fringes of the Adirondack Mountains. Once apprised of this fact, I noticed people with the McFarland surname appearing in the lists of those arrested for poaching deer in the forest reserve in the 1880s and 1890s.[4] This finding embarrassed Mom, but as my readers will soon see, I have come to take a much more measured assessment of such lawbreaking.

The loss of my mother has made me treasure the remainder of my family all the more. Dad, Dean: thank you for all your years of love and support. *Un abrazo de mucho cariño.* Thanks, too, to my new family, Grace and William Lee, who, along with their children Victor, Leonard, and Michelle, have been welcoming in-laws and enthusiastic cheerleaders in all my academic endeavors. The most recent addition to our family, Jason Jacoby Lee, arrived just as this book was reaching its final stages. His presence has proven to be a great distraction from the long hours in the archives and in front of the computer that writing a history book entails, but I would not have it any other way. As for you, Marie, what can I say? You have been a continual inspiration, not only as a writer but also as the person who makes life worth living.

The Hidden History of American Conservation

Of all the decisions any society must make, perhaps the most fundamental ones concern the natural world, for it is upon earth's biota—its plants, animals, waters, and other living substances—that all human existence ultimately depends. Different cultures have approached this challenge in different ways, each trying to match their needs for natural resources with their vision of a just and well-ordered society. The following pages explore how one culture—that of the United States—attempted to balance these often competing objectives during a key moment in its environmental history: the late nineteenth and early twentieth centuries, when in an unprecedented outburst of legislation known as the conservation movement, American lawmakers radically redefined what constituted legitimate uses of the environment. Over just a few short decades, state and federal governments issued a flurry of new laws concerning the hunting of game, the cutting of trees, the setting of fires, and countless other activities affecting the natural landscape. We live amid the legacy of these years, which has bequeathed to us many of the institutions—parks, forest reserves, game laws, wardens, rangers, and the like—that even today govern our relations with the natural world.

Among historians, the conservation movement is best known for what Richard Grove once termed its "pantheon of conservationist prophets": celebrated figures such as George Perkins Marsh, John Muir, Gifford Pinchot, and Theodore Roosevelt, who collectively laid the political and intellectual groundwork of the movement.[1] Although scholars have traditionally paid far less attention to the responses of ordinary folk to conservation, the movement's arrival sparked sharp social unrest in many of the areas most directly affected by conservation policies.[2] In New York's Adirondack Mountains, for instance, state officials frequently found their pathbreaking plans for protecting the region's forest and wildlife frustrated by local resistance, which ranged from surreptitious violations of game laws to arson and even murder. In Yellowstone National Park, a formative territory for the development of federal conservation, unauthorized intrusions into the park by whites and Indians alike reached such pronounced levels by the 1880s that administrators were forced to call in the U.S. Army to restore some semblance of order. At many of the national forests created around the turn of the century, the situation was much the same: squatting, timber stealing, and illegal hunting all proved endemic.

Law and its antithesis—lawlessness—are therefore the twin axes around which the history of conservation revolves. To achieve its vision of a rational, state-managed landscape, conservation erected a comprehensive new body of rules governing the use of the environment.[3] But to create new laws also meant to create new crimes. For many rural communities, the most notable feature of conservation was the transformation of previously acceptable practices into illegal acts: hunting or fishing redefined as poaching, foraging as trespassing, the setting of fires as arson, and the cutting of trees as timber theft. In many cases, country people reacted to this criminalization of their customary activities with hostility. Indeed, in numerous regions affected by conservation, there arose a phenomenon that might best be termed "environmental banditry," in which violations of environmental regulations were tolerated, and sometimes even supported, by members of the local rural society.[4]

To the conservationists who found themselves arrayed against such outlaws, the most common explanation for these illegal acts was that they were manifestations of the "malice" and "criminal instincts" of a backward rural populace. Lawbreaking, after all, was deviance; those who engage in unauthorized uses of the environment must therefore be "depredators" and "degenerates."[5] Historians have largely concurred with such judgments, viewing rural folk as operating with a flawed understanding of the natural world. "The appreciation of wilderness…appeared first in the minds of sophisticated Americans living in the more civilized East," writes Roderick Nash. "Lumbermen, miners, and professional hunters...lived too close to nature to appreciate it for other than its economic value as raw material."[6] Framed in this manner, the history of conservation has become little more than a triumphant tale of the unfolding of an ever-more enlightened attitude toward the environment. The result has been a narrative drained of all moral complexity, its actors neatly compartmentalized into crusading heroes (conservationists) and small-minded, selfish villains (conservation's opponents).[7]

In the chapters that follow, I have tried to reveal the complicated reality that the prevailing narrative about conservation has long obscured. In particular, I seek to recreate the moral universe that shaped local transgressions of conservation laws, enabling us to glimpse the pattern of beliefs, practices, and traditions that governed how ordinary rural folk interacted with the environment—a pattern that, paraphrasing E.P. Thompson, I have come to term the participants' *moral ecology*. This moral ecology evolved in counterpoint to the elite discourse about conservation, a folk tradition that often critiqued official conservation policies, occasionally borrowed from them, and at other times even influenced them. Most of all, though, this moral ecology offers a vision of nature "from the bottom up," one that frequently demonstrates a strikingly different sense of what nature is and how it should be used.[8]

If historians have largely shied away from such an approach, no doubt part of the reason has been the difficulty involved in illuminating the rural demimonde that nurtured these alternative visions of nature. In contrast with the voluminous body of documents generated by conservationists—sporting journals for the well-to-do such as *Forest and Stream*, travel accounts written by upper-class tourists, and the countless letters, memos, reports, and regulations produced by the government agencies charged with executing conservation policy—there exist few sources produced directly by those who engaged in acts such as poaching or timber stealing. These were by definition clandestine activities—deeds that one tried to commit surreptitiously, leaving behind as few traces as possible. Moreover, even if some of those who engaged in violations of conservation law had been willing to leave a written, potentially incriminating record of their actions and beliefs, it is not clear they could have done so. Literacy was by no means universal in the American rural periphery during the nineteenth century, especially among the Indians and poor whites who made up the largest portion of the transgressors of the laws relating to conservation.[9] While many of the regions affected by conservation possessed a rich oral tradition

commenting on the conflicts between country people and state authorities, this tradition, because of its sensitive nature, was typically shared
only among confidants. Shielded from outsiders, it seldom made the
leap to written form. The little that did was often recorded years after
the events in question, once passions had cooled and memories had
faded.[10]

Nonetheless, the "unofficial mind" of rural Americans need not be
completely closed to us. There exist a number of often-overlooked
sources that can transmit to us the voices of rural folk: court cases, the
few newspapers from rural areas, the scattered personal accounts
written by country people. These materials can be supplemented by an
informed rereading of the documents produced by conservationists. By
turning these documents on their heads, as it were, it is possible to peer
beyond the main text (the attitudes of conservationists toward nature)
to glimpse the counternarrative embedded within (the attitudes of country people toward nature). This counternarrative is perhaps clearest in
the various state investigations into lawbreaking in rural areas, which
were often little more than official attempts to eavesdrop on the "hidden transcripts" of the local populace.[11]

We can also reach a fuller understanding of the encounter between
rural folk and American conservation by situating the history of conservation within its larger context. Involving as it does factors such as
the rise of the state, the development of natural resources, and conflict
with Indian peoples, the story of conservation may at first glance seem
to fit neatly into the larger tale of the American West, the region where
many early conservation projects were located. Yet, as notable as the
ties between conservation and the West surely are, there were also
significant conservation experiments east of the Mississippi, perhaps
the most important being the forest preserve located in New York's
Adirondack Mountains. Furthermore, it is important to recognize that
conservation was a transnational phenomenon. The movement's roots
can be traced back to Europe, where scientific forestry first developed
in the 1700s. Several leading American conservationists, such as Gifford Pinchot (who would head the Forest Service under Theodore Roosevelt and help to found the Yale Forestry School in 1900), went to Europe for their training. Others, such as Bernhard Fernow (the chief of
the federal government's Division of Forestry from 1886 to 1898) and
Carl Schenk (the founder of the first forestry school in the United
States), were direct imports from the famed forestry academies of Prussia and Saxony.[12]

Along with many other early American conservationists, these figures held up the environmental measures already in place in Europe as a model to be emulated in the United States. As the Prussian-trained Fernow argued in 1887: "The forestry problem presents itself for consideration to every nation, and nation after nation has recognized its importance and acted accordingly.... All the European governments have properly equipped forest administrations. Russia, the English colonies in Asia and Australia, Japan, and even China have recognized the necessity for action in this direction, and have acted. The United States alone, among the civilized nations, has as yet failed to perceive the wide bearing which a proper forestry policy has on the material and moral development of a country."[13]

Such calls to emulate European conservation were not, however, without their perils. The parks and forest preserves of the Old World might appear to be peaceful pastoral landscapes, but such institutions in fact precipitated numerous episodes of social unrest. Among the most notable of these were the actions of the armed poachers known as "Blacks," who roamed Great Britain's woods during the 1720s, to which we might add the "Captain Swing" riots that flared up in England in 1830–31 and the "War of the Demoiselles" staged by French peasants in the Pyrenees against the National Forest Code of 1827.[14]

Less spectacular, but no less significant, were the everyday manifestations of resistance that European peasants made to the new state regulation of the environment. During the 1800s, for instance, Prussia, the birthplace of modern forestry, experienced a steep rise in forest crime as peasants engaged in widespread poaching of wood, fodder, and game from lands that had once been under village oversight but which were now state controlled.[15] This bitter clash attracted, in turn, the attention of a young Karl Marx, whose first published articles included a defense of Prussian peasants prosecuted for the theft of wood.[16] After European colonialism exported conservation to Africa, Australia, India, and much of the rest of the world, it inevitably spawned new conflicts in these regions as it crossed swords with preexisting ways of interacting with the environment.[17]

What made conservation so controversial in such locales was the fact that it ultimately concerned far more than mere questions of ecology—how many trees to cut and where, what animals to hunt and for how long. In redefining the rules governing the use of the environment, conservation also addressed how the interlocking human and natural communities of a given society were to be organized. Conservationists might present themselves as dispassionate technicians concerned only with solving neatly confined scientific problems, but their proposals possessed profound social implications. With their emphasis on the need for expert oversight of the environment, conservationists endeavored to concentrate the decision-making power of the state in the hands of a corps of highly trained technocrats. Conservation thus extended far beyond natural resource policy, not only setting the pattern for other Progressive Era reforms but also heralding the rise of the modern administrative state.[18]

It is much harder, of course, to understand the country people who contested conservation measures. The writings of such folk are diffuse, their actions frequently cloaked in secrecy. But understanding how these individuals imagined their world and their place in it is no less important—for, like their opponents, these folk were trying to determine what kind of society they should inhabit and how this society should relate to the natural world around it. That many of the inhabitants of the American countryside came up with a distinctly different set of answers to these questions than did conservationists underscores the divergent visions of the economic and social order—and ultimately of nature itself—that competed with one another in the United States at the turn of the century. Recent scholarship has done a great deal toward illuminating these alternative perspectives by recapturing such voices of radical agrarian dissent as the National Farmers' Alliance, the Populists, and the Knights of Labor. Yet we know far less about that vast substratum of society composed of the inarticulate and the unorganized, among whose ranks some of the most marginal inhabitants of the rural United States could be found. Examining the struggles that took place over conservation in the American countryside offers a rare opportunity to place such previously overlooked folk in the forefront of our historical analysis, allowing us to better understand their lives and the landscapes they called home.

It is to these landscapes that we now direct our attention. In order to root my discussion of conservation in the specifics of time and place, I have selected three geographically bounded locales around which to weave the narrative that follows. The first is New York's Adirondack Mountains, site of one of the first attempts at applied conservation in the United States and a telling illustration of conservation's evolution in the east. The second is Yellowstone National Park in northwestern Wyoming, where the federal government took its initial, faltering steps toward implementing a conservation policy in the late nineteenth century.

The third is Arizona's Grand Canyon, which, in addition to being one of the earliest forest reserves, provides an especially valuable example of the impact that conservation had on American Indians, the community most affected by the arrival of conservation. Although there is some temporal overlap between case studies, each advances the narrative chronologically. The section on the Adirondacks discusses the rise of the conservation movement in the post–Civil War era; Yellowstone covers the span from the 1870s to the 1910s; and the Grand Canyon brings the story further into the twentieth century.

Telling the tale of conservation in this manner inevitably produces a narrative at odds with standard discussions of the movement. National policy makers fade into the background, while local actors seize the foreground. Certain highly charged issues, such as poaching, arson, and squatting, reappear at several key points. Although the result may be a less tidy narrative, it is also, I believe, a more honest one—a narrative that reflects the vastness and complexity of a world that, until now, has remained lost in shadow.[19]

PART I

Forest

The Adirondacks

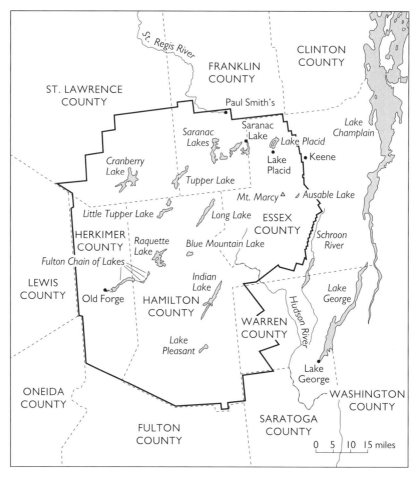

Map 1. Adirondack Park, 1892

CHAPTER I

The Re-creation of Nature

When the New York City minister Joel Headley collapsed in 1849 from a nervous breakdown, he was ordered by his doctor to try what was, for a mid-nineteenth-century American, a most unusual undertaking: a vacation. As a destination for this peculiar endeavor, Headley selected the little-known Adirondack Mountains, a series of heavily forested peaks that crowned New York's northernmost counties. The Adirondacks' clean air, tranquil scenery, and remoteness from urban centers, Headley reasoned, would provide a tonic for his shattered nerves. Although at the time upstate New York was better known for its hardscrabble farms and lumber camps than for its recreational opportunities, the frazzled minister had made a wise decision. A few weeks in the "vast wilderness" of the Adirondacks rejuvenated Headley's constitution, leading him to pronounce the region's "glorious woods" the perfect antidote to the stresses of urban life. "I could hardly believe," he exulted, "I was in the same State of which New York was the emporium, whose myriad spires pierced the heavens."[1]

These cries of amazement were echoed by several other nineteenth-century observers, all of whom, like Headley, puzzled over the existence of extensive forestlands only two hundred miles from New York City. As one anonymous author put it in 1865, "One might expect to find it [the Adirondacks], or its fellow, somewhere in the far-off West, that mythical land which is every day drawing nearer to us,—but not on the Eastern side of the continent,—not in the Northern States, and assuredly not in the great State of New York, where its existence to-day is little short of a miracle." Many of those who sought to explain this "miracle" could only conclude that nature must have set forth unalterable laws preventing the development of the region. Following a visit to the Adirondacks in 1880, for example, A. Judd Northrop posited that "the law—not of New York but of Nature—has set apart this wilderness irrevocably to purposes which find little recognition in the marts of trade and the necessities of a population struggling for subsistence." According to such logic, the Adirondacks' harsh topography and sandy soils represented nature's way of enforcing its rule over the area. "This region has always been and will always be under the dominion of Nature," remarked Nathaniel Sylvester in 1877. "Its altitude renders its climate cold and forbidding, while its rugged surface and light soil render it in a great measure unfit for cultivation."[2]

Headley, Northrup, and Sylvester were just a few of the many voices joining in a debate that had by the mid-nineteenth century assumed an increasingly prominent place in American culture. The discussion's core questions were deceptively simple: What is nature? And how does it shape human affairs? But at perhaps no time in United States history were the answers the source of so much intellectual ferment. The Anglo-American world of the nineteenth century witnessed an efflorescence of works seeking to plumb nature's inner workings: the transcendentalism of Ralph Waldo Emerson and Henry David Thoreau; the American school of landscape painting, developed by artists such as Thomas Cole, Frederic Church, and Thomas Moran; the rise of natural history, heralded by the founding of journals such as *Nature* and the *American Naturalist* in the 1860s; the eugenics movement led by Herbert Spencer and Francis Galton; even the popular books of Henry William Herbert, who in the 1830s immigrated to the United States, renamed himself Frank Forester, and introduced the American elite to the upper-class European tradition of sports hunting. Nature, as the historian David Arnold has aptly observed, was "one of the principal metaphors of the age, the prism through which all manner of ideas and ideals were brilliantly refracted."[3]

Yet in spite of this shared subject matter, the era's nature studies did not always cohere in any clear or consistent manner. At the same time that A. Judd Northrup might reason that the law of nature protected the Adirondacks from development, a far more pessimistic—and influential—series of natural laws was being promulgated by a onetime schoolteacher, newspaper editor, and diplomat from Vermont named

George Perkins Marsh, in a work entitled *Man and Nature*. The American minister to Turkey during the Crimean War and later to the Kingdom of Italy from 1861 to 1882, Marsh had long been puzzled by the environmental conditions he encountered during his postings abroad. How was it, he wondered, that the Mediterranean basin—a landscape that at the time of the Roman Empire had been lush and fertile—was now so barren? The connection between the region's current aridity and the decline of its preeminent civilization, Marsh concluded, was not coincidental. In *Man and Nature,* published in 1864 and "the most extensive work on land management to appear in the English-speaking world up to that date," Marsh ventured a compelling new explanation of the region's past: the Romans and the other peoples of the Mediterranean basin had doomed themselves by recklessly cutting the forests surrounding their settlements. Deprived of the leaves that had once regulated temperatures and of the roots that had once anchored topsoil, the region's deforested lands had experienced erosion, desertification, and ultimately, ecological collapse. Human folly had, in short, "changed millions of square miles, in the fairest and most fertile regions of the Old World, into the barrenest deserts."[4]

Marsh's grim scenario both explained the past (making Marsh arguably the first environmental historian) and predicted the future. The same environmental catastrophe that had devastated the Old World, Marsh asserted, now threatened to spread to the United States and the rest of the globe, with potentially apocalyptic consequences: "The earth is fast becoming an unfit home for its noblest inhabitant, and another era of equal human crime and human improvidence...would reduce it to such a condition of impoverished productiveness, of shattered surface, of climatic excess, as to threaten the depravation, barbarism, and perhaps even extinction of the species."[5]

One spot that Marsh singled out as being in urgent need of protection was Headley's beloved Adirondack Mountains, which contained the headwaters of several of New York's most important rivers, including the Hudson. While the region's remoteness had so far prevented its development, Marsh feared that with each passing year settlers and lumber companies were whittling away more of the Adirondacks woodlands. Left unchecked, Marsh maintained, such actions would place New York in grave danger: "Nature threw up those mountains and clothed them with lofty woods, that they might serve as a reservoir to supply with perennial waters the thousand rivers and rills that are fed by the rains and snows of the Adirondacks, and as a screen for the fertile plains of the central counties against the chilling blasts of the north wind." Deforestation in the Adirondacks would dry up New York's principal rivers, causing "irreparable injury" to the mills and transportation networks that depended upon them.[6]

To prevent such disaster, Marsh proposed a novel solution: New York should "declare the remaining forest [of the Adirondacks] the inalienable property of the commonwealth" and become the forest's administrator and protector. The current land policy in the United States—converting the public domain into private property—was, in Marsh's opinion, a grave mistake. "It is a great misfortune to the American Union that the State Governments have so generally disposed of their original domain to private citizens," he wrote. "It is vain to expect that legislation can do anything effectual to arrest the progress of the evil [of the destruction of woodlands]...except so far as the state is still the proprietor of extensive forests."[7]

Marsh advocated this radical shift in policy for two reasons. The first was a distrust of the inhabitants of the countryside, particularly the small-scale farmers who made up the bulk of the residents in places like the Adirondacks. In keeping with his Whig political beliefs, Marsh viewed these members of the lower classes as lacking the foresight and expertise necessary to be wise stewards of the natural world. *Man and Nature* thus included pointed critiques of "the improvident habits of the backwoodsman" and "the slovenly husbandry of the border settler." Second, Marsh believed that in a world dominated by the search for short-term private gain, only the state had the long-term public interest at heart. Marsh pointed approvingly to Europe, where coalescing national bureaucracies had established state forest academies, carefully regulated forests, and the new science of silviculture. "The literature of the forest, which in England and America has not yet become sufficiently extensive to be known as a special branch of authorship, counts its thousands of volumes in Germany, Italy, and France," he noted. If the Old World's ecological disasters had something to teach the United States, then so did its recent successes in uniting science and the state.[8]

Undergirding *Man and Nature*'s critique of backwoodsmen and its appeals to the lessons of European forestry lay a powerful new vision of nature. In Marsh's view, the natural world existed in a state of balance and stability. "Nature, left undisturbed, so fashions her territory as to give it almost unchanging permanence of form, outline, and proportion," he wrote in a passage anticipating twentieth-century ecology's concept of the self-perpetuating climax community. Within this static model, environmental decline came about almost exclusively from human intrusions. "Man is everywhere a disturbing agent," declared Marsh. "Wherever he plants his foot, the harmonies of nature are turned to discords." (So strongly did Marsh embrace this point, in fact, that he originally proposed titling his work *Man the Disturber of Nature's Harmonies*.)[9]

Man and Nature's unique perspective on the natural world not only made the book a best-seller, it established the text as, in Lewis Mumford's words, the "fountainhead of the conservation movement." Indeed, Marsh's work originated the degradation discourse that would dominate conservationist narratives about landscape change for the next century. The discourse's essential ingredients were a natural world that was stable, predictable, and manageable; a rural populace engaged in "unwise" environmental practices that would have potentially catastrophic ecological consequences if left unchecked; and an interventionist state armed with technical and administrative expertise. Combined with one another, these narrative elements formed the central story of conservation—a tale that prophesied imminent ecological doom, unless natural resources were removed from local control and placed in the hands of scientifically trained governmental managers.[10]

With its dire predictions of what deforestation in the Adirondacks would mean for the state's waterways, *Man and Nature* attracted immediate attention in New York. As early as 1872, the state legislature, prodded by an unlikely alliance of sports hunters who wanted to preserve New York's northern counties as a permanent hunting and camping ground, and industrialists concerned about maintaining an adequate flow of water for the region's mills and canals, formed a committee to look into the feasibility of adopting Marsh's recommendation to establish a park in the Adirondacks. The following year, the committee issued a report concluding "that the protection of a great portion of that forest from wanton destruction is absolutely and immediately required" and calling for the creation of a "timber reserve and preserve" in the Adirondacks. While the committee members drew much of their discussion directly from Marsh, they appended to his argument an additional point of their own: "[Besides] these weighty considerations of political economy, there are social and moral reasons which render the preservation of the forest advisable.... The boating, tramping, hunting and fishing expedition afford that physical training which modern Americans—of the Eastern

States—stand sadly in need of, and which we must hope will, with the fashionable young men of the period, yet replace the vicious, enervating, debasing pleasures of the cities.... To foster and promote these natural and healthful exercises among the young men of the State, it is necessary in some measure to preserve the game, and the forest which affords it shelter."[11]

This linkage of an environmental crisis (deforestation and water loss) and a social crisis (urbanism and the undermining of traditional models of masculinity) captures the modern and antimodern impulses that, in uneasy combination, lay at the core of the nascent conservation movement. On the one hand, conservation, with its emphasis on using the power of science and the state to rationally manage natural resources, represented a quintessentially modern approach toward the environment. On the other, conservation frequently invoked the Romantic search for authentic experience, in which nature was offered as the antidote to an increasingly industrial, "overcivilized" existence. These two positions did not necessarily contradict one another; it was possible to be an industrialist during the week and a sports hunter on the weekend (as many of the leading proponents of conservation in fact were). But tensions between the two perspectives would, at times, prove difficult to reconcile. As a result, conservation never traveled a simple trajectory. Although its central beliefs remained remarkably consistent—an emphasis on professionalization, on governmental ownership and management of the environment, and on the inherently stable and predictable character of the natural world—conservation charted an irregular orbit around these positions, as first one force than another exerted its gravitational pull on the movement.[12]

In the case of the Adirondacks, recommendations for state action languished until 1883, when a severe drought gripped New York and the water level in its principal rivers, the Hudson, the Mohawk, and the Black, dipped to alarmingly low levels. Concerned with the effect this decline could have on the Erie Canal and downstream mills, the New York Chamber of Commerce and the New York Board of Trade added their weight to calls for state management of the Adirondacks. In response, the New York legislature passed a measure in 1883 forbidding any further sales of state lands in the Adirondacks. Over the next few years, state control over the region ratcheted steadily upward. In 1885, the legislature reorganized its holdings in the Adirondacks into a forest preserve, overseen by a forest commission. In 1892, lawmakers consolidated these efforts into the three-million-acre Adirondack Park, made up of both the Forest Preserve and adjoining private lands. An 1894 constitutional amendment stating that the Forest Preserve was to be "forever kept as wild forest lands" helped ensure the permanence of the state's experiment in conservation. The legislature also took steps to tighten the region's game laws during this period. In 1886, hunters were limited to three deer per year, a number that in 1895 dropped to two per year. Other legislation restricted such traditional hunting practices as jacking (hunting at night using a bright light to blind deer) and hounding (hunting with dogs). In fishing, the use of nets was outlawed in favor of the rod and reel. To enforce this new array of rules, the state created a "forest police," empowered "without warrant, [to] arrest any person found upon the forest preserve violating any provisions of the act creating the commission."[13]

The ultimate result of these actions was to turn the Adirondacks of the mid-1880s into the most advanced experiment in conservation in the United States. Many of the people who would later lead the national conservation movement—Franklin Hough, Bernhard Fernow, Teddy Roosevelt, and Gifford Pinchot among them—gained their first insights into the challenges of American forestry in the woods of northern New York.[14] Moreover, for conservationists, New York's Forest Preserve established a viable new role for the state: active supervisor of the environment. Inspired by the example of the Adirondacks, several prominent conservationist organizations, including both the American Forestry Congress and the federal Division of Forestry (which at the time possessed only an educational function, since there were no national forests to administer), held up New York's Forest Preserve—"this first attempt at making a reality of forest preservation"—as a model to be emulated nationwide.[15] Congress eventually accepted such suggestions in 1891 when it passed the Forest Reserve Act. But during conservation's early years, it was New York's unprecedented undertaking in the Adirondacks that set the pace for the rest of the nation.[16] "Here [in the Adirondacks], then, for the first time on the American continent, had the idea of State forestry, management of State lands on forestry principles, taken shape," observed Fernow in his 1911 textbook, *A Brief History of Forestry.* "A new doctrine of State functions had gained the day."[17]

One point, however, was frequently obscured amid such celebrations: the consequences that the coming of conservation would have for the approximately 16,000 people already living in the Adirondacks.[18] On those rare occasions when New York authorities pondered the impact that their new policies would have on these people, they generally believed that the residents of the Adirondacks—a "scanty population which…struggles to compel the inhospitable soil to yield it a miserable existence"—would welcome the benefits that were sure to follow increased state supervision of the environment.[19] The region, after all, was not a flourishing one. It had already experienced considerable out-migration, as many families, tiring of trying to wrest a living from the Adirondacks' cold climate and poor soils, headed for more fertile lands elsewhere. As early as 1825, the town of Lake Pleasant in Hamilton County had experienced a 30 percent decline in population, and by 1860 the town of Morehouse, also in Hamilton County, had dwindled from 250 people to just four families. This widespread depopulation had turned the Adirondacks landscape into an artifact of what might be termed the "de-frontier" process. Noted the Forest Commission in 1885, "The traveler through this region is struck by a certain peculiarity, and that is, the constant recurrence of deserted homesteads; in many cases he will encounter whole villages, abandoned and going rapidly to decay as if struck by a blight."[20]

Given such conditions, officials assumed that the region's residents would readily embrace conservation. "The little settlements already existing in the region are not incompatible with the project [of a park]," concluded the 1873 report of the Commissioners of State Parks. Recognizing the money to be made from the increased tourism that an Adirondacks park would attract, the inhabitants of the region would, the commissioners predicted, "take a direct interest in the welfare of the park" and "would voluntarily protect the game and timber from unlawful destruction."[21]

There was a grain of truth to this hypothesis. When the Forest Commission dispatched agents in 1885 to interview local inhabitants about their reactions to the newly created Forest Preserve, it found many residents ignorant of the specifics of the reserve but in agreement with the larger project of protecting the Adirondacks' forests. "I have lived here forty-five years, being a hunter and passing a large portion of my time in the woods," declared one local. "The woods must be taken care of if they want any left worth calling a forest. I am in favor of the best plan." Offered another: "We depend on the woods and the attractions of the place for our living, and don't want to see either destroyed or marred." "People through this valley are very much in favor of the work of the Forest Commission," added a resident of Keene Valley in Essex County. "We need the protection, as the woods are our one source of income."[22]

Despite this promising start, however, relations between conservationists and Adirondackers quickly soured. Following their first patrols, the Forest Commission's newly appointed foresters reported "gross infractions" of the state's new game, timber, and fire laws. Noting the frequent hostility the foresters encountered whenever they tried to arrest those responsible for such crimes, the New York Fisheries Commission concluded that "in the whole Adirondack region...the utmost lawlessness prevail[s]." Contemporary newspaper accounts added to the sense of crisis. In 1889, for example, the *New York Times* published a string of articles bearing such lurid headlines as "Pirates of the Forest," "Stealing Is Their Trade," and "Useless Forestry Laws" that depicted violations of the state's conservation code as common throughout the Adirondacks. As such accounts multiplied, many conservationists began to fear that their celebrated new plans for the region were on the verge of being swept away by a wave of inexplicable popular disorder.[23]

Perhaps in no nation are agrarian fantasies as complex and contradictory as in the United States. Nineteenth-century discussions of the Adirondacks, for instance, pivoted on two countervailing agrarian tropes. The first, which might be called the pastoral, stressed the simplicity and abundance of rural life. "An easy life is theirs," remarked Headley upon encountering some settlers at Raquette Lake: "No taxes to pay— no purchases to make—and during most of the year, fish and deer and moose ready to come almost at their call." William Murray—whose popular 1869 book, *Adventures in the Wilderness: or, Camp-Life in the Adirondacks,* brought a stream of tourists to the region—offered a similar vision: "A more honest, cheerful, and patient class of men cannot be found the world over. Born and bred, as many of them were, in this wilderness, skilled in all the lore of woodcraft, handy with the [fishing] rod, superb at the paddle, modest in demeanor and speech, honest to a proverb, they deserve and receive the admiration of all who make their acquaintance....Uncontaminated with the vicious habits of civilized life, they are not unworthy of the magnificent surroundings amid which they dwell."

A second trope, which might be called the primitive, focused on the backwardness and privations of rural life. J. P. Lundy, who visited the Adirondacks in the 1870s, saw only the region's "hard and grinding poverty." The typical Adirondacker, Lundy reported, "looked upon all physical and mental superiority with aversion or disdain.... He trapped a little, and too often sold the pelts for whiskey and tobacco instead of procuring food for his hungry wife and children." "The present population [of the Adirondacks] is a sort of immovable sediment, a weedy sort of folk attached to the soil in a blind way," agreed Elizabeth Seelye. "[They] seem to strive only to solve the problem of how to exist with the least possible amount of bodily exertion." In the South, a similar set of images would coalesce during this time into the figure of the shiftless hillbilly. While rural Northeasterners were never subjected to a stereotype as well-defined as this one, the parallel nonetheless existed. "There is in the backwoods of New England an element as untamed and brutal as in any of the new counties of the West and Southwest," proclaimed *Forest and Stream* in 1892. "It is these fellows...who are continually poaching on the lakes of northern New York."[24]

Of course, neither pole—the pastoral nor the primitive—offered more than a crude approximation of a place like the Adirondacks. Both interpretations, by seeking to capture the unchanging essence of rural life, missed the dynamism that had long marked the region and its shifting human populations. For much of the 1600s and 1700s, the Adirondacks had been a lightly inhabited border zone fought over by the Iroquois to the south and Huron and Algonquin to the north. Bands from these nations sometimes hunted for moose and beaver in the Adirondacks, but because of the risk of attack and the short growing season, they rarely established permanent villages. Warfare under these circumstances functioned as a sort of crude conservation policy, limiting the ability of native peoples to exploit the region's resources for any extended period of time.[25]

Once the power of the Iroquois was broken in the aftermath of the American Revolution, a variety of newcomers drifted into the area: Yankees from Vermont and the more southerly parts of New York, and French Canadians from the north. Preceding these pioneers were Indian settlers, many of them refugees from tribes such as the Penobscot (an eastern Abenaki people originally from Maine) and the St. Francis (a western Abenaki group originally from Vermont and southern Canada) displaced from homelands farther east. As the settler Harvey Moody recalled in 1860, a number of Native American families were already well established in the Adirondacks when he arrived in the region as a young boy: "When I fust come to the S'nac [Lake Saranac] with father, there was nobody else about there but Injins. I used to meet 'm on the lakes fishin' in their bark canoes, and trappin' about the streams, and huntin' everywheres."[26]

TABLE I. OCCUPATIONS OF MALE AND
FEMALE RESIDENTS OF HAMILTON COUNTY,
AGE 18 AND OLDER, 1880

Male

Agriculture (farmer, hired hand)	564	(48.6%)
Timber industry ("worker in lumberwoods," shingle maker)	228	(19.6%)
Crafts (mason, boatbuilder, blacksmith, carpenter)	56	(4.8%)
Laborer (unspecified)	180	(15.5%)
Professions (minister, teacher, surveyor, clerk)	40	(3.4%)
Services (hotel keeper, guide, gamekeeper)	86	(7.4%)
Miscellaneous (pauper, hermit)	8	(.7%)
TOTAL	1,162	(100%)

Female

Homemaker ("keeping house," "keeping shanty")	731	(94.7%)
Professions (teacher, nurse)	14	(1.8%)
Domestic service (servant, hotel maid)	19	(2.5%)
Trades (glove maker, dressmaker)	8	(1.0%)
TOTAL	772	(100%)

SOURCE: 1880 Population Census, Manuscript Schedules, Hamilton County, New York, Roll 837, T9, Records of the Bureau of the Census, RG 29, National Archives.

Encroaching white settlers both feuded and intermarried with the Indian peoples they encountered in the Adirondacks.[27] By the time federal census takers arrived in the region in the mid-nineteenth century, New York–born whites had become the predominant group in the region, but there remained Indian families, wives, and husbands scattered throughout the communities of the central Adirondacks. The 1880 census, for example, records that Hamilton County—the only one of New York's northern counties located completely within the Adirondack Park—was home to eleven Indians, eight living at Indian Lake and three at Long Lake.[28] For whites and Indians alike, the most common occupation for men listed in the federal censuses of the 1800s was "farmer," while the activities of women were typically classified as "keeping house." (See Tables 1 and 2.) Neither category illuminated the diversity of economic life in the Adirondacks with much precision. The region's women undertook countless domestic chores, from gardening to gathering medicinal herbs to maintaining the networks of mutuality and

TABLE 2.   BIRTHPLACES OF RESIDENTS
OF HAMILTON COUNTY, 1880

New York		3,449	(87.8%)
Northeastern United States		129	(3.3%)
Connecticut	11		
Maine	4		
Massachusetts	16		
New Hampshire	9		
New Jersey	4		
Pennsylvania	12		
Rhode Island	3		
Vermont	70		
Southern/Western United States		5	(.1%)
Illinois	3		
South Carolina	1		
Virginia	1		
Canada		144	(3.7%)
Europe		200	(5.1%)
England	36		
France	12		
German States	44		
Holland	3		
Ireland	87		
Scotland	16		
Switzerland	2		
TOTAL		3,927	(100.0%)

SOURCE: 1880 Population Census, Manuscript Schedules, Hamilton County, New York, Roll 837, T9, Records of the Bureau of the Census, RG 29, National Archives

borrowing so vital to rural life at the time. Similarly, Adirondacks men relied on a number of activities to support their families, of which farming was, ironically, one of the less important, as the region's harsh climate and lack of transportation made the production of crops for market a risky undertaking. "There is no inducement for the settler to clear up more land than will furnish him with grass and vegetables for his two or three cattle and his family," explained Headley in 1875. "He can raise nothing for market, for the transportation out costs more than the article is worth." Because neither corn nor wheat grew well in the Adirondacks, the favored crop was potatoes ("Our food was mostly fish and potatoes then for a change we would have potatoes and fish," recalled one early inhabitant), occasionally supplemented by peas, rye, buckwheat, or oats. Crops were planted in late spring—the exact timing often determined by the phases of the moon—and fenced in to prevent the incursions of deer or the settlers' own livestock, which were allowed to roam loose in the surrounding forest.[29]

These same forests provided Adirondackers with much of their annual support. In spring and summer, men collected wild ginseng *(Panax trifolius)* for resale to outside traders, while their wives and children gathered medicinal herbs such as sweet fern *(Comptonia peregrina)* and the wild leeks *(Allium tricoccum),* cowslips *(Caltha palustris),* adder tongues *(Botrychium virginianum),* and berries that Adirondacks families used to supplement their diets. "When the berries came it was nothing but pick berries with mother and the children that were old enough to go," recalled Henry Conklin, an early resident of Herkimer County. In the fall, men—and, upon rare occasion, women—went into the woods in pursuit of deer, bear, or partridges. Younger boys occupied themselves closer to home by setting snares for smaller game like rabbits or woodchucks. All caught fish for their families' tables in the multitude of streams and ponds throughout the Adirondacks. In the winter months, local males ventured into the woods yet again, lacing on their snowshoes to collect valuable forest products such as spruce gum or wild furs. It was not unusual for Adirondacks men to be gone for a week or more on such expeditions, during which they usually camped in bark shanties that they erected wherever they happened to be at the time.[30]

The far-flung character of these undertakings reflected themselves in turn in local property rights. Although state officials in the 1880s charged Adirondackers with looking upon the forests as "a piece of 'commons,' or as a public crib where all may feed who choose," matters were more complex than this assessment implied. In keeping with the common-rights ideologies prevailing elsewhere in the rural United States at this time, locals did regard undeveloped lands, whether state or private, as open to hunting and foraging. Engaging in such activities on another's property "we would not call a trespass," admitted the Adirondacks resident Freeman Tyrrell in 1895. "I know I don't when they go on my lands."[31] These "rights in the woods," however, were hedged by numerous constraints. Inhabitants often considered certain features of the woods, such as game blinds, fish weirs, or traplines, to be—like homesteads or other "improved" areas—exclusive property. Interference with these could prompt violent confrontations, as happened in the late 1800s, when H. Dwight Grant and his

friends had an armed standoff with two brothers named Johnson over
the right to hunt on Fifth Lake.[32] More important, even those resources theoretically open to all were governed by certain conventions.
Adirondacks local David Merrill recalled some of the hunting traditions that prevailed in Franklin County during the late nineteenth century: "In the good old days we went deer hunting, primarily, to get
food for the household, and like the Indians we did not pay much attention to the game laws of which there were not very many at that
time. However there was a universal code that deer should not be disturbed while 'yarding,' or in the breeding season, and this applied to
game birds as well." Ellsworth Hayes of Lake Placid recollected learn-
ing a similar "law of the woods" from his grandfather, who told him,
"Never kill anything that you do not need." In the absence of laws governing such behavior, these customs sustained themselves through informal norms, enforced through community sanction.[33] Fellow residents might subject those perceived to be violating local practices to
everything from ostracization and ridicule—acts which in the region's
small, tight-knit villages could have serious consequences—to wrecked
boats, killed dogs, and physical assaults. Inhabitants also took measures to exclude those seen as nonmembers of the community from
gaining access to local resources, a phenomenon reflected in Adirondacks
folklore, which abounds with tales of chasing tourists, Indians, "half-
breed" French Canadians, and other interlopers off local forestlands.[34]

This common-rights ideology persisted in the Adirondacks despite
the changes that, in the years following the Civil War, pulled the region
with increasing force into the expanding national economy. Unlike
much of the rest of the American countryside, the economic modernization of the Adirondacks did not center on agriculture—the region remained too remote and its soil too thin to support intensive farming—
but rather on the forests themselves. By the 1860s, northern New York
had become home to an extensive forest industry composed of tanneries
(which used bark from the area's abundant hemlocks to cure hides) and
lumber operations (which regularly hired crews of local men to cut and
skid logs during the winter months). Although these companies purchased vast portions of the Adirondacks landscape after the Civil War,
they seldom tried to close their property to local hunting and foraging,
as such activities posed little threat to the spruce, pine, and hemlock
that the lumber companies sought. Moreover, these corporations seldom sought to exercise their property rights for very long. Typically,
they would cut the marketable timber; then, rather than holding the

lands for the decade or two required for a fresh crop of lumber to appear, they would abandon the property, which would eventually be claimed by the state for nonpayment of taxes. Although this practice would leave the region with a legacy of confusing land titles that would take years for the Forest Commission to sort out, the lumber companies' narrow exercise of their property rights also meant that their operations seldom encroached on the uses that Adirondackers had long made of the forest.[35]

Technological limitations posed an additional barrier to the Adirondacks timber industry in the immediate post–Civil War years. Today, the term "lumbering" may conjure up images of vast clear-cuts, but up until the late 1880s most timber operations in the Adirondacks logged on a selective basis. Because companies transported logs to saw mills via streams, only those trees located within a few miles of a waterway could be cut—and then only those species that floated well. Softwoods such as black spruce *(Abies nigra)* and white pine *(Pinus strobus)* were the lumberman's favorites, while hardwoods such as the sugar maple *(Acer saccharinum)*, red oak *(Quercus rubra)*, red beech *(Fagus ferruginea)*, and white birch *(Betula populifolia)*, all of which floated poorly, were rarely cut, except for local consumption. These circumstances ensured that only a limited number of the region's trees were felled. "The lumberman did not take more than eight trees to the acre, on an average," explained the Forest Commission in 1891.[36] "The phrase 'lumbered land' is a somewhat misleading one. It does not imply that such land is cleared, devastated, or even stripped of timber. The term is used, locally, to describe lands from which the 'soft wood' (spruce, hemlock, pine and tamarack—one or all) has been taken, leaving the hard wood (birch, cherry, maple, beech, etc.) standing. Generally there is so much of this hard wood left on a 'lumbered' tract that an inexperienced eye glancing over it would scarcely detect the work of an axe. The woodsmen expect to see such land covered with spruce again, large enough to be marketable, in about fifteen years."[37] In fact, Forest Commission records from 1897 indicate that for all the dire accounts of deforestation circulating at the time of the Forest Reserve's creation, most lands in the Adirondacks retained their tree cover, and many never felt the woodsman's ax.[38] (See Table 3.)

Lumbering nonetheless set in motion profound ecological changes in the Adirondacks. The opening up of the forest canopy that accompanied timber operations promoted what ecologists have come to term the edge effect: a transition zone between open land and woodland,

TABLE 3.   CLASSIFICATION OF LANDS
WITHIN ADIRONDACK PARK, 1897 (IN ACRES)

Cleared for agriculture		75,819	(2.5%)
Wild meadow		724	(>.1%)
Water		59,111	(2.0%)
"Wastelands"		22,424	(.7%)
Burned areas		18,220	(.6%)
"Denuded lands"		61,009	(2.0%)
Forested, soft timber removed		1,627,955	(54.2%)
Untouched forestlands		1,139,593	(37.9%)
	TOTAL	3,004,855	(100.0%)

SOURCE: New York Fisheries, Game, and Forest Commission, *Third Annual Report, 1897*, 269.

rich in grasses and young plants. Such conditions were ideal for deer, which thrive on disturbed habitats, and their numbers rose sharply in the Adirondacks during the nineteenth century. This increase led, in turn, to a decline in the moose. The dominant ungulate in the Adirondacks throughout the 1700s, the moose had all but disappeared by the 1860s. While many contemporary observers attributed the moose's demise to overhunting by local residents, this was not the only factor contributing to the plummeting moose population. Deer carry brain worm, a parasite that, while relatively benign to them, is fatal to moose. Thus, an increase in the deer population usually has negative repercussions for their larger cousins. As the numbers of moose declined—and as newly arriving settlers began to kill predator species such as wolves and mountain lions—the deer population in the Adirondacks continued to climb, transforming the whitetail into the region's leading game animal.[39]

This growth in the whitetail population had a significant impact on another forest industry taking shape in the Adirondacks in the 1860s: the tourist trade. Headley had been an anomaly when he visited the region in the 1849, but following the Civil War, members of a growing urban elite began to flock to the Adirondacks. Many of these visitors were what local residents called "sports"—well-to-do professional men who hoped to indulge in the masculine pastimes of hunting and fishing in one of the largest extant forests in the Northeast. These sports rarely ventured into the Adirondacks' woods without hiring local guides, whose job it was to conduct hunters to likely hunting spots, set up camp, and track deer and other game. Much to their delight, Adirondacks men discovered that at a time when laboring in a lumber camp usually earned only a dollar a day, tourists would pay a guide two or three times that much for a workday that was considerably shorter and less dangerous. Since sports often took meals at, or spent the night at, Adirondacks homes, tourism also gave local women an opportunity to bring their domestic skills as cooks and housekeepers into the marketplace. Indeed, some popular Adirondacks stopping places, such as "Mother Johnson's" and "Aunt Polly's," came to be identified with the female figures who ran them.[40]

For all its monetary benefits, however, tourism unleashed new pressures as well. The arrival of large numbers of sports placed increased demands on the Adirondacks' limited supply of fish and game, while the rise of the tourist industry created fresh class divisions in the region, with a few locals capitalizing on the trade to become large landowners and employers. Perhaps the most successful of these entrepreneurs was Apollos "Paul" Smith, a onetime trapper and guide. In 1852, at the suggestion of one of his clients, Smith built a small "hunter's retreat," where he and his wife could take in eight or ten sports as boarders. Bit by bit, Smith added to his holdings, until by the time of his death in 1912 he owned some thirty-five thousand acres and a four-story hotel overlooking lower St. Regis Lake that could accommodate a hundred guests. Smith's clientele included such members of the eastern upper classes as Gifford Pinchot, who as a child summered in the Adirondacks with his family in 1879, and a young Theodore Roosevelt, who stayed at Smith's when he made his first visit to the Adirondacks in 1871. Besides running a hotel and employing many of his neighbors to wait on his guests, Smith sold lots to wealthy vacationers who wanted to construct summer homes nearby. Although these homes were euphemistically called "camps" after the rough cabins occupied by the region's inhabitants, many became luxurious and exclusive estates. "The guide told me that in some of these 'camps' there was hot and cold water, and in one electric lights," remarked one visitor in 1898. "It all seemed to me like playing at roughing it." Even Smith, in his more candid moments, admitted his bewilderment at the odd business in which he found himself: "I tell you if there's a spot on the face of the earth where millionaires go to play at housekeeping in log cabins and tents as they do here, I have it yet to hear about."[41]

Such developments made the Adirondacks of the late nineteenth century a region that defied easy categorization. It was a place of abandoned farms and of grand new estates, where daily rhythms were set by commercial timber operations and by subsistence agriculture, by wage labor and by household chores, by summer tourism and by winter trapping, foraging, and lumber camps. Asked to state their occupations, many residents thought it best to respond by naming a variety of undertakings. Some, such as guiding, linked them to the emerging tourist economy; others, such as hunting and fishing, were holdovers from previous practices. William Helms of Long Lake, for example, described his occupation as "guiding, hunting and fishing, and anything that a man could turn his hand to in the woods." Seth Pierce phrased it much the same way: "My occupation is guiding, fishing and hunting, and once in a while I take my tools and go at carpenter work." These varied roles testify to the hybridity and unevenness that governed the capitalist transformation of the nineteenth-century American countryside. Seasonal work patterns in a place like the Adirondacks both directed the region's residents inward toward family subsistence and outward toward market production, generating a lifestyle that was neither completely subsistence- nor market-oriented but rather an improvised combination of the two. Already precarious, this arrangement would be subjected to new and profound stresses in the Adirondacks as state officials took their first steps in turning their conservation plans for the region into a reality.[42]

CHAPTER 2

Public Property and Private Parks

"The people, as a rule, know nothing of the existence of a Forest Commission." So reported one of the commission's agents following a special investigative tour of the Adirondacks in the summer of 1885, in a comment that portended the enormous challenges facing the region's newly appointed managers. It had been a relatively easy matter for officials in Albany to draw a "blue line" around some three million acres of state and private land in northern New York and to proclaim this space a park and forest preserve governed by a new series of environmental regulations. But landscapes do not magically reshape themselves in accordance with the desires expressed in legislation. Establishing a functioning conservation program would require not just new laws but new mechanisms of enforcement as well, for, as New York officials soon discovered, managing the ecology of the Adirondacks was possible only if one monitored the daily interactions of local residents with the natural world.[1]

To facilitate the expanded state supervision of the countryside that conservation required, the Forest Commission embarked upon a program of what the political scientist James Scott has termed "state simplification," in which officials standardized and rationalized local practices to make them more comprehensible—and ultimately more controllable—by government agencies.[2] Creating a simplified Adirondacks, however, was far from a simple process. The new agencies charged with overseeing the region's ecology often lacked basic knowledge about local conditions. Even data that one imagines to have been easily accessible to state officials had rarely been assembled in a manner convenient for a fledgling bureaucracy like the Forest Commission. One of the first tasks facing the commission, for instance, was simply figuring out what lands it was supposed to manage. Because the Adirondack Park was a patchwork of private and state lands, environmental regulations in the region varied considerably from one location to the next. While it was illegal to settle, farm, or cut trees on state property, for example, such activities remained permissible on private lands within the park.

Differentiating between state and private lands was therefore essential if the Forest Commission was to apply the state's conservation laws in the appropriate manner. Yet instead of organizing its property documents in one central place, New York had long left this task to each county, which kept track of its records in whichever way seemed to best fit local practice. As a result, simply to compile an accurate list of the lands in its domain, the Forest Commission had to spend almost fifteen years sorting through the often confusing and contradictory land titles and tax records filed with the six counties that had lands located within the Adirondack Park. Not until 1901 did the commission complete this project, releasing what the superintendent of state forests considered to be "the most important and valuable publication issued by the Department": a definitive, 367-page list of all "the 5,934 separate parcels of land which constitute the Forest Preserve."[3]

In addition to clarifying the title to its lands in the Forest Preserve, the Forest Commission also needed to locate each of its holdings—a task complicated by the lack of a standardized grid of lot lines in the region. Most of the Adirondacks had been surveyed only roughly, sometimes not since the 1700s. Furthermore, many parcels were bound by idiosyncratic limits, which, while they made sense to those on the ground, often confused state officials and other outsiders. One plot in Herkimer County, for example, was delineated at one corner by "a large rock marked (+)"; another by "a soft maple tree at the end of Brown's Tract road marked 13 1/4 miles from Moose River." A 737-acre parcel of public land in Hamilton County began at the northwest corner of a farm owned by one Charles Fisher and then proceeded in a northwest direction until it reached the shore of "Mud or Gilmour's Lake." From here it continued north along the shore of the lake until reaching "a hemlock tree marked for a corner." It then went south along a roadway until touching upon Charles Fisher's farm again, at which point it traced an eccentric arc marked by a birch tree, a beech tree, and two township lines.[4]

Those not familiar with local geography often found it tedious and time consuming to chart the unusual boundaries of such plots. As Verplanck Colvin, the state official who headed the Adirondack Survey throughout the 1880s, observed, the "old reference points" mentioned in property documents frequently eluded his survey team. "While there are numerous references to 'a stake' or a 'heap of stones,' it has been found by experience in the field that the stakes have in most places entirely decayed and disappeared and the 'heap' of stones are generally quite indistinguishable from other stones, scattered throughout the woods." Because of such conditions, it was, "extremely difficult in all, and impossible in many cases, to establish the exact boundaries of the various tracts and subdivisions [of the park]." In 1896, Forest Commission officials admitted that even after a decade they had yet to find and mark all the boundaries in the region: "It should be understood that the lot lines which are so distinctly shown on our Adirondack map are not always so apparent in the forest itself, where, at the best, they can be traced only by the occasional faint 'blaze,' made in most cases fifty, and perhaps ninety years ago,—marks discernible only by those experienced in this peculiar woodcraft. In fact, the boundaries of the 160 or 200-acre lots in some townships never existed except on the map of some early surveyor who, having surveyed the outer lines, contented himself with making a 'paper allotment,' and doing nothing further in the way of surveying and marking these interior lines on the ground itself." While these conditions rarely interfered with local residents' uses of the forests, they often placed the Forest Commission in the awkward position of being unable to locate, let alone manage, its holdings.[5]

To counter such obstacles, the Forest Commission embarked on one of the essential practices of state simplification: the creation of a new, more detailed map of the region to be supervised. A cartographic representation of the Adirondack Park, the commission reasoned, would condense the information necessary for its conservation policies into a single page, thus providing a handy synoptic overview of the region and facilitating many of the chores associated with administration: "Ever since the organization of this Commission the necessity of a map which would show correctly the allotments of the various townships in the Great Forest of Northern New York has been felt, both in our office business and in our field work.... The Wardens, Inspectors and Foresters have been greatly impeded in their work by the lack of some accurate diagram which would show on one sheet the complete allotment of that territory. The Commission has accordingly directed that a map be compiled from the records of the various State offices.... It will be of great value in the routine work of this Bureau, in the preparation of forest statistics, in the purchase of lands, and in the final situation of the Park lines." In 1893, the commission released a *Map of the Adirondack Forest and Adjoining Territory Compiled from Official Maps and Field Notes on File in the State Departments at Albany*. Updated every few years, it detailed the location not only of the lands in the Forest Preserve and the outer boundary of the park (or "blue line") but also of ranger camps, fire observation stations, waterways, and paths; it even specified the composition of the park's woodlands, including information, for example, on how susceptible certain stands were to fire.[6]

Besides making the Adirondacks more legible to outside agencies like the Forest Commission, such maps also played an important role in the region's reorganization. The Forest Commission's official maps documented the agency's idealized conception of the Adirondacks under conservation as a tidy grid of property units and forest types. At the same time, the agency neglected to record local uses of these same woodlands—the locations of traplines and hunting shanties, of areas frequently used for hunting, fishing, or gathering wild plants, of favorite spots for cutting firewood or building supplies, and so on—that might cloud the state control that the Forest Commission sought to achieve. For these reasons, many inhabitants viewed the agency's mapping efforts as a threatening first step toward erasing all local claims to the forest. When asked by surveyors for information on the location of local lands within the Forest Preserve, therefore, residents frequently responded by feigning ignorance or giving intentionally misleading responses. As investigators for the Forest Commission fumed in 1895, "Few persons of those examined have appeared to know of the exact locations or bounds of State lands in any township." Other locals, as soon as the survey left their vicinity, burned, cut down, or otherwise destroyed the blazed trees and other monuments that surveyors had erected to indicate boundaries—so frequently, in fact, that the New York legislature in 1888 increased its penalties for anyone who "willfully or maliciously remove[s] any monuments of stone, wood or other durable material, erected for the purpose of designating the corner, or any other point, in the boundary of any lot or tract of land."[7]

By destroying monuments, which in turn obscured the location of the state's landholdings, locals hoped to preserve their access to the resources on nearby public woodlands. Indeed, as one exasperated warden noted, those arrested for trespassing on state lands often defended their activities by pointing to the state's lack of borderlines, "boldly ask[ing,] 'Where is your line?' and 'Why is it not marked?' " "The absence of lines, or plainly marked boundaries," claimed the commission in 1890, "is often the occasion of an unintentional trespass; but, more often, the pretext for a willful one. The establishment of new lines, and the re-marking of old ones, has the effect of lessening the number of trespasses by removing the pretext under which they may be committed."[8]

Of all the issues associated with the state's efforts to delineate its territory in the Adirondacks, by far the most volatile concerned the location of local homesteads. Throughout the nineteenth century, Adirondackers had tended to establish homes and farms on any available plot of land, often neglecting, because of the costs and difficulties involved, to obtain any title to their holdings. In place of a system of property rights that flowed from the state downward, such folk substituted a property system based on usufruct rights—rights based on use and occupation, in which lands that were unused were unneeded and therefore open to settlement by others. This "homestead ethic," which derived its authority from the republican belief that the ownership of land was crucial to one's political and economic independence, had been workable when the state was a remote presence. But after the arrival of conservation in 1885, many settlers suddenly found themselves at risk of occupying the wrong space on the Forest Commission's new map and being recategorized as squatters.[9]

By 1891, the Forest Commission's chief warden, Samuel Garmon, had identified squatting on state lands as one of his most pressing concerns.[10] Subsequent reports from the Forest Commission bewailed "the occupation of land in the Forest Preserve…[as] one of the most perplexing and complicated questions with which this Commission has to deal." With the boundaries of so much of the Adirondacks in question, it was difficult even to determine the exact scope of the problem. Official tallies varied widely, with the total number of illegal dwellings ranging from ninety-eight to more than nine hundred. Squatters also came from a surprising variety of backgrounds. While many of those dwelling on state land were longtime inhabitants of the region ("farmers who have occupied the premises as homes for over thirty, and, in many instances, forty years"), other squatters were wealthy tourists who had built vacation homes on plots purchased from Adirondacks locals.[11] Consequently, in the words of the Forest Commission, "these occupancies range all the way from the most primitive shanty to costly and beautiful summer homes." Since many of the wealthy summer home owners were politically well connected and difficult to dislodge, the commission initially focused its attention on the poorer class of squatters. The shanty of someone from this class, argued the commissioners in 1897, was "apt to be an unsightly thing, marring the beauty of some charming spot. Its owner, too often, is not a desirable neighbor. His abode is not only an eyesore, it is too often surrounded with a litter of old tin cans, fish scales, offal, hair and hides, with some howling cur tied to a tree." But the Forest Commission soon discovered that ejecting the owners of such "eyesores" was not as easy as expected, for attempting to do so risked sparking violent confrontations with the people affected. "While these people have no legal rights to their homes," noted *Forest and Stream*, "the removing of them is likely to engender a spirit of resentment and revenge which would lead to the burning of forests and the destruction of fish and game."[12]

In the face of such dilemmas, the Forest Commission adopted a policy of benign neglect for much of the nineteenth century, limiting new settlements but doing little to oust longtime squatters. Not until the early 1900s did the commission begin to push more aggressively to reclaim control of its lands. In 1901, for example, the state issued ejection notices to a large number of residents of the Raquette Lake area. Many squatters, however, refused to leave their homes. After several delays, the commission finally dispatched foresters to tear down and burn the offending structures. In November of 1905, District Game Protector John B. Burnham and fifteen men went into Raquette Lake with orders to destroy some fifty houses on state lands, only to be met by angry locals: "threats of violence to the state officers if property was harmed by them were freely given out at the village, and it was expected that there would be trouble," noted a reporter for the *New York Times*. Residents tried to counter the state's attempt to eject them by emphasizing the public nature of the park as well as their lengthy residence in the area. "[The squatters] offer as a defense that the Adirondack forest park was created at the expense of and for the use and enjoyment of the people of the State, and that they, as citizens, are entitled to such use as they now make and always have made of it." While the Forest Commission did end up expelling a significant portion of the squatters after 1910, some settlers continued to resist their removal, with the result that property rights in certain portions of the Adirondack Park, including Raquette Lake, remain contested even today.[13]

To project its authority in these and other tense situations, the Forest Commission relied on its "forest police," or foresters. Adopting a policy that *Forest and Stream* summarized as "set[ting] the guides to catch the guides," the commissioners selected its "policemen of the woods" from among the "experienced woodsmen" of the Adirondacks. State authorities concluded early on that hiring Adirondackers to patrol the region was unavoidable, for catching lawbreakers in the vastness of the northern forest required a number of skills seldom found in outsiders: a familiarity with the best hunting and fishing spots; a knowledge of some of the tricks poachers might use to kill game illegally, such as creating salt licks or planting turnip patches to attract deer; an ability to cover an enormous territory, much of it unmarked by trails, and to camp out for days at a time; and an understanding of how to track both humans and animals for long distances, while leaving few tracks oneself. Moreover, foresters had to be able to accomplish these duties "under cover of nightfall, for it is at that time that nearly all violations occur with fish pirates and pot-hunters."[14]

In 1886, the Forest Commission hired an initial force of 25 foresters. Although this number dipped to 15 the following year because of budget shortages, the next several decades witnessed a steady upward progression in the force. In 1892, the number reached 20; in 1895, 38; in 1902, 50; in 1910, 90; and in 1912, 125. Despite such growth, there were never enough foresters to satisfy many conservationists. Outraged letters to the editor complaining of continued violations of the game and timber laws were standard features of such leading conservation journals as *Forest and Stream* and *Garden and Forest* throughout the late nineteenth and early twentieth centuries. The Adirondack Park was so large and the lawbreaking by local people so incessant that some letter writers suggested that only by radically expanding the force to 400 or even 1,000 foresters could the state prevent violations of the conservation code.[15]

To be sure, the vast territories that foresters had to cover often hindered their abilities to enforce the forestry laws. Isaac Kenwell, the fish and game protector based in Indian Lake during the 1890s, for example, was assigned to a district that included not only much of Hamilton County but portions of neighboring Essex County as well. During the winter of 1893–94, Kenwell reported to his superiors that he had traveled an average of 481 miles per month (his high being 738 miles in January 1894). Because of the lack of trails, much of this patrolling was slow, laborious work. "There is a large part of my district so situated that it is impossible to get from one section to another very quickly," explained Kenwell. "Large parts have to be travelled on foot." Even in later years, when the number of wardens was larger, the distances to be covered were still quite extensive. In 1908, A.P. Williams, a writer for *Field and Stream,* accompanied the protector Emery Kinsman on one of his routine patrols. The two spent thirteen days in the woods, covering a circuit of some 150 miles. According to calculations published by *Forest and Stream* in 1911, despite the expansions in the force, the average forester in the Adirondacks still had to oversee a territory of approximately 200 square miles.[16]

But there were other factors beyond a simple calculus of square miles per forester that inhibited the enforcement of state forestry laws in the Adirondacks. While the hiring of local people as foresters provided the Forest Commission with individuals who possessed a detailed knowledge of the Adirondacks forest, it also meant that foresters possessed strong allegiances to the rest of Adirondacks society and, as a result, often felt the tug of local loyalties. Since it was impossible for the Forest Commission to monitor every facet of their daily behavior, foresters often had considerable latitude in deciding how to enforce—and *not* enforce—the forestry laws. As *Forest and Stream* charged in 1885: "The constables being appointed from the country round and knowing many of the guides, it is a generally understood thing that if no venison is in sight there will be no search for any. As soon, therefore, as a deer is killed the carcass is buried or hidden in the underbrush, and if a constable should pay a visit to the camp he and the campers have so many pleasant topics of conversation that it seems a pity to introduce unpleasant ones."[17] Fourteen years later, the situation, according to the journal, remained much the same: "The game protectors realized the hardships which a thorough and effective execution of their powers would entail, and in most cases it was more than their positions were worth to buck up against public sentiment and antagonize the community in which they lived by a strict enforcement of the text [of the law]."[18]

Indeed, a standard feature of Adirondacks folklore was the "good" forester. This figure might overlook certain violations; or, rather than arresting an offending local immediately, he would first issue a warning, giving the lawbreaker an opportunity to mend his or her ways and thus avoid arrest. Ira Gray, born in the Adirondacks in 1886, recalled one such story about a protector who paid a visit to a local who was well-known for hunting deer out of season. After the two had enjoyed a friendly dinner together, the forester asked the man to poach deer no longer, confessing, "I would be awfully sorry to catch you." Similar tales celebrated game protectors who, when aware of lawbreaking, informed the locals involved, "Now don't make me do something I don't want to do." Such stories should be read on two levels. On the most immediate, they reflect how difficult it must have been for foresters to arrest fellow community members for violations of park regulations. "It's pretty damn hard for a game protector to say we've got to fine you for doing it, or catch you for it," explained the Adirondacks resident Clarence Petty. "So you know darn well that some of these people just overlooked it." But no doubt some stories about "good" foresters were apocryphal. Such tales—an expression of how locals thought the relationship between foresters and local people *should* function—were likely employed as a way to reinforce community solidarity while also nudging present foresters toward more accommodating modes of behavior.[19]

Such stories, however, formed only a small portion of the strategies that local people employed to regulate the behavior of foresters. One other common tactic was the social ostracization of an overzealous forester. Fletcher Beede, the district game and fish protector of Essex County, charged that after arresting several locals for hunting deer out of season and for using illegal fishing devices, his family's position in the local community had become quite difficult, for he was "getting to be the most cordially hated man in the county." Locals relied on more direct forms of intimidation as well. One frequent strategy, according to Adirondacks folklore, was to warn the protector that he looked like a deer out in the woods and that he might therefore get shot "by accident." "Mighty easy to think it's a deer if the game constable's around.... What can anybody do? The man shoots at a deer and the game constable happened to be there." At times, such threats crossed the line to direct action. As the Forest Commission admitted in one of its annual reports, attempted shootings were a persistent feature of the foresters' profession: "It is not uncommon for protectors to be shot at while in pursuit of their duties. There are few protectors who have served any length of time on the force who have not had an experience of this kind."[20]

Foresters also found themselves constrained by local surveillance. Bill Smith, recalling his childhood in the Adirondacks in the early 1900s, remembered that when a new game warden arrived in their township, the first reaction of those living nearby had been to learn as much about him as they could: his habits, his tracks, his schedule. "The poor man, of course, he probably didn't have any idea he was being watched anywhere near as close as he was. But we wanted to know about this fellow," recounted Smith. Inhabitants often maintained an informal network that relayed information on the warden's whereabouts. "It's a funny thing," declared one local, "but no matter when a game constable comes along the news of his coming always gets ahead of him.... Fellows get wind that he's on the trail, and they pass the word along." As *Forest and Stream* complained in 1899, "Their [the foresters'] approach is announced hours before they arrive, and everyone is ready to receive them when they arrive."[21]

From time to time, a clever forester might find ways to avoid such surveillance. Seymour Armstrong, for instance, once pretended to be a traveling salesman for *Quain's Dictionary of Medicine* as he patrolled his district. More often, however, Adirondacks communities were so familiar with their local warden that it was necessary, as one forestry official put it, "to send the forester into an entirely new district where he wasn't known for the purpose of catching or getting on to the evidence of trespasses." "They [the foresters] have to be transferred from their home counties, at much expense, to other and distant counties to work incognito where the local protector is known to every citizen, and word is sent of his coming in advance of his movements," grumbled the Forest Commission in its 1901 report. "Habitual law violators soon become acquainted with the habits of the local protector, and devise clever schemes for keeping tabs on the protector's movements. It is, therefore, often necessary to bring in from other sections men who are not known locally, in order to secure convictions of this class of violator."[22]

The peculiar pressures bearing upon foresters highlight the new social and political relationships that the rise of conservation generated in the Adirondacks. Foresters played a dual role in the region: not only were they the means by which state power was projected into the countryside, they were also the means by which local influence penetrated into the state. As a result, foresters had to navigate between several competing allegiances. On the one hand, the Forest Commission sought to make the forester an extension of its conservation program; on the other, the forester's friends and neighbors often tried to render him an accomplice in their efforts to evade the state's environmental regulations. While the forester who became too aggressive in pursuing his duties risked being ostracized or shot by local residents, the forester who was found to be too cozy with lawbreakers could lose his job or even be arrested for corruption, as happened on several occasions to foresters who were alleged to be taking bribes to ignore the illegal cutting of timber in their districts. The daily dilemmas that foresters faced in trying to balance these competing claims convey worlds about the distance that often existed between the simplified categories of conservation and the messy realities of everyday life in rural America.[23]

As central as state simplification was to New York's conservation program for the Adirondacks, not all of the region's conservation efforts at the turn of the century were, in fact, state directed. By the 1890s, one of the dominant features of the Adirondacks landscape was the *private* park. Even before the Forest Preserve's creation, wealthy sports hunters had upon occasion bought up large tracts of abandoned timber land and converted these still-wooded plots into hunting preserves. The size and number of private parks, however, surged during the 1890s, as the New York State Legislature, reluctant to authorize the funds necessary for the repurchase of all private lands in the Adirondack Park and seeing the interests of estate owners as "identical with those of the State," revitalized a preexisting law allowing for the creation of preserves on private land. This statute permitted people or clubs who wanted to "encourage the propagation of fish and game" to set up private parks from which they could exclude trespassers at greatly increased penalties. (In 1892, the state even flirted briefly with a program which would have exempted estate owners from taxes if they agreed to restrict timber cutting on their holdings.)[24] By 1893, there were some sixty private parks in the Adirondacks, containing more than 940,000 acres of private lands, including many of the region's best hunting and fishing grounds, at a time when the state-owned Forest Preserve contained only 730,000 acres. As *Forest and Stream* observed the following year, "Private parks in the Adirondacks today occupy a considerably larger area than the State of Rhode Island....a man might travel ninety miles in a comparatively straight line without being fifteen minutes out of sight of a trespassing notice." Many of these parks were owned by wealthy individuals such as William Rockefeller. Others, such as the Adirondack League Club's (ALC), belonged to associations of well-to-do sports hunters. To increase their hunting opportunities, the new owners of these parks frequently stocked their ponds and streams with fish, engaged in large-scale feeding programs for deer and other wildlife, or imported exotic game animals, such as boar, caribou, western elk, or English deer.[25]

Although they initially faced many of the same problems with setting boundaries and enforcing regulations as the state, most private parks surmounted these obstacles through expenditures of funding and manpower that far exceeded the state's efforts during this same time.

Edward Burns, the general manager of Ne-Ha-Sa-Ne Park, a 112,000-acre private estate, detailed some of the steps taken by his employer, William Seward Webb, to secure his new holdings: "Webb had the land surveyed and had a topographical map of it made, running lines in each direction at 1/2 mile intervals. Also had notices posted around the exterior lines of his tract and on the lines of [Townships] 37 and 38. The substance of these notices were [sic] that people were forbidden to trespass, hunt or fish. Trails were cut out on the lands and a fence was built around a part of it. Men were detailed to patrol and watch it; they were hired for that purpose. There were during the first few years as many as fourteen or sixteen men."[26] If state lands were seldom well marked, the boundaries of private parks, in contrast, tended to be ringed by barbed-wire fences and warning signs. The fences kept unofficial visitors out and deer and other wildlife in, while the signs threatened trespassers with prosecution under the expanded penalties of the Fisheries, Game and Forest Law. The overall impression was, as intended, quite imposing. "This fence [of Ne-Ha-Sa-Ne Park]," explained Louis Yell, a resident of Upper Lake, "is composed of wire material. It is about eight feet high fastened to posts and trees. These notices... are posted around forbidding people from going on the ground, hunting, fishing, trespassing, building fires and felling trees and cutting timber. I knew that the land was being watched."[27]

As Yell's reference to "the land being watched" implies, almost all private parks employed a number of guides who acted both as a private police force and as a supplement to the Forest Commission's foresters. By the late nineteenth century, the Adirondack League Club alone had a contingent of over twenty guides, all of whom were required as part of their employment to sign a pledge that they "shall consider themselves game protectors." According to the ALC's handbook, the guides in the club's employ were to report all cases of trespassing and poaching and to "use every effort for the successful apprehension and punishment of every such offender." To reinforce the guides' role as law enforcers, the ALC distributed to each of its employees a silver, star-shaped badge that bore the words *Police Guide*. Despite such regulations, the guides at many parks, much like their counterparts in the state's forester corps, seem to have demonstrated a certain ambivalence about their new role as law enforcers. Many guards were efficient enough to earn the enmity of local communities. But examples do exist of conflicts between guides and private park owners. At the ALC, for instance, there were sporadic attempts among the guides to unionize for better wages and, on at least one occasion, ALC guards were caught poaching deer on the club's grounds.[28]

Among Adirondackers, private parks soon became the most hated facet of conservation. In little more than a decade, private park owners had sealed off many of the region's best hunting and fishing areas, defying the previous convention of leaving undeveloped forestland open to hunting, fishing, or foraging by local community members—a restriction that not even the Forest Commission, which still permitted public passage and the taking of game on Forest Preserve lands during the hunting season, had attempted. Private parks' stringent efforts against trespass, combined with their concentrated landholdings and extensive corps of guards, made them, for many rural folk, a powerful symbol of the class biases lurking at the heart of conservation. Observed an investigative committee of the New York State Assembly in 1899, "The poor [in the Adirondacks], as well as the men of moderate means, are complaining that our forest lands are rapidly being bought up by private clubs, and are closely watched by alert game keepers, and thus, as they claim, and not without some reason, our [woods] are all being monopolized by the rich; that we are apeing the English plan of barring the poor man from the hunt, etc."[29]

In 1903, the resentment of private parks long bubbling beneath the surface of Adirondacks life finally boiled over. On September 20, Orrando Dexter, an estate owner in Franklin County who had launched numerous lawsuits against local trespassers, was shot dead as he drove his carriage down a once-public road that he had enclosed within his estate. Dexter's outraged father, the wealthy founder of the American News Company, offered a five-thousand-dollar reward for information and hired a team of Pinkerton detectives to search for his son's killer, but the murderer was never located. All evidence, however, indicated that the killer must have been a local resident. Not only was the bullet that killed Dexter of a type commonly used for deer hunting, but near the murder scene were several footprints made by a "coarse shoe or boot such as are worn a great deal by the workmen, woodsmen and hunters of the Adirondacks." Seizing upon such clues, many newspapers trumpeted Dexter's death not as an isolated incident but as "only one demonstration of the hatred that exists in the woods." Editorialized the *New York World,* "Dexter's murder illustrates and must intensify the bitterness felt by the small farmers and woodsmen in the Adirondacks, and by those who have been long accustomed to hunt and fish where they wished, against the rich men who have established great estates in the forest, fenced them with wire and dotted them with signs: 'No trespassing,' 'No poaching.'" Indeed, the killing seems to have emboldened many residents of the Adirondacks to voice sentiments they had previously suppressed. Preserve owners and members of the Forest Commission alike reported receiving threats: that they "would receive the same fate that Dexter did"; that "if you're not careful there'll be another Dexter case up here. Somebody else is liable to be shot in the back." In response to such pronouncements, many private park owners hired additional guards, while the Forest Commission expanded its force of foresters, turning the Adirondacks of the early 1900s into a tense, armed camp.[30]

Although few cases reached the extremes of Dexter's, the unpopularity of private parks did, as one local newspaper put it, have "the effect of breeding lawlessness." Local people ripped down the "no trespassing" signs that ringed the parks' boundaries. They cut the elaborate wire fences that enclosed many estates, hoping that the deer and other game within might escape. They set fire to private parklands, sometimes with the intention of damaging fences, other times with the apparent desire to make the preserve an undesirable refuge for game animals.[31] And they shot at the guides hired to protect the private parks. "The position of guard on the vast forest preserves of William Rockefeller is not one to be much desired," observed the *New York Times* dryly in 1904: "Several of these guards have been fired at recently while patrolling their lonely beats in the dense forest, and one who had a bullet pass through his coat sleeve, narrowly missing his shoulder, has resigned, declaring the job too strenuous for him. As smokeless powder has been used in every case, all efforts to locate and capture these 'snipers' have proved futile." Even Rockefeller's house did not prove immune from such attacks. On several occasions, locals fired late-night shots at the buildings on Rockefeller's estate, leading the Standard Oil heir—who already took the precaution of never leaving his grounds without several bodyguards—to erect bright floodlights all around the perimeter of his Adirondacks "camp."[32]

Although vandalism and shootings were by far the most common forms of resistance to private parks, a few locals challenged the estates by means of the court system. The ALC was the target of one such case in 1898. As the club's manager wrote in his annual report, "We reported last year seven convictions of trespassers on the preserve. Several of them threatened reprisal and in some cases bloody revenge. George Thomas, who had unwillingly paid us $58 after staying seventeen days in jail, brought suit for false imprisonment. George did not get anything."[33]

The best-known court case concerning private parks grew out of an extended confrontation between William Rockefeller and the inhabitants of the town of Brandon, located almost completely within Rockefeller's private park. Founded in 1886, Brandon had originally been a lumbering center with a largely French-Canadian population of almost twelve hundred. But as the marketable timber within the village's vicinity decreased, making it no longer profitable to run Brandon's sawmill, Patrick Ducey, the lumberman who owned much of the land surrounding Brandon, sold his holdings to Rockefeller, who planned to make a private park out of them. Ducey was not able to sell all of Brandon to Rockefeller, though: some of the land in the village center belonged to the town's residents. Anxious to leave, many willingly sold their homes to Rockefeller, who "to the amazement and concern of the remaining inhabitants" tore them down and allowed the forest to grow back over the old housing sites—an action that led *Collier's* to dub Rockefeller the "Maker of Wilderness."[34]

Within a few years, some two to three hundred of Brandon's homes had disappeared, along with the village's hotel, church, and mill. The fourteen families remaining in the town relied mainly on hunting and fishing in the surrounding forest to survive—or, in the words of Oliver Lamora, one of the holdouts, "my occupation is, well, doing nothing." A veteran of the Civil War, Lamora received what one observer termed "a pension enough for a plain subsistence, which he ekes out with trout from the streams, partridge and deer from the forest, and berries from the mountainside." Such activities brought Lamora and the other residents of Brandon into inevitable conflict with Rockefeller, on whose lands any hunting, fishing, or foraging had to occur, since Rockefeller's park completely surrounded the village.[35]

In late April 1902, Lamora took one of the paths leading out of Brandon and crossed into Rockefeller's park, where he began to fish in the St. Regis River. He did so, Lamora later admitted, "with full knowledge that Mr. Rockefeller had...forbid me to go there." One of Rockefeller's guards, Fred Knapp, spotted Lamora and ordered him to leave the park. Lamora replied that he would go when he was ready. He spent a little less than two hours at the river, catching nineteen fish, before he returned home. As this was not the first time that Lamora had engaged in such behavior, Rockefeller decided to have the bothersome French Canadian prosecuted under the Fisheries, Game and Forest Law for trespass.[36]

Lamora demanded a jury trial, and the result was a series of lawsuits that dragged on for the next four years. Lamora won many of the early

rounds, but, in the words of the *New York Times*, "the case was carried
from one court to another until a decision was rendered in favor of Mr.
Rockefeller." At the first trial a jury in Saranac Lake found no cause for
action, and Rockefeller had to pay court costs of $11.39 for bringing a
frivolous suit. Rockefeller also lost his first appeal in a case that took a
local jury only thirty minutes to decide. In the second appeal, the jury
awarded Rockefeller damages of just 18¢, although by finding Lamora
guilty of trespass (as the judge in the case had ordered the jury to do),
this decision required Lamora to pay Rockefeller's court costs of
$790.31.[37]

The case of *Rockefeller v. Lamora* commanded considerable attention throughout the Adirondacks, with many residents viewing the case
as a pivotal challenge to the power of private park owners to restrict
public passage and hunting on their lands. Seeing Lamora's cause as
their own, a number of inhabitants began a popular subscription to
raise money for the pensioner's mounting court costs. Lamora's initial
victories also emboldened many locals to assert claims of their own
against private parks. "Mr. Rockefeller's men have taken the names of
upward of fifty different persons who were found fishing in the Rockefeller park," reported the *Times* in 1903. "The success Lamora had in
the lower courts prompted fishermen in other localities to enter private
parks, and the gamekeepers of the preserves of William C. Whitney, Dr.
W. Seward Webb, Edward Litchfield, and others were troubled as they
had never been before by poachers."[38]

Within the courtroom, the case hinged on two key issues. The first
was whether Rockefeller had the right to make private the preexisting
pathway that Lamora had taken to reach the St. Regis River, a route
that some inhabitants of Brandon testified had been in use since 1886.
Lamora maintained that he had always respected Rockefeller's property
rights; he had always stayed on this pathway, which he considered public property, when on his way to the St. Regis River. (Although Lamora's
argument concerned this one path, a friend of Lamora's, Fred McNeil,
stated outside the courtroom that for the past several years he had been
traversing all the trails on the Rockefeller estate to demonstrate that
they were still in public use.) The second issue was what right Rockefeller had to the wild game found within his park. Lamora's lawyers
argued that since the state had in past years stocked the waters of the St.
Regis with fish, the fish in the river were public property, not the private
property of Rockefeller. Thus, as long as Lamora fished in season, there
was no cause for his arrest. This issue of who had stocked the waters of

the St. Regis opened up, in turn, the larger question of who owned the wildlife in the Adirondacks. Wild animals in "a state of nature," Lamora's supporters asserted, had no ownership. They became property only when one invested the time and labor necessary to capture them, not simply because one happened to own the land on which the animals might be found. As one of Lamora's supporters summarized the case, "wild game, wild fish and wild birds belong to the people. . . . [Rockefeller] is suing a man who followed a public highway to which the public has as much right as to the air they breathe, and caught trout which Rockefeller did not plant, but some which the State did plant, and the rest of which were propagated naturally."[39]

The opposition to private parks manifested by locals such as Lamora in the early 1900s even struck a chord with a growing number of sports hunters. Originally, most visiting sports had celebrated estate owners as the saviors of the region's game. "[The deer] would long ago have been exterminated, if it were not for the large areas of private parks, where they do receive protection," declared *Forest and Stream* in 1894. But as it became apparent that the expansion of private parks meant that those sports hunters who could not afford to buy large estates or to become members of clubs were being excluded from significant portions of the Adirondacks, the attitude of many outsiders began to shift. By the time of Dexter's murder in 1903, several New York newspapers had begun to argue against the private park law. In the words of the Albany *Press-Knickerbocker,* "William G. Rockefeller, J. Pierpont Morgan, Dr. Seward Webb, Alfred G. Vanderbilt, and other landed proprietors in the Adirondacks are only doing with our woods what they have already done with our industries. They are bringing forests and streams under the control of a few, for the benefit of a few, and at the expense of many." Within a few years, even *Forest and Stream* was running angry articles with titles such as "Private Parks Do Not Protect Game" and protesting preserve owners' efforts to "restrict the common-law right of . . . citizens to take wild game."[40]

As a result of their mutual opposition to private parks, sports hunters and local residents occasionally forged alliances with one another against their common foe. One such example occurred in 1896, when William West Durant enclosed the South Inlet entrance to Raquette Lake within his private park. The first to challenge Durant's efforts was a visiting sport from New York City named John Golding. Golding and his guide, Ed Martin, dragged their boat over the log barrier that Durant had erected across the South Inlet and proceeded to fish in Durant's

TABLE 4.   ACREAGE OF THE
ADIRONDACK FOREST PRESERVE,
1886–1910

Year	Acreage
1886	681,374
1888	803,164
1891	731,674
1894	731,459
1897	801,473
1898	852,392
1899	1,109,140
1900	1,290,987
1901	1,306,327
1902	1,325,851
1906	1,347,280
1907	1,415,775
1908	1,438,999
1910	1,530,559

SOURCE: Association for the Protection of the Adirondacks, *Eighteenth Annual Report of the President,* 7.

NOTE: The preserve's recorded size varied in the late 1880s and early 1890s because of inaccuracies in the property records of the time.

park, attracting the attention of one of Durant's watchmen. Arrested and fined twenty-five dollars for trespassing, Golding retreated back to Manhattan. Nonetheless, his prosecution demonstrated to local residents Durant's intentions to restrict all access to his park. In response a few days later, two inhabitants of Raquette Lake, Charlie Bennett and Jack Daly, used a crosscut saw to destroy the log boom that Durant had used to prohibit entry to the stream. Durant repaired the boom and sent a large force of armed guards to protect it from further damage, but the cost and hassles involved led Durant to sell this portion of his park to the state shortly afterward.[41]

As the resolution to this particular standoff suggests, the combined outrage of locals and sports hunters over private parks did eventually lead the state to alter some of its conservation policies in the Adirondacks. In 1897, the New York legislature established a new fund to buy additional land for the Forest Preserve. Within four years, this effort raised the number of state-owned acres in the park to more than a million, surpassing for the first time the acreage of private preserves, which dipped during this same time from 900,000 to 705,000. Many of these new holdings came from some of the largest of the private parks:

75,000 acres from Ne-Ha-Sa-Ne, 35,392 acres from the ALC, and 30,000 acres from the Santa Clara Reserve. By 1907, the state had spent $3,500,000 on new purchases, almost doubling the size of the Forest Preserve.[42] (See Table 4.)

Despite such measures, the repurchase program was far from a total victory for the region's inhabitants. Adirondackers never eliminated the hated private preserves: even today, significant portions of the park remain in the hands of private owners, who continue to post their land against local trespass. Moreover, in certain respects, local opposition to private parks reinforced the state's control of the region—for, as the Lamora case evinces, in voicing their opposition to private parks, the region's residents frequently resorted to a vocabulary of public property and public rights that echoed the language used to legitimize state conservation. Although this congruence was often unintentional, at other moments locals consciously advocated state ownership as a more attractive alternative to private parks. As one inhabitant of Brandon put it in 1903, he hoped "Mr. Rockefeller will sell out to the State....then we will be allowed to make our town again what it once was."[43]

Such expressions of local support for New York's conservation program, however, often proved fleeting at the turn of the century. No doubt residents preferred state conservation to the vast and exclusionary estates of a Dexter or Rockefeller. But if New York's purchase program prevented a rash of Orrando Dexter–style murders from erupting across the Adirondacks in the early 1900s, it still left many of the central tensions of conservation unresolved. Adirondackers would soon find that the state control over the environment that the Forest Commission sought posed almost as great a challenge to their land use practices as had the region's hated private parks.

CHAPTER 3

Working-Class Wilderness

In planning the Adirondack Park, conservationists had envisioned nature as stable and predictable, an entity that followed fixed laws easily comprehensible to trained experts. If park supporters had initially focused little attention on the people inhabiting their new conservation experiment, they soon concluded that the region's human populace possessed few of the qualities that characterized its natural systems. In place of nature's order and harmony, Adirondackers seemed to be governed by a "peculiar moral attitude" that manifested itself in unpredictable, lawless behavior. "I have not found a single instance in which the State forestry laws are obeyed or even respected," reported an outraged correspondent to the *New York Times* in 1889. "Instead of the employees of the State guarding against violation of the statutes or trying to enforce their provisions they assist in breaking them. The statement that the Commonwealth owns certain portions of the territory upon which they live has no apparent meaning to the mountaineers....Not alone are the laws forbidding the cutting of timber upon State lands violated, but the game restrictions are never thought of by the mountaineers."

This "opposition from the inhabitants of the northern counties...to every serious attempt made for the care and protection...of the North Woods" seemed inexplicable to most conservationists, given the benefits they believed the movement was bringing to the region.[1] As a committee of the New York State Assembly stated following an investigative tour of the park in 1899, "[We encountered much] grumbling by the old hunters and guides, they claiming that private ownership of forest lands, which are turned into hunting preserves and carefully guarded by a keeper, and too stringent regulations if carried out on state lands, deprive them of the rights and privileges they have freely enjoyed since their birth, all of which some of them claim are unAmerican and wrong. Wide open laws in regard to our forest is what that class seem to desire, which would result, ultimately, in a barren waste, and an early extinction of their fish and game."[2] The committee's conclusion—that rural folk favored a rapid and relentless exploitation of the natural world—became a standard refrain not only of nineteenth-century conservation but of many twentieth-century environmental histories as well. In their influential works *Changes in the Land* and *Dust Bowl,* for example, the environmental historians William Cronon and Donald Worster argue that early settlers viewed nature through a narrow capitalist prism, one that reduced complex ecosystems to discrete bundles of marketable commodities. In *Wilderness and the American Mind,* the environmental historian Roderick Nash asserts that Euro-Americans possessed a cultural antipathy toward all undeveloped landscapes—a "wilderness hatred."[3]

There is, to be sure, much that is correct about such analyses. The settlement of the American countryside was accompanied by tremendous ecological devastation as settlers endeavored to find marketable goods and remake the "wild" nature they encountered into a more familiar world of fields and fences. Yet the current scholarship remains elusive on a number of critical issues. Above all, while many environmental historians place capitalistic economic relations at the center of their analyses, they frequently treat capitalism as little more than a marketplace for the buying and selling of natural resources. Rarely do their discussions touch upon capitalism's social or cultural dimensions: its division of labor, its contesting classes with their distinct ways of conceptualizing the world. Submerging these differences has lent environmental history tremendous rhetorical power, but at the cost of obscuring the diversity of relationships that Americans forged with the natural world. Moreover, by failing to engage the perspective of non-elites, environmental historians have inadvertently recapitulated much of the degradation discourse of early conservation, especially the movement's leaders' vision of themselves as saving nature from "the ignorant or unprincipled."[4]

The timber stealing and game poaching in the Adirondacks that so troubled the New York Forest Commission provide useful vantage points from which to reexamine this scholarly consensus. After all, at first glance the region's widespread lawlessness would seem clear evidence of a rural community so committed to the exploitation of nature that it clung to such behavior despite all regulations to the contrary. Upon closer examination, however, it becomes increasingly difficult to maintain the stark dichotomies—rule versus chaos, careful stewardship versus ruthless development—animating such interpretations. The inhabitants of the Adirondacks may not have been innocent rustics living in quiet harmony with the natural world, but neither were they blind to the effects that their actions had on the environment around them. During the closing decades of the nineteenth century, Adirondackers would experiment with a variety of strategies designed to regulate the uses that could be made of the region's natural resources. In so doing, however, they would bring to the surface a number of the region's deepest tensions—not only the ones between the region's residents and outside conservationists but those between the competing elements of Adirondacks society itself.[5]

Because maintaining the region's tree cover was a central rationale for conservation in the Adirondacks, one of the Forest Commission's initial goals was simply to prevent the illegal cutting of timber on state lands in the park. As Theodore B. Basselin, the prominent lumberman appointed forest commissioner, recounted, "When we took office in 1885, we knew but very little of the State management of the forest." Upon surveying their new holdings, however, Basselin and the other commissioners "found a large number of trespasses, some very large and some small—the number so large that we were very much surprised." Equally alarming, many residents appeared to consider the theft of wood from state lands a perfectly acceptable practice: "We also found that the people around the borders of this wilderness had been educated from time immemorial, that is, from the first settlement of the country, that what belonged to the State was public property, and that they had a right to go in there and cut as they wanted to; their fathers and grandfathers had been doing that, and that they had a birthright there that no one could question." Finding it impossible to prosecute so many trespassers all at once, the commission "endeavored to single out the more glaring ones and endeavored to strike terror, as it was, into the people who were trespassing in that way."[6]

To their dismay, however, Basselin and his colleagues encountered frequent difficulties in persuading locals to testify against the "timber poachers" in their midst. The inhabitants of the Adirondacks, the Forest Commission charged, "often profess to be unable to recognize their nearest neighbors while cutting State timber a few rods away; they do not know their neighbors' horses and oxen, nor the location of roads and lots, although familiar with all these things....Every conceivable evasion is resorted to."[7] On those occasions when officials were able to secure evidence of timber stealing, they did so only after internal rivalries had torn the web of local complicity. In the words of John H. Burke, an inspector for the Forest Commission: "It is almost impossible to obtain evidence against any individual in a locality unless there is some man in that section who has some ill will against him; if they are all friendly it is almost an impossibility, because the persons who go there, the State officials, are strangers; the men who live in the locality expect no favors from them and if they tell what they know in regard to these trespasses to the State officials they subject themselves to the annoyance and to the ill will of their neighbors[;] and it makes their life unpleasant for them at home...and perhaps leave [sic] them, the men whom they reported against, their enemies for life."[8] Added another forester, "They are all neighbors and they all want to trespass some if they can get a chance, and, as a rule, they won't squeal on one another. If a man does and it is known[,] they turn him down pretty quick."[9]

The Forest Commission's enforcement problems arose, however, not only from the mixture of neighborliness and intimidation prevailing in many Adirondacks villages but also from an even more fundamental cause: a profound disagreement with local residents over the definition of timber stealing. While conservation officials, in keeping with their program of state simplification, insisted on classifying all cutting of trees on public lands as theft, local residents considered such "crimes" to be, under certain circumstances, perfectly legitimate. These differing perspectives emerged in sharp relief during the investigation into lumber trespasses that the Forest Commission conducted in 1895. Asked about the frequent timber theft in the region, Robert Shaw, a farmer in Long Lake, retorted, "This country has been wild, you know, until within a few years, and the owners of lands here used to let the people, for their own use, cut any timber they were a mind to, anywhere; that was the former practice, and it never has been fully abandoned." Flabbergasted, state officials queried Shaw as to whether the felling of trees on another's property was not a crime. "No, sir; it is not considered by the majority of the people a heinous crime at all," replied Shaw. "Half of the people haven't got any wood of their own that lives around the vicinity....and so they never have considered it any crime."[10]

Adirondackers typically justified such behavior by claiming a natural right to subsistence. Under this logic, many of the acts recorded in the Forest Commission's trespass files—the cutting of "17–18 cords of stove wood," the theft of "hard wood for fire purposes," the stealing of state timber "to build a house and barn"—were not crimes at all but legitimate appropriations of necessary household resources.[11] "Men we would call in this locality honest, straight, law-abiding citizens," noted Burke, "would consider it no crime whatever to take a few logs from State land." Indeed, to those Adirondackers who depended on state woodlands for firewood, building materials, and other supplies, New York's Forest Preserve appeared less an exercise in the wise stewardship of nature than the callous denial by the Forest Commission of local access to essential resources. In numerous Adirondacks communities, almost all the nearby woodlands belonged to the state, leaving residents with little option but to steal timber from the new Forest Preserve. "In many localities, e.g., Raquette Lake, Long Lake village, and Saranac Lake village, the State owns nearly all the forest land, thereby making firewood and lumber scarce and high priced," acknowledged the Forest Commission at the turn of the century. "Consequently, the inhabitants, becoming somewhat desperate, felt justified in obtaining their wood and lumber where it was most convenient, without regard to ownership."[12]

Although conservation officials realized that many such trespasses were committed "for the sole purpose of obtaining firewood," they nonetheless insisted that "the people who did the cutting [be] arrested, convicted and fined.... These parties, all of whom were very poor, pled in their defense that the State owned all the land in their vicinity, except for some small private preserves whose owners would not sell to them any timber for fuel. They claimed that they had gathered all the dead or fallen timber for a long distance, and that to go farther for such fuel made it cost more than firewood of any kind was worth. They complained loudly of the worthless quality of the old, fallen trees, which they dislike to burn, accustomed as they have been all their lives to using good 'body wood' in their cook stoves." Several Adirondackers even dispatched anguished letters to the Forest Commission, asking officials to rethink their policies. As William Dunham of Piseco, Hamilton County, wrote in 1899, "I have been informed by one of the officers of your Commission that the people of this vicinity are forbidden to cut any firewood on State lands.... As a good many of the people here have no woodland of their own and cannot buy any of their neighbors, it be-

comes quite necessary for them to cut what wood they want to burn—
which does not exceed twenty-five cords for each family for a whole
year—on the State [lands]." But to the frustration of local residents, the
Forest Commission remained unwilling to amend its single, simple
definition of timber theft. "The action of the State officials in refusing to
allow families in many localities to obtain fuel has occasioned un-
friendly criticism and aroused a feeling of bitter resentment among the
settlers in some localities," admitted commissioners in 1900.[13]

Many locals defended their thefts of trees not only by stressing their
right to subsistence but by placing their activities outside of the market
nexus. As the Adirondacks native Henry Bradley explained in 1895,
residents considered it perfectly legal to take firewood or building
supplies from state lands if the materials were used for one's immediate
household subsistence. From the local perspective, such activities only
achieved the status of crimes if, in Bradley's words, one cut trees "for
the purposes of marketing and selling the logs again." "Though the cutting of timber from State lands for the market has been recognized as
done in violation of the law," agreed an investigative committee of the
Forest Commission, "it seems not to have been considered a crime or
offense of any kind for trespassers to cut timber upon State lands for
firewood or for building purposes, chiefly of hardwood." In keeping
with this division between subsistence and market activities, local
people also distinguished between which species of trees might legiti-
mately be cut. To fell spruce, pine, or any other marketable softwood
remained questionable (the only notable exception to this trend being
the special cuts of cedar and pine essential for the construction of guide
boats). In contrast, to take nonmarketable hardwoods was considered
perfectly acceptable, as William Dunham's letter to the Forest Commission on his need for firewood suggests: "All the woods used as fire-
woods are hardwoods, no evergreen timber being used."[14]

If the persistence of this subsistence, nonmarket ideology illustrates
the reluctance of many rural folk to embrace a completely capitalist
orientation, it also reveals the uncertain ethical terrain Adirondackers
had come to inhabit by the close of the nineteenth century. Residents
might, in keeping with enduring agrarian notions of simplicity and self-
sufficiency, give moral primacy to subsistence practices. But by the
1880s, none lived a completely subsistence lifestyle. Thus, as much as
holding up subsistence as a moral ideal may have appealed to Adirondackers' image of themselves as independent pioneers, it curtailed their
ability to address the true dilemmas that they faced—issues such as

how to interact with the market yet still preserve some element of personal independence or responsibility to the larger community.

As a result of this confusion, residents found it difficult to arrive at a consensus as to what constituted an appropriate middle ground between subsistence and capitalist engagement. In the case of timber theft, some Adirondackers reasoned that if the taking of firewood and building supplies for subsistence was a reasonable practice, it should also be justifiable to sell stolen timber if the resulting cash was used to buy household staples. Such logic held a particular appeal for residents with few other means of generating revenue, and throughout the 1880s and 1890s one could find a "mostly...poor class of citizens who own little or no land of any character" pilfering logs from the Forest Preserve. One of the most common targets for such thieves was trees stolen for shingles or "fiddle butts" (the bottom part of large spruce, used to manufacture sounding boards for fine pianos). Those who committed such crimes often claimed that since they possessed little property of their own, they had few alternatives but to sell resources from state lands. When Inspector Seymour C. Armstrong confronted a man he caught stealing logs from the Forest Preserve in 1895, for example, the thief responded that he was "a poor man and was obliged to take the timber to get something to live on." Foresters reached a similar conclusion about the timber thief Charles Barney: "Barney has no means of support except cutting and selling wood and timber from state lands on which he resides." Local juries, the Forest Commission soon learned, displayed frequent sympathy to such arguments. "If this man happens to be a poor man who is being prosecuted," grumbled one inspector, "he has the sympathy of his friends and neighbors, and the very men who are on the jury are men possibly who have been engaged in some such operations themselves."[15]

Residents may have also tolerated the theft of trees for shingles or fiddle butts because they recognized that neither activity posed an overwhelming threat to local forests. Only a few trees were suitable for either product, forcing trespassers to cut selectively. Furthermore, after felling their trees, the thieves still had to invest a considerable amount of time and labor to transform the raw timber into a marketable commodity. Shingles, for instance, were produced using a shaving horse, on which the shingle maker would sit and, using a drawing knife, shave shingles from a carefully trimmed log. Fiddle butts required less intensive reworking prior to sale, but, unlike other logs, they could not be floated to downstream mills, as water was believed to damage the wood's sound quality. Local residents instead had to use horses or oxen to drag each log to the nearest mill.[16]

Although the Forest Commission devoted much of its resources to stopping such practices, the stealing of trees for fiddle butts or shingles did not constitute the Adirondacks' most common form of timber theft in the 1880s and 1890s. Measured in terms of quantity of trees stolen, by far the most common form of timber theft was in fact the large-scale cutting of timber by crews working for lumber companies. Such trespasses were typically planned in advance and sifted through several layers of oral contracts. "A contract to cut timber usually passes through many hands before it comes to the man who actually does the work," charged state investigators in 1895. "An effort to shift the responsibility for cutting over the lines is shown....In general the jobbers have cut the timber wherever employed by contractors or lumbermen to do so, without investigation or concern as to whether the land belongs to the State or not; and the common workmen have been, if possible, even more indifferent to the ownership of the land, so long as they have made a living from their work." These arrangements enabled timber concerns to shield their involvement while leaving the woodsmen who did the actual trespasses on state lands to face the risk of fine or arrest alone. Observed the *New York Times* in 1889, "The scheme of 'letting jobs,' as it is known here, is partly responsible for the difficulty of fastening the guilt of the illegal cutting upon the persons who authorize it. A boss lumberman will direct a lumberman to cut a specified tract. The lumberman employs his men and they henceforth go on with the work not in any sense subject to the direct control of his employer....Should proceedings be taken by the State, [the subcontractor] is compelled to show his instructions very clearly or he is the man who is regarded as responsible."[17]

The rise of this widespread theft occurred at much the same time as several other key shifts in the timber industry, which would in the 1880s transform lumbering in New York into an enterprise far different from the one Adirondackers had known just a few years before. While earlier timber operations had focused on cutting large softwoods located within a few miles of waterways, the rise of the railroad and the pulp mill in the closing decades of the nineteenth century altered this long-standing pattern. Liberated by the train from their dependence on rivers for transportation, lumbermen expanded their activities dramatically, cutting many previously untouched portions of the Adirondacks and taking many of the hardwoods that timber crews had previously left unharvested because of the difficulties of transport. At the same time, pulp mills, which manufactured paper using finely ground softwoods of any size, led to much more extensive cutting of local evergreens. Consequently, even after the creation of the Forest Preserve, the production of lumber in the Adirondacks almost doubled between 1885 and 1910 as timber concerns expanded their legal (and illegal) cutting operations.[18]

Because of the pressure that these changes placed on wildlife habitats and their own wood supplies, a number of Adirondackers began to insist, in the words of resident D. F. Sperry, on the need "to protect the state lands from the vandalism of the lumberman." "There is no prejudice existing in Franklin county in favor of lumbermen," observed the county's chief fish and game protector, J. Warren Pond, in 1891. "On the contrary they are regarded with some suspicion on account of the desire of people to preserve the forests and [waters] and the game therein." That same year, in a move that would have surprised those who believed that rural folk uniformly favored the rapid exploitation of natural resources, the *Adirondack News* called for stricter supervision of the region's lumber industry. "Let the state appoint wardens to supervise the cutting of timber and allow no trees of less than twelve inches in diameter to be cut; and let the most stringent enactment be made against charcoal manufacturers and the establishment of pulp mills," editorialized the *News,* "and there will always be forests."[19]

As a result of this local opposition to the timber industries' rapid expansion, those working for illicit timber crews did not always enjoy the same popular acceptance as the region's other timber thieves. To those Adirondackers worried about lumbering's growing impact on their region, such groups seemed too cozy with the timber industry that, in their eyes, constituted the real bandit in the region. Nathan Davis, a local surveyor, contended that it was such companies, not the poor resident taking some firewood or building supplies for his or her own use, that were the Adirondacks' true criminals: "Trespasses are done by men of some considerable means, lumbermen.... ordinary people, as a general thing, do not steal timber from State lands." To contain such local unease, a few black marketeers took the precaution of organizing themselves into gangs—some sporting names such as the "State Troops" and the "Grenadiers" that offered ironic commentary on the Forest Commission's conservation efforts—and issuing threats designed to keep residents from interfering with their activities. A favorite territory of one gang in Herkimer County, for instance, was posted with the warning that "anybody that comes here to watch, their bones will be left in these woods, so help us, Jesus!"[20]

Despite such measures, the heyday of the Adirondacks timber gang lasted little more than a decade. The Forest Commission's ability with each passing year to map and patrol its holdings with greater precision soon made it difficult for organized groups to steal the large quantities of logs that the timber industry sought. By 1900, the Forest Commission could report that of the forty-six cases of trespassing it had prosecuted that year, only one had been connected to a lumber company. Instead of stealing timber outright, many lumber concerns began to exploit the weaknesses of conservation in other, more subtle ways. A number of companies seized upon the confused status of property titles in the region to strike sweetheart land deals with sympathetic members of the commission (several of whom, like Basselin, were drawn from the ranks of New York's prominent lumbermen). In 1894 and again in 1910, such scenarios led New York to investigate charges of fraud in the Forest Commission and to dismiss several leading conservation officials.[21]

Yet, even as theft by the lumber industry declined sharply at the turn of the century, subsistence pilfering continued unabated in the park. Exasperated commission members admitted in 1897 that "petty trespassing" remained widespread throughout the Adirondacks, especially "by residents who wanted some building material or fuel." Well into the twentieth century, the bureau found itself plagued by "the poorer class of residents who t[ake] trees for firewood," with thefts of fuel constituting the vast majority of the trespass cases the commission investigated. Because of their detailed knowledge of local conditions, these thieves proved nearly impossible for the commission to apprehend. Typically, local timber poachers slipped onto state holdings late at night, bringing along their dogs to warn them of the approach of any strangers. After tying a coat or blanket around the trunk of a tree to muffle the sound of the ax, they would cut a few logs, which they would then spirit out of the preserve as quickly as possible. "A man will go with his boy or his neighbor and cut two or three trees and take them away in the middle of the night," declared Warden Samuel Gorman. "There is no way of getting hold of them."[22]

Although this ongoing pilfering posed little threat to the survival of the Adirondacks forest, it stood as a potent symbol of the standoff that had developed between the Forest Commission and local residents. In spite of its foresters and its attempts at simplification and surveillance, the commission still found itself incapable of exercising the complete administrative control over the Adirondacks that it sought. Most locals for their part saw the Forest Commission as having seriously undermined their customary uses of the region's woodlands, turning many otherwise honest and law-abiding citizens into squatters and timber thieves. Even after more than two decades of interaction, the groups continued to disagree over which one possessed the more legitimate claim to the Adirondacks forest.

For all the controversies surrounding timber theft, no facet of conservation proved more contentious in northern New York than the game law. To the deer and other animals of the chase, it doubtless mattered little who was trying to kill them. But to the other participants in the process—sport hunters and local residents alike—who was hunting, how, and why mattered a great deal, turning the pursuit of game into a flash point over the questions of who should control the Adirondacks' natural resources, and to what ends.

Sports' approach to hunting was derived from a curious amalgam of British upper-class tradition, imported to the United States by English expatriates such as Frank Forester, and a homegrown desire to recreate the imagined world of the American frontier through "occasional relapses from the restraints of civilization into the primitive conditions of the backwoods."[23] Out of this peculiar mixture of history, militarism, and upper-class pretense, there developed during the late nineteenth century a sportsman's code in which *how* one hunted was almost as important as *what* one hunted. This approach led, in turn, to impassioned debates among sports hunters over what constituted the best test of the manly skills that hunting was supposed to measure. Some sportsmen contended that "driving with dogs" represented "the fairest, manliest and most interesting" way of hunting, while others asserted that the still hunt (the unaided stalking of game) was "the only fair and manly way of hunting anything."[24]

If there was one point that sports did agree upon, it was that their behavior was not the cause of game scarcities in popular hunting spots like the Adirondacks. "We believe that more deer are killed by the few score guides in [the Adirondacks]...than by all the sportsmen put together," declared *Forest and Stream* in 1874. This indictment of local practices, echoed repeatedly in the pages of the leading sporting journals of the day, pointed toward an obvious conclusion: that protecting the wildlife in the Adirondacks depended on setting stricter limits for locals rather than on outside sports hunters. In the words of J. H. Wood-ward of New York City: "I, for one, do not believe that the solution of the problem [of a shortage of game in the Adirondacks] lies in still fur-ther restricting the sportsman."[25]

As might be expected, most Adirondackers strongly disagreed with such interpretations. Residents pointed out that wealthy sports hunters did not need the game they killed—hunting, after all, was for tourists a leisure activity. By contrast, hunting was for locals an integral compo-nent of household subsistence. "We lived off the land, and the deer were there, and you ate them the year around," noted resident Bill Smith.[26] To such folk, it seemed unfair that New York's game law failed to dis-tinguish between rural need and elite leisure. Rather than passing laws for "the benefit of the cities alone," argued Christopher J. Goodsell of Old Forge, the legislature should "make the game laws for the poor as well as the rich."[27] Many inhabitants fondly recalled an earlier era when the state had not meddled in their hunting practices. "Times is dif-ferent now," grumbled Alvah Dunning in 1897: "In them days nobody said a word ef a poor man wanted a little meat an' killed it, but now they're savin' it until the dudes get time to come up here an' kill it an' some of 'em leave a deer to rot in the woods, an' on'y take the horns ef it's a buck, or the tail ef it's a doe, just so's they can brag about it when they go home, an' they'd put me in jail ef I killed a deer when I needed meat." To Dunning and others like him, this contrast between the se-riousness of local subsistence and the frivolity of outside sport high-lighted the obvious inequities of the game law.[28]

By the close of the nineteenth century, the growth of tourism had propelled such issues to center stage in the Adirondacks. One glimpse of the resulting clash in perspectives can be found in the brief exchange that took place between Charles Hoffman, a visiting sport, and John Cheney, his guide. The two were out hunting and had already killed some birds and a deer when Hoffman spotted a covey of partridges. To Hoffman's suggestion that they increase their bag by shooting some of the partridge, Cheney replied, "It's wrong, it's wrong, sir, to use up life in that way; here's birds enough for them that wants to eat them; and the saddle of venison on the buckboard will only be wasted, if I kill more of these poor things."[29] Adirondacks local David Merrill offered an even more caustic critique of sports hunting as a wasteful, even cruel, activity. On several occasions, foresters arrested Merrill, his father, and brother for netting fish in the lake near their home. Yet the Merrills maintained that a net, while illegal under the new game law,

was a far more humane way to catch fish, for it allowed fish to be captured more quickly and ensured that only mature specimens were
killed. "My father did not believe it was right to catch fish for sport,
but for food only," Merrill observed. "And the right method for fishing
was with a net that would take only larger fish. The hook and line
method for fishing takes mostly small fish, and in this way you are killing some six fish to get a pound of food, whereas with a net you kill
one fish and get two pounds of food. However if the fish were put here
for the purpose of providing sport for pleasure seekers, the net would
not be the proper equipment for they [the tourists] prefer to torture the
fish for the fun they get out of it. A fish as well as a man has a sense of
feeling and suffers after being hooked, and the longer this period of
torture can be extended, the more fun the so-called 'sportsman' can get
out of it."[30] A more oblique yet no less critical view of sports hunting
runs through the poem composed in the 1890s by Patrick Sheehy, an
inhabitant of Schroon Lake. Sheehy's poem lamented the death of "Old
Golden," a large buck "granted immunity from harm" by the local
people of the area "out of respect for his great size, endurance, and
beauty":

> A party of young gentlemen came north to kill some deer;
> They did not know Brave Golden was well known to hunters here;
> They struck his track with well-bred dogs and boasted of the same.
> Lo! soon the king through grove and glen proved both grit and game.
>
> For three long days they chased him o'er hills and mountains high,
> Till hounds and men surrounded him, each moment pressing nigh;
> He seemed to plead for mercy. Alas! it was in vain;
> He was shot and shed his life's blood on the bosom of Champlain.
>
> We miss Brave Golden from his herd, we miss him from his home,
> We miss him from each grove and glen through which the king did roam;
> Our hounds will never strike his track to make the valley ring;
> The stranger's cruel, deadly shot laid low our noble king.[31]

The regret running through Sheehy's poem was not only for the demise
of Old Golden but also for the loss of the system of local controls over
the environment that the Adirondackers had once exercised. Residents
found their environmental practices under attack on several fronts during the 1880s, first by a loss of legitimacy to the state's conservation
code and then by the scores of sports hunters, "strangers" unfettered by
community ties, pouring into the region.

Initially, most Adirondackers viewed New York's new game laws as
offering few solutions to these problems. Locals were quick to observe

that throughout the nineteenth century the legislature designed its regulations in favor of visiting sports hunters, confining the hunting season to the late summer and early fall, the period when tourism in the region was at its peak. Residents also noted that while the state's legal bag limit was often too low for those who depended on wild game for their annual meat supply, it nonetheless allowed visiting sports to wreak serious havoc on the local wildlife population. The *Boonville (N.Y.) Herald* exposed one such case in the 1880s:

> Information reaches us that along the Moose river and in many parts of the Adirondack region, deer are being slaughtered in a great number by certain parties who hunt and shoot these beautiful creatures for mere sport. A week or more ago hunters from Utica and Holland patent killed twelve deer near Moose river and the carcasses of the animals were left in the woods to rot. Such "sportsmen" as these should not be permitted to pursue their cruel and destructive business, which will soon rid the forests of the game that is so prized and ought to be in some manner protected from the wholesale slaughterers....Altho' the letter of the law does not prohibit such unnecessary slaughter, the spirit of it certainly does. The man who shoots more game or catches more fish than he can make use of, is not a sportsman in any sense of the word.

There was only one solution, according to the *Herald:* "persons who are interested in preserving the game in the Adirondacks should band together for the purpose of keeping out the deer slayers."[32]

Apparently, others agreed. The closing decades of the nineteenth century witnessed a number of collective efforts by residents to control the hunters in their midst. During a return trip to the Adirondacks in 1875, for example, Headley learned of one sportsman who had recently visited the region, killing large numbers of deer. His overhunting so enraged "the scattered settlers and guides" that "at length [they] sent him word that if he ever came there again they would make an example of him, and he has since prudently stayed away." Local outrage coalesced into more formal modes of action at this time as well. In early 1883, for instance, a number of the inhabitants of Boonville, upset by the "unscrupulous butchers in the guise of sportsmen [who] have unmercifully slaughtered hundreds of deer in this section of the country," formed a club to watch over their local forestlands. The club members raised money among themselves to pay for "two able and efficient guides...to secure evidence against parties who engage in illegally killing deer." Three years later, a similar movement took place in the Keene Valley area of the Adirondacks. Despite the opposition of those residents involved in the tourist trade, a number of locals formed a club "for the protection of game" and dispatched several of their members to gather evidence about tourists "engaged in unlawful pursuit of deer."[33]

Such developments complicate the prevailing interpretation of game laws as an unwelcome sanction from above, imposed on a restive and resisting rural populace. To be sure, many Adirondackers manifested open hostility to the new laws that governed when and how they could hunt. But others came to find ways in which the state's conservation program could be used in place of the region's earlier, community-based regulatory regimes. The forester John Hunkins noted just such a shift in his territory in St. Lawrence County. "On my first trip," Hunkins recalled, "I was unable to obtain a boat or any accommodations from these people for any consideration. Our lives were in constant jeopardy, either from those we had prosecuted or from those who feared being called to account for their many misdeeds." With the passage of time, however, some residents began to see Hunkins as a useful ally against those who abused local resources. "Now," declared the forester, "some who had been the most outspoken are my most valuable and able assistants; ever ready to carry me from point to point and give any information they possess."[34]

Adirondackers were especially quick to direct foresters against unpopular outsiders such as sports hunters and preserve owners. In the 1890s, for example, people living near Lieutenant Governor Woodruff's private park in the Adirondacks tipped off local foresters that Woodruff was keeping a pack of dogs for deer hunting, in violation of the law against hounding. At much the same time, locals employed at J. Pierpont Morgan's private park confided to the Raquette Lake game protector that Morgan had been fishing out of season. The protector's search of Morgan's camp revealed thirteen lake trout, resulting in a $155 fine. In 1903, the *Adirondack News* celebrated the fact that "twenty-four violators of the game laws, who were hunting on state lands in the Adirondacks, the number including prominent business and professional men of New York, Albany, Troy, Schenectady and Saratoga, have been arrested as the result of good work done by Protectors Mattison and Hawn." And, in 1906, in what was perhaps their crowning achievement, some friends of Oliver Lamora brought about the arrest of John Redwood, the superintendent of William Rockefeller's private park, and Harry Melville, one of Rockefeller's gamekeepers, on charges of deer hounding, causing them to be fined one hundred dollars apiece.[35]

By exposing elite lawbreakers, Adirondackers sought not simply to punish certain individuals but also to undermine a key assumption of conservation's degradation discourse. While conservationists might depict rural folk as ignorant and environmentally destructive, residents pointed out that many violators in the Adirondacks were in fact drawn from the ranks of ostensibly enlightened sports hunters. "Sportsmen come here and force their guides under penalty of dismissal to fish out of season," charged C. H. Larkin, a guide from St. Regis Falls. "What is a guide to do under such circumstances? A guide has no influence to inforce [sic] the laws or prevent the infraction of them, particularly when opposed to sportsmen who are oftimes among the richest law-givers of opulent cities." In a similar vein, when the inhabitants of Tucker Lake formed a club to "fight Rockefeller's men" in 1903, they called themselves the Adirondack Game and Fish Protective Association—a name that appropriated the very language of conservation to articulate the residents' vision of themselves as the genuine protectors of the Adirondacks wildlife against rapacious private preserve owners.[36]

Yet if Adirondackers insisted on strict enforcement of game laws against outsiders, they rarely applied the same standards to fellow community members. As *Forestry Quarterly* noted in 1902, residents frequently overlooked violations when "bound by the ties of kin, of friendship, of neighborliness.... The game wardens are prompt against a stranger, but the local offenders who go unpunished are numberless." Even when foresters did arrest locals for breaking the game law, sympathetic courts often refused to punish the wrongdoers. "It has been said that a Hamilton county jury would not indict a resident for violation of the game law," griped Seymour Armstrong, the game and fish protector in Hamilton County, in 1887. The career of Isaac Kenwell, Armstrong's replacement, demonstrates the validity of Armstrong's observation. Of the seven people that Kenwell prosecuted in 1894 for violations of the game law, three were acquitted, one never showed up to trial, and one, having pled guilty to killing a deer out of season, received only a suspended sentence. Only two suffered any penalty: fined ten dollars apiece for "illegal fishing," the defendants never paid, serving ten days of jail time instead. Concluded Kenwell, "It is very hard to get a conviction in the County Court of Hamilton for violation of the Game Law, as the jurors are most all old violators or are friends of the violator, and their sympathy is with the offender."[37]

To justify their violations of the game law, Adirondackers called upon a complex of beliefs that linked hunting to the proper ordering of social and political relations, derived in part from an attenuated but still vital republicanism. Americans had long celebrated the fact that unlike in European monarchies such as Great Britain, where the hunt was limited to the landowning aristocracy, in the United States all citizens had an equal and common right to pursue wild game. Not only did this open access stand as a powerful symbol of New World freedom, but by providing rural families with hides and meat it also helped to preserve the agrarian self-sufficiency that republican ideology so prized. Even at the close of the nineteenth century, such beliefs resonated with many Adirondackers, who viewed New York's efforts to restrict their hunting as "un-American." Queried in 1897 about the game law, Alvah Dunning, for instance, could only mutter, "I dunno what we're a-comin' to in this free country."[38]

In addition to asserting their right to this republican ideal, residents claimed—just as with the cutting of trees for firewood or building supplies—that they also had a natural right to subsistence. "If I'm hungry, I've a right to furnish myself with venison," maintained one local when asked about his violations of the game law. "The law of [nature] and necessity permits it, and that I say, again, is higher than the statut' book." "[The deer] were given to us for food, and it matters not how we kill them," contended another. Adirondackers asserted that this right to subsistence predated and preempted any claims the state might have to the same resources. As one longtime resident quipped, "When they made the game laws down in Albany, somehow they skipped Spruce Mountain," his favorite local hunting area.[39]

The ethical framework that residents applied to hunting paralleled their approach to timber cutting in other respects as well. In much the same manner that Adirondackers considered the felling of trees for non-market uses to be the most justifiable form of timber trespass, they viewed the taking of game to be most morally defensible when the hunter used the animals for family subsistence rather than selling them. Recalling his boyhood hunting in Herkimer County, Henry Conklin declared, "Everybody got them [white-tailed deer] and supposed they were free as water. There was never any wasted, for they were not killed expressly for their saddles to supply the market. No, they were killed because we were poor and had to have meat." Questioned in 1885 about conditions in the region, Ernest H. Johnson of Tupper Lake ventured a similar preference for nonmarket hunting: "Stop the hunting and fishing (out of season) for market, and pass an act making it unlawful to buy or offer for sale any venison in the Adirondacks. I would urge that the sale of venison within the boundaries of the State Park be prohibited." Concurred Arvin Hutchins of Indian Lake, "If there was a law to make it a fine to offer fish or venison for sale, I think that would be all the additional law that would be necessary." That same year, asserting that "it is the market hunter who will exterminate the deer of the woods," the inhabitants of Conklin's Herkimer County circulated a petition that asked the county supervisors to prohibit all killing of deer for market.[40]

Much as occurred with lumbering, however, the moral certainties of this subsistence position began to erode in the late nineteenth century. As the market cast an increasingly long shadow over the region, a number of inhabitants fastened upon market hunting as a preferable alternative to other, seemingly more dependent and less profitable forms of capitalist engagement, such as wage labor. Both such factors exhibit themselves, for instance, in the thinking of Albert Page of Lake Pleasant, who enthused after killing a partridge in the early 1900s that "he had...made a good day's wage as he was going to sell [the bird] for $1." At the same time, the activities of market hunters such as Page placed them at odds with residents who adopted other economic strategies during this period—especially guides, who sought to preserve their relatively well-paying jobs by maintaining a pool of wildlife that would attract employers to the region.[41]

As such divisions reveal, the conflicts that unfolded in the Adirondacks over the game law pitted residents against not only outside conservationists but also against members of their own communities. The peculiar mixture of subsistence, lumbering, and tourism that prevailed in the Adirondacks left the region's inhabitants with a number of tensions that were difficult, if not impossible, to reconcile. As a correspondent for the *Hamilton County Record* reported in 1895, "After a deliberate and diligent inquiry with the people, regarding the proposed changes in the game laws of the state that are now agitating people here...I am forced to the opinion that no law can be framed which will be satisfactory to all." Some residents hoped to preserve their economic autonomy through market hunting. Others wanted to outlaw market hunting completely because of its potentially devastating effect on the region's game population. Some residents preferred to hunt by hounding and jacking because of the efficiency of such techniques. Others feared that these practices enabled sports hunters to decimate local wildlife. Some residents were willing to accept the larger quantities of deer that sports killed with hounding and jacking, because these successes attracted more tourist dollars to the region. Others worried about the possibility of overhunting. These debates acquired a further layer of complexity because activities such as jacking and hounding did not allow for much selectivity as to the animal one was killing (when jacking, all one saw was the illuminated eyes of the deer; when hounding, it was the dogs that chose which deer to follow). Recognizing the stresses that recent developments had placed on the game supply, a number of Adirondackers began to argue that the hunting of does should be outlawed, which would also mean outlawing jacking and hounding. Those involved in the tourist trade tended to favor a ban on the killing of does for another reason as well: the regularity with which guides were mistaken for deer and shot by inexperienced and overexcited sports hunters. Many guides believed that such tragedies could be prevented if the law required hunters to check whether an animal was male or female before they fired.[42]

Much like the timber law, then, the game law became the terrain on which Adirondackers negotiated the new circumstances governing their lives. If they were never able to resolve all the competing agendas of their fellow community members, the considerable energy that Adirondackers devoted at the turn of the century to debating game legislation demonstrates that they were not, as conservationists often imagined, opposed to laws per se. Moreover, in many cases residents advocated not "wide open laws" but regulations, such as those against market hunting or the killing of does, that were far more restrictive than New York's existing statutes. Viewed from this context, Adirondackers' violations of the forest code emerge not as a manifestation of their inherent disregard for all law but as a sign of their frustration with a simplistic regulatory regime that failed to take into account their wants and needs. As one resident put it, "The laws were made by men who don't know what we need here. Give us some laws we can take care of and we'll put them through."[43]

As a result of the coming of conservation, the residents of the Adirondacks inhabited a landscape that, by the mid-1890s, was far different from the one they had known only a decade or so earlier. Many of the forests where locals used to cut firewood and building supplies had become part of New York's Forest Preserve and were now patrolled against trespass by the state's new forester force. The wildlife in the region was now subject to an array of new state laws that limited the season and manner in which game could be hunted. The building of homesteads on unused state land had become criminalized as squatting. The spread of private parks denied Adirondackers access to lands where they had long hunted, fished, and foraged for wild plants. Observed the state surveyor Verplanck Colvin sympathetically in 1896, "The enclosure of large private parks, the reservation of the forests, the narrowing limitation of laws relative to the wild forest game, all indicate a changed condition of affairs." In a number of other rural areas such as British India and the post-Reconstruction American South, lawmakers instituted similar regulations over natural resources to drive country folk into the labor market. Even though New York's conservation code was not designed with the same end in mind, its effect was almost identical. By impeding residents' access to the local environment, conservation inevitably magnified the importance of wage labor as an alternative means of support.[44]

Wage work assumed a variety of forms in the Adirondacks, from sawing logs in a lumber camp to cleaning dishes in a hotel. But the guiding of sports emerged as the most avidly sought position, for it offered comfortable working conditions and, by regional standards, relatively high pay. As the competition for employment increased in the closing decades of the nineteenth century, guides responded by establishing a number of local clubs designed to increase their control over hiring and wages. A correspondent to *Forest and Stream* explained in 1883 that the Adirondacks' guides had become "nearly all members of associations.... There are Blue Mountain guides, Saranac guides, Long Lake guides, Fulton Chain guides, St. Regis, Raquette, and I don't know how many others, and a migratory sportsman finds that he cannot depend upon a cordial reception being given to his guide if he takes him into the limits claimed by a body of which he is not a member."[45] Over time, these clubs established a system of work rules that was closely followed throughout the Adirondacks. These practices subdivided the region into different districts, each served by a corps of guides drawn from the local community. "Adirondack guides do not roam aimlessly through the entire wilderness in search of employment," noted the New York State superintendent of forests, William Fox. "Each one attaches himself to some particular locality. They strictly adhere to the rule that the guides in each locality are entitled to the patronage of all tourists, travelers, or sportsmen starting from within the precincts of certain guides' territory." Under this system, a guide who lived in the vicinity of Blue Mountain Lake, for instance, would guide only visitors to that area. If his sport subsequently decided that he wanted to journey on to the lakes of the Fulton Chain, the guide would convey his client to a place where he could engage a Fulton Chain guide. The Blue Mountain Lake guide would then return to his home territory; the wages he collected from his sport would include a payment covering the time necessary to complete this return journey. Besides reflecting the many community-based "micro-localities" that had long governed resource use in the Adirondacks, this system yielded two additional benefits: it ensured that employment was more equitably shared among guides, and it meant that sports often had to pay more in wages, since they might pay for the return trips of several guides.[46]

Guides followed other rules as well. No guide, for example, accepted employment for less than a day. Nor did guides rent out untended boats. Visiting sports who wanted the use of a boat were required to hire a guide to accompany them. Should these controls be threatened, it was not unknown for guides to take violent measures to protect what they took to be their prerogatives. When a man named Theodore White brought a steam-powered boat, the "Lake Lily," to Lake Placid in the 1880s, for example, it was consumed not long afterward in a suspicious blaze, said to have been ignited by angry guides who considered transporting tourists to be their exclusive right and the hand-rowed guide boat the only acceptable vessel for doing so.[47]

Localistic, informal associations throughout the 1880s, the guide clubs reshaped themselves in the 1890s as conservation heightened the importance of wage labor. In 1891, representatives from the region's various clubs gathered together in Saranac Lake to form the Adirondack Guides' Association (AGA)—the first time all the guides in the Adirondacks had ever been unified into a single organization. While the exact membership varied over the years, over 200 guides attended the AGA's formative meeting, and a broadside that the association published in 1897 lists 233 guides as members.[48]

Although the AGA carefully avoided calling itself a union, in a number of key respects it paralleled the craft unions founded by artisanal workers during this same period. Like a craft union, the AGA provided sickness, death, and disability benefits to members and their families, and it strove to maintain a uniform rate of pay: three dollars a day plus expenses. "The rates asked by the guides are uniform throughout the entire region...and firmly fixed," noted the Forest Commission in 1893. "The tourist and sportsman will find that there is nothing to be gained by haggling over them." Most important, the AGA sought to limit membership, and thus employability, to a select few. Potential AGA members had to pass through a rigorous accreditation process.

Only long-standing community members—those who had lived in the Adirondacks for at least fifteen years and who had previously worked as a guide for at least three years—were eligible to join. Each potential member also had to approved by one of the AGA's twelve regionally based subcommittees, carryovers from the earlier system of local clubs.[49]

Despite these resemblances to other craft unions, the AGA possessed several features that set it apart from the typical labor organization. By far the most unusual concerned membership. While the AGA accepted only guides as full members, it invited sports hunters to join as "associate members" who paid dues but were unable to vote on any of the association's resolutions. Following his election in 1891, the AGA's first secretary, J. Herbert Miller, initiated an aggressive mailing campaign to attract as many prominent sportsmen as possible to join the AGA. Surprisingly, many sports—perhaps because of the appeal of rubbing shoulders with manly Adirondacks hunters—responded enthusiastically to the opportunity to become dues-paying, nonvoting members of what was, in effect, a rural craft union. In the words of *Forest and Stream,* "Many of the most prominent citizens of New York State have enrolled. Among them are State officials, hotel men, prominent physicians and attorneys, members of the press and of the various Adirondacks clubs." Another of the AGA's unusual features was its creation of the post of honorary president, which was held not by a local guide but by a prominent outsider. For most of the AGA's early years, Verplanck Colvin, the head of the Adirondack Survey, filled the position. Colvin's main duty was delivering annual addresses, in which he typically celebrated the AGA as a unique organization, able to bridge the class divide that so troubled American society elsewhere. "In this form of association you have set a wonderful example to the labor organizations of the world," he remarked at the AGA's first annual meeting. His annual speech four years later struck a similar note: "You have brought about ... the preliminary steps toward that combination of capital and labor which has been the dream of some political economists and the hope of patriots."[50]

As Colvin's words underscore, the fact that the AGA was willing to accept both laborers (guides) and their employers (sportsmen) would seem to make it a curious union indeed, one that scarcely seems to demonstrate the class consciousness that, according to some definitions, is essential to a workers' organization.[51] As peculiar as it was, however, this arrangement offered several tactical advantages. The first and most

obvious was that accepting associate members expanded the pool of
funds available to the AGA. Associate members not only paid dues but
were often appealed to for extra sums to finance special endeavors of
the AGA. Some of these associate members (of which there were 107 in
1898, compared to approximately 280 regular members that same
year) could be quite lavish in their support of the union.[52] When the
AGA sent representatives to the annual sportsman's show at Madison
Square Garden in 1902, for instance, the financier William Whitney
took the AGA's delegation of twelve guides to a Broadway show
(Beauty and the Beast) before treating them to a banquet at the exclusive New York Athletic Club, where the party drank a champagne toast
"to the Adirondack Guides' association."[53] The acceptance of sportsmen within the AGA also reflects the peculiar character of the guides'
profession. In an industry with a diffuse set of employers, for whom
hunting and fishing were not moneymaking operations but were instead
leisure activities, it would have been difficult for guides to pursue such
traditional union tactics as slowdowns or strikes. Inviting sportsmen
into the AGA was a way to nudge them toward a greater appreciation
of the concerns of guides, while diffusing any fears the sports may have
had about a conspiracy among the guides. (Anxieties about the AGA
nevertheless surfaced from time to time. Following the murder of Orrando Dexter in 1903, for instance, one Albany paper reported that "a
number of guides who are foremost in the Guides' union are being
watched by the police. It is almost certain, it is said, that arrests will be
made and the secrets of the union delved into.")[54]

A final incentive for including sportsmen in the AGA was the lever-
age that sports provided in the union's efforts to shape regulations in the
region. Each year at their main meeting, AGA members voted on resolutions recommending changes in the state's timber and game laws. In
1895, for example, the AGA voted in favor of a measure urging the
New York State Legislature to enact a law "that no brook or lake trout,
or venison, be sold or offered for sale in any of the counties comprising
the forest preserve at any season of the year."[55] Other measures passed
in subsequent years by the AGA and by the Brown's Tract Guides' Association (BTGA, a group from the Fulton Lake district that split from
the AGA in 1898 over the issue of hounding) called for increasing the
quantity of state land in the park, for an end to the killing of
does, and for more protection of the black bear.[56] The inclusion of
well-connected associate members provided both groups with a con-
duit through which such resolutions could reach an audience beyond

the Adirondacks. One notable success came in 1899, when Teddy Roosevelt, then governor of New York, invited representatives from both the AGA and the BTGA to meet with him in Albany to discuss possible amendments to the conservation laws.[57]

Through such measures, the members of the AGA and BTGA sought not simply to improve their immediate working conditions but also to articulate their own vision of conservation. Members stressed their ties to the Adirondacks, which, they argued, made them especially sensitive to the condition of local plants and wildlife. Rather than threatening the region's natural resources, as conservation's degradation discourse posited them as doing, the guides envisioned themselves as "the true game-keepers of the magnificent park in which most of their lives have been spent." While conservationists believed that rural folk's economic dependency led them to embrace destructive practices, guides turned this dependency into a positive good, arguing that it forced them to steward local resources. A guide "sees in the forests, in the fish, in the game his stock in trade," explained J. Herbert Miller, the AGA's secretary, in 1895. "The forests," Miller added, "can best be protected by those residing within their borders, especially by those who are interested in their preservation that their means of livelihood may be retained."[58]

With their allusions to virtuous locals and misguided outsiders, the AGA and BTGA shared some of the anticonservationist, antisportsman rhetoric of other Adirondackers.[59] But the guides' language of protection and their economic and social links to prominent sports also gave them the ability to forge alliances with conservationists. In fact, in the 1890s and early 1900s the AGA and the BTGA were active participants in several conservationist schemes to restore the Adirondacks wildlife. The most successful was an effort to increase the beaver population in the Adirondacks, which by 1900 had dipped to an estimated twenty animals, all located in Township 20 in Franklin County. In 1904, the Forest Commission bought seven Canadian beaver. The animals wintered in Old Forge, where they were cared for by the BTGA at its own expense. The following spring, an "Army of Liberation" composed of BTGA members released the animals at various promising spots within the park. In 1906, the Forest Commission purchased twenty-five more beaver, this time from Yellowstone National Park. The BTGA again oversaw the care and release of the animals, which took so readily to their new surroundings that by the 1920s the beaver population within the park had climbed to an estimated twenty thousand.[60]

The guides' associations were instrumental to several other restocking attempts as well. In 1901, the members of the BTGA, pledging "we will protect them," urged the state to restore moose to the region.[61] In response, the New York State Legislature appropriated five thousand dollars to purchase and ship moose to the Adirondacks, and by 1902 at least fifteen animals had been released near Raquette Lake and the promisingly named Big Moose Lake. That same year, the BTGA solicited a donation of five elk and paid to have the animals shipped to the Adirondacks. Members cared for the elk over the winter before releasing the animals the following spring.[62] Although the BTGA subsequently posted notices throughout the region warning of the increased penalties for killing an elk or moose (a fine of one hundred dollars plus a sentence of three months to one year in jail), some residents nonetheless targeted the transplants.[63] Less than a year after the BTGA released its elk, one was hit by a train and the remaining four were killed by local hunters and left to rot in the woods. "The shooting," fumed the BTGA in its annual report, "was without doubt intentional and from pure malice."[64] The reintroduced moose fared little better. Habitat change, brain worm, and poaching sealed their fate, and by 1908 the experiment was pronounced a failure.[65]

The fact that some Adirondackers would maliciously shoot the very same animals that other community members were caring for testifies to the deep fissures that had developed within Adirondacks society by the turn of the century. Ironically, at the very moment that the region's guides had begun to accommodate the new conservationist order, other inhabitants were unleashing a wave of spectacular protests against conservation, of which the killing of the unfortunate moose and elk comprised just one example. In 1899, 1903, 1908, and again in 1913, vast forest fires swept across the park, burning more than a million acres of state and private land. While many of these fires could be attributed to the fire hazards created by the region's spreading railroad system, a significant proportion was the work of arsonists. (See Table 5.) After the forest fires of 1903, for example, which scorched over 450,000 acres in the Adirondacks, the Forest Commission declared that "some conflagrations were started by incendiaries and degenerates, prompted by malice, revenge, or criminal instincts." Commissioners charged that "in nearly every [Adirondacks] village there is a disreputable class whose presence is inimical to the preservation of our forests. They are the men who, having been arrested at some time for violation of the Game Law or timber stealing, have a grievance against the authorities.

They hang around hotels or taverns and when any so-called 'State man' is in hearing, delight in making threats that, 'The State has got to look out or there will be more fire in the woods,' to which the bystanders listen with smiles or nods of approval."[66] Making sense of this widespread arson remains one of the most challenging problems confronting any history of conservation. Unlike the poaching of timber or game—crimes that rewarded their perpetrators with obvious benefits—setting vast portions of the Adirondacks forest ablaze would seem to yield no clear advantage to anyone. In fact, given that arson sometimes resulted in raging conflagrations that destroyed not only trees but topsoil, it would seem inimical to the interests of the region's residents.[67]

One potential answer to this puzzle comes to us from other nations' experiences with conservation. The scholar Ramachandra Guha, for example, has proposed that the frequent arson in India's forest districts reflects an alienation from nature produced by state forestry policies. According to Guha, peasants excluded from woodlands where they had once foraged began to view the forest not as source of sustenance but "as an entity *opposed* to the villager"—a symbol of their displacement and disempowerment. Consequentially, peasants retaliated by burning the woodlands they had once depended upon. In much the same manner, the historian Eugen Weber has explained the massive fires that greeted the rise of forestry in France by arguing that the French peasantry "had come to hate the forests themselves, and hoped that if they ravaged them enough they would get rid of their oppressors."[68]

Revenge certainly explains a substantial portion of the arson in the Adirondacks. Asked years later about the region's frequent forest fires, one longtime inhabitant recalled, "Hell, we had to wait for droughts to get even. I remember my father cursing the rain that seemed to be always falling on the Adirondacks. We didn't get much chances, but we took them when we got them."[69] Residents had multiple reasons for seeking vengeance: the state's restrictive new hunting law ("If they don't stop bothering us with this game law business, the people will burn down the whole north woods"); the Forest Commission's efforts to uproot squatters ("Threats have been made by certain squatters that if ejected they would seek revenge by burning up the North Woods"); and the prosecution of timber thieves ("If the State attempted 'to slaughter' these men, it would be the worst thing the State could do to preserve the lands....the trespassers would retaliate by *firing* state lands").[70] Such threats, which transformed the forest into a hostage whose very survival depended on the state not antagonizing local residents, often proved

Year	Number of Fires	Acreage Burned	Causes						
			Careless- ness	Fisherfolk	Berry Pickers[a]	Smokers	Hunters[b]	Railroads	Clearing Land[c]
1891	65	13,789	4	5		2	1	7	18
1892	33	1,030		1				8	18
1893	13	8,790			1			2	5
1894	50	17,093		6			1	10	14
1895	36	2,448	2	2	1		1	4	14
1896	116	29,817	4		4	3	2	9	41
1897	98	26,187		6	1	1	5	3	11
1898	98	9,648	3	6	1	1	4	16	28
1899	322	51,565	7	15	30	11	62	24	31
1900	127	14,893	6	5	2	6	8	21	19
1901		7,780							
1902		21,356							
1903	643	464,189	6	47	3	23	7	121	89
1904	101	2,627	3	8		14	9	21	20
1905	126	4,795	9	2	2	18	10	31	8
1906	142	12,500	1	14	2	14	8	20	9
1907	198	5,653	6	10	6	5	2	48	21
1908	596	368,072	15	19	14	34	100	89	21
1909	356	11,759	28	14	31	25	19	45	38
1910	277	12,680	12	23	3	39	37	60	24
1911	595	37,909	40	35	38	72	10	109	35
1912	383	6,990	13	37	7	59	10	93	17
1913	688	54,796		120	31	224	14	78	43
TOTAL	5,063	1,186,366	159	375	177	551	310	819	524
PERCENT OF TOTAL NUMBER OF FIRES			3.1	7.4	3.5	10.9	6.1	16.2	10.4

[a] Berry pickers set fires to encourage the growth of a fresh crop of berries.
[b] Hunters set fires to drive game and to create new browse for deer.
[c] Farmers used fire to prepare their fields for planting.
[d] Bee hunters used fire to smoke bees out of their hives.
[e] Many cases of arson or of fires set to clear farmland may have gone unrecorded by local fire wardens who did not want to antagonize fellow community members by reporting their crimes to the Forest Commission.

SOURCE: Howard, *Forest Fires*, 19.
NOTE: Forest Preserve counties were located both in the Adirondacks and in the Catskills.

Causes

Arson	Campers	Lightning	Burning Buildings	Children	Logging Engines	Sawmills	Bee Hunters[d]	Blasting	Unknown[e]
3	2			1	1				21
1			1				1		3
2									3
4	3						1		11
	5								7
6	4	1					1		41
8			2	3					58
1	1				1				36
9	47	9	5	7			3		62
13	6	3	1	1			1		35
6	6	1	6	1					327
4	4	1		2				1	14
5	2		6	1		1			31
11	6		1	4				1	51
5	8	1	3						83
48	27	9	1	6		1		2	210
21	47	4	3	5			1	1	74
22	23	11	9	2	2				10
37	29	65	1		1			1	122
20	32	34	5	4		1	2	1	48
30	64	26	8	7	2		1		40
256	316	165	52	44	6	4	11	7	1287
5.1	6.2	3.3	1.0	.8	.1	<0.0	.2	.1	25.4

quite effective in restraining officials. One reason that the Forest Commission tarried so long in ejecting squatters from state lands, for instance, was out of concern for what "a man who had a spite could cause to the State by fires."[71]

But to focus exclusively on revenge obscures some of the other reasons Adirondackers set forest fires. Timber poachers, for example, frequently burned the area where they had illegally cut wood in the hope of erasing any traces of their trespasses. Other Adirondackers, adopting a long-standing Indian practice, burned local woodlands to encourage the growth of berries or fresh browse for livestock or wildlife. Others set fires on the private parks within the Forest Preserve with the intention of damaging estate property or driving deer and other game animals onto lands where they might be hunted.[72] And still others set fires because they sought the cash wages that employment on a fire-fighting crew could bring or, once on a fire-fighting crew, hoped to prolong their employment. "The poor people of a certain community cut wood on State land last winter and were fined for it," reported *Forest and Stream* in 1903. "Partly to 'get even' and partly to earn money to make up the fines by fighting fires, the poachers were believed to have set the fires."[73]

In addition, any full understanding of the arson that gripped the Adirondacks at the turn of the century needs to situate such acts in relation to the fire control laws that New York instituted in the region in the mid-1880s. Prior to the coming of conservation, Adirondackers had traditionally set "fallow fires" to prepare their fields for planting. This practice came under new state regulation in 1885, when Bernhard Fernow wrote the fire code for New York's new Forest Preserve. (The "first effective law against forest fires" in the nation, Fernow's code was later copied by Maine, New Hampshire, Wisconsin, and Minnesota, among other states.) Because fallow fires sometimes strayed into nearby forests, the code required that all agricultural burning be limited to certain seasons and conducted under the supervision of fire wardens. Should any large fires break out in the vicinity, the law mandated that all residents participate on fire-fighting crews, with anyone who refused being subjected to a fine of up to twenty dollars.[74]

These changes proved unpopular with many residents, for they conflicted with the exigencies of local agriculture. Previously, Adirondackers had fired their fields in the spring, before planting, and in the fall, after the harvest. But as these were also the dry seasons in the region, the new regulations required that locals instead burn their plots in

Figure 1.   Mitchell Sabattis, an Abenaki Indian and longtime
resident of Long Lake, standing between two examples of the
hybrid European–Native American material culture that developed in the Adirondacks during the nineteenth century: the
pack basket and the Adirondack guide boat. (Photo courtesy
of Adirondack Museum.)

Figure 2.   A guide transporting his "sport" in the distinctive Adirondack guide boat, which combined elements of both the Native American canoe and the European rowboat. (Photo courtesy of Adirondack Museum.)

Figure 3. Two Adirondackers "jacking" deer. The man in the bow of the boat used the bright light from the lantern on his head to blind his prey. Although popular among many of the region's residents, this form of hunting was outlawed by the New York State Legislature in 1897. (Photo courtesy of Adirondack Museum.)

Figure 4. Shingles made from trees illegally cut on the Forest Preserve, abandoned by timber thieves fleeing state authorities. (Collection of author.)

Figure 5. Forest Commission officials (note the figure by the stump at right) investigating the theft of a large pine log from state lands near Raquette Lake in 1901. (Collection of author.)

Figure 6.   A sign from a private park in the Adirondacks. Most estates in the region were ringed by scores of such signs, which prohibited locals from hunting, fishing, or otherwise using private parklands. (Photo courtesy of New York State Archives.)

Figure 7. One of the many signs detailing New York's regulations for the use of fire that the Forest Commission posted throughout the Adirondacks at the turn of the century. (Photo courtesy of New York State Archives.)

Figure 8.   A new fire tower. Following a devastating series of forest fires in
1903 and 1908, New York authorities constructed towers such as this one at
many high points in the Adirondacks, enabling Forest Commission employees
to expand their surveillance of local conditions. (Photo courtesy of New York
State Archives.)

Figure 9.   The remnants of a poacher's cabin in Yellowstone. This particular structure was so well hidden that it was not discovered by park authorities until the 1960s. (Photo courtesy of National Park Service, Yellowstone National Park.)

Figure 10. "The National Park Poacher." The buffalo poacher Ed Howell is on the far right, with his dog curled up by his feet; the scout who brought him in, Felix Burgess, is on the left; two of the U.S. Army soldiers assigned to the park appear between them. All are outfitted with the long wooden skis that patrollers and poachers alike favored for getting around during Yellowstone's harsh winters. (Photo courtesy of National Park Service, Yellowstone National Park.)

Figure 11. Ed Howell being escorted into Fort Yellowstone by army patrollers, following his arrest. (Photo courtesy of National Park Service, Yellowstone National Park.)

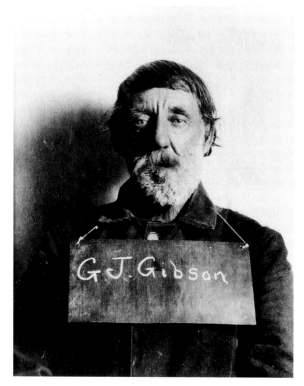

Figure 12. G. J. Gibson, arrested by the army in 1908 for trapping beaver in Yellowstone National Park. (Photo courtesy of National Park Service, Yellowstone National Park.)

Figure 13. Joseph Stukley, a former miner from Electric, Montana, following his arrest for hunting deer in Yellowstone. Stukley had lost his right arm in a mining accident and presumably turned to poaching because his injury made it difficult for him to find employment as a miner. (Photo courtesy of National Park Service, Yellowstone National Park.)

Figure 14.
A mug shot of William
Binkley, taken by army
photographers shortly after
Binkley's 1907 conviction
for poaching elk in the park.
(Photo courtesy of National
Park Service, Yellowstone
National Park.)

Figure 15. Army officers posing at Fort Yellowstone with buffalo heads
confiscated from park poachers at the turn of the century. (Photo courtesy
of National Park Service, Yellowstone National Park.)

Figure 16.   A Havasupai woman photographed in the 1890s. She is wearing clothing made of calico and carrying mescal shoots in the basket on her back. (Photo courtesy of Grand Canyon National Park Museum Collection.)

Figure 17. Chickapanyegi as he appeared in 1898 in a photograph most likely taken on the plateau above Havasu Canyon. Note his rifle and the deer antler at his feet. (Photo courtesy of Grand Canyon National Park Museum Collection.)

Figure 18.   Havasupai men putting the finishing touches on a new trail along the Grand Canyon's South Rim. (Photo courtesy of National Archives and Records Administration.)

Figure 19.   One of the cabins constructed by the Havasupai in the early twentieth century from materials salvaged from the Grand Canyon Village dump. (Photo courtesy of Grand Canyon National Park Museum Collection.)

Figure 20. A Havasupai family photographed in the early 1930s at the camp near Grand Canyon Village. (Photo courtesy of Grand Canyon National Park Museum Collection.)

Figure 21. Another cabin in the Havasupai camp near Grand Canyon Village. The assorted barrels and jugs were used to store drinking water, while the automobile—a relatively recent addition to Havasupai life—enabled the tribe's men to search for seasonal wage labor over a much wider geographical area. (Photo courtesy of Grand Canyon National Park Museum Collection.)

the summer and winter. In summer, however, any fire risked destroying just-planted crops, while in winter, fallow fires frequently had to contend with a thick blanket of snow. Claiming that "the law is no good" and that "they can burn on their own land when they have a mind to," Adirondackers seldom honored the new law. "Less than one-half of the persons setting fires to burn fallows have given notice to me or to the district-wardens," complained the Minerva fire warden Daniel Lynch in 1890. Two years later, William Meveigh, the fire warden for the town of Lake Pleasant, confronted Charles Leston, "who [had] set fire to his fallow in positive defiance of the law." "When I discovered it," Meveigh recounted, "I went down and told him [Leston] it was a violation of the law, and to extinguish it. He told me that he would put it out when it burned out, as the land was his, and he would do as he liked on it; the State had no right to prevent him. I think it is meant to be a test case, and that Leston is incited by others to go ahead and see what the State can do about it, as the fire law meets with little favor in this town." Other locals angrily told forestry officials, "We have got to burn this fallow because we have got to plant potatoes.... it is the only means of subsistence we have."[75]

Given such regulations, the Adirondacker who set local woodlands on fire was engaging in an act that was deviant on a multitude of levels. Not only was he (arsonists, like poachers and timber thieves, seem to have been overwhelmingly male) asserting his disregard for the state's attempts to control the time and space where fires were permissible, he was also rejecting the model of civic duty proposed by the Forest Commission, in which "good citizens" participated on fire-fighting crews. The arson that periodically swept the region can therefore be interpreted not simply as a manifestation of revenge but as an effort by those residents who believed that the Forest Commission's regulations had unfairly deprived them of their rights to hunt, farm, or lumber to assert their—and the forests'—freedom from state supervision.[76]

Unable to halt such arsonists ("the miscreants who start these fires... enter the forest alone and unobserved...and then, aided by their knowledge of the wilderness, emerge at some point many miles distant"), the Forest Commission could only increase its fines, which by 1910 reached two thousand dollars or ten years in prison, and try to limit the fires' spread once they started. Following the devastating conflagrations of 1903 and 1908, the commission erected "observation stations" from which watchers could spot blazes as soon as they began. By 1914, there were fifty-one towers located at strategic high points throughout the region, each equipped with "strong field glasses, range finders, maps made especially for the purpose," and special telephones that allowed the watchers to report any fires to officials as quickly as possible. To facilitate their occupants' views of the surrounding territory, the stations rose far above the surrounding tree line. Starkly silhouetted against the Adirondacks sky, each stood as a prominent symbol of the heightened state surveillance that conservation had brought to the region and of the restive and divided populace now dwelling within the Adirondack Park's borders.[77]

PART II

Mountain

Yellowstone

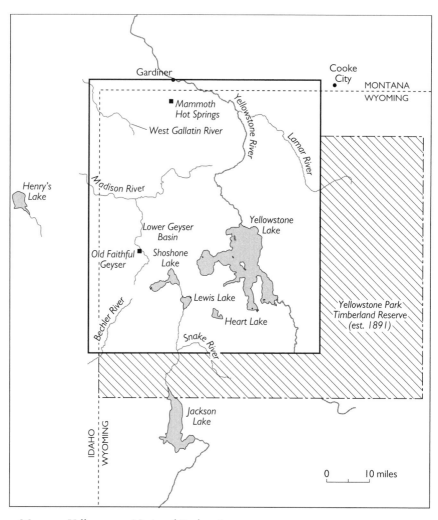

Map 2.   Yellowstone National Park, 1872

CHAPTER 4

Nature and Nation

On the morning of August 24, 1877, Frank Carpenter awoke to a sight unlike any other he had encountered in Yellowstone National Park: five mounted Indians riding into his camp in Yellowstone's Lower Geyser Basin. For the past two weeks, Carpenter, along with several friends and family members, had been sightseeing in the nation's first park, created some five years earlier to protect Yellowstone's unique natural features. Dramatically situated on a high plateau, the new park boasted thousands of geysers, boiling springs, mud pots, fumaroles, and other geothermal oddities—all testimony to the region's location over a rare volcanic hot spot in the earth's crust. Like the handful of other sightseers trickling into the area in the 1870s, Carpenter and his companions quickly became enchanted with Yellowstone's strange geological formations, which had already earned the park the nickname "Wonderland" after the recently released *Alice's Adventures in Wonderland*.[1]

Tourists at a time when the industry was in its infancy, Carpenter's party met few other visitors during their initial days in Yellowstone. This situation changed abruptly, however, in the early hours of August 24. Shortly after dawn, just as the travelers were beginning to awaken, a party of five Nez Perce Indians, led by a man who called himself Yellow Wolf, rode into view. The Indians demanded food and ammunition and, after unsuccessfully attempting to pass themselves off as Shoshones, admitted to being members of Chief Joseph's Nez Perce band. This was a shocking revelation, for as both the Indians and the tourists knew, the Nez Perce were fighting a running battle with U.S. Army troops, sparked by heavy-handed federal efforts to force the tribe onto a reservation in Idaho. Alarmed, Carpenter and his fellow sightseers attempted to pack up camp, only to be seized by the Nez Perce, who feared that the tourists might tell the army of the Indians' position and thus prevent the tribe's flight to Canada. For the next several days, Carpenter, his sisters, and his friends were held hostage by the Nez Perce and forced to accompany some eight hundred tribe members on their journey across the park into Montana.[2]

This encounter between tourist and Indian was scarcely the sort of interaction that Congress had intended when it established Yellowstone National Park in 1872. Rather, the chief goal in setting aside some two million acres at the junction of Wyoming, Montana, and Idaho territories as "a public park or pleasureing-ground [sic] for the benefit and enjoyment of the people" had instead been to preserve the region's unusual geothermal features, both as a "laboratory" for natural scientists and as a unifying national emblem for a nation just emerging from a bloody and divisive Civil War.[3] At the time, so little was known about Yellowstone's topography (one of the remotest places in the continental United States, it would not be mapped until the mid-1880s) that lawmakers, not wishing to leave any of "the greatest wonders of Nature that the world affords" outside of the future park, drew its boundaries generously, taking in much of the area surrounding the known geysers and fire holes.[4]

As a result, even though the congressional debate leading up to Yellowstone's creation involved little reference to Marsh or the other early conservation thinkers who had proved so instrumental to New York's efforts in the Adirondacks, the nation's new park was expansive enough to encompass not only the headwaters of several major western rivers and extensive herds of elk, deer, and mountain sheep but also one of North America's last surviving buffalo populations. Once later investigations revealed Yellowstone's potential for conservation, federal officials, at the urging of eastern conservationists such as George Bird Grinnell, Teddy Roosevelt, and the elite, New York–based Boone and Crockett sports hunting club, expanded the park's timber and wildlife regulations. By 1895, a congressional report on Yellowstone could speak of the park as serving three central functions:

> First. As a region containing some of the chief natural wonders of the world.
> Second. As the largest of the forest reserves.
> Third. As the greatest existing game preserve.[5]

Despite the haphazard manner in which conservation began at Yellowstone, the park nonetheless marked a turning point in federal land policy. In keeping with the goal of fostering the independent yeoman farmers so prized by republican ideology, previous federal programs had focused on converting the public domain into small-scale, privately owned plots of land. But the creation of a two-million-acre park signaled a significant shift in federal priorities. No longer was the national government to be merely a temporary caretaker of the American countryside, eager to surrender its role to private property owners: henceforth, it would be an ongoing presence in the landscape, the permanent manager of vast portions of the rural United States. And Yellowstone, as the location where the federal government first undertook this new role, would serve as proving ground and template for federal efforts elsewhere.[6]

Federal planners, however, were not the only people with designs for the Yellowstone landscape during the late nineteenth century. In ways that the nascent conservation movement seldom cared to acknowledge, Yellowstone was also part of a preexisting native world. The Nez Perces' unexpected arrival at Frank Carpenter's camp in 1877 testifies to at least one aspect of this Indian Yellowstone: the network of Indian trails lacing the new park. In their flight to Canada, the Nez Perces were following a familiar route, one they had used many times before to cross the Rocky Mountains and reach the once buffalo-rich prairies of the northern Great Plains.[7] This pathway, rutted from the passage of countless travois and Indian ponies over the years, fanned out in the Yellowstone region into a dense web of Indian trails. Some led to the game grounds surrounding Yellowstone Lake, others to the sites where one could quarry obsidian, a glasslike stone created by volcanic action, out of which Indian peoples fashioned knives, arrowheads, and other tools. In the words of Hiram Chittenden of the U.S. Army Corps of Engineers, "Indian trails...were everywhere."[8]

These trails reflected the passage of a wide spectrum of native groups, of which the Nez Perce, who spent most of the year in present-day Idaho and Washington, were far from the most prominent. The Yellowstone Plateau was situated at the point where several different Indian nations overlapped and contested one another. To the north were the Blackfeet, who occasionally ventured into the area to hunt elk or trap beaver. To the east were the Crow, whose territorial claims, although battered by the incursions of the expansive Lakota, took in both sections of the Great Plains and the foothills of the Rocky Mountains.

To the west and south were loosely associated bands of the Shoshone and Bannock, who in the course of a year might range through a number of Yellowstone's ecological zones, from its well-watered river bottoms to its subalpine meadows, in search of game and wild plants. While relations between these groups ran the gamut from peaceful trade to hostile raids, intertribal tensions appear to have increased in the nineteenth century as some groups, amid the instability brought by epidemic disease, European trade, and heightened warfare on the plains, attempted to increase their spheres of influence at the expense of their weaker neighbors.[9]

Perceptive nineteenth-century observers found the Yellowstone landscape saturated with traces of these Indian groups. Early park managers discovered abandoned Indian shelters—"circular upright brush heaps called wickeups"—"in nearly all of the sheltered glens and valleys of the Park," and in most every meadow they found "extensive pole or brush fences" designed to funnel deer, mountain sheep, and other animals to canyons or enclosures where they could more easily be killed.[10] Other visitors encountered even more direct evidence of Yellowstone's Indian presence. Near the confines of the present-day park, the members of an 1869 survey of the area met "a band of Indians—who, however, proved to be Tonkeys, or Sheepeaters." The following year, another party of "explorers" not only followed "an old Indian trail" into the area, along which the group found "plenty of Indian 'signs,'" they also spotted a number of Crow Indians keeping a wary watch on the party's progress. During a U.S. Geological Survey mapping expedition in 1871, surveyors "accidentally discovered...the camp of a family of the Sheep-eater band of Bannacks [sic]." Because of such peoples' detailed knowledge of local geography, later expeditions frequently employed Bannocks or Shoshones as guides. (For their part, members of these bands were not above capitalizing on their intimate knowledge of the landscape by stealing horses from Yellowstone's early surveying parties.)[11]

Despite such encounters, park backers nonetheless persisted in describing the Yellowstone region as existing in "primeval solitude," filled with countless locations that "have never been trodden by human footsteps." The native peoples of the area, supporters maintained, seldom visited the lands bounded by the newly created park, for they were afraid of its spouting geysers and boiling hot springs. "The larger [Indian] tribes never enter the basin, restrained by superstitious ideas in connection with the thermal springs," proclaimed Gustavus Doane, an army officer who accompanied an 1870 expedition to the region. "The unscientific savage finds little to interest him in such places," agreed Doane's fellow "explorer," Walter Trumbull. "I should rather suppose he would give them a wide berth, believing them sacred to Satan." Ironically, such pronouncements had persuaded Carpenter and his companions that they had nothing to fear from the Nez Perce during their tour of Yellowstone. Army officers, recalled one of Carpenter's sisters, "assured us we would be perfectly safe if we would remain in the [Geyser] Basin, as the Indians would never come into the park."[12]

As the Carpenter party soon discovered, however, the Nez Perce exhibited little superstitious awe of Yellowstone's geothermal formations. Shortly after his capture, Carpenter ended up chatting with one curious Nez Perce about the source of the geysers' energy ("Heap fire down under the ground," explained Carpenter in what he considered to be the appropriate Indian terminology). Carpenter's companions noted that female members of the tribe used the region's hot springs to cook and clean their meager supplies of food. Other Indian peoples seem to have a similarly nonchalant response to Yellowstone's geysers. In fact, Yellowstone's volcanism may actually have drawn Native Americans into the region: the warmth given off by its ten-thousand-odd hot springs and other geothermal oddities encouraged snowfree winter grazing zones and extensive meadows, both of which made the area unusually rich in elk, deer, bison, and other game animals.[13]

Ultimately, the effort by park backers to disavow any Indian connection to Yellowstone National Park reveals far more about Euro-American conceptions of Indian land tenure than it does about the realities of Indian life. Drawing upon a familiar vocabulary of discovery and exploration, the authors of the early accounts of the Yellowstone region literally wrote Indians out of the landscape, erasing Indian claims by reclassifying inhabited territory as empty wilderness. Those "explorers" who, during the course of their travels, encountered Indian peoples within the confines of the park simply dismissed these natives as transitory nomads. Neither the Bannock, the Shoshone, the Crow, nor the Blackfeet practiced agriculture, and seeing no landscapes in the Yellowstone region that had been "improved" through farming, many Euro-Americans conveniently concluded that the area's Indians were rootless beings, with no ties to the lands they roamed across.[14]

What this ideology of dispossession overlooked was that Indian migratory patterns were not a series of random wanderings but rather a complex set of annual cycles, closely tied to seasonal variations in game and other wild foodstuffs. Moreover, while they were not farmers, local Indian peoples nonetheless "improved" the landscape around them through the setting of fires. Native Americans used fire for multiple purposes: to keep down underbrush, facilitating travel; to rid camping areas of insect pests; and to aid in hunting. Among many Indian peoples, including the Bannock, Shoshone, and Crow, it was customary for experienced tribe members to kindle fires in order to drive game animals toward locations where they might be killed by waiting hunters. By burning underbrush and dead wood, low-level fires of this sort also helped to recycle nutrients into the soil and create a mosaic of plant communities at varying levels of succession, raising the level of vegetational diversity and opening up a variety of ecological niches for wildlife. The benefits of fire were therefore not only short-term (facilitating travel and the taking of game) but long-term as well (maintaining a higher population of wildlife than would have occurred otherwise).[15]

Following their adoption of the horse in the early 1700s, the region's Native Americans expanded their use of fire, setting periodic blazes to improve the grazing lands available for their growing herds of ponies. This heightened proscriptive burning may explain the large blazes that, according to the archaeological record, swept through Yellowstone's upland forests in the 1700s as well as the repeated fires that took place in the lower lying grasslands during this same period. Eyewitness accounts suggest a link between Indian peoples and several fires that took place within the park during the 1870s and 1880s. During his 1870 survey of the park, for example, Doane observed that "the great plateau had been recently burned off to drive away the game, and the woods were still on fire in every direction." In 1881, another army officer, the Civil War hero Philip Sheridan, similarly discovered "the forests on fire for miles, at five or six different places."[16]

Not understanding the role that it played in increasing plant diversity or forest reproduction, nineteenth-century conservationists considered fire a uniquely dangerous and unpredictable force. Sheridan, for instance, considered the fires he witnessed in Yellowstone evidence of the "indifference shown by the government" toward the park, while John Wesley Powell, in his famous *Report on the Lands of the Arid Region of the United States,* released in 1878, asserted that Indian burning represented the largest single threat to forests throughout the American West. "The protection of the forests of the entire Arid Region of the United States," wrote Powell, "is reduced to a single problem. Can these forests be saved from fire?" For Powell, the answer was clear: since "in the main these fires are set by Indians[,]...the fires can, then, be very greatly curtailed by the removal of the Indians."[17]

Powell's suggestions dovetailed with already existing arguments in favor of confining Indians to reservations, which stressed the need for Native Americans to abandon their migratory practices and to adopt a settled, agricultural lifestyle modeled on that of the self-reliant Euro-American yeoman farmer. As one agent to the Shoshone wrote his superiors in 1865, "This people have never turned their attention to agricultural pursuits, nor can it be expected of them until they are placed upon a reservation....If they are not provided with such a home, they are destined to remain outside of those influences which are calculated to civilize or christianize them...[and to render them] useful members of society. Wild Indians, like wild horses, must be corralled upon reservations. There they can be brought to work, and soon will become a self-supporting people, earning their own living by their industry, instead of trying to pick up a bare subsistence by the chase." The rise of conservation added another imperative to such arguments. Not only would the sedentarization of Native Americans on reservations teach Indians how to be "civilized," it would limit the risk of further Indian damage to the environment.[18]

It was more than coincidental, then, that the 1872 proclamation setting aside Yellowstone park took place amid a flurry of reservation building, during which the Blackfeet, Crow, Bannock, and Shoshone were confined to reservations in Montana, Wyoming, and Idaho. The vision of nature that the park's backers sought to enact—nature as prehuman wilderness—was predicated on eliminating any Indian presence from the Yellowstone landscape. Whether or not the tourists who later came to the park realized it (and most, of course, did not), Yellowstone's seeming wilderness was the product of a prior, state-organized process of rearranging the countryside, in which native peoples and nature were slotted into distinct categories and separated from one another.[19]

In theory, this compartmentalization of the countryside—the creation of what the historian Sarah Deutsch has called a "landscape of enclaves"—should have eliminated any further Indian presence at Yellowstone.[20] Ironically, though, the setting aside of reservations may have helped set the stage for continued Indian incursions into Yellowstone. Not only did reservations consolidate Indian bases of operation close to the park, the limitations of the reservation system—most notably the frequent shortages of rations—often left the hungry inhabitants with little choice but to set off on protracted autumn hunts, both for meat for themselves and for hides and furs that could be traded for "flour, bacon, coffee, sugar, and other necessaries." "The supplies furnished by the government are not sufficient alone for their maintenance," reported the Indian agent on the Wind River Reservation in 1882. "But they [the Bannock and Shoshone] are fortunately situated in a game country, and support themselves two or three months each year in hunting during the winter season."[21] Furthermore, for several tribes, such hunts were a right protected by the very treaties that established the reservation system. "In the treaty made with the Bannocks and Shoshones at Fort Bridger in 1867 or 1868," reported the agent at the Fort Hall Reservation in Idaho, "they were granted the privilege of hunting on any unoccupied public land. Being short-rationed and far from self-supporting according to the white man's methods, they simply follow their custom and hunt for the purpose of obtaining sustenance."[22]

Each fall, hunting bands from nearby reservations gravitated toward Yellowstone—in part out of habit and in part because the area bordering the park was one of the largest open spaces remaining in the region. These incursions attracted little notice in the park's early years, when the number of visitors was small (only an estimated five hundred tourists came to Yellowstone in 1876, for instance) and official oversight limited. But by the 1880s, as the number of visitors crept upward and as administrators began to assume a more permanent presence at the park, it became increasingly obvious that "raiding Indians," evincing no superstitious fear of Yellowstone's strange geological features, were making yearly forays into the park. "[Having] discovered that the best hunting grounds are on the borders of the National Park," noted *Forest and Stream* in 1889, "the Crows on the east, the Shoshones on the south and east, the Bannocks from Fort Hall and Lemhi on the south and west all send annually their hunting parties into the region surrounding the Park for a winter's supply of meat."[23]

Rather than looking upon these native hunting expeditions as part of a seasonal cycle that predated the park's existence, Yellowstone's managers viewed any Indian presence in the park as a new and artificial intrusion. Park superintendents labeled Indians invaders, their hunting expeditions "an unmitigated evil," their setting of fires an affront to the "spirited cautions against fire" posted throughout the park. All constituted, in the eyes of Yellowstone officials, clear evidence that the inhabitants of nearby reservations were allowed "entirely too much liberty."[24]

What made these Indian actions all the more galling to park administrators was their apparent depravity. Indians did not just hunt, according to Yellowstone authorities; they overhunted. The Bannock, fumed one Yellowstone superintendent, used such "wasteful and improvident methods" that during their "protracted hunts of several months duration" they killed a staggeringly "large number of game animals." *Forest and Stream* issued similar accusations, charging the Bannock with "slaughtering [game] in such quantities as to have tons of meat hanging on their scaffolds" and the Crow with "killing what[ever] they could find." To conservationists, such behavior proved Indians' "love of game-butchery." But the prolonged hunts by the Crow, Bannock, and Shoshone on the fringes of the park may, in fact, have been signs of communities in crisis. Deprived of their traditional quarry, the buffalo, and forced to cope with the diminished resource base of the reservations, Indian peoples doubtless had to make much more intensive use of the game in Yellowstone National Park than ever before.[25]

Park authorities responded to such behavior in a manner similar to that of their counterparts in the Adirondacks: by drawing a sharp contrast between upper-class sports hunting, with its elaborate code of the chase, and the excesses of local hunters: "These Indians have no knowledge of the law, and submit to no restrictions; and it is believed that a single one of these hunting parties works more destruction during a summer's hunt than all of the gentlemen sportsmen put together who annually visit this region."[26] Although park officials considered the Native Americans hunting in Yellowstone little more than common criminals, neither the Shoshone nor the Bannock nor the Crow seem to have believed they were doing anything illegal. Instead of moving surreptitiously in small bands, as white poachers at this time did, the members of these tribes hunted as they always had: in large kin groups that often numbered fifty or a hundred individuals.[27] These sizable camps, along with the Indians' practice of setting fires when hunting, made native groups relatively easy for park authorities to locate. But lacking any jurisdiction over Indian peoples, officials could do little more than insist that hunting parties move outside the park's boundaries.[28] Supervisors found this a less than satisfactory solution, for Yellowstone's ecosystem did not fit neatly within the park's rectilinear borders. A fire that Bannocks set while hunting outside the park, for example, could easily stray inside the park and burn its forest cover. Similarly, as game animals migrated out of the park to lower elevations in the early fall, they were often killed by waiting Indian bands—a scenario unattractive to park authorities, who had not envisioned protecting Yellowstone's game for much of the year only to see it "contribute to the support of the surrounding Indian tribes" each autumn.[29]

Frustrated park supervisors spent much of the nineteenth century searching for a more permanent solution to such dilemmas. In his 1878 report to the secretary of the interior, Superintendent Philetus Norris made the first of several attempts to enlist the U.S. Army and the Bureau of Indian Affairs in his efforts to prevent Indian incursions into Yellowstone: "The few Sheepeaters, Bannocks, or Shoshones who alone once resided within the park, now belong at their agencies with the other annuity Indians. Hence, no Indians now visit the park save as a haunt for the purposes of plunder, or of concealment after bloody raids upon the ranchmen, pilgrims, or tourists. Therefore, I urge the necessity of the agency Indians of all the surrounding tribes being officially notified that they can only visit the park at the peril of a conflict with each other and the civil and military officers of the government."[30] Although Norris never achieved the absolute ban on Indian visits that he sought, his actions did help precipitate a fresh round of treaty making with the Crow. One particular source of confusion had been the overlap between the northern edge of Yellowstone National Park and the Crow Indian Reservation as established by the Treaty of Fort Laramie in 1868. A new treaty in 1880, in which the Crow ceded the western portion of their homeland, erased this conflict. Norris seized upon this agreement—as well as upon a treaty signed with the Shoshone and Bannock at the same time that reduced the size of the Lemhi Reservation—as an excuse to visit several of the surrounding Indian agencies and to extract "a solemn promise" from the "aboriginal owners of, or occasional troublesome ramblers in portions of the Park ... to abide by the terms of their treaty" and "not enter the Park."[31]

What the Indians who issued this "solemn promise" thought they were doing remains unclear. It may be that they were merely making a polite gesture in the hopes of dismissing Norris. It is equally possible that they were offering a sincere commitment not to pursue game within the park. It does seem that in subsequent years the region's Indians frequently confined their hunting to Yellowstone's poorly marked periphery. However, this compromise (if that is what is was) only partially mollified park administrators, who had hoped to stop native peoples from even "approaching the park boundaries."[32]

In their campaign to discourage Indian "raids" into the park, Yellowstone authorities received valuable aid from a number of eastern conservationists. George Bird Grinnell, whose magazine, *Forest and Stream,* had played a central role in creating the Adirondack Park, published several articles on the threat that "bands of roaming savages" posed to Yellowstone National Park. Grinnell's good friend Teddy Roosevelt also spoke in favor of stricter supervision of the Bannock, Shoshone, and Crow, who, as he saw it, threatened to "waste and destroy" the park. In 1889, at the urging of Roosevelt and Grinnell, the Boone and Crockett Club adopted a resolution labeling the "destruction of forests and of game caused by these Indian hunting parties...a serious evil" and calling for prompt governmental action to control native hunting and use of fire at Yellowstone.[33]

These efforts were rewarded by the tightening of some reservation regulations. In 1888, for example, the Commissioner of Indian Affairs forbade the Bannocks and Shoshones on the Wind River Reservation from hunting off reservation without written permission from the Indian Bureau in Washington, D.C. But stricter rules did not in and of themselves reduce hunting in the park. As the Indian agent at Wind River admitted, "The bad element...steal away and disobey the order, as it is almost impossible to detect them." "I refused to give them passes and [warned them] that if they went and didn't behave themselves they were liable to get into trouble," reported the equally frustrated agent at the Lemhi agency in Idaho. "They say they don't get enough to eat and that it is necessary for them to go hunting....An agent is powerless to compel Indians to remain on their Reservation unless he has some substantial support."[34]

Except for extraordinary events such as the Nez Perces' seizure of Carpenter and his companions in 1877, however, the struggles between park authorities and native peoples over access to Yellowstone largely took place offstage, out of sight of the growing number of tourists to the park in the 1880s and 1890s. In 1886, the same year that Yellowstone's superintendent was sending desperate telegrams to his superiors at the Department of the Interior about dozens of Bannocks hunting in the park, the travel writer George Wingate confidently stated that in Yellowstone "the Indian difficulty has been cured, the Indians have been forced back on their distant reservations, and the traveler in the Park will see or hear no more of them than if he was in the Adirondacks." At best, Wingate's analysis was only half right. It was true that visitors to the park seldom encountered Indians near Yellowstone's famous geysers and hot springs. But the Native American presence in the park had not ended; it had simply shifted to Yellowstone's outer fringes. Indians would continue to hunt and set fires along the periphery of the park for years to come.[35]

Given the prevailing frontier ideology of the time, one might expect that park officials celebrated the changes taking place in the Yellowstone region in the late nineteenth century. After all, the creation of the reservation and the subsequent opening of new territories to Euro-American settlement would seem to represent pivotal milestones in the triumphant tale of progress and civilization that Americans have come to expect of their western lands. In reality, however, park supervisors manifested a rather ambivalent attitude toward such changes. Rather than establishing prosperous, independent farms, many newly arriving settlers seemed to devote much of their time to illegal hunting or trapping in Yellowstone, leading many park officials to conclude that there was little to distinguish the "lawless whites" filtering into the region from the "raiding Indians" they were supplanting.

As a result, rather than drawing a sharp racial distinction between local Indians and rural whites, park managers and their supporters often lumped the two into one uniformly dangerous class. At times, this linkage could be subtle, as when park supporters, using terms that had no distinct racial component, spoke of the "western nomads, who would rather kill one elk in the Park than three outside of it" and the "savage barbarism" of buffalo poachers.[36] But often the parallels were drawn more explicitly. In 1891, for example, *Forest and Stream* warned its readers that Yellowstone was fast becoming "a hunting ground both for whites and Indians, and the forests which cover its mountains are in constant danger of fire from these wandering and often careless invaders."[37] On occasion, park authorities even claimed that whites and Indians were actively cooperating with one another to undermine conservation at Yellowstone. In 1886, the park's superintendent blamed "squaw-men" (white men married to Indian women) for recent fires in the reserve, claiming that the Indians troubling Yellowstone had been "incited to hunt in the Park by unscrupulous white men."[38] Such formulations led to a peculiar blurring of the standard categories of race in much of early conservation literature. Accounts of poaching at Yellowstone, for instance, feature frequent mentions of "Indians red and Indians white" and of "red or white Indians"—usages that suggest that the privilege of whiteness could depend on one's environmental practices.[39]

In certain respects, park authorities considered "white Indians" to constitute even more of a threat to Yellowstone than Indians did. Not only did white settlers elude the forms of social control, such as reservations, intended to restrain Indians, their actions could not be dismissed as "ignorance" the way that Indian behavior often was.[40] Noted *Forest and Stream,* "It is popular to make a great fuss about the harm done to game and forests by the Indians and to say nothing about that done by whites, who, by virtue of the color of their skins, are supposed to have the right to burn and destroy at will.... [Yet] it is a matter of common knowledge that whites kill game out of season and for hides, and are seldom or never punished for it."[41] The magazine urged its readers not to "save up all their indignation for Indians and half-breeds, when white men, who understand the law and the real magnitude of such an offense [poaching], are guilty of the same misdemeanor."[42]

Given its surreptitious character, it is difficult to gauge the precise extent of white poaching in Yellowstone's early years. Some visitors, however, ventured enormous estimates. Superintendent Norris supposed that "at least 7,000" elk had been "slaughtered between 1875 and 1877 for their hides," while the army officer William E. Strong reported in the summer of 1875 that "over four thousand [elk] were killed last winter by professional hunters in the Mammoth Springs Basin alone. Their carcasses and branching antlers can be seen on every hillside and on every valley."[43]

Strong directed his criticism not only toward the "human vultures" who committed such acts, but also toward the park's administration. "How is it that the Commissioner of the Park allows this unlawful killing?" he demanded. "It is an outrage and a crying shame that this indiscriminate slaughter of the large game of our country should be permitted. The act of Congress setting aside the National Park expressly instructs the Secretary of the Interior to provide against the wanton destruction of the game and fish found within the limits of the Park, and against their capture or destruction for the purposes of merchandise or profit. No attempt has yet been made, however, to enforce the act in the Park."[44] Strong's charges point toward what was indeed Yellowstone's greatest weakness: its lack of an enforcement mechanism for the park's environmental regulations. If events in the Adirondacks demonstrated how difficult it could be to enforce game and timber laws despite a year-round Forest Commission and a corps of experienced foresters, this difficulty was compounded at Yellowstone, where no administrative force existed at all. For many years, Congress did not even set aside funds to cover the salary of the park's superintendent. Consequently, Yellowstone's first superintendent, Nathaniel Langford, maintained a full-time job elsewhere as a bank

examiner, sometimes not even visiting the park for years at a time. Philetus Norris, who replaced Langford as superintendent in 1877, spent only
the summer and early autumn at Yellowstone, passing the other half of
the year at his home in Michigan.[45]

Not until 1883 did Congress designate funds to set up a force of ten
"assistant superintendents" to help protect the park. Even so, these assistants had only a limited impact on violations of the park's regulations. Largely out-of-state political appointees, they found it difficult to
apprehend Indians, poachers, and other rule breakers, most of whom
possessed a far more complete knowledge of the park's geography than
they did. "The Government has not the kind of men holding the position of assistant superintendents that it should have," concluded an
agent for the General Land Office after an investigative tour of Yellowstone in 1883. "The duties of the office require men possessing both
judgment and nerve, men who have the physical courage to do their full
duty in the face of the rough element which is to be found in the Park,
and which has not yet been made to realize that the regulations of the
Interior Department for the government of the Park must be respected
and observed. In making selections of men to fill these positions, I think
the interests of the Government would be subserved by taking those
who have lived on the frontier and are accustomed to hardships."[46] But
the Interior Department neglected to follow these suggestions, leaving
the park's superintendent to plead two years later for the funds to hire
"mountaineers able to anticipate the wary 'skin hunter.'...Even now
there are parties hunting in the park because I haven't enough men of
the right kind to cover the large extent of hunting ground that I am
compelled to protect."[47]

Yellowstone's lack of game wardens was only part of its enforcement
problem. The act creating Yellowstone National Park had also neglected to include any method for administering punishments to wrongdoers. "Under the law as it now stands...I have not the legal right or
power to arrest and detain any person charged with a violation of any
of the rules governing the Park," lamented Yellowstone's superintendent in 1883. "Now what am I to do?"[48] On those occasions when assistants did catch violators of the park's rules, the severest penalty that
the wrongdoer faced was expulsion from the park with orders never to
come back. Should the offending party return, all park authorities could
do was to expel that person yet again. Unsurprisingly, park managers
came to view expulsion as a toothless punishment, a measure that was
almost more of an incentive to wrongdoing than a check. Stated one su-

perintendent, "All sorts of worthless and disreputable characters are attracted here by the impunity afforded by the absence of law and courts
of justice."[49]

Casting about for a way to end this impasse, the Interior Department
arrived at an unusual solution. In 1884, it persuaded the Wyoming territorial assembly to place the park under Wyoming jurisdiction, an action that gave the Department of the Interior's regulations at Yellowstone the force of law in Wyoming. The territory appointed two
constables and two justices of the peace to the park, supplementing the
existing force of ten assistant superintendents. Although this arrangement had the potential to cloud whether the territory or the federal government exercised ultimate control at Yellowstone, it was seized by the
park's beleaguered superintendents as their long-awaited opportunity to
counter the "hard cases getting in to the Park." Yellowstone authorities
soon boasted of having made the first arrest of a poacher in park history
("a fellow by the name of George Reeder," who was "killing elk and
trapping beaver in the Park") and of moving against squatters and other
"vagabonds and tramps that under various pretenses are trying to obtain some sort of a foothold or settlement in the park."[50]

These advances in administration, however, had to contend with a
rapidly growing local populace. When the park was first established in
1872, there had been few centers of population nearby. The two closest
towns—Bozeman and Virginia City, each claimants to the title "Gateway
to the National Park"—were both more than seventy miles away. With
each passing year, however, the tide of settlement lapped a little closer. In
the early 1880s, the arrival of the Northern Pacific Railroad led to the
founding of Livingston, Montana, fifty miles to the park's north. A growing number of homesteads soon clustered along the Yellowstone River
valley between Livingston and the park. Then, in 1883, Gardiner, Montana, a "village of rough board shanties and log cabins" with a population of approximately a hundred and fifty, sprung up on Yellowstone's
very border—so close, in fact, that the front doors of many of the residents' homes opened up directly onto the park.[51] (See Tables 6 and 7.)

To worried Yellowstone officials, this new neighbor, which fast became a trading center for nearby ranches and a supply stop for visiting
tourists, represented a grave threat to park security. "The disorders of
the neighboring town of Gardiner..., which now overflow into the park,
are a constant and serious source of annoyance," complained one.
"[Gardiner is] destitute of all means for the preservation of law and
order..., the resort of hard and worthless characters who assemble to

TABLE 6.   POPULATION OF GARDINER,
MONTANA, 1900

Women	46	(30%)
Men	107	(70%)
TOTAL	153	(100%)

SOURCE: 1900 Population Census, Manuscript Schedules,
Park County, Montana, Roll 913, T623, Records of the Bureau
of the Census, RG 29, National Archives.

TABLE 7.   OCCUPATIONS OF MALE
RESIDENTS OF GARDINER, AGE 18
AND OLDER, 1900

Agriculture (farmer, hired hand)	6	(7.1%)
Mining (coal miner, quartz miner)	6	(7.1%)
Laborer (unspecified)	18	(21.5%)
Crafts (blacksmith, carpenter, mason)	10	(11.9%)
Professions (engineer, landlord)	5	(6.0%)
Services (saloonkeeper, barber, park guide)	19	(22.6%)
Transportation (teamster)	20	(23.8%)
TOTAL	84	(100.0%)

SOURCE: 1900 Population Census, Manuscript Schedules, Park County, Montana, Roll 913,
T623, Records of the Bureau of the Census, RG 29, National Archives.

prey upon the visitors to the National Park, and who have been excluded from the Park by my order."[52] Eastern conservationists likewise portrayed the village as a nest of poachers and outlaws. In the words of William Hornaday, the director of the New York Zoological Society, "In the town of Gardiner there are a number of men, armed with rifles, who toward game have the gray-wolf quality of mercy....If the people of Gardiner can not refrain from slaughtering the game of the Park...it is time for the American people to summon the town of Gardiner before the bar of public opinion, to show cause why the town should not be wiped off the map."[53] The deeper source of such unease was that Gardiner's founding signaled the end of the buffer zone of unoccupied territory that had once insulated the park from the outside world. No longer did the park gradually shade out into the surrounding territory. With Gardiner's arrival, issues long dormant in the federal management of Yellowstone— the setting of boundaries; the prevention of timber stealing, squatting, and other unauthorized uses of the park's environment; the arrest of wrongdoers—all acquired a sudden urgency.

To cope with these new challenges, Yellowstone's authorities could only resort to an odd, improvised administration divided between federal superintendents and territorial constables and justices of the peace. Had this peculiar arrangement held together, it might have set a precedent for a national conservation program based on power-sharing between federal and local governments. But it quickly disintegrated, a victim of corruption among the Wyoming constables assigned to the park. In 1885, the botched arrest of a visiting congressman, Lewis E. Payson of Illinois, revealed that the constables were using their position to extort fines from passing tourists. Embarrassed by the ensuing controversy, the Wyoming territorial assembly quietly revoked its previous measures for the park. Violations soon soared, as local residents realized that Yellowstone's officials once again had no way to enforce the park's regulations.[54]

Even before this latest crisis, a number of observers had argued that only the institution of martial law would enable the federal government to counter the Indians, poachers, and other wrongdoers ravaging Yellowstone. As early as 1875, the army officer William Ludlow had suggested that "the cure for...[these] unlawful practices and undoubted evils can only be found in a thorough mounted police of the park. In the absence of any legislative provision for this, recourse can most readily be had to the already-existing facilities afforded by the presence of troops in the vicinity and by the transfer of the park to the control of the War Department. Troops should be stationed to act as guards at the lake, the Mammoth Springs, and especially in the Geyser Basin."[55] Other conservationists soon arrived at a similar conclusion. In 1882, Samuel S. Cox, representative from New York, proposed placing Yellowstone National Park "under the exclusive care, control and government of the War Department." That same year, General Sheridan recommended that troops from nearby forts be used to "keep out skin hunters...and give a place of refuge to our noble game."[56]

This domestic deployment of American armed forces was not unique to conservation. Throughout post–Civil War America, the army was the police of choice for restive areas: the Reconstruction South; urban areas beset by labor strikes; a West still engaged in wars against various Indian nations. With such precedents already in place—and with many of the same perceived opponents (Indians, lower-class white lawbreakers)—it was but a small step to expand the army's role in the "defense of national property" to include conservation sites.[57] Perhaps the sole official to express any disquiet with this proposed shift was the secretary of the interior, who perceived in the transfer a loss of power for his own department. Even after the passage of an act authorizing the army "upon the request of the Secretary of the Interior...to make the necessary details of troops to prevent trespassers or intruders from entering the park," the secretary held off making any such a request for two years.[58] But following Wyoming's withdrawal of protection for Yellowstone in 1885, and a budget battle in Congress the subsequent year that stripped the Department of the Interior of the funds necessary to administer the park, the secretary was left with few other options. On August 17, 1886, Captain Moses Harris and fifty cavalrymen from Fort Custer, Montana, marched into the park. In short order, Harris, the park's first military superintendent, could glory in "the visible power and force of the National Government as represented by the military garrison in the Park" and speak of Yellowstone as "a military reservation."[59]

Although the army's presence was intended to be only temporary (Harris and the other officers who oversaw Yellowstone all bore the title "acting superintendent" on the assumption that they would soon be superseded by civilian officials), the military ended up remaining at the park for the next thirty-two years. During its prolonged tenure at Fort Yellowstone, the army would reshape federal conservation in its own image, turning a once inchoate venture into a well-organized bureaucracy, complete with uniforms, armed patrols, and detailed record-keeping procedures. If only a few years earlier Yellowstone had been one of the most remote spots in the continental United States, its destiny had now become linked to one of the agencies at the forefront of building the modern administrative state.[60]

CHAPTER 5

Fort Yellowstone

To most nineteenth-century conservationists, the military's arrival at Yellowstone marked a clear turning point in the park's fortunes. John Muir, for instance, rejoiced at seeing Yellowstone "efficiently managed and guarded by small troops of United States cavalry." "Uncle Sam's soldiers," the Sierra Club president enthused, are "the most effective forest police."[1] "I will not say that this Rocky Mountain region is the only part of the country where this lesson of obedience to law is badly needed," agreed Charles Dudley Warner in *Harper's* magazine, "but it is one of them." Like Muir, Warner saw Yellowstone's military administration as a notable improvement on its civilian predecessor: "Since the Park has passed under military control, fires are infrequent, poaching is suppressed, the 'formations' are no longer defaced, roads are improved, and the region is saved with its natural beauty for the enjoyment of all the people.... The lawless and the marauders are promptly caught, tried (by a civil officer), fined, and ejected." The conclusion to be gathered from such evidence was clear: "The intelligent rules of the Interior Department could only be carried out by military discipline."[2]

Sharing Muir's and Warner's enthusiasm for "military discipline," many conservationists soon suggested that much of the rest of the federal government's conservation program be delegated to the military. In 1889, the American Forestry Association (AFA) passed a resolution recommending that the army "be employed to protect the public forest from spoliation and destruction."[3] The following year, Charles Sargent, a professor of arboriculture at Harvard University and an adviser to the New York legislature when it created the Adirondack Forest Preserve, took up the AFA's suggestion in the pages of his journal, *Garden and Forest.* The posting of troops to Yellowstone, Sargent wrote, "has proved the most efficient means of protection which has yet been tried. It is our belief that neither the national reservations nor the public forests will be safe until the United States Army is actively engaged to protect them."[4] Noting the prominent role the British Army was playing in forestry in colonial India, other conservationists soon joined the call for the militarization of conservation, in which poachers would be subjected to military tribunals and forestry would become a regular course of study at West Point. In 1890, in partial response to such pressures, the Department of the Interior dispatched army units to the three other existing national parks: Yosemite, General Grant, and Sequoia.[5]

Yet at the very moment that the national press was holding up the military at Yellowstone as a model to be emulated nationwide, quite a different perspective was being voiced in the newspapers from the small Montana villages bordering the park. To the correspondents for this local press, the sight of armed soldiers patrolling the park represented not a triumph of conservation but rather the unwarranted imposition of martial law. "Military rule in time of profound peace is distasteful to the American people under any conditions," charged the *Livingston Enterprise,* a newspaper whose general assessment of the army's involvement with conservation was perhaps best conveyed by the headline "Military Government and How It Is Employed in Yellowstone Park to Work Hardship on Law-Abiding Citizens of Montana."[6] Even the *Livingston Post,* typically the *Enterprise*'s ideological sparring partner, viewed the army's presence at Yellowstone with alarm. Noting "the American sentiment against a military law," the *Post* portrayed the various army officers who served as Yellowstone's acting superintendent as authoritarian despots.[7] A favorite target of abuse was Captain George S. Anderson, the park's superintendent from 1891 to 1897. An avid sportsman and a member of the Boone and Crockett Club, Anderson was particularly aggressive in his efforts to rid the park of lawbreakers, for which he was regularly lionized in the pages of sporting journals such as *Recreation* and *Forest and Stream.*[8] Locally, however, the captain's endeavors earned him the nickname "the 'Czar of Wonderland' "—a moniker no doubt designed to underscore the "un-American" character of the army's conservation policies—and the scorn of newspapers such as the *Post:* "Capt. Anderson's greatest activity has taken the form of arresting reputable citizens of Montana and charging them with various offenses which he has failed to prove. When he isn't doing that he is bothering his alleged brain trying to invent some new form of oppression under the authority of his shoulder straps, or to pick out the next citizen whom he will arrest."[9]

The animosity behind such critiques derived in large part from the confrontations between residents and the army that began almost immediately after the military arrived at the park. Under Yellowstone's previous, weak civilian administration, many settlers had treated the park much as they did undeveloped property elsewhere in the American countryside—as land open to timbering, grazing, hunting, and foraging by local community members. Such practices, however, conflicted with the army's attempts to institute the technical oversight and state simplification that conservation demanded. Thus, even though the villages surrounding Yellowstone were founded after the park's creation in 1872, the result was a situation not unlike that in the Adirondacks, where many of the region's inhabitants perceived conservation as interfering with their preexisting rights to the natural world.[10]

As in the Adirondacks, one early point of conflict concerned the park's timber. Because of Yellowstone's remote location, regulations against the cutting of trees had lain dormant until 1883, when the establishment of Gardiner on Yellowstone's northern border propelled the issue to center stage. Alarmed at the removal of lumber by the park's new neighbors, the Department of the Interior tightened its ban on tree cutting. Yellowstone's civilian superintendent, Patrick Conger, placed the town's residents under close surveillance ("near the village of Gardiner I found it necessary to place some men, not only to watch the hunters, but to keep the villagers from stealing wood from the Park"), but with limited success.[11] Although Conger's force of ten assistants did catch a few inhabitants of Gardiner loading up wagons with firewood and building supplies, many residents, when informed that "they would have to stop cutting and hauling wood off of the Park," responded in a manner similar to that of a "Mr. Wannakee" of Gardiner: "He said he did not care what you [Conger] said, if he wanted a load of wood he would go and get a load, and I could report him if I wanted to. He said that he would not be afraid to stand trial or such words to that effect."[12]

Viewing their cutting of wood as a justifiable subsistence use of the environment, Gardiner's residents circulated a petition calling on the Department of the Interior to revise its policies. Signed by fifty male residents of Gardiner and submitted to the secretary of the interior in 1884, the petition stated: "About midway between the village of Gardiner and Mammoth Hot Springs there is a belt of timber which has been killed by forest fires several years ago. The old dead timber is either rotting on the ground or standing a black, unsightly, obstructive encumbrance of the soil; serving no human use while it prevents the growth of young trees and grass. Your petitioners ask the privilege of entering upon this land for the removal of the dead timber to be used for fuel, fencing and other purposes, subject to such limitations as the Superintendent might deem judicious for the public interest, both in the protection and improvement of the park and for the good of the people who reside contiguous thereof."[13] Although framed in the language of deference, this petition offered an implicit bargain: if Yellowstone's managers would permit the inhabitants of Gardiner to gather fallen timber for their household use, the townspeople's cutting of living trees would cease. Perhaps hoping to avoid further confrontations, the Department of the Interior accepted the arrangement, which the town's inhabitants soon reinterpreted as the general right "to get all the down wood for their winter use" wherever it might be found in the park.[14]

From the perspective of the park's newly arrived military commanders, this practice of letting locals gather wood in Yellowstone was far too open-ended. It allowed residents too much discretion in deciding what constituted "down wood," and it gave poachers and other wrongdoers a pretext for wandering, unsupervised, throughout the park. In its place, the army instituted a system of permits, which required the town's residents to get approval in writing before gathering wood from parklands. Besides allowing for the more precise dictation of where and when wood could be gathered, this arrangement enabled Yellowstone's superintendents to exercise a form of social control over Gardiner in which informers and others sympathetic to the park authorities were rewarded with permits while poachers or other lawbreakers could have their wood-gathering privileges withheld.

The mass of correspondence that this new policy generated documents Gardiner residents' reliance on park timber for a variety of subsistence uses. Joseph Duret asks that he be allowed to gather two loads of driftwood from along the Gardiner River to be used as firewood; Richard Randall requests permission to cut logs "to be used in building a house and stable at Gardiner"; S. C. Gassert inquires whether the superintendent would "send me a permit to get some wood for fuel out of the Park"; Joseph Duret writes again to ask "that I be permitted to take some dry wood from the Park for use as fuel."[15] The correspondence also details some of the conditions that park officials attached to their permits. In April of 1891, for instance, Yellowstone authorities distributed five permits to inhabitants of Gardiner to take wood out of the park, of which the permit granted to Charles B. Scott was typical. Scott was allowed to take "80 logs for the construction of a house for your own use." But, his permit added, "these logs must be cut from *dead* timber and in such a locality as not to mar the scenery of the park." In addition, many permits were only good for a specified period of time, generally two weeks or less.[16]

In 1898, apparently dissatisfied with its permit system, the military declared all gathering of wood in the park illegal. "Another order of this season," reported the *Livingston Enterprise,* "prohibits the towns-people from hauling wood for domestic uses from a burned tract on the slopes of Sepulcher Mountain, which had hitherto been permitted.... citizens of Gardiner are prohibited from getting wood for home consumption from the limits of the Park."[17] Local residents opposed to the measure continued to sneak wood out of the park (an activity for which Joseph Duret, among others, was arrested and fined in 1908). But access to timber never became as bitterly contested an issue at Yellowstone as it did in the Adirondacks. Nor did there arise in Gardiner organized gangs of timber poachers akin to the "State Troops" or "Grenadiers" that during this same period challenged the authority of conservation officials in New York.[18]

Understanding why the local response to the ban on timber cutting developed so differently in the Adirondacks and in Yellowstone reveals a great deal about the distinctive character of conservation in each region. It was not that the residents of each area differed markedly in outlook—indeed, inhabitants of both places seemingly agreed that there was little illegal about the appropriation of game or wood for subsistence purposes. But whereas conservation in the Adirondacks had involved the placing of state controls over a preexisting grid of human communities, Gardiner had been founded after Yellowstone's creation. (There were, of course, human communities that predated Yellowstone National Park, but these had been Indian communities, whose rights to parklands the federal government had extinguished.) This difference alone created quite different spatial arrangements at the two locales. Gardiner, for instance, was situated on the edge of the park, rather than being surrounded on all sides by state land as were many communities

in the Adirondacks. Thus, while Yellowstone was a close and convenient source of timber for those living in Gardiner, it was never the only
available resource. Moreover, Yellowstone's status as a solid block of
land, rather than a mosaic of state and private lands, facilitated enforcement efforts. Instead of having to patrol a multitude of poorly
marked plots as their counterparts in the Adirondacks did, Yellowstone's officials had only to guard the park's outer periphery, where
timber poaching was invariably concentrated because of the difficulties
of transporting logs over long distances.

The final reason why the theft of timber never achieved the prominence in Yellowstone that it did in the Adirondacks had to do with the
relative ecologies—and resulting economies—of the two regions. Unlike
upstate New York, the area abutting Yellowstone never developed an
active timber industry. (In fact, when Gardiner was founded in 1883,
the first homes erected in the village were all constructed out of un-
milled logs because of the lack of any local sawmill.) While such conditions were in part a reflection of Yellowstone's remoteness, they also
had much to do with the composition of the region's forests. The park's
dominant tree, the lodgepole pine *(Pinus contorta),* was only marginally
marketable—indeed, elsewhere in the West, foresters, considering the
lodgepole something of a pest, devoted considerable energy to eradicat-
ing it and encouraging more valuable species of trees to grow in its
place. Consequently, there were few outlets for timber poached from
Yellowstone and no especially valuable cuts of lumber—like the "fiddle
butts" of the Adirondacks—that made particularly tempting targets for
thieves.[19]

In contrast, because many of the settlers around Yellowstone established ranches on the grass-rich plains of the Yellowstone Plateau, park
officials found themselves faced with an issue that had rarely troubled
their counterparts in the Adirondacks: the grazing of livestock within
park borders. Prior to Gardiner's founding, park authorities had not
even anticipated such an issue arising. As a result, there were no standing regulations about grazing when the town was created. As in many
other rural communities, Gardiner residents often let their animals
roam loose. Since the boundary with the park was unfenced, domestic
stock from the village soon made its way into Yellowstone, just as wildlife from Yellowstone often ventured out of the park.

Initially, Yellowstone's military superintendents, continuing the
policy of their civilian predecessors, tolerated the incursions of livestock
into the park. But as the region's populations of antelope, deer, and elk

rebounded, placing greater stress on Yellowstone's grazing lands, officials took steps to exclude livestock from the park. In the late 1890s, Yellowstone's authorities initiated a policy of impounding all stock found wandering in the park and fining the animals' owners—a move that most inhabitants of Gardiner construed as using the nation's troops to attack its own citizens, particularly those with little property of their own on which to graze their animals. As one resident fumed in an article entitled "Military Government," "Nice business, is it not, for U.S. troops to be engaged in, driving a poor man's cow five miles, then charging him a dollar for the privilege of taking her home....The last season's orders relative to stock found in the Park has entailed a real hardship on those owning cows, who could not afford to buy feed, there being no good grazing ground on the opposite side of the Yellowstone adjacent to the town."[20]

Nevertheless, many locals continued to graze their animals in the park, leading the army to increase its penalties. In 1900, Colonel Samuel B.M. Young implemented a policy of driving any loose domestic animals found in the park out through the distant Wyoming entrance, escalating Gardiner residents' complaints about being subject to an un-American tradition of martial law. "In days gone by the National Park has been ruled over by many an autocrat, many who would make the Czar of Russia ashamed that he ever ascended the throne," wrote one Gardiner inhabitant; "but of the long list of those who have made life miserable for residents of the upper Yellowstone country none could compare with Col. S.B.M. Young." Residents expressed particular frustration with the army for allowing a seemingly arbitrary boundary to curtail a well-established right to graze local public land:

> For years the cows and horses at Cinnabar and Gardiner had been permitted to graze on the public domain without molestation. Only an imaginary line divided the world from the czar's domain, and, as long usage had made all grass look alike to the animals around Gardiner, it not infrequently happened that some strayed across this imaginary line and clipped a few mouthfuls of bunch grass from Uncle Sam's possession. But this was too much for the colonel. The idea of a plebeian cow or horse eating off the same domain with the petted animals of the Park rankled in his bosom to such an extent that an order was soon issued that any animal caught grazing on the Park side of Gardiner would be driven to Mammoth Hot Springs and from there escorted out of the Park on the Wyoming side. From the point of exit back to Gardiner, outside the confines of the Park, meant a nice jaunt for the unfortunate animals of a couple of hundred miles, and while it no doubt added greatly to their digestive qualities it provoked an epidemic of indigestion among upper Yellowstone residents that made the colonel the victim of more

choice epithets than had ever been hurled at any former ruler of Wonder-land.[21]

Despite several other punitive measures, roaming livestock plagued Yel-lowstone officials well into the twentieth century. In 1903, rather than increasing its penalties further, the army tried a new approach: erecting a wire fence for about four miles along the northern boundary of the park. "This fence has long been needed, and it now affords a means of keeping stock of all kinds off that section of the park." In 1914, soldiers replaced much of this woven wire fence with an even more imposing barrier: a set of five-foot-high steel spikes designed "to keep cattle and dogs out of the park."[22]

Such fence building reinforced another project of the army's: the de-lineation of all of Yellowstone's boundaries. As early as 1878, officials had acknowledged that, much as in the Adirondacks, conservation reg-ulations could be enforced only if the spaces where they applied were clearly bounded: "That the special rules and regulations, necessarily anomalous and conflicting with the roving-hunter habits of the sur-rounding mountaineers, cannot be effectively enforced without the lim-its of their operations (the boundaries of the park) being established and plainly marked, is too evident for controversy." But attempts by the ci-vilian administration to mark the park's borders had stalled, leading Captain Harris, after taking office in 1886, to plead for funds to com-plete such a project: "The present uncertainty [of the boundaries] is a constant invitation to lawless hunters and others to encroach upon the Park, and adds greatly to the annoyance and labors of those charged with its protection."[23]

Later superintendents were to echo Harris's pleas, for it was obvious that making any official judgment about the legality of certain prac-tices—such as when hunting constituted poaching, when the cutting of a tree was stealing, or when the building of a home represented squat-ting—hinged on fixing these activities in space. Complicating this task was the peculiar nature of the park's borders. Since the congressmen who had originally set Yellowstone's perimeters in 1872 had had only the vaguest idea of the topology of the area, the park's rectangular bor-ders did not follow any convenient, "natural" boundaries such as rivers but rather cut across streams, mountain ranges, and other geographical features in a way that often proved disorienting when viewed from the ground.

As in New York's Forest Preserve, mapping and marking boundaries therefore emerged as fundamental to establishing administrative control of the park. The military officials at Yellowstone floated a number of plans designed to accomplish this mission. Some favored the construction of "a suitable fence...inclosing the entire reservation," while other supervisors were partial to a scheme to cut "a wide swathe... along the entire boundary line wherever timber exists." Both plans proved unworkably expensive, but between 1900 and 1903 the army did dispatch surveyors from the Corps of Engineers, who mapped the park's borders and erected stone boundary markers every half mile along Yellowstone's perimeter.[24]

During this time, the army also embarked upon a program to simplify the trails within the park. Upon its arrival at Yellowstone, the military had discovered a latticework of paths, some produced by Indian peoples, others "originally made by hunters, trappers, and prospectors," crisscrossing the park. In place of this dispersed network, the army established a system that funneled travelers through just four entrances, corresponding to Yellowstone's north, east, south, and west sides—an arrangement that allowed soldiers to monitor closely the comings and goings of visitors. At each entrance, "as a precautionary measure against violations of the laws relating to hunting and forest fires," troops took down the name, address, and intended length of stay of every visitor.[25] Those who journeyed through Yellowstone after the summer tourist season were subject to even more checks. "All persons traveling through the park from October 1 to June 1 should be regarded with suspicion. They will be closely questioned and carefully inspected, and, if necessary, will be watched from station to station."[26] Even if one possessed the requisite permit for off-season travel, it had to be "presented at each station passed and...carefully scrutinized by the man in charge of the station," who then had to endorse the permit on the back. Those who lacked the proper permission or endorsement, or who were deemed to have tarried unnecessarily between checkpoints, were liable to be detained by park authorities.[27]

The establishment of official entrances also allowed the army to control what visitors brought into the park. To prevent Yellowstone from becoming "a thoroughfare for sportsmen, hunters, and game slaughterers," the army forbade the transportation of game (even that killed legally outside the park) across park borders, prompting "much adverse criticism by hunters and guides."[28] The military also issued orders that any dog seen running loose in the park should be shot on sight, since poachers often used dogs to track game and warn of approaching strangers. And even though "the custom of carrying firearms through the park has been almost universal among those who live in the neighboring states," after 1897 the army required all visitors to surrender their firearms at the entrances or to have their weapons sealed for the duration of their stay in the park—a process that involved the soldiers "tying the lock of the gun securely with a piece of 'red tape' and sealing the knot with wax, on which is stamped the great seal of the United States."[29]

The fact that many locals learned how to slip this red tape off their rifles and to hunt in the park as before provides an apt illustration of the ability of the region's residents to elude the army's controls. This resistance manifested itself in many ways, most dramatically in the creation of a shadow landscape of surreptitiously erected footbridges and "unfrequented and little known trails," used by those who wanted to sneak past the official entrances and gather an illegal load of wood or poach some game.[30] A number of poachers even built cabins or dugouts in the park, where they could hide for the night and hastily preserve any illicit game before smuggling it out over Yellowstone's borders. These structures were secreted at regular intervals in the densest forests of the park where they were unlikely to be stumbled upon by passing tourists or Yellowstone officials. Although its traces were, as intended, indistinct, this shadow landscape extended throughout the park, an illicit counterpoint to the officially sanctioned tourist landscape of hotels and campsites that spread across Yellowstone in the late nineteenth century.[31]

If most of the ever-increasing numbers of tourists to Yellowstone were unaware of the network of hidden trails and cabins throughout the park, so, too, were park officials. It was not that the various army officers who served as the park's acting superintendents during the late nineteenth and early twentieth centuries were ignorant of the violations that occurred within Yellowstone's bounds. As Captain Anderson admitted in 1891, "I am satisfied that both hunting and trapping are carried on within the limits of the Park." But the shadow landscape of poachers and other wrongdoers nonetheless remained difficult for Yellowstone's military managers to penetrate. Contrary to the predictions of conservationists, many soldiers did not immediately take to their new roles as law enforcers. "The enlisted men of the Army," explained Colonel Samuel B. M. Young, "are not selected with special reference to the duties to be performed in police patrolling, guarding...and in protecting against the killing or frightening of the game and against forest fires." Indeed, a fair proportion of the soldiers at the park seem to have evinced little enthusiasm for conservation. "While I found some excellent, intelligent, and conscientious noncommissioned officers and privates who have taken interest in carrying out their instructions in park duties," added the colonel, "the majority are indifferent and appear to resent being required to subserve both the military interest and the interest of the park."[32]

All too often, the soldiers guarding Yellowstone resembled the unit that Lieutenant Elmer Lindsley inspected in 1898: "absolutely unfamiliar with the country and their duties as game wardens." Even under the best of circumstances, the constant transfers involved in military life meant that just as the soldiers at the park had begun to master Yellowstone's rugged geography and the cumbersome cross-country skis used in winter patrolling, their tour of duty at Yellowstone had drawn to a close. "The troops assigned from time to time for guard duty in the park can scarce all become familiar with its topography and trails ere a just regard for the proper maintenance of organization and discipline and division of duties...require their withdrawal," noted Young. These shifts in personnel did not go unnoticed by local residents, who often timed their lawbreaking so that it occurred when the troops stationed at the park were unseasoned new arrivals. "From many sources information comes to this office that preparations are in progress by lawless characters for poaching on a large scale during the present season," wrote the colonel in 1897. "These people are encouraged by the knowledge that all my soldiers are new and untrained in the duties necessary to protect the Park properly."[33]

The inexperience and indifference of many of the soldiers assigned to guard Yellowstone also appear to have made them susceptible to various forms of petty corruption. Army records from 1902 reveal repeated instances of soldiers colluding with local lawbreakers. In February of that year, Colonel John Pitcher, the park's acting superintendent, notified the secretary of the interior that a Sergeant Knapp at the park had been caught trafficking in elk teeth.[34] The following month, Pitcher received a series of letters from Ed Romey, a scout assigned to patrol the park's southern boundary, detailing several cases of corruption among Yellowstone's enlisted men. In one instance, a poacher traded a pistol to two soldiers for the skins from several moose. In another, "a soldier named Flegal...made a deal with two poachers to drive two buffalo out of the park so that poachers could get them."

Romey also told of soldiers who pointed out to local hunters where they had spotted buffalo and moose in the park and of poachers who stayed with the soldiers at one station while their commanding officer was away.[35] Similar accusations of corruption surfaced in a letter that an outraged inhabitant of Wyoming sent to Pitcher in February of 1902. "It is common talk here," the informant declared, "that the soldiers let the trappers stay with them for a week or ten days at a time and the soldiers keep the trappers posted as to when the Park Scouts will come so that the trappers will keep away."[36]

Although all the available evidence indicates that the majority of soldiers performed their duties in an honest manner, local newspapers preferred to emphasize the "venal and corrupt" features of the army's management of the park.[37] "The acceptance of bribes," maintained the *Livingston Post,* "is 'so open and notorious that westerners have ceased to express surprise at it.'" The *Post* even charged one enlisted man with soliciting so many illicit payments during his tour of duty that he was able to buy a large ranch near the park upon his discharge.[38] On the most immediate level, such accusations reflect the antagonism that many residents felt toward the park's military supervisors. But they can also be read as attempts to disprove a key element of the logic of conservation. Rather than delivering the enlightened oversight of natural resources that its advocates had promised, conservation seemed instead to create new opportunities for corruption and mismanagement. As one resident of Gardiner put it, "the military up at the Park was all a fake....it didn't protect the Park and was no good."[39]

One reason the soldiers posted to Yellowstone may have been so vulnerable to corruption was the necessarily decentralized nature of law enforcement at the park. To counteract the hidden network of paths and hideouts used by local poachers, the army erected its own far-flung system of trails, cabins, and guard posts, designed, in the words of Frederic Remington, to leave "the track of the cavalry horse-shoe in the most remote parts of the preserve, where the poacher or interloper can see it, and become apprehensive in consequence of the dangers which attend his operations."[40] At each guard post, the army deployed "three to ten enlisted men," often leaving the soldiers isolated for weeks at a time with little official oversight. During the 1890s, the military supplemented these posts with a network of log cabins spaced a day's journey from one another. Nicknamed "snowshoe cabins" because they were primarily used for winter patrolling, these structures allowed the army to extend its reach into the remoter, previously unguarded sections of

Yellowstone and heighten its surveillance during the crucial winter months, when poachers were most active.[41]

This adoption of winter patrolling highlights a central component of the army's tenure at Yellowstone: the appropriation of tactics used in Indian warfare for peacetime conservation. The flow of techniques from combat to conservation was no doubt reinforced by the frequent shifts between the roles of Indian fighter and park policeman that many soldiers engaged in during Yellowstone's early years. Several troops serving at the park, for instance, came directly from assignments against "hostile tribes," while others were "ordered into the field on account of . . . Indian troubles" during their tours of duty at Yellowstone.[42] But this appropriation of military tactics for use in conservation likely made sense to army officials for other reasons as well. To capture elusive Indian opponents, for example, the army had found winter campaigns and the use of regularly spaced supply depots invaluable. The establishment of "snowshoe cabins" and winter patrols at Yellowstone enabled the military to apply these familiar tactics against another elusive target: poachers. Similarly, having discovered its unfamiliarity with the geography of the Far West to be a hindrance in Indian campaigns, the army began after the Civil War to employ Native Americans and other locals as scouts whenever possible. This policy, first made official under the Army Act of 1866, was also well suited to Yellowstone, where the army found itself lacking "men who are accustomed to the mountains." Following wartime precedent, the park's military superintendents soon hired scouts from among the local populace—men capable of guiding army patrols and of "measur[ing] wits, experience, and mountain skill with [the] other mountain men who constitute by far the most dangerous class of poachers."[43]

In certain respects, the peculiar demands of conservation expanded the role of the park's scouts. Unlike wartime scouts, whose duties seldom extended beyond directing army columns to hostile encampments, Yellowstone's scouts often worked undercover in the communities abutting the park, tapping into the rumors and gossip about violations of park rules that circulated among the region's residents yet remained inaccessible to Yellowstone's authorities. When seeking to capture a "gang [of poachers] who had been operating from Idaho" in the 1890s, Captain Anderson turned to secret operatives, "who went among the residents of that country, and brought me back a full report of their names, and their places of operation."[44] Anderson's successor as acting superintendent, Colonel Samuel B. M. Young, continued this policy, employing special scouts to "visit the settlements adjacent to the Park boundaries and ascertain the names and present occupations of well known poachers and their associates." Through such tactics, the military intended to determine "the location of all persons who in past years have been guilty, or thought guilty of poaching, and never let them get beyond the surveillance of park authorities."[45]

Not surprisingly, such undercover operations generated considerable unease in many of the villages surrounding Yellowstone. One Montana newspaper complained that Yellowstone authorities had "spies at every turn"; another spoke derisively of the park's "mysterious scouts." As one officer explained to his superiors, "The people are very suspicious of us and it is hard to get information, and harder still to get *reliable* information."[46] Added the scout Ed Romey:

> Why they [the local inhabitants] all say how is it. We never yous [used] to see a scout or a soldier in this section of country. And now they have soldiers stationed on Bechler [River] and we don't know when we are talking to a scout.[47]

Not that such confusion always lasted for long. Locals were often quick to discern who was on the army's payroll. Much as happened with New York's foresters, many of Yellowstone's scouts became "so well known that their presence in the section of country where these men [poachers] live is the sign, either for them to clear out, or to surround themselves with such safeguards that it is impossible to secure evidence against them."[48]

Like their New York counterparts, Yellowstone's scouts occupied a contested place in the region's social order. To many residents, the park's scouts functioned simultaneously as emblems of an intrusive state and as guardians of the local community. Rarely able to reconcile these roles with much success, the scouts often found themselves criticized by fellow residents for failing to fulfill one or another of their responsibilities. "There is a great deal of game killed in and out of the Park[,] and the scouts never made a pretense of capturing the hunters," complained a correspondent in Gardiner's short-lived newspaper, *Wonderland,* in 1903. "Instead of being out on the line watching the game, as they are told to do, they loaf around the saloons in Gardiner and Cinnabar until evening; then ride to the post and report…that everything is O.K." A few locals even charged that the scouts were not as law-abiding as they pretended. As one sarcastic inhabitant of Gardiner put it, he hoped to "trap the beaver and kill the buffalo and get on as a scout, and ride a sorrel horse and wear a big six-shooter with 'U.S.' on it."[49]

Despite such charges of corruption, several of the locals volunteering for the scout position professed an apparently genuine desire to restrain the environmental abuses of fellow community members. "I know all of the pochers that live at Henerys lake and the Madison Bason and I would like to have them stoped if posiable," wrote one resident, offering himself for the position.[50] Another settler from Jackson Hole presented as his credentials the fact that he had "incurred the displeasure of nearly all my neighbors through my upholding the protection of the game[,] for the majority of them are trappers.... I will do so to a much greater extent if I can receive the appointment of warden." A subsequent letter clarified the reasoning behind the would-be scout's position: "This is one of the best game countries that I know of.... Now with a good game warden here and the Park on the north, we can do much in the way of preserving the game."[51]

A more detailed portrait of the scouts can be found in the diaries that the army required all scouts to keep during the late 1890s. Generally, while on duty, the scouts followed a well-established routine. Accompanied by a few enlisted men, the scouts would ride—or, if the snows were deep, ski—from point to point in the park, checking on the location and well-being of Yellowstone's wildlife, and looking for the tracks that might indicate the presence of poachers in the park. The diary entry of the scout James Morrison for November 24, 1897, was typical: "Took back trail down Fawn Creek about 4 miles, thence south along Quadrant Mountain to Indian Creek and up it about 4 miles to snowshoe shack, where we camped. Saw about 150 elk; many signs of beaver on this creek. Distance traveled, about 15 miles." For the most part, scouts focused their patrols along Yellowstone's periphery, where they would search for "fresh trails leading to the park" and listen for the gunshots that indicated that poachers were in the vicinity.[52]

While the scouts searched for poachers, the park's poachers, in turn, searched for the scouts. Noted one resident to Yellowstone authorities, "People who make a business of poching have studied the moovements of your Patrole." Astute lawbreakers soon learned how to turn many of the scouts' tactics against them. The army's regular system of patrol cabins, for instance, made the location of scouting parties easy to predict. "Experiance has tought them [poachers] that the patrole plan on getting back to their quarters by dark if not earlier, and they ar not far from their station before 8 AM. So they [poachers] do their hunting early morning but more often leight of an evening."[53] In addition, poachers discovered that firing a shot into the air could often trick patrols into revealing their position. As one scout, George Whittaker, recorded in his diary after hearing rifle shots during one patrol, "My opinion is that the two shots were fired just to draw us out of our camp and to find out if we were still camped here." Whittaker's suspicions were confirmed the following day when, after hearing a shot, he spotted a man looking for them with field glasses.[54]

To counteract such tactics, the army soon ordered the scouts to conceal their movements and camping spots. "During the winter period," mandated the army's regulations of 1907, "patrolling and scouting will be constantly carried on, and when camps are made they will, if possible, be selected so as to be hidden from poachers who may be in the park. Patrols and scouts will avoid the regular trails as far as possible, and will vary their different trips as much as the character of the country will allow."[55] To achieve such goals, patrols would often split up and approach their destination from several directions or switch their locations under cover of darkness. Explained one scout, "My idea for doing this [breaking camp] at night is to keep the hunting class of people thinking the camps were still out where they were."[56]

If one part of the scouts' job was making extensive, unobserved reconnaissances of Yellowstone, the other involved remaining in place, watching and waiting. Occasionally, scouts would situate themselves on a high ridge from which they could watch the park's borders, as Scout Whittaker did on a peak overlooking Gardiner on November 11, 1898. From this vantage point, he was able to witness two men using a clever subterfuge to mask their attempts at poaching in the park. They began by deliberately driving a herd of horses into the park: "My opinion," wrote Whittaker in his diary, "is they are men who intend to kill some antelope and if caught they will say they were looking for horses that will be their excuse." A few hours later, Whittaker spotted the men herding the horses back out of the park—and, while so doing, trying (unsuccessfully) to drive some of the park's antelope out with them.[57] More commonly, long waits ensued whenever scouts happened upon a poacher's campsite or a freshly killed animal. The scouts would stake out these positions, hoping that the poachers might make a return appearance to reclaim their prey. In the winter of 1898, Sergeant M.J. Wall had several such experiences. At one point he discovered a "poachers' cabin on Buffalo Mountain.... There was a fire burning inside, but no one at home. I looked all around and saw some mink skins and what I thought to be fox skins." Wall "waited to see if anyone would show up," but his arrival must have spooked the occupants, for they did not return. (Wall's diary does not record what happened to the cabin, but park authorities usually burned such structures whenever they found them.) Wall made a similarly unsuccessful hunt for wrongdoers a few months later, when he heard several gunshots and, going to investigate, encountered a dead mule deer. The following day, Wall watched the deer for several hours in the hope that whoever had shot it would come back, but the poacher never showed himself.[58]

While the scouts' duties were largely routine ("monotonous, toilsome, and uneventful work," in Frederic Remington's words), lurking beneath the daily tedium of patrolling and surveillance lay the potential for violent confrontation at any time.[59] An excerpt from the diary of Scout Whittaker provides a vivid illustration of the suddenness with which such incidents could occur. On November 24, 1898, Whittaker, hearing some shooting near the antelope herd that wintered along Yellowstone's northern boundary, went with one of the park's soldiers to investigate: "We struck the trail of two men they went within ten feet of the line then followed along the line toward Reese Creek I sent sgt Wall off to my right and told him to watch for anybody that might come that way while I would follow the trail made by the two men I did not go over 3/4 miles when two shots were fired directly at me after the first shot I droped down on my knee and got ready to shoot but I did not see where the first shot came from but I saw the flash of the second one and whoever it was that did the shooting got up and ran down a little draw or ravine by the time I got to where the shot was fired they were all of 300 yds away but I fired two shots at them don't believe I hit either."[60] The scout Jim McBride related a similar incident from the early 1900s: "Two of us found a fellow near Snake River, whom we suspected of possessing furs. I started up to him and he shot at me. I dropped on the ground and lay behind a rock while he fired seven times. When he had emptied his rifle I knocked him off his horse with the butt of my gun."[61]

Perhaps the most significant insight to emerge from the scouts' diaries, however, is an awareness of how difficult it was for Yellowstone authorities to catch wrongdoers. The diaries are filled with references to hearing gunshots, finding dead or wounded animals, encountering the campsites and tracks of poachers, and the remains of trees cut by timber thieves. Yet, despite near-constant patrolling, the scouts were able to capture only two wrongdoers during the winter of 1897–98—a rate consistent with present-day studies of poaching, which conclude that authorities typically apprehend only 2 or 3 percent of all game-law violators.[62]

The first of those arrested was the colorfully nicknamed "Horse Thief Scotty" Crawford, whom a patrol led by Scout Whittaker seized on the park's northern border. Some days earlier, Whittaker and his men had spotted Crawford's camp, located some "five hundred yards outside of the north boundary, conveniently close to watch both the mountain sheep, elk, and antelope on Gardiner flat and Mount Everts," and had kept it under steady surveillance. Only when it seemed as if Horse Thief Scotty, rifle in hand, had crossed over into the park in pursuit of game, did Whittaker and his escort emerge from their hiding place. Crawford quickly dropped his rifle in the snow and tried to cover it up, but it was found by one of the soldiers of the patrol, as were some six hundred pounds of elk meat that Crawford had hidden underneath a blanket in a nearby aspen grove. This seemingly airtight case against Horse Thief Scotty quickly fell apart, however, when it turned out that he had been apprehended several yards outside of the park. The army turned Crawford over to the county sheriff on charges of violating Montana's game laws, but "a jury composed of men more or less engaged in breaking the Montana game laws" soon acquitted Horse Thief Scotty of all charges.[63]

The case of Thomas Miner, the other man Scout Whittaker arrested during the winter of 1897–98, came to an only slightly more satisfactory conclusion. Miner, who inhabited a small cabin near Gardiner, was hunting legally outside of Yellowstone when he spotted an elk. Miner's first shot only wounded his target, and the elk fled several hundred yards south into the park, where Miner finally killed and butchered the animal. For such behavior, Scout Whittaker felt "duty bound to arrest" Miner, who ended up spending thirty days in the guardhouse at Fort Yellowstone.[64] Judging from newspaper coverage of the incident, local sympathy was on the side of Miner, who seemed less like a rapacious poacher than an ordinary citizen tripped up by an unusual set of circumstances. "The offense was slight and should have been condoned," opined the *Livingston Enterprise*. "[Miner] has always been regarded as an honest, truthful man."[65]

In retrospect, then, neither of the apprehensions during the winter of 1897–98 culminated in a clear-cut victory for park authorities. Horse Thief Scotty eluded all punishment, thanks to a sympathetic jury, while the arrest of Tom Miner—a man who would seem to fit only the narrowest definition of a poacher—doubtless reinforced local perceptions that Yellowstone's military administrators cared more about legal fine points than about the well-being of the rural folk living near the park. Other years witnessed similarly mixed results, leading some conservationists to reassess the military's ability to police the park. "It is evidently impossible for two troops of cavalry to so thoroughly cover more than 5,000 square miles of this rugged mountain country as to keep poachers out or to make their capture, in flagrante delicto, certain," noted *Forest and Stream* in 1898. Frederic Remington struck a similar note, concluding that the existing forces at the park "could not entirely prevent poaching in the mountain wastes of the great reservation."[66]

Such assessments were more accurate than their authors may have realized. From a present-day perspective, even a number of the military's supposed successes at Fort Yellowstone appear far more limited than most nineteenth-century conservationists recognized. Indian incursions into Yellowstone, for instance, did decrease significantly during the military's years at the park. But closer examination suggests that this was as much the product of changes going on outside Yellowstone as it was of any actions taken by the army. Each passing year, increasing numbers of Euro-Americans settled in the areas abutting the park, claiming the open public lands on which Indians had previously hunted. These newly arrived ranchers and farmers had little tolerance for the annual hunting expeditions of the Bannock, Shoshone, and Crow—especially since native peoples were not bound by the same game laws that non-Indians were theoretically obliged to obey. Observed the Commissioner of Indian Affairs in 1894, "Complaints were [recently] received from Idaho, Wyoming, and Montana that parties of Indians were continually leaving their reservations with passes from their agents to make social and friendly visits to other reservations; that en route they slaughtered game in large quantities merely for the sake of killing and for the hides, particularly in the country adjacent to the Yellowstone National Park.... if such depredations were allowed to continue, it would probably result in a serious conflict between the white settlers and the Indians."[67] As predicted, "serious conflict" did indeed erupt, most notably in July 1895, when a self-proclaimed posse of twenty-seven men from Jackson Hole "arrested" several families of Bannock Indians "for wantonly killing game" to the south of Yellowstone park. On previous occasions, local settlers had confronted Indian hunting parties with little violence. This time, however, when the alarmed Bannocks tried to escape into the woods, posse members opened fire, wounding five and killing one of the fleeing Indians.[68]

Although this unprovoked assault occasioned both a federal investigation and considerable public outcry, it was the settlers who emerged as the ultimate victors. The shooting led to a court case, *Ward v. Racehorse,* in which a Bannock chief named Racehorse contested the legality of Wyoming's game laws. Arrested for killing an elk out of season, Racehorse maintained that he was within his treaty rights, as the 1868 Treaty of Fort Bridger had granted the Bannock "the right to hunt on the unoccupied lands of the United States so long as game may be found thereon." The case proceeded all the way to the U.S. Supreme Court. In a judgment issued on May 25, 1896, the justices ruled that upon its admission as a state, Wyoming had acquired the right to regulate hunting on its lands, irrespective of preexisting Indian treaties. Other states soon seized upon this precedent to curtail the hunting rights of their own Indian populations. Even before this judgment, however, many Crows, Bannocks, and Shoshones had become reluctant to hunt off their reservations because of the potential for further violence, effectively diminishing the flow of Indians to the Yellowstone region.[69]

If in this instance the army exercised less control over events than most conservationists realized, in other cases the military's policies produced outcomes far different than intended. Such was the case for the army's aggressive campaign against forest fires, initiated the very day that troops marched into the park (indeed, the first sight to greet Captain Harris and his soldiers when they arrived at Yellowstone in 1886 was "three large fires raging in the Park," and Harris's first order as acting superintendent was to direct his forces to extinguish the blazes).[70] Previous civilian superintendents had also made attempts to prevent fires in the park, but the army, by setting up a "ceaseless and numerous system of patrols" and by mobilizing the two to four hundred enlisted men posted to the park, soon established an impressive record of locating and stopping forest fires before they could spread (a record no doubt facilitated by the decrease in fire-setting Indian hunting parties during this period). In 1888, the army limited the fires in the park to one hundred; the following year, this number was down to seventy, with most of them being small, localized blazes. By 1895, the officer in charge of Yellowstone could boast that "in the four seasons during which I have been in the Park but one fire of any magnitude has occurred."[71]

The full effects of this campaign did not become apparent until decades later. Army officers believed that by preventing forest fires they were defending Yellowstone against destruction, but their policy actually led to dramatic alterations in the park's ecosystem. In the lower elevations, sagebrush and conifers invaded grazing areas, diminishing the quality and quantity of the grass available to the park's wildlife. In the forests that dominated Yellowstone's middle elevations, the suppression of fire disrupted the reproductive cycle of the lodgepole pine, the park's most common tree, whose serotinous cones released their seeds only when exposed to intense heat. Furthermore, by preventing forest fires the army allowed dead plant matter to accumulate, so that when fires did erupt they proved uncommonly fierce and difficult to control.[72]

The army's management of Yellowstone's wildlife had similarly un-expected results. Hoping to increase the park's ungulate population, the military launched periodic campaigns against mountain lions, coyotes, wolves, and other predators.[73] Combined with the army's efforts against Indian hunters and white poachers, these measures reduced many of the checks that had long restrained the park's elk population. As early as 1895, Captain Anderson noticed that the elk at Yellowstone were growing so plentiful as to "possibly make them more numerous than the food supply could well support." By 1909–10, superintendents estimated that the park's elk herd ranged from 30,000 to 40,000 animals. (Later ecologists, expressing some reservations about the army's census techniques, have revised these figures downward, suggesting that the elk population may have climbed from some 5,000 to 6,000 animals in the 1880s to around 10,000 by the early 1900s.)[74] The soaring number of elk heightened the pressure on the park's grazing lands, triggering soil erosion and a decline in the aspens and willows that were among elks' favorite browse. The park's beaver population, which relied on aspens and willows to build their dams, proved unable to compete with the resurgent elk, leading Yellowstone to lose many of these aquatic rodents, and with them, the ecologically rich wetlands that their ponds had once sustained.[75]

This array of undesired outcomes to the army's policies at Yellowstone points to a central danger of conservation's program of state simplification. In theory, concentrating decision making in the hands of a few highly trained officials ensured that natural resources were administered in the most enlightened manner possible. In practice, however, this centralization increased the potential for disaster, especially when those in power misjudged—and *over*simplified—complex natural systems. While such perils existed everywhere conservation policies were enacted, they loomed especially large at Yellowstone during the years it was under the military's management. With little other training to guide

them, the army officers that John Muir and others so esteemed approached their new roles from a martial perspective. Drawing on tactics
learned in Indian warfare and elsewhere, they reduced natural resource
management to a battle, one in which forest fires, predators, and human
intruders alike became little more than enemies to be attacked and van-
quished.[76]

CHAPTER 6

Modes of Poaching
and Production

As the fall of 1892 drew to a close, Yellowstone's acting superintendent, Captain George S. Anderson, paused to reflect on recent events at the park. The past year had witnessed a number of developments: the erection of a new army barracks at Mammoth Hot Springs; heavy rains that had washed out many of the park's roads and discouraged tourist travel to Yellowstone; an early September snowstorm. Still, one issue above all preoccupied the captain. "Trouble with poachers," railed Anderson, "continues to be one of the greatest annoyances the superintendent has to contend with. There is gradually settling about the park boundaries a population whose sole subsistence is derived from hunting and trapping." It especially irked the superintendent that the poachers surrounding Yellowstone operated with the knowledge—and seeming co-operation—of the local population. "In most civilized countries the occupation of such vandals as these is held in merited contempt," grumbled Anderson. "But it is not so in the region of which I have made mention." The captain identified numerous violations during the previous months: "All the people are thoroughly cognizant of the location of the boundary lines, but only respect them in the presence of some member of the park force. Live elk, deer, antelope, and bears are caught and sold; the various fur-bearing animals are trapped for their pelts, and hunting parties are guided into the best game region."[1]

More than any other phenomenon, it was Yellowstone's prolific poaching that defined the relationship between park officials and the local populace. To Yellowstone's superintendents, the apparent support that illegal hunters enjoyed among the folk living near the park provided an unwelcome reminder of how limited their command over Yellowstone truly was. The ultimate source of such problems, officials contended, was the territory's raw frontier condition. "The Park is surrounded by a class of old frontiersmen, hunters and trappers, and squaw-men," explained Moses Harris in 1886. "As the game diminishes outside the Park, [they] increase their efforts and resort to all sorts of expedients to get possession of that which receives the protection of law."[2] Prominent conservationist William Hornaday expanded upon such interpretations in a series of lectures delivered at Yale Forestry School, in which he described poaching as a regressive phenomenon that plagued the entire western United States: "In the Western third of the United States, and especially on the so-called 'frontier,' it is a common occurrence for a sympathetic jury of neighbors and friends to acquit a red-handed violator of the game-law by saying: 'Not guilty! He needed the meat!' ... Any community which tolerates contempt for law, and law-defying judges, is in a degenerate state, bordering on barbarism; and in the United States there are literally *thousands* of such communities! The thoroughness with which one lawless individual who goes unwhipped by justice can create a contempt for law and demoralize a whole neighborhood is both remarkable and deplorable. That way lies anarchy."[3] For Hornaday, this "anarchy" imperiled conservation's goal of a natural world rationally managed by the state. "Out West, there is said to be a 'feeling' that game and forest conservation has 'gone far enough.' ... Many men of the Great West,—the West beyond the Great Plains,—are afflicted with a desire to do as they please with the natural resources of that region."[4]

Settlers near Yellowstone typically responded to such critiques in much the same manner as their counterparts in the Adirondacks. Stressing their natural right to subsistence, residents argued that conservation laws unfairly interfered with the frontier custom of "killing for the table." As one Wyoming resident contended in 1895, "When you say to a ranchman, 'You can't eat game, except in season,' you make him a poacher, because he is neither going hungry himself nor have his family do so.... More than one family [here] would almost starve but for the game."[5]

This defense of poaching as a pioneer tradition, however, simplified local practices almost as much as did many conservation policies. By the turn of the century, poachers killed game for many reasons besides simply the need for sustenance. As a result, poaching at a place like Yellowstone exhibited a remarkable variety of forms. Some poachers, for example, hunted by themselves; others poached as members of organized groups. Some poachers were protected by their local community; others found themselves the targets of informers and lynch mobs. Some poachers killed only a few animals per year; others slew dozens and did not even take the hides or meat of the animals they killed. To understand the sustained poaching that took place at Yellowstone and other conservation sites, we therefore need to examine each of these many facets—for only by surveying all of the forms that poaching assumed can we glimpse what it was that made poaching one of the most routine yet complex of rural crimes.[6]

At daybreak, March 14, 1894, Scout Felix Burgess located what he had been searching for: a set of ski tracks confirming official suspicions that a lawbreaker was lurking somewhere in the park's northeastern corner. For some time, rumors had hinted that someone from Cooke City was in Yellowstone killing buffalo for their hides and heads, which could bring from one hundred to four hundred dollars in nearby Montana towns. In addition, the soldiers at one of the army's outposts on the park's eastern edge had recently found tracks indicating that a man pulling a toboggan had slipped by their station late one night in the middle of a blizzard. After efforts to locate this mysterious traveler had failed, Captain Anderson had directed Burgess to make periodic patrols of the area where the tracks had been discovered. But days of searching had yielded nothing—until this morning.[7]

Together with Private Troike, an enlisted man posted to the park, Burgess followed the tracks a short distance. The two soon stumbled across a "teepee" and, bundled in gunny sacks and hoisted into a tree to keep them away from the park's scavengers, the heads of six buffalo. Burgess and Troike also picked up a fresh set of ski tracks, which they pursued to "a newly-erected lodge" where the poacher had been staying. The next question—figuring out where the poacher himself might be—solved itself shortly afterward: the pair heard six rifle shots in rapid succession. Upon investigation, Burgess and Troike spotted five dead buffalo several hundred yards away. The animals had been driven into the deep snow and shot. Hunched over one of the carcasses was a man removing the buffalo's hide with a knife.[8]

Despite the two hundred yards separating him from the poacher, Burgess decided he needed to act before the wrongdoer detected the patrol's presence and slipped away yet again. The scout raced across an open field toward the poacher, a high wind helping to drown out the noise of his skis. Given the possibility of violence when arresting an armed assailant, this was a potentially reckless act, but fortunately for Burgess, the man never looked up from his work. Nor was Burgess detected by the poacher's dog, which, unknown to the scout, lay curled up next to one of the buffalo carcasses. Not until he heard the words "Howell, throw up your hands!" did the hunter, a sometime sheep shearer from Cooke City named Ed Howell, know, as one subsequent account put it, that "he was not alone in the buffalo country."[9]

Howell's capture became an immediate national sensation. Not only was this the first instance of a poacher being caught in the park in the act of killing and dressing an animal, but, through a curious twist of fate, the arrest came at the same time that Emerson Hough, a correspondent for *Forest and Stream*, happened to be visiting Yellowstone. Hough telegraphed his editor, George Bird Grinnell, with the news of Howell's capture, and Grinnell, with the help of the Boone and Crockett Club, publicized the event as incontrovertible evidence of the need for expanded protection of Yellowstone.[10] Grinnell and his supporters found it especially galling that Howell, after killing at least eleven buffalo in the park, could be punished only by expulsion—the same weak penalty that civilian superintendents had complained about years earlier. "The man Howell, who has just been arrested, has destroyed property belonging to the Government—that is, to the people—which was worth from \$2,500 to \$5,000; yet if we may judge the future by the past, he will be allowed to go on his way practically without punishment," fumed *Forest and Stream*. "If he had committed a similar act anywhere else—if he had destroyed Government horses or mules or grain or supplies of any sort to this extent—he would have served a long time in prison. So long as these lewd fellows of the baser sort...know that they will not be punished for their invasions of the Park, ten regiments of troops could not protect it against their raids." The only solution, according to Grinnell and his associates, was to greatly increase the penalties for violating the regulations governing Yellowstone National Park.[11]

In their effort to compensate for the weakness of the park's official penalties against poaching, Yellowstone's military superintendents—Captain Anderson in particular—had over time cobbled together a variety of semi-legal sanctions. As one local newspaper phrased it, "It has been the custom...for Capt. Anderson, superintendent of the Park, to exercise his own pleasure with reference to the punishment of persons who have been arrested for killing game within the boundary lines of Wonderland."[12] The first such penalty was confinement to Fort Yellowstone's guardhouse, sometimes for a month or more, during which time prisoners were typically served a diet of bread and water and forced to endure solitary confinement in a large cage. As Anderson himself admitted to the secretary of the interior when discussing the case of E. E. Van Dyke (like Howell, a poacher from the fifty-person town of Cooke City), there was no legal basis for such imprisonment. Nevertheless, the captain saw confinement as the only way to deter lawbreakers: "I realize that under your regulations I had no authority to imprison Van Dyke, but simple removal has absolutely no effect on such characters, and *he* would have been back at the same business within 24 hours." "A tour there [in the guardhouse] will take the taste of game out of his mouth," added Anderson, "even if nothing more serious happens to him."[13]

The second penalty concocted by the park's military authorities was the confiscation of all goods that lawbreakers had used in committing their crimes. Unlike imprisonment, this measure at least had some basis in Department of the Interior regulations. At first, the officers in charge of the park had construed confiscation as applying only to rifles, traps, and other items of hunting equipment. Under Anderson, however, this policy expanded to include horses, saddles, harnesses, sleds, tents—anything of value that wrongdoers might have in their possession. When the captain compiled an inventory of the goods taken from poachers in 1893, the list made for "quite an array of confiscated property," including seven or eight horses. Many poachers, however, soon learned how to take the sting out of this penalty by claiming that whatever they had with them at the time of their capture was the property of someone else. When George and Henry Rockinger, from Gardiner, were apprehended in the park at midnight on December 17, 1894, with a sled load of freshly killed elk, for example, the army initially confiscated all the Rockingers' equipment. Not long afterward, though, another resident of Gardiner came forward to state that the horses, sled, harness, and butcher cleaver taken from the Rockingers actually belonged to him; he had lent them to the Rockingers without knowing that they were going to use his property to poach elk. Park authorities had no alternative but to return the items. Similar scenarios occurred with such frequency that Anderson could only observe that "it seems strange to me that whenever a thief is caught poaching in the park everything he has with him, but his skin and bones, belong to some good citizen."[14]

Howell's well-publicized arrest created the ideal opportunity to re-place this improvised, legally questionable system of enforcement with a more comprehensive and permanent arrangement. Building on their net-work of well-placed allies in Congress, Grinnell and the Boone and Crockett Club sped through both houses "an Act to protect the birds and animals in Yellowstone National Park, and to punish crimes in said park." Signed into law by Grover Cleveland less than sixty days after Howell's capture, this measure declared all violations of the Department of the Interior's regulations at the park to be misdemeanors, punishable by a fine of up to one thousand dollars and two years in prison. The act also assigned a magistrate to the park with the power to try and punish offenders. "In one sense it [Howell's killing of park buffalo] was the most fortunate thing that ever happened in the Park," enthused Captain Anderson, "for it was surely the means of securing a law so much needed and so long striven for."[15]

Many of those living on the park's perimeter, however, drew a differ-ent set of lessons from Howell's arrest. A few inhabitants, in keeping with the view that violations of the game laws were forgivable when done to meet basic subsistence needs, expressed sympathy for the press-ing hunger that, they felt, must have pushed Howell to his "perilous" deed. Asked the *Livingston Post,* "Was he, like many another man in these times, out of employment and destitute of the means of securing clothing, a bed, or perhaps even food? Indeed, it would seem that he must have been surrounded by some such circumstances to induce him forward." While the *Post* did not think Howell's "slaughter of buffalo" should go unpunished, the newspaper did raise mitigating circum-stances: "The plea of ministering to his own necessities ought certainly to have some weight in determining Howell's punishment."[16]

Far more common, however, were expressions of local disgust at Howell's killing of rare animals (by the 1890s, there were only two hun-dred to three hundred buffalo at Yellowstone) simply to sell their heads and hides to the commercial trophy market. Howell "will find no apol-ogists in this section...for his nefarious work," declared the *Livingston Enterprise.* "The sentiment here is universal that the small remnant of American bison still in the Park should be protected by rigid laws to pre-vent their extermination at the hands of poachers whose only object is to secure the valuable consideration offered for their scalps and hides."[17] More often than one may suspect, such public declarations were sup-ported by private gestures. During the 1890s, park authorities received a steady trickle of notes from anonymous local sources, providing tips about threats to Yellowstone's wildlife, especially its buffalo. "I will drop you a few lines as a favor for the Buffaloes as they are about extinct," read one such letter, bearing a Gardiner postmark, that told of the capture of several buffalo calves in the park and was signed "A Friend to the Buffalo." A similar missive told of a group of four men who, with several dogs and a sled, had gone into the park to kill buffalo. The writer urged the park authorities to capture the men, whom he or she dismissed as "scalp hunters and game slaughterers in general."[18]

Other residents fretted that deeds such as Howell's only confirmed the harsh opinions of them voiced by conservationists, and thus provided a justification for the army's unwanted presence in their midst. As one inhabitant of Cooke City griped, "This place has a bad reputation as a roost for poachers.... everybody living here is held responsible for the trespassing of a few men[,] and the general opinion prevails that we are nothing else but a whole community of outlaws." "The residents of Park County do not desire to have odium cast upon them or any justification given for the obnoxious and unjust rules of the Park military authorities by the lawless acts of buffalo slayers," agreed the *Livingston Enterprise.* "They will stand upon their rights as citizens of Montana in the matter of killing game in this state in the open season, but very few if any will be found to condone so open and flagrant a violation of the laws of Montana as the killing of the few remaining buffalo."[19]

Intriguingly, Howell, who was by no means silent in this debate, chose not to describe his actions in the economic terms employed by his defenders. Instead, in the chatty letters to the editor that he contributed to the newspaper, he attempted to defuse popular impressions of him as "a desperate, bad man" by focusing on the skill and daring that had enabled him to elude park patrols for so long and to survive a harsh Yellowstone winter over a hundred miles from the nearest settlement. "I was doing what a great many more would do if they had my courage and ability," he contended in one letter.[20] Delighting in his notoriety as the "National Park Poacher," Howell indulged a correspondent for *Forest and Stream* with a detailed description of the techniques he and other poachers used to outwit Yellowstone's patrols when hunting elk: "It is the simplest thing in the world. When the snow begins to fall in September and October, we wait until a nice snowstorm has set in, and then taking a saddle horse and two or more pack horses, we start for the Park and travel fast. After reaching the ground we have previously selected to hunt over, we make a long detour and cross our tracks perhaps

ten miles from camp so as to ascertain whether the soldiers are following our trail or not. If no other tracks are seen we go back to camp feeling safe, for we know that the new snow will obliterate all tracks before
dawn. We then secure enough elk to load our pack horses and are soon
on our way out of the Park."[21]

As his account underscores, poaching for Howell involved more than
simply the killing of game. It was a test of his bravery, of his knowledge
of the local landscape, of his skill as a hunter and tracker—in sum, an
exercise that called upon many of the qualities at the core of rural masculine identity. This connection between poaching and manliness may
help explain why poachers, despite the care they took to hide their lawbreaking from Yellowstone's authorities, so often bragged about their
risk-taking to fellow community members, an activity that frequently
appears to have taken place in the male venue of the local saloon. Several of the anonymous notes received by park authorities tell of over-
hearing poachers in barrooms "mak[ing] their bosts [sic] of hunting in .
. .the park" and "remark[ing] that he was 'too cute for any park policeman to take him in.'" Trial transcripts reveal that some poachers avidly
displayed the results of their illegal hunting to bartenders and other saloon regulars.[22] Such evidence suggests that poaching satisfied a
number of masculine functions. Not only did it allow local men to fulfill
their idealized male role as provider of food and income, but the risk
that illegal hunting involved gave it—in certain circles, at least—a
manly cachet. Poaching's many similarities (killing, the use of weapons,
the risk of encounter with armed opponents) to the quintessential male
activity, warfare, can only have amplified these connotations, especially
once the army assumed control of the park in 1886.[23]

Because of such factors, even those who decried poachers as outlaws
were not immune to admiring their masculine qualities. *Forest and
Stream* might sniff that Howell was "a most ragged, dirty and unkempt
looking citizen...dressed in an outer covering of dirty, greasy overalls,"
but the magazine still expressed amazement at his skill in constructing
his own skis and in hauling a heavily loaded, 180-pound toboggan
across the frozen Yellowstone landscape. Impressed that Howell had
endured harsh winter conditions during his surreptitious foray alone in
the park, one correspondent for *Forest and Stream* termed Howell "in
his brutal and misguided way a hero in self-reliance....Howell, or any
like him, I hate instinctively, but I salute him."[24] Even the park's scouts,
who as local residents doubtless realized better than anyone else the
hazards involved in venturing into the park during its harsh winters,

admitted to a certain grudging admiration for Yellowstone's poachers. As Thomas Hofer, a onetime scout, later put it, "All these hunter[s] earned all they got on their trips. Hard work and exposure."[25]

Yet manliness was not the sole province of poachers, as the curious coda to Howell's experience at Yellowstone reveals. In 1897, following a stagecoach robbery in the park, acting superintendent Colonel Samuel B. M. Young hired Howell, "who knew all the bad men and poachers around the park," as a scout. Howell's skillful tracking soon led park authorities to the robbers' trail, and after their capture Howell received $150 in reward money (despite Theodore Roosevelt's strenuous objections to any sort of payment to the former poacher). During his time as a scout, Howell also patrolled Yellowstone's western perimeter, reporting to Young that "I would like to locate all the buffalo I can on this trip that I may know where to go to protect them during the hunting season."[26]

On one level, Howell's apparent change of heart—from poacher of buffalo to the animals' protector—may seem like an extraordinary leap in moral perspective and in mode of relating to nature. On another level, though, there were inescapable continuities between the two positions. Tracking and other outdoor skills, the competitive challenge of outwitting an opponent, toughness, and physical bravery: all were qualities that poachers and scouts alike called upon to perform their assigned roles. Paradoxically, many of the same qualities that animated poachers could animate the park's local defenders as well.[27]

While Howell's arrest rid Yellowstone of "a notorious poacher" and helped establish a stricter enforcement policy, it did not, as Captain Anderson had initially hoped, signal the end of poaching in the preserve. Game continued to be killed in the park, not only by solitary poachers like Howell but also by organized groups of lawbreakers. The most daring and dangerous of these bands was the "merciless and persistent lot of head and skin hunters" that headquartered itself in Henry's Lake, a small Idaho village of ninety-eight people located not far from the park's western boundary.[28] As one army officer put it, "[At Henry's Lake there] lives a gang of hardy mountain pirates who make a scanty living by hunting, trapping, and fishing.... Natural poachers, they are banded together and work in concert, completely dominating the sparsely settled section, adjoining the Park, in which they live. Such skilled robbers are they and so minute their knowledge of the country that it is almost impossible to convict them."[29] Attempting to build on

the momentum Howell's arrest provided, Anderson soon initiated a renewed campaign against "the worst and most daring and desperate
gang of poachers who ever defied the park laws and the vigilance of the
authorities."[30]

Whether or not the target of Anderson's attention can best be described as a criminal gang remains open to interpretation. There is little
question that a number of the inhabitants of Henry's Lake were participants in a systematic poaching operation that sold meat, heads, and
hides to area taxidermists and mining camps. But whether this group
was a just a loose association of familiars or a hierarchically arranged
band with a clearly defined membership—a true gang—is less clear. The
group at Henry's Lake was certainly less organized than the "poaching
fraternities" active in rural Great Britain at much the same time. Such
fraternities, which often had as many as forty members, possessed a
highly developed hierarchy of armorers, treasurers, and other officers
and a complex initiation process that usually involved swearing oaths
of loyalty and secrecy.[31] By contrast, the lawbreaking at Henry's Lake
appears to have been much less structured, with the prevailing unit of
organization being the family. Two of the leaders of the supposed gang
were the brothers James and Al Courtenay; their father-in-law, Silas
McMinn, and his step-son, Jay Whitman, also participated from time to
time in their poaching activities, as did McMinn's neighbor, Dick Rock.
This reliance on family and neighbor recurred in other Yellowstone
poaching operations, no doubt because of the heightened loyalty such
arrangements offered. A pair of well-known poachers from Idaho,
George and John Winegar, were also brothers; William Binkley, the
leader of a band of poachers in Jackson Hole, often hunted with his
son-in-law.[32]

Although the group from Henry's Lake endeavored, like poachers
everywhere, to avoid keeping a predictable routine, they did have a rep-
ertoire of favorite techniques. Typically, the village's poachers hunted in
the southwestern corner of the park, particularly in the Madison River
basin and the Bechler River basin. Their standard procedure was to
haul a sled or wagon up to Yellowstone's western border, then slip
across on horseback, often following a streambed so as not to leave any
tracks. After killing whatever game they could find, the poachers would
then load their packhorses and use the cover of darkness to steal back
out of the park, trusting their horses to remember the route. Occasionally, the band relied on other tricks to fool the park authorities. One
common technique was to cache one's rifle and ammunition in the park

in the late autumn. This way, if caught while going into the park later in the winter, there was no evidence of having done so with the intention to hunt. Another technique to get around the illegality of possessing firearms in the park was to ride into Yellowstone unarmed and to drive some of the wildlife over the park's border, where it could then be legally killed with rifles that had been hidden nearby. The poaching parties that engaged in such strategies could be fairly large. During the winter of 1895, for example, an army patrol along Yellowstone's Idaho border stumbled across a group that appeared to contain four or five poachers, triggering a shoot-out in which one of the poachers' horses was killed.[33]

One frequent target of the Henry's Lake poachers was elk. After killing an elk in the park, the poachers would butcher the animal, taking only the best cut of meat (the "saddle") back to the village with them. Once at Henry's Lake, the poachers would box the meat or cover it in burlap and then ship it via stagecoach to nearby mining camps such as Virginia City disguised as "beef or domesticated elk." (The McMinns' neighbor, Dick Rock, owned a number of domesticated elk, providing a convenient cover for the steady shipments of elk meat from the village.) Another of the poachers' favorite targets was buffalo. The risks involved in killing a buffalo in the park were such that poachers seldom took the time to butcher the animals for their meat but would smuggle the heads and hides out, as these could be sold for several hundred dollars on the trophy market. In addition, during the spring some of the residents of Henry's Lake would try to capture buffalo calves, which they would then corral in remote locales outside the park. Once the buffalo were full grown, the poachers would arrange for the sale of the animals' heads to one of the not overly scrupulous taxidermists with whom they did business.[34]

Although many of the people of Henry's Lake apparently knew what the poachers in their midst were doing ("there is no secret made about these hunting expeditions," remarked one inhabitant to park authorities), this knowledge did not equate with full support of the group's activities.[35] In fact, at the same time that some of the inhabitants of Henry's Lake's were slipping into the park to poach, other inhabitants were slipping notes to park authorities, urging the army to curb the poachers' activities. "What is the game warden doing?" queried one such letter. "Is he going to let a few men kill all the elk in the Park[?] they come across the line to fead and they are killing them bye the four horse load and shiping them."[36] "Dick Rock of Henry's Lake Idaho has in his possession three young Buffalo calves supposed to have been caught in the Park," read another note, signed "A citizen." Stated another missive, "If you make an investigation and search about the hunters and fishermans cabbins about Henry Lake you will find where some of your Bison has gone to from the Y. N. Park. Believe me a true Citizen."[37]

Almost without exception, those who passed such information to the authorities at Yellowstone either ended their letters with a plea that their identities be kept secret or chose to shield themselves behind pen names. (Intriguingly, like the letter writers above, many of those who selected this latter option signed themselves "a citizen," providing suggestive, if fragmentary, evidence that such informers viewed the control of game to be connected to issues of community and civic responsibility.)[38] The authors of these letters offered a harrowing litany of the woes that could befall those known to have informed on poachers to park officials. "Keep my name still if your man ketch them," pled one informant. "I have horses here on the range and if they should find me out they wood run them off." "This must be confidential," added another. "If it were known my house and stock would not be worth a cent, we have some hard citizens here." A third letter writer was even more alarmist: "You will pleas keep this *perfectly secret* if they should find out that I have given you any information [I] would be in danger of my life as there is some tough cases up here."[39]

As such pleas reveal, the public acceptance that the Henry's Lake gang enjoyed masked considerable private resentment. While community members may have been afraid to confront the poachers directly, they proved more than willing to work behind the scenes to bring about the group's downfall. Once they realized the extent of the efforts against them, the village's poachers, much like timber gangs in the Adirondacks, attempted to intimidate local residents into halting the flow of information to conservation officials. "After you was at the lake they [the gang members] tried very hard to find out where you got yor information from," explained one informant following a surprise patrol of the village by park scouts. "Be very carefull don't let yor best friend no our business."[40] During a subsequent patrol, the military interrogated Henry's Lake's lone storekeeper. The man, while apparently anxious to dislodge the poaching operation in his village, was afraid of appearing to cooperate with park authorities. "I think Sherwood [the storekeeper] will give up any information he gets," reported the officer in charge, "but only in secret, as he claims—and I think truly—that they would burn his store and saw mill if they knew he informed on them." Such fears of violent retaliation do not appear to have been baseless: in 1898, Al Courtenay, one of the ringleaders of the poaching band in Henry's Lake, shot and killed an accomplice nicknamed "the Panama Kid" during a petty squabble.[41]

With Idaho authorities doing little to restrain the dangerous cast of characters in their midst, the residents of Henry's Lake turned to one of the few alternatives available to them: the conservation forces at Yellowstone. Inhabitants' behind-the-scenes information enabled the military to put together one of its most successful antipoaching campaigns ever. Thanks to its improved intelligence on the poachers and their compatriots, the army broke up the group's distribution network, arresting some of the taxidermists to whom the gang had sold heads. Similarly, after locals identified the poachers' favorite hunting spots, the army stepped up its patrols of the affected areas and resurveyed the boundaries in the park's southwestern quadrant, eliminating the ambiguity that had previously allowed poachers to argue that they had captured their game outside Yellowstone's borders.[42]

Such measures allowed park administrators to celebrate the new century with their first successful prosecution of any of the poachers from Henry's Lake. In 1900, James Courtenay and Jay Whitman were arrested and fined three hundred dollars apiece for killing an elk in the park. Deciding that "Park authorities had it in for him," Courtenay and his brother left the area shortly afterward, while Whitman moved to the new town of West Yellowstone, Montana, where he eventually opened a tourist campground. In 1902, their companion Dick Rock, having eluded all attempts by the army to catch him poaching, suffered a more poetic form of justice: he was gored to death by one of his captured buffalo. As such losses mounted, the gang at Henry's Lake, if a gang it was, dwindled to a shadow of its former self, its participants no longer able to inspire the terror that had once so gripped their village.[43]

In 1899, Edwin Daniel, a businessman from Chicago, wrote to *Forest and Stream* about a strange new poaching practice he had encountered during a recent hunting excursion to Wyoming. Just outside Yellowstone, Daniel reported, he had discovered a large number of elk that had been "simply shot recklessly and wantonly, and without any object whatever, except it might be perhaps to get their teeth." To Daniel as well as to many of *Forest and Stream*'s other subscribers, such behavior could only be described as bizarre. As one of the magazine's puzzled readers put it, "I kept wondering what these felows [sic] wanted with a collection of elk teeth."[44]

There was nonetheless a rational explanation for such goings-on. Elk teeth—or, to be more precise, the prominent upper canines, or "tusks," of the adult elk—had long been used by the Assiniboine, Cheyenne, Shoshone, and other Indian peoples as a form of adornment. The women of the Crow tribe, for example, ornamented their buckskins with hundreds of elk teeth, so that a single costume might weigh as much as ten or twelve pounds. Following the rise of the reservation, these practices became increasingly rare among Indian peoples. In their place, however, there arose another group whose members decorated themselves with elk teeth: the Benevolent and Protective Order of Elk, a fraternal organization founded in New York City in 1868. With growing numbers of club members wearing elk tusks—favorite fashions included using the teeth as watch fobs, rings, cuff links, and hat pins—the price of the teeth shot upward. "Five years ago I bought them in Idaho for 50 cents," lamented one club member, "whereas now a pair of fine teeth cannot be had for $5." Other commentators placed the price even higher, from ten to fifty dollars a pair, depending on the size and coloration, with the larger tusks from mature bulls bringing the best money.[45]

For the inhabitants of the Yellowstone region, who had the good fortune to live near some of the largest remaining elk herds in the United States, this booming market in elk tusks was an unexpected windfall. Under Wyoming law, residents could kill two elk during hunting season. The teeth from these animals, which previously might have been discarded, could now be sold for a tidy sum. In addition, if one chanced across the remains of a dead elk—a none-too-infrequent occurrence during the region's harsh winters, when elk sometimes died by the hundreds—it was a simple matter to collect additional tusks with the aid of a pair of pliers.[46]

Yet not all the settlers living near Yellowstone were content to gather tusks through legal means. Some, as *Forest and Stream*'s correspondents had discovered, killed elk simply for the animal's two canine teeth. Such illicit "tusking" could often be quite extensive. In 1916, for instance, park scouts reported finding "the bodies of 257 elk which had been killed for their teeth" by "certain lawless individuals" near Gardiner. Trial records from this period tell of tooth hunters who were observed with anywhere from 24 to 270 elk teeth in their possession.[47]

Even more than earlier poachers like Howell or the gang from Henry's Lake, tuskers proved difficult for park authorities to apprehend. Since elk teeth were small, the fruits of one's lawbreaking could easily be hidden in a shirt pocket or tobacco sack, where they were safely out of view of any passing park official. Once safely outside of Yellowstone, it was simple to conceal one's loot amid one's personal possessions. The compact size of elk teeth made selling them easy as well. Rather than smuggling a cumbersome animal head or hide to a nearby taxidermist or having to preserve and market large cuts of meat, the tusker could simply mail a small package to any one of the dealers in elk teeth who advertised in local papers. And because elk teeth did not spoil, they could be gathered year-round, whereas most other forms of hunting were pursued in the winter months when the cold weather ensured that animals' pelts were at their thickest and that whatever meat one killed would not spoil.[48]

In addition to these inherent advantages, many tuskers utilized a variety of tricks that enhanced their elusiveness, as the career of one notorious tooth hunter, William Binkley of Jackson Hole, Wyoming, demonstrates. Like most inhabitants of the Yellowstone region, Binkley made a living through a variety of means. Besides "prov[ing] up on a home-stead," where he ran a few cows and "raised some garden," he also worked from time to time as a butcher, a guide for visiting sports hunters, and, according to the 1900 census, a teamster.[49] But Binkley seems to have spent most of his time tusking, an undertaking in which he was frequently joined by a number of accomplices from Jackson Hole. (Park authorities dubbed the group the "Binkley-Purdy-Isabel gang," in honor of its primary participants.) When poaching, Binkley relied on a small-caliber rifle, a weapon that could seldom be heard from more than fifty yards away. (Other poachers, concerned that their shots might attract the attention of passing army patrols, fashioned homemade silencers that muffled the noise of their rifles.)[50] After he killed an elk, Binkley seldom removed the teeth right away. Rather, as one game warden explained, the standard practice for Binkley and his compatriots was "to shoot an elk, and probably not go to him for a week. His teeth wouldn't be hurt, at all. His teeth would be just as good in a week, and the elk would be partly ate up by animals, and then the man would be plumb safe to go back and get the teeth. There would be no evidence agin him." When it did come time to extract the elk's teeth, Binkley often took the added precaution of using a "skee"—"a flat piece of board and two mounted elk feet on it"—so that if he walked "where a band of elk had passed in the snow or mud...it resembled the track of the elk."[51]

The careers of Binkley and his partners in crime also offer some tantalizing clues as to their motivations. One piece of evidence comes from a Wyoming saloon, where Binkley showed the bartender his finger, telling the man that it had a callus from "pulling the trigger, shooting elk." Binkley proudly noted that this callus was the only one on his hand because he "didn't work."[52] A similar contrast between poaching and work was drawn by one of Binkley's compatriots, Oscar Adams. Telling an acquaintance that "he was making more money [tusking] than by working on a ranch," Adams added that he believed it "was foolish to work for wages."[53]

Binkley and Adams's positioning of poaching and work as opposed categories may initially appear peculiar. After all, to be successful, a poacher had to exert considerable physical effort. He might spend days in the saddle or on snowshoes, making long, surreptitious journeys through rough terrain. To avoid encountering any of the scouts or soldiers patrolling Yellowstone, a poacher frequently operated at night or during snowstorms and other bad conditions. Moreover, neither Binkley nor Adams belonged to the one group for whom hunting truly was play: upper-class sports hunters, such as the members of the Adirondack League Club or the Boone and Crockett Club, who found the chase most glorious when it fulfilled a cultural rather than economic function. For Binkley and Adams, poaching was no amusing pastime; it was the source of much of their annual income.[54]

Where tusking did diverge from the world of work for Binkley and his compatriots was in the contrast that it posed to wage labor. When he stated that it was "foolish to work for wages," Adams was no doubt celebrating the poacher's freedom from the dependency and time discipline of the workplace. Despite the risk of arrest (apparently never overwhelming: Binkley and Adams, like many of Yellowstone's poachers, evaded capture for years), poaching allowed its practitioners to embrace many long-standing producerist ideals—to work with a rhythm, and at the time, of their own choosing; to avoid subservience to bosses and employers—while also earning far more than the typical wage laborer.[55]

Because of such factors, poachers at Yellowstone were predominantly drawn from the region's growing working class. Although the army kept no precise data on the occupations of the poachers it arrested in the park, observers noted that a large number were agricultural and industrial laborers, the latter often from the coal and quartz mines that opened on the park's northern edge in the early 1900s. Explained one informant to park authorities, "I know there is a great many people of the working class that will not hesitate in going for game where ever they can find it up to a resonable [sic] distance in to the Park."[56] While some of these poachers, like Binkley and his accomplices, hoped to use poaching to avoid the workplace altogether, many others found illegal hunting a valuable supplement during economic downturns. Historians of Great Britain, for example, have discovered that poaching in nineteenth-century England peaked during times of high unemployment or high food prices.[57] The rate of poaching at Yellowstone seems to have moved in a similar rough accordance with larger economic trends. Howell's foray, for instance, occurred during a depression year. Similarly, following the panic of 1907 the number of arrests for hunting in the park increased fivefold, to ten from just two the year before.[58]

Drawing upon republican traditions that equated hunting with independence and self sufficiency, many of those arrested for poaching in the park defended themselves by pointing to the debilitating circumstances that had driven them to their illegal acts. After his capture in 1914, for instance, the unemployed worker Harry McDonald maintained that he had hunted in the park only because he was "broke all the time." McDonald noted proudly that he had never poached for trophies; he "wanted no heads but wanted some meat whether it was a deer, elk or [mountain] sheep." Although unsympathetic to McDonald's plight, park authorities were not unaware that hunting often provided a subsistence cushion for local laborers. As Yellowstone's superintendent acknowledged in 1912, many of the elk killed after migrating out of the park went "to families that otherwise might have had a slim meat ration for the winter due to dull times for workingmen in this section of country."[59]

This use of poaching to distance oneself from the strictures of the workplace, however, left its practitioners vulnerable to charges that they lacked the appropriate commitment to the work ethic and to community improvement. "We have a splendid game country here, but there is a certain element who seem to be doing the best they know how to deplete it," contended one Montana resident in 1897. "There are men here engaged in trout fishing and selling, in the open market, which is against the law....Elk meat was brought in by the wagon load, for sale, last winter. There are men here who are always at such work; but would not do an honest day's work." A correspondent for

the *Livingston Enterprise* struck a similar note, asserting that those
who supported themselves solely by poaching devalued other, more
honorable forms of labor: "some men would rather spend a month or
more time in trapping a beaver or two, or killing an elk at the risk of
fine and imprisonment, than earn a few honest dollars by manual
labor."[60]

Because of such factors, disputes over poaching often brought to the
surface local class tensions. William Simpson of Jackson Hole, for example, explained the activities of Binkley and other neighborhood
poachers by dividing the community's inhabitants into "two classes....
One is those who see in the country a future for themselves and families,
and who are particularly anxious to protect the game within the borders
of Uinta and Tremount counties. The other class is those who have no
permanent interest, no property, nor anything to keep them, outside of
being able to kill game for the meat, hides, heads and teeth; and in this
manner they make a partial living without work." For Simpson and
others like him, poaching spoke of the larger struggle between agrarian
modernizers and backward rural holdovers (whose primitivism merited
the charge of "white Indian"). Yet in certain respects the two groups
were not as far apart as they may have appeared. A poacher like Binkley
might resist entering the labor market, but he did so by intensifying the
sale of natural resources. Thus, both the poacher and his detractor
sought to capitalize on the spread of market relations. Indeed, by certain
measures, a poacher like Binkley could be considered even more attuned
to modern economics than his critics: through his intensive sale of game,
Binkley was commodifying a good that many other residents resisted
bringing entirely within the marketplace.[61]

For all of Binkley's ability at eluding park authorities, he had less
success in evading the volatile emotions that poaching excited among
the members of his own community. Jackson Holers' first effort to control the poachers in their midst came in 1899, when the town's inhabitants took up a collection to hire an additional game warden, primarily
to prevent outsiders from hunting illegally in the area. Three years later
residents formed a "Game Protective Association" designed, in the
words of one participant, to "make it hot for the game hogs."[62] Despite being early targets of the association, Binkley and his accomplices
did not alter their behavior. By 1906, the wily tuskers' neighbors had
had enough. Some twenty-five Jackson Holers formed a "citizens' committee" to bring the poachers to justice. After a brief meeting to debate
the merits of a summary lynching, the group decided to offer Binkley,

Adams, and their partners an ultimatum: vacate the area within the next forty-eight hours or they would be "left dead... for the scavengers to devour." Binkley and company fled within the time allotted, although not without first engaging in an elaborate ruse that enabled them to sneak into Idaho with a wagon load of elk and moose heads.[63]

Even after this close call, Binkley professed ignorance as to why his actions had triggered the wrath of his fellow residents. After all, he observed, many other members of the "citizens' committee" also hunted illegally. Thus, "they are not any better than I am.... They have been doing just the same." While it was certainly true that many other Jackson Holers ignored local game laws, Binkley overlooked the distinctions that rural folk had long drawn between different modes of poaching. Viewing subsistence as a natural right, the residents of Jackson Hole—much like country people in the Adirondacks and elsewhere—rarely opposed poaching done for necessities such as meat, hides, or tallow. On an earlier occasion, in fact, Binkley had been a beneficiary of this local tolerance of subsistence poaching. A few years before his near-lynching, Binkley shot an elk out of season for an ill neighbor who needed meat, an act for which he was arrested not long afterward by the state game warden. Outraged at what they considered to be Binkley's unjust treatment, Jackson Holers took up a collection and paid his hundred dollar fine.[64]

These same residents, however, were far less willing to be similarly tolerant of Binkley's foray into tusking. The distinctions rural Americans had attempted to draw between subsistence activities and commercial behavior may have been breaking down in the increasingly cash-based economy of the late nineteenth century. But Binkley's tusk hunting presented few such ambiguities. His slaughter of hundreds of elk—at the time of his arrest, Binkley had close to three hundred tusks in his possession—simply for their teeth represented an unmistakable example of destructive market engagement that, if allowed to continue unchecked, would destroy the natural resources upon which all the village's inhabitants depended. (These same fears about overexploitation—about "a few men kill[ing] all the elk in the Park"—no doubt played a large role in animating local opposition to the poachers at Henry's Lake as well.)[65]

In creating a "citizens' committee" to discipline Binkley, Jackson Holers drew upon a lengthy, if informal, tradition of community control over local resources. Most often, this control had taken the form of excluding those seen as outsiders—Indians such as the Bannock and

Shoshone, settlers from other towns, migratory shepherds—from the village's game or grazing areas. For many years, for example, a sign posted in the pass leading into Jackson Hole admonished:

Sheep Men Warning
We will not permit sheep to graze upon the elk range
in Jackson's Hole. Govern yourselves accordingly.
Signed: the Settlers of Jackson's Hole

Those shepherds brave or foolish enough to enter the valley were beaten and had their sheep killed by Jackson Holers determined to protect the local elk habitat. While attacks on fellow community members were rarer, the relentless tusking of Binkley and his compatriots eventually placed them outside the communal circle, making them targets for the same sort of violence.[66]

Binkley's forced exile from Jackson Hole did not end his connection with the region. Following their flight from Wyoming, Binkley and Charles Purdy were arrested in Los Angeles, where a California game warden discovered their stash of "hides and horns underneath the floor of an unused room" in a local taxidermy shop. Tried on charges of having violated the 1900 Lacey Act forbidding the transportation of illegally killed game across state lines, the two were fined the maximum amount allowed, $200 apiece. The pair were then sent to Yellowstone, where they faced a second trial on charges of having poached game in the park. Found guilty on these counts as well, Binkley and his compatriot were fined another $933 and confined to the park's guardhouse for three months. Binkley's confinement, however, did not last for long. In October 1907 he managed to escape from his cell. Calling upon the detailed knowledge of Yellowstone's hiding places and secret pathways that he had acquired during his many years as a poacher, he eluded all attempts to recapture him.[67]

Having made good his escape, Binkley may—or may not—drop from the historical record. A number of clues—hair color, height, and a raspy voice—point to Binkley as the masked man who, on the morning of August 24, 1908, undertook the most daring robbery in Yellowstone's history: the armed holdup of several of the park's tourist stagecoaches. Perhaps Binkley needed money to finance a final escape from the region. Or perhaps he wanted to "show" park authorities, as he had threatened during his confinement. But if the robber was indeed Binkley, his concern over the inequities of the wage labor system apparently remained intact: when the first stagecoach pulled into view, the robber announced that he was robbing only tourists. "If you drivers have got anything," the man declared, "you keep it, for you have to work for your money."[68]

If many park observers thought tusking an odd endeavor, they found the events that took place at Yellowstone in early February 1915 even more bewildering. The incidents began around midnight on February 1 when "some miscreant" cut the woven wire fence that ran along the park's border with Gardiner. The following evening, one or more figures slipped into a holding pen of elk located near Yellowstone's northern entrance, "in sight of the town of Gardiner." Fashioning an impromptu spear from a knife tied to a long stick, the trespassers proceeded to stab to death seven of the elk stored in the pen. The savageness of the attack as well as its lack of any understandable motive baffled park officials. "Scarcely any of the meat had been taken," noted the park's superintendent, who speculated that "it appeared likely that the work was done by some one for spite, possibly by the same persons who cut the fence."[69]

This assault on the park's elk, for which no one was ever arrested, remains one of the oddest episodes of poaching in Yellowstone's history. Unlike the illegal hunting undertaken by Howell, the Henry's Lake gang, and Binkley and his colleagues, it was a crime without a clear beneficiary. Why kill so many elk, especially if one was to leave the most valuable parts of the dead animals, the teeth and the meat, behind? Given this seeming senselessness, it is tempting to dismiss the attack as an irrational act of animal cruelty—the work, in the words of one observer at the time, of a "fiend." Such a position becomes harder to maintain, however, once we piece together the conditions prevailing at Yellowstone during the early 1900s. It seems that a certain grim logic may indeed have underlain the actions that unfolded on those cold nights in February 1915.[70]

Our investigation starts with the prologue to the elk stabbing: the cutting of the fence running along the park's border with Gardiner. As we have seen, the army began construction of this fence in 1903. Although its initial purpose was to serve as "a means of keeping stock of all kinds off...the park," the fence also helped prevent wildlife from wandering out of the park—especially Yellowstone's antelope herd, which often wintered on the grassy plain abutting Gardiner. Making the fence serve this second function, however, required constant adjustments. Elk regularly tore down or leapt over fences designed for livestock, while antelope, because of their small size, often slipped through openings that would have restrained horses or cows. In response to such problems, in 1907 and again in 1909 the army supplemented the fence near Gardiner with wire netting, as "it was found that [the antelope] would crawl beneath the fence where even small holes could be found."[71] In spite of all these efforts, antelope and other wildlife still managed to drift out of the park every winter, requiring soldiers to drive them back across Yellowstone's borders. During the winter of 1911, for instance, the park's superintendent found it necessary "on eleven different occasions...to send detachments of troopers of from 10 to 30 men each to assist the scouts in herding [the antelope] back into the park." The following year, a scout and an enlisted man passed the entire winter watching over the animals grazing near Gardiner, making sure that the antelope did not stray out of Yellowstone's confines. In 1913, in an effort to eliminate such laborious duty, the army erected a "new 7-foot Page woven-wire fence" for four miles along the park's border with Gardiner.[72]

This fence building was part of a larger program by Yellowstone's superintendents to limit the mobility of the park's game animals (a rare example of a program of state simplification aimed not at local residents but at wildlife). The first effort in this direction came in the mid-1890s, when park authorities endeavored to build a "tame" buffalo herd from animals purchased from commercial ranches. These buffalo were corralled at all times as a protection against poachers like Howell and the "gang" from Henry's Lake. A more indirect form of controlling animal mobility was the winter feeding program that the army initiated in the early 1900s. Each year, the military harvested several tons of hay from alfalfa fields the soldiers planted in the park. Soldiers then fed this pasture to Yellowstone's deer, antelope, mountain sheep, and elk during the winter months in an attempt to dissuade the animals from wandering to the lower elevations outside of the park in search of forage, where they might be killed by local hunters.[73]

As might be expected, those living on Yellowstone's fringes seldom appreciated these policies, which pinched off much of the area's animal supply. The ensuing shortages of game exacerbated tensions over Yellowstone's borders, particularly over the issue of how one determined when an animal had left the protection of the park and become fair game for passing hunters. While settlers considered any animal that strayed even momentarily beyond Yellowstone's confines a legitimate target, park authorities took a more expansive view. As Major Harry Benson explained to the secretary of the interior in 1909, "It is not believed that the State authorities intended game to be killed by these people simply because it had gotten through the fence and strayed a few yards beyond the limit of the Park." In keeping with such logic, super-intendents often punished locals for killing game that was technically outside park boundaries. During the winter of 1897, for example, a band of antelope "drifted across the northern boundary line of the Park but a short distance on account of the stormy weather." Before "a de-tachment of 20 men and 2 scouts" could drive the animals back, the an-telope "were fired into by lawless persons and ten were killed." After identifying the hunters, Colonel Young, Yellowstone's acting superin-tendent at the time, issued "instructions [that] if found inside the boundary lines of the park they shall be arrested and ejected there-from—not necessarily at the nearest point."[74]

Protesting that they were "neither the ignorant or lawless element as charged by Col. Young," several of the participants pointed out that their killing of the antelope had been legal under Montana's game laws: "A law-abiding citizen of Montana tried, convicted and sentenced be-cause it was rumored that he had killed game in his own county and state. Can, then, a superintendent of the Park or commander of a mili-tary post deprive a citizen of an adjoining state of the rights vested in him by the constitution? It is not claimed that the offense (?) was against the rules, and within the jurisdiction of the Park authority or military reservation. Game is migratory."[75] Despite such arguments, Yellow-stone authorities maintained that many of the animals that strayed be-yond the park's boundary were only out of the park temporarily and therefore should not be hunted. In 1908, the army barred thirteen people charged with "killing park antelope that had escaped through [the] fence near Gardiner" from any future access to the park. Two years later, the military issued a similar judgment against Shirley Brown of Gardiner for killing a deer "that had just jumped over the park fence into Mont[ana]. . . . This [shooting] was not in violation of the letter of any law but was in violation of spirit of same."[76]

In light of such policies, the cutting of the fence in February 1915 can perhaps best be understood as a rebellion against the army's efforts to control the region's wildlife. There were reasons both practical (to allow animals out of the park) and symbolic (to demonstrate one's disregard for the army's attempts to impose its own boundaries on the landscape) that could have motivated a disgruntled local to damage the barrier that was the most visible marker of Yellowstone's northern limit. The timing was equally significant: the attack came shortly after the army had re-placed the previous fence with a seven-foot, woven-wire version, which

TABLE 8.   ELK SHIPPED FROM
YELLOWSTONE NATIONAL PARK,
1911–1918

Winter 1911–12	137
Winter 1912–13	538
Winter 1913–14	99
Winter 1914–15	375
Winter 1915–16	618
Winter 1916–17	496
Winter 1917–18	145
TOTAL	2,408

SOURCE: U.S. National Park Service, *Annual Report of the Director of the National Park Service, 1917,* 132; U.S. National Park Service, *Annual Report of the Director of the National Park Service, 1918,* 127.

doubtless had the combined effect of cutting off whatever leakage of animals out of the park had previously occurred while also serving as a much more prominent symbol of the army's attempts to shape the local landscape.

But what about the attackers' choice of target—the elk corralled near Yellowstone's northern entrance? It may have been that these were simply the closest and easiest park animals for the poacher to kill, but there are also reasons why attacking such animals would have resonated symbolically with some of the local population. Herding elk into pens was a recent development at the park—an outgrowth of official concerns that Yellowstone's elk population was rising to unmanageably high levels. But rather than revising the antipredator and winter-grazing policies that had led to this surge in the elk's population, the army opted instead to ship thousands of "surplus" elk via railroad to zoos, parks, and other conservation sites. (See Table 8.) The collection point for these shipments was situated just across the border from Gardiner—a location convenient to the town's railroad station but also one that gave the village's inhabitants a prominent vantage point from which to watch the removal of the region's most popular game animal. Moreover, many of those who witnessed the army's shipments doubtless disagreed with the park authorities' belief that the region was suffering from an oversupply of elk. Because of the military's fence and feeding policies as well as some uncooperative winter weather, the game supply beyond the park's borders had been quite sparse of late. "Hunting has been very poor during the last two seasons," noted Yellowstone's superintendent in 1915.

"Cold, stormy weather did not come in time to drive the elk down before the close of the hunting season."[77]

Under such circumstances, the attack on the penned elk at Gardiner may well have represented a protest against the army's conservation policies. Once integral to local subsistence, the park's elk had instead come to symbolize the new conservation order taking shape at Yellowstone. Viewed from this perspective, the stabbing of the penned elk constituted not an attempt at illegal appropriation of resources but rather a crime against property: the destruction of something belonging to Yellowstone officials (much as the setting of forest fires in the Adirondacks at this same time sometimes appeared to be intended to destroy state-controlled forestlands).[78] Perhaps the stabbing even represented, as the historian John Archer has argued in his study of incidents of animal maiming in nineteenth-century rural England, "a form of symbolic murder," in which the animals were killed in place of a despised park administration. This theory would help explain why the killers took "scarcely any of the meat" from the dead elk: the deed they were performing was more akin to assassination than to hunting.[79]

It is even possible that the attack on the elk was a form of vengeance against the animals themselves. To some locals, it may have appeared as if Yellowstone's wildlife, having become comfortable with the protection the army provided, did not venture outside the park as they once did and still should have. As one resident of Gardiner lamented in the early 1900s, the animals, having learned "where the line is," no longer allowed themselves to be hunted as before. The killers' decision not to take any of the meat or teeth from the dead elk may therefore have been an act of revenge designed to demonstrate local outrage at the animals' seeming betrayal of their preexisting relationship with the region's inhabitants.[80]

Yet for all the elements of possible social protest underlying this savage attack on the park's elk, apparently not everyone in Gardiner shared the perpetrators' motives. After the stabbing, several of the village's inhabitants, expressing revulsion at the slaughter of "a large number of... helpless animals," started a popular subscription that raised over three hundred dollars in reward money for the arrest of the elk killers. Other residents hinted at an even darker fate for the animals' assailants. "It would not be lucky for the guilty person or persons if some of the citizens of Gardiner apprehended him, so incensed are they with the cowardly crime," observed a local newspaper.[81]

Such a response—Gardiner's residents raising money to help capture a poacher—was not the sort of local behavior that Captain Anderson had predicted in 1892. However, in his haste to lambaste the "people who live on the borders of the park" for "intentionally and purposely... depredating" in Yellowstone, Anderson had missed an important truth. At no time did the poachers plaguing Yellowstone enjoy the total acceptance that Anderson and other park officials imagined. In fact, on many occasions illegal hunters found themselves the targets of popular efforts designed to restrain their efforts. Thus, rather than divide rural folk and park authorities into two mutually exclusive camps as early conservationists often did, it is more telling to emphasize the extent to which each category flowed into the other, complicating any easy moral tale about conservation. There were, for instance, those associates of the park, such as the soldiers who cooperated with local poachers, who evinced little interest in the goals of conservation. And there were those local inhabitants who aided the Yellowstone administration, either by seeking employment as scouts, by passing along information on poaching or other wrongdoing, or, as in the case of the stabbed elk, by raising money to support the arrest of lawbreakers.[82]

In the end, the fact that the American countryside produced both prolific poachers and a moral ecology that criticized certain poaching practices should not prove surprising. Poaching touched on many issues at the heart of turn-of-the-century rural life—the desire for self-sufficiency, the drive to prove one's manliness and daring, the hope of avoiding the dependency of the workplace—as well as on abiding notions of community responsibility and of one's right as an American to the hunt. These factors sometimes coincided but often conflicted, prohibiting rural folk from reaching any easy consensus about poaching's moral stature. In subtle yet unmistakable ways, Yellowstone by the early 1900s had become as much a monument to such tensions as it was to the geothermal energies that powered its famous geysers.

PART III

Desert

The Grand Canyon

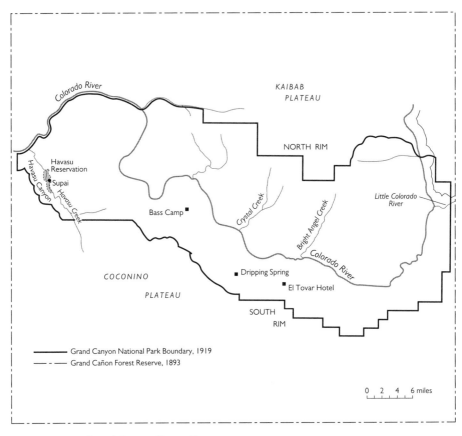

Map 3. Grand Cañon Forest Reserve, 1893

CHAPTER 7

The Havasupai Problem

In the fall of 1915, Captain Jim, a member of the Havasupai tribe of northern Arizona, dispatched an urgent letter to the Commissioner of Indian Affairs. Captain Jim opened his missive by detailing the close relationship that had once existed between his people and the wildlife of the region, particularly mule deer, the area's most plentiful game animal: "A long time ago the Gods gave the deer to the Indian for himself. The women and children all like deer meat very much. The Indian men like buckskins to trade for grub, saddles, horses, saddles, blankets, and money. A long time ago...the Indians all go out on the plateau and hunt deer for two or three months and then all come back to Supai [the Havasupais' main village] to stay." But recent changes, Captain Jim observed, had disrupted this long-standing pattern: "Now the Indians are all afraid about the hunting and never go far away. I want you to send me a hunting license and tell me good and straight that I may hunt deer.... The white man should now help the Indians by giving him permission to hunt deer as there be no trouble with the Game Wardens.... This is all."[1]

In its own abbreviated way, Captain Jim's letter summed up the altered circumstances that conservation brought to many Indian peoples. It was above all a narrative of loss—of the deprivation of traditional resources; the breakdown of seasonal cycles and of customary gender roles; the undermining of belief systems—at the conclusion of which Native Americans found a bewildering array of licenses and game wardens mediating between them and the natural world. Yet, in more subtle ways, it was a tale of Indian reinvention and resistance, too. The initiative that Captain Jim demonstrated in dictating a letter to the Bureau of Indian Affairs and his efforts to link the traditions of his tribe to the strange new world of hunting permits suggests something of the creativity that Indian peoples evinced as their previous ways of interacting with the environment collided with a new system of state controls.

For Captain Jim and his people, the challenges conservation posed were especially dramatic. Two decades earlier, in 1893, the federal government had created the Grand Cañon Forest Reserve (later, Grand Canyon National Park), which encompassed the territory that the Havasupai people had long claimed as a hunting ground for game, a gathering area for wild foodstuffs, and a grazing spot for their horses. The establishment of this reserve left the tribe with a reservation completely surrounded by national forestlands, so that any effort by the Havasupai to venture outside their reservation—for hunting, the gathering of plants and firewood, the grazing of animals, or other activities—risked bringing them into conflict with the forest's new federal managers. Unsurprisingly, the Havasupai, much like the rural folk in the Adirondacks and at Yellowstone, continued their customary use of the resources now enclosed within conservation lands. But they did so now as outlaws who often had to dodge the rangers sent to enforce the reserve's regulations (as Captain Jim's reference to "trouble with the Game Wardens" reflects).

While the Havasupai may seem like an extreme example of the displacement that Indian peoples experienced with the coming of conservation, theirs was not an isolated case.[2] The files of the Bureau of Indian Affairs (BIA) bulge with letters authored by Native Americans protesting the limits that game laws and forest reserves placed upon the ways in which they had previously interacted with the natural world. In 1897, for example, twenty-two Lac du Flambeau Indians in Wisconsin sent the bureau a petition protesting that when tribal members had sold their land "they were not selling the deer and game that belonged to them.... they were always to have them." "It is not the Indians that have killed all the game and deer, it is the white men," added the petitioners, "[yet] when they catch us killing deer or game they lock us up in jail." In 1903, Charley Bailey, an Indian from Michigan, expressed a similar objection to the limits that game laws had placed upon natives' hunting: "I...write these few lines to request you to give me a privilege to kill the deer for my food, as the Government promised us when [it] bought our land[,] for [it] did not bought our animals that we should have all ways for our food." Other BIA documents tell of the violent confrontations that occasionally broke out when authorities tried to prevent Indian peoples from gathering traditional resources. In 1895, for instance, a Ute hunting party engaged in a shoot-out with Colorado game wardens intent on driving the Utes back onto their reservation. Two years later, a group of Chippewa Indians in Minnesota killed a game warden after he tried to arrest them for trapping muskrats.[3]

Through such deeds, Indian peoples offered a powerful collective dissent from the official mores of conservation. Native Americans were not alone, of course, in finding their customary use rights rendered obsolete by state planners, their foraging areas reborn as parks and forest reserves, and their hunting practices and use of fire decried as environmentally destructive. Many non-Indians, such as the squatters evicted from the Adirondacks Park, could recount similar tales of dispossession. The settlers near Yellowstone were also disparaged as examples of people who engaged in the wasteful, disorderly use of the environment that conservation intended to replace. Yet of all the inhabitants of nineteenth-century rural America, it was Indians who were the most powerless, and consequently, it was Indians whose lives were most remade by the coming of conservation. As events at Yellowstone illustrate, the movement's arrival shut off vast portions of tribal hunting and foraging areas while also inhibiting Native Americans' use of fire to shape the landscape around them. Even more strikingly, conservation interlocked on multiple levels with other, ongoing efforts—treaties, the establishment of reservations, allotment—to displace Indians' claims upon the natural world in order to open up such areas to non-Indians. In this sense, conservation was for Native Americans inextricably bound up with conquest—with a larger conflict over land and resources that predated conservation's rise. Any discussion of the consequences that conservation had for Indian peoples thus needs to take these coterminous incidents into account. From the perspective of Native Americans, conservation was but one piece of a larger process of colonization and state building in which Indian peoples were transformed (in theory, at least) from independent actors to dependent wards bound by governmental controls.[4]

As dramatic and wrenching as these efforts to remake Indians proved, they also remained incomplete. Despite the unequal balance of power between themselves and non-Indian society, native peoples were able through a variety of tactics to elude the controls placed on them and even, at other times, as Captain Jim's letter to the commissioner demonstrates, to challenge them. In the case of the Havasupai, the tribe's continued resistance to conservation efforts at the Grand Canyon repeatedly forced reluctant authorities to confront what they came to term "the Havasupai problem"—which was, writ small, the problem lying at the heart of conservation itself.[5]

According to one of their stories, the Havasupai learned how to cultivate their staple agricultural crop, corn, from Coyote. Coyote planted the first kernels of the plant near the canyon creek from which the Havasupai took their name for themselves: Havsuw 'Baaja, people of the blue-green water. (Later visitors would corrupt this term into Yavasupai, Suppai, and finally the name by which the tribe is known today, Havasupai.) But Coyote did not have enough seeds. The Havasupai, he told the tribe, could farm only part of the year. The rest of the year they would have to hunt for their food as he did.[6] As a result, during the prereservation era the Havasupai lived an existence divided between intensive agriculture and extensive hunting and gathering. The farming portion of the tribe's seasonal cycle began each spring, when the Havasupai would clear and plant their fields in Havasu Canyon, a narrow tributary of the Grand Canyon, located some three thousand feet below the surrounding plateau lands. Here, on the limited land available between the steep cliffs on either side, the tribe developed a system of dams and irrigation ditches that enabled them to use Havasu Creek— one of the few sources of permanent water in the area—to nourish their crops of corn, beans, sunflowers, squash, and other plants.[7]

The tribe's crops typically began to mature sometime in June, and in late summer, once most of the crop was in, the Havasupai held their annual harvest festival. This celebration also marked the onset of an intensive period of trading, as the Havasupai exchanged their seasonal abundance with the members of neighboring bands: the Walapai (a closely related group with which the Havasupai frequently intermarried); the Hopi; the Mohave and the Paiute (two nearby groups with whom the Havasupai had sporadically hostile relations); and, after they began to filter into the area in the mid-1800s, the Navajo.[8] Of all these trading relationships, the most crucial was with the Hopi, whose village was located several days' journey to the east. In exchange for Hopi specialties such as pottery, jewelry, and blankets and other woven goods, Havasupai women would trade baskets and the fruit of the agave cactus, as well as salt and a red paint made from minerals gathered in the Grand Canyon. Havasupai men traded skins from deer killed on the plateau to the south of the Grand Canyon. Tanned according to Havasupai custom, these buckskins became favored trade items with many Indian groups in the area. In the words of Mark Hanna, a tribe member born in 1882, "Hopis came down here [to the Havasupais' summer village] with a lot of blankets and some jewelry. They wanted buckskins.... The Supais had lots of buckskins then because they hunted all over. There weren't any rangers around here [at that time]....Lots of Indians came down here to trade for buckskins."[9]

As fall arrived and the trading season drew to a close, much of the Havasupais' crop was dried and stored in granaries built into the sheer stone face of Havasu Canyon. The tribe then broke up into smaller units and spent the winter on the mesa lands above, where each family had its customary camping ground. As Big Jim, a Havasupai born sometime around 1860, recollected years later, on the plateau south of the Grand Canyon there were "certain areas that each family [had]... place[s] that they used a whole lot, known as permanent places." Because of the aridity of the Havasupais' homeland, most of these family-use areas centered on "tanks"—the scattered springs that for much of the year were the sole sources of water in the area and were therefore accorded special prominence in Havasupais' mental maps of the plateau. "They usually come back to [the] same destination every year where the permanent waters [are]," observed Big Jim. Added fellow tribe member Allen Akaba, born in 1881, "There is springs just all along that country. That is where the tribe used to go to stay."[10]

Moving onto the plateau for the winter enabled the Havasupai to tap the annual bounty of the Coconino Forest that bordered the south rim of the canyon. Using their intimate knowledge of the local ecology, the women of the tribe would gather wild plant foods ranging from piñon nuts to the seeds of grasses such as goosefoot *(Chenopodium)*, mutton grass *(Poa fendleriana)*, and Indian millet *(Oryzopsis hymenoides)*. For their part, Havasupai men engaged in extensive hunting expeditions along the south rim, especially after the first snows, which facilitated their tracking of the deer, rabbits, porcupine, antelope, and other game animals that inhabited the area. "That is when the hunting season [was] fair, during the snow," explained Big Jim.[11]

Coyote's plan for the Havasupai had been a wise one, then, for such an arrangement enabled the tribe to take advantage of two different ecosystems: the first, the well-watered semitropical setting in Havasu Canyon; the second, the arid, game-rich highlands that characterized

much of northern Arizona. Moreover, inhabiting two different landscapes in this manner buffered the Havasupai against any one resource
base becoming depleted. If, as happened in some years, Havasu Creek
overflowed and ravaged the tribe's fields, they could turn to the gathering of wild plants and wild game on the plateau. If game was scarce, the
community could rely upon the corn and other foods stored in its granaries. Trade with neighboring Indian peoples further broadened this resource base. Not only did it make accessible goods and foodstuffs that
otherwise would have been unavailable, it also built relationships that
provided the Havasupai with outside support in times of extreme
crisis—as in the early nineteenth century, when many of the Havasupai,
hoping to avoid raids that the Yavapai Indians had launched upon
them, spent several months living with the Hopi.[12]

Even the *entrada* of Spain into the Southwest in the sixteenth century,
which was to have a major impact on groups such as the Pueblo, Hopi,
and Navajo, did little to disrupt the Havasupais' annual cycle. Isolated
by the fastness of their rugged canyon home, the tribe, unlike their trading partners to the east, had little direct experience of Spanish (and later,
Mexican) colonialism. Instead, for the Havasupai, the Spanish presence
was notable principally for the gradual diffusion of European material
culture into the region—tools, plants, domestic animals, and the like. By
providing a whole new array of valuable goods to be exchanged, the
Spanish may, in fact, have infused new vitality into preexisting trade
networks between the native peoples of the Southwest. The Havasupai
soon became an important link in an east-west trade route in which
goods from New Mexico—cloth, metal, new crops, and horses and
other livestock—obtained by the Hopis and other groups in close contact with the Spanish were traded from tribe to tribe, passing to the Havasupai and then to the Walapai, the Mohave, and even remoter groups.
Although the Havasupai did not adopt every piece of European material
culture that this trade made available, they quickly accepted peach and
apricot trees, which flourished in the semitropical environment along
Havasu Creek, and the horse, prized because it greatly aided the tribe's
mobility while hunting, trading, or traveling between the plateau and
their agricultural plots in Havasu Canyon.[13]

The geography that insulated the Havasupai from the impact of
Spanish colonialism in the 1600s and 1700s also limited the immediate
repercussions of 1848, when Mexico, the theoretical ruler of the Havasupai homeland, ceded political control of the region to the United
States. However, if the first years of the American conquest of the

Southwest passed relatively unnoticed, it did not take long before the Havasupai received a number of signals that the outside world was changing in disturbing ways. In 1863, for example, desperate Navajos fleeing an army campaign to move them to the Bosque Redondo in New Mexico straggled into the Havasupais' summer village in Havasu Canyon. Some ten years later, several members of the Walapai tribe fled to Havasupai settlements in the Grand Canyon to escape U.S. Army efforts to confine them to a reservation. Not long afterward, Mexican-American shepherds appeared on the plateau, briefly contesting the Havasupais' right to water holes in the area.[14]

The pace of change accelerated in the 1880s, as the Atlantic and Pacific Railroad snaked its way across northern Arizona, opening the territory to outside settlers and markets. Miners searching for precious metals began to probe the inner recesses of the Grand Canyon, polluting the local water supply and intruding into areas that the Havasupai claimed as exclusively their own. In 1879, for instance, two miners, W. C. Beckman and H. J. Young, located a lead-silver mining claim along Havasu Creek, just a short distance downstream from the Havasupais' summer fields.[15] The Havasupai lost further territory during this time to the incipient tourist industry that began to develop along the south rim of the Grand Canyon. In 1883, a sometimes asbestos miner named John Hance constructed a log cabin on the canyon edge and advertised himself as a guide for visiting tourists. He also laid claim to a Havasupai path that led into the Grand Canyon, which he widened and renamed the Hance Trail.[16] At much the same time, two brothers, Ralph and Niles Cameron, part-time prospectors and sheep ranchers, seized control of another Havasupai pathway, renamed it Bright Angel Trail, and proceeded to charge a toll to any passing tourist who wanted to take the trail into the canyon.[17] Even more wrenching disruptions followed, as the diseases that miners and tourists left in their wake devastated the Havasupai. The tribe's population, which had probably hovered around 300 in the eighteenth century, dropped to 265 in 1886. By 1906, it had reached a low of 166, with a disproportionate share of the decline resulting from deaths of the tribe's women and children.[18] (See Table 9.)

In enumerating the many losses that the Havasupai endured during this era, one needs to take care not to miss the other side of the story: the remarkable resilience that the tribe displayed in the face of the limited opportunities available to them. One telling example of the Havasupais' creativity amid strange new circumstances can be seen in the adaptations that the tribe members made in their mode of dress. The 1880s witnessed

TABLE 9.   HAVASUPAI POPULATION,
1900–1910

	1900		1910	
Women	111	(44.4%)	75	(43.9%)
Men	139	(55.6%)	96	(56.1%)
Under 15 years old	116	(46.4%)	50	(29.2%)
15–45 years old	90	(36.0%)	90	(52.6%)
Over 45 years old	44	(17.6%)	31	(18.1%)
TOTAL POPULATION	250	(100.0%)	171	(100.0%)

SOURCE: 1900 Population Census, Manuscript Schedules, Coconino County, Arizona, Roll 48, T623, Records of the Bureau of the Census, RG 29, National Archives; 1910 Population Census, Manuscript Schedules, Coconino County, Arizona, Roll 39, T624, Records of the Bureau of the Census, RG 29, National Archives.

the tribe's widespread adoption of manufactured clothing, much of it "cast-off soldier and other American clothing" apparently obtained by scavenging around forts and other settlements. By 1892 a visitor to the tribe could report that "every man was well dressed, and I counted fifty pairs of pants hanging in the different wickiups. There were also shirts, vests, coats, dresses, shoes, boots, muslin, calico in abundance, some flannel, and some linen."[19] "The men run to overalls and a jumper and the large western hat," noted another visitor, "while the women wear long, wide-skirted dresses of calico which they make themselves." Although the Havasupai seem to have considered the Euro-American style of dress relatively unattractive, they did find manufactured wool and cotton goods warmer. "It may not look better," observed Chief Navajo, one of the Havasupais' tribal leaders, "but it is warmer than the buckskins." Perhaps more important, with this style of dress the deerskins that would have previously been used to make clothing for tribe members were now available for trade.[20]

However, as a result of the radical changes in the region, trade no longer flowed in the same channels as before. The Navajo, Hopi, Walapai, and other groups, confined to reservations, often had fewer goods to trade than before, while the array of controls erected by the Bureau of Indian Affairs frequently hindered travel between Indian communities. Intertribal exchange still continued—as late as 1898, the travel-book writer George Wharton James could report that "every summer trading-parties of both Hopis and Navahoes come down to the [Havasupai] village, bringing blankets, ponies, pottery, and the like"—but such dealings gradually assumed less and less importance for the tribes involved. Recalled Mark Hanna, "The Hopis and Navajos didn't come down here [to the Havasupais' summer village] much anymore. A lot of them used to come down here, but they don't come no more."[21]

In response to such shifts, during the 1880s and 1890s the Havasupai began to redirect their trade to white merchants in such newly created railroad towns as Williams, Peach Springs, and Ash Fork, where tribe members found a ready market for the deerskins, dried peaches, baskets, and other goods they had once traded with the Hopi and other Indian groups. Soon, Havasupais "go[ing] down to the railroad [to] trade for clothes and money" became a familiar sight to settlers. Observed the *Arizona Journal-Miner* in 1890, "[Tribe members] visit all the towns along the Atlantic and Pacific railroad, as well as Prescott, and trade with citizens of them." Added Clarkson Thurston of Flagstaff, "[The Havasupai] manufacture and sell [many] articles—baskets, etc. They also sell deer skins, antlers, venison, arrowheads, etc., and are very shrewd in trade." Although it is difficult to gauge the precise magnitude of this trade, it appears to have been substantial. Asked in 1893 to describe his dealings with the Havasupai, John Davis, a store owner in Williams, responded, "We buy from them skins and dried peaches and would suppose their trade with us amounts to about $500 or $600." Other merchants in the area gave similar answers.[22]

With the money they received from these merchants, the Havasupai frequently purchased the manufactured goods that they had been able to procure before only through the Hopi, as well as such previously unknown luxuries as matches, coffee, sugar, and tobacco. As early as the 1880s, visitors to the tribe reported that most every family was well equipped with brass kettles and iron knives and hoes. During this same period, Havasupai men, according to Frank Hamilton Cushing, "universally possess[ed] repeating rifles of the most improved models and an abundance of ammunition," which they used during their annual hunts on the plateau lands. Perhaps the most eloquent summary of the changes in material culture that the Havasupai experienced during this era comes from the tribal leader Navajo (so named for his killing of a Navajo Indian). Gazing around at the ample supply of manufactured goods among his people, Navajo observed to Cushing, "You know that we were a poor people; we used the flint knife, the stone axe, and in our agricultural operations we took a deer horn and a pointed stick. This day, look around you, you see the iron hoe, the pick, shovel, the knife of steel."[23]

On one level, then, the Havasupais' shift from intertribal trade networks to the newly developing railroad towns of northern Arizona can be seen as an astute improvisation—a demonstration of how the tribe, in the face of United States conquest, managed to expand its trade networks in fresh directions, acquiring valuable new goods in the process. But this trade with non-Indian merchants also carried increased risks for the Havasupai, for such dealings brought the Havasupai into the cash economy—and, however peripherally, into the national market as well. In this setting, the value of trade goods could often fluctuate markedly, as the Havasupai found when preserved peaches from California pushed aside the dried peaches from the Indians' orchards, relegating them to stores that specialized in the "Mexican trade." In the same manner, the value of Havasupai deerskins suffered when forced to compete with both commercially tanned leather and machine-woven cloth, while the red paint that tribe members had made from minerals collected in the Grand Canyon lost its value when manufactured paints became readily available in the region. Moreover, this new trade network existed outside the networks of reciprocity that had characterized the trading relationship between the Havasupai and the Hopi, where each group might support the other in times of need.[24]

Nevertheless, given their skill as hunters, agriculturists, and traders, the Havasupai might have been able to weather the instabilities that resulted from their insertion into the national marketplace had their resource base not been declining at the very same time. There were several reasons for this decline, most of them linked in some way to federal attempts to place the Havasupai on a reservation in Havasu Canyon. The first step in this process had taken place in 1880, when, following Havasupai protests about the intrusions of miners near their fields, President Rutherford B. Hayes issued an executive order setting aside a block of land five miles wide by twelve miles long as a reservation for the Havasupai.[25] The following year, the officers in charge of mapping this new reservation, finding it nearly impossible to plot such a shape amid the jagged landscape of the Grand Canyon, "gave up all idea of marking upon the ground the boundaries as set forth in the Executive Order [creating the reservation]." Instead, after consulting "with Navajo, chief of the Yava-Suppais, as to the lands occupied or desired by him," Lt. Carl Palfrey of the Army Corps of Engineers decided just to mark the two-mile-long segment of Havasu Canyon that contained the tribe's summer village and irrigated fields. As a result, the Havasupai found themselves the possessors of a plot some two miles long by a quarter of a mile wide, containing only 518 acres—the smallest reservation in the nation. Moreover, since this reservation enclosed only the Havasupais' summer fields, it accommodated only one-half of the tribe's seasonal cycle. It did nothing to protect the springs and campgrounds that the Havasupai used when up on the plateau in the autumn and winter.[26]

Given these shortcomings, it may seem odd that, as one of the officers involved put it, "all the Supais seemed much gratified when the monuments [marking the reservation's boundaries] were erected." And it may seem stranger still that the army erected its monuments "at points they [the Havasupai] themselves indicated," in one instance even making the boundaries more expansive than those Navajo suggested. One should be careful, though, not to assume, as the federal government and many non-Indians in the region did, that, because the Havasupai were active participants in the laying out of their new reservation, the tribe willingly surrendered all claims to lands elsewhere. Rather, to Navajo and his people, a reservation simply represented recognition from the federal government that the Havasupai had an inalienable right to their farmland in Havasu Canyon. As the Havasupai envisioned it, their newly created reservation was to serve as a protective curtain around their crops and water, shielding them from the intrusions of miners and other newcomers. Thus, even after one of the floods that periodically swept through Havasu Canyon obliterated the stone monuments erected by the army to mark the reserve, the Indians continued to remember where the monuments had been placed and to point out their location to arriving prospectors.[27] In addition, tribe members also insisted that the military, having created the reservation, preserve its integrity. Chief Navajo, for instance, asked that the army "send him an order directing white people to keep off his reservation," complaining that "there are many miners constantly trespassing upon him; that they spoil his water and make mining locations in his country, and when he tells them it is a reservation, they pay no attention to him. He wants to have no trouble with the whites, but wishes the General to protect him." Displaying their typical inventiveness, the Havasupai were attempting to co-opt the army and federal government, turning them into allies whom they could call upon to protect them from the disruptions of the outside world.[28]

While tribe members may have acquiesced to the proffered reservation because it promised to secure at least one part of their resource base against intrusions, they continued to see other places—particularly the forested plateau to the south of the Grand Canyon—as crucial to their existence. A revealing illustration of the Havasupais' continued claims to lands outside of Havasu Canyon can be seen in the story that Big Jim offered of what really transpired during the initial surveying of the tribe's reservation: "Quasala [a Walapai interpreter] told them, the Supais, that the reservation marked out was not a regular reservation but just the area of their farming land. . . . Quasala said that the white people would get our farming land if we did not get this reservation. Captain Navajo told General Crook that he needed the land outside of the Canyon for his hunting and General Crook gave him a pass to continue his hunting there." As a result, even after the establishment of their reservation, tribe members persisted in returning to the plateau south of the Grand Canyon, believing that it still belonged to them.[29]

By the late 1880s, however, the campsites that each family had once possessed on the plateau had begun to slip out of their control. Following establishment of the tribe's reservation in 1881, Euro-American ranchers began to move onto the grazing lands bordering the canyon's south rim, which they now viewed as territory to which all Indian title had been extinguished. Inevitably, the competing sets of claims put forth by these ranchers and the Havasupai gave rise to a number of conflicts, focused in particular on access to the area's limited number of water tanks. One notable clash occurred in 1888, when, according to alarmed army officers, "a party of citizens [were] ordered away by the Suppai Indians from some tanks about 60 miles north of Prescott Junction." Navajo and some of his family members had been staying at a spot known as Black Tanks, when several cattlemen arrived, led by an individual named John Duke. The Havasupais did not initially object to Duke and his companions camping at the site. (On other occasions, members of the tribe even "rented" water holes to passing non-Indians for small sums of money.) But when the men "commenced to build a corral for the purpose of driving in cattle, [the Havasupai] considered that an infringement upon their rights and ordered the citizens away." Interviewed shortly afterward by army officials, who questioned the Havasupais' claim to a water hole some thirty-five miles off their reservation, Navajo invoked both custom and utility to defend his position. He told the officers that "for many years he had camped at the black tanks and hunted in that locality, that if the white[s] drove in cattle they would drive the game away, and the cattle would drink up the water, which lasts but a short time." The investigating officer professed sympathy for Navajo's plight, but "explained to him that he had no right to the tanks or to the country outside of his reservation." With no outside support, Navajo could do little to prevent Duke's takeover of the tank. Within a few months, Duke and a partner named Carrell had constructed a corral near the tanks, where they quartered some 125 head of livestock.[30]

Similar conflicts soon followed. In 1890, for example, a nearly identical scenario unfolded involving Captain Tom, a Havasupai who had long camped at Rain Tank, one of the few water holes along the trail to the Hopi villages to the east. No doubt hoping to give the impression of a more permanent Indian presence at Rain Tank, Captain Tom had begun to build himself a log cabin at the tank and had enlarged the basin around the spring so that it would hold more water for his horses. Yet during one of Captain Tom's periodic absences, "a party by the name of E. Randolph set up a claim to the place and took the logs from the uncompleted house and built one for himself." "Intimidat[ing] the Indians with threats," Randolph set about establishing a sheep ranch on the location. In response, Captain Tom and some of his friends went to Flagstaff to demand that the authorities remove Randolph. But as the tank was not on the Havasupai reservation, Captain Tom "met with but little encouragement from any source." He, like Navajo, lost his site on the south rim.[31]

Given such incidents, it should not prove surprising that when late nineteenth-century visitors queried the Havasupai about their conditions, the Indians' first complaint was of "the constant persecution of cattle men on the mesa."[32] Reported an army officer who encountered the band during the winter of 1890, "[The Indians said that] as long as they could remember the custom had been to cultivate the land during the summer in Cataract [Havasu] Canyon, and in the winter to hunt on the high mesa lands. . . . Now all the game in the country had been killed off and white men were driving in cattle and taking all the water. Their hereditary winter camp at Black Tanks had been taken from them two years ago. In a little while all the water would be taken up and the Indians would have no place to go."[33] In their own accounts of past events, the Havasupai preserved a palpable sense of outrage over what they viewed as their unjust displacement from their customary spots on the plateau. As Allen Akaba recalled, "They [the Havasupai] gave up their place on top due to white settlers, homesteaders, cattle owners, would come in here and the Indian would have a spring back in the hills, the cattle owner would come along, he would water his stock where the Indians were. He would stay along with them; told them later on that this spring water hole was his. The Indian had nothing to do with it; chase them out. Gave them a few things and told them to go home, 'Paid you for it.'...[The Havasupai] didn't give up territories on top, but they drifted back for fear if they stayed up there they thought maybe the white settlers would kill them all off." As such accounts suggest, tribe members viewed their movement off the plateau as being made under duress. In their minds, their displacement was illegal; the lands were still theirs.[34]

What made the arrival of cattle and sheep ranchers on the plateau all the more disturbing for the Havasupai was the fact that the outsiders' livestock usurped much of the water and browse that would have otherwise supported the deer, antelope, and other animals that the Havasupai customarily hunted on the south rim.[35] In the face of such competition, the game population plummeted. Observed one Arizona legislator, C. C. Bean, to the Commissioner of Indian Affairs in 1885, "The introduction of herds of cattle and flocks of sheep, of miners, prospectors and tourists have all combined to render [the Havasupais'] vast hunting ground useless."[36] Not only did the loss of game mean less meat for tribe members, it also meant fewer deerskins to trade for supplies. According to W. W. Bass, a rancher and tourist-camp owner who sometimes hired Havasupai Indians as guides or packers, "Game is so scarce that their [the Havasupais'] supply of meat has become a serious consideration, while Buckskin which was their source of revenue has become so scarce that they cannot procure enough to use for Mockazins *[sic]*, while formerly it was traded to other tribes for blankets."[37] No longer did the Havasupai "have buckskins that could be traded to the Moquis [Hopi] for seeds or sold for cash," wrote another observer at much the same time. What meat the tribe did consume appears to have come from marginal sources. Visitors to the tribe in 1890, for example, reported that instead of dining on deer or antelope, the Indians were eating "rats and mountain squirrels which they dig from their dens." The following winter, others noted that because of the scarcity of game, the Havasupai were "killing and eating their horses and burros."[38]

By the early 1890s, the dire circumstances in which the Havasupai found themselves had attracted the attention of the Bureau of Indian Affairs, the federal bureau within the Department of the Interior that was the tribe's theoretical protector. But rather than restoring the Indians' hunting grounds as the tribe itself urged (and as several army officers sent to investigate the condition of the Havasupai suggested), the BIA proposed that the tribe's salvation lay in their becoming intensive agriculturists. In keeping with this logic, in February 1892 the agency assigned the first federal official to the Havasupai reservation: an instructional farmer named John F. Gaddis, whose orders were to encourage "a spirit of industry" among the Havasupai by teaching them "a knowledge of agricultural pursuits." BIA administrators believed that by giving the Havasupai new crops and by instructing them in farming techniques, the tribe could use its existing land more efficiently, thus making up for its loss of territory. For example, bureau officials argued that instead of cultivating "small, irregular 'patches'" of land, the tribe should extend its irrigation ditches throughout Havasu Canyon, bringing all available land into production. As one administrator explained, "I have instructed the farmer to get these Indians to clear their land, to reopen and repair their irrigating ditches, to plant larger and more varied crops, and to carefully preserve their surplus for future use."[39]

Gaddis's attempts to teach the Havasupai to be yeoman farmers met with only limited success. No doubt feeling that they already knew how to plant crops, tribe members often proved resistant to Gaddis's earnest efforts to enlighten them. "The introduction of the plow did not meet with as much approval as I had anticipated," he wrote to his superiors in 1892. "They were slow to catch on, they still cling on to their former ways." While tribe members readily accepted the "variety of fruit trees and vines which were supplied them by the Government," using these plants to expand their already substantial orchards of peaches and apricots, they demonstrated much less enthusiasm for the goats that the BIA insisted they adopt as a substitute for wild game. "They will not have them [the goats] nor will they look after them," complained Gaddis. "I left them in charge of an Indian when I left before. He paid no attention to them but let the dogs kill several and scatter them all over the cañon."[40]

While the Bureau of Indian Affairs interpreted such opposition to its policies as stubborn backwardness, this behavior likely had more to do with tribe members' belief that agriculture alone was not an adequate replacement for their traditional seasonal cycle. With flash floods a fact of life in Havasu Canyon, it made little sense for the Havasupai to devote all their energies to cultivating crops that might be destroyed at any time—indeed, in 1898 "their crops were nearly all washed away" as a result of "disastrous floods." In addition, radically expanding the amount of lands that they planted, as Gaddis urged, meant that the tribe would have to sacrifice the brushlands bordering their village—which, given the small size of the Havasupais' reservation, served as important reservoirs of firewood, basket-making materials, and building supplies. And goats not only competed with the tribe's horses for the limited amount of pasture available in Havasu Canyon but also required constant care so that they did not fall victim to predators or wander into the Indians' fields.[41]

Instead of becoming totally dependent on agriculture as the BIA advocated, the Havasupai adopted a modified seasonal cycle of their own devising. Each fall, even though many of their old camping sites had been taken up by settlers and large game was increasingly scarce, tribe members returned to the plateau south of the Grand Canyon. Here in the Coconino Forest there were smaller game animals, such as rabbits, in relative abundance. Here, too, were also ranchers' cattle, which the Havasupai may have clandestinely killed from time to time as a substitute for the deer and antelope they had once hunted. (Recalled tribe member Mack Putesoy, "Too many cattle, no more game. So sometimes we'd have to get a big steer.") Moreover, the plateau possessed thick growths of junipers and piñons, which furnished the tribe with plentiful firewood, and grass, which served as pasture for the Havasupais' horses. In the absence of water holes, drinking water could be supplied by melting snow.[42]

To supplement this annual cycle, many Havasupai men turned to seasonal wage labor. Finding work at nearby ranches, mines, or along the railroad, the men would typically work just long enough to buy whatever supplies their families needed to tide them over until the fall harvest—at which point they would quit and return to their reservation. "The Havasupai are good workers, and are eagerly sought after by surrounding ranchmen," declared one BIA employee, "but their love for their canyon home prevents their remaining away very long at a time." As Mark Hanna, whose own experiences with wage labor varied from herding cattle to picking crops to washing dishes at one of the hotels that sprung up on the south rim of the canyon during the late 1800s, explained, "I never stayed out too long. I always came back and checked if my mother was out of food or wood and helped in the garden." Wage labor thus functioned as only a partial insertion into the cash-based economy of the outside world, not so much dissolving the Havasupais' communal obligations and preexisting seasonal cycle as reworking and reinforcing them.[43]

Despite such adaptations, Havasupai society remained under great stress during this period. Game was scarce, most families had lost their water holes on the plateau, disease had ravaged the tribe. White ranchers had even begun to round up the Havasupais' ponies, which they considered to be unowned and free for the taking because the animals bore no brands.[44] Such dire conditions made the tribe receptive to the millennialism of the Ghost Dance movement, which swept the Havasupai in 1891 with its promises to undo the tragedies that Indian societies had suffered in recent years: "All Indians who have died in the ages that are gone will be restored to life.... Simultaneously will reappear the game that has existed in past ages, while the white people and all other races, except the American Indian, will perish."[45] The dance's acceptance among the Havasupai seems to have been initiated by Chief Navajo himself, who in early 1891 made a special trip to witness a ceremony among the Walapai (who, in turn, had learned the Ghost Dance from its originators, the Paiute). That summer, the Havasupai held the first of their four-day Ghost Dance ceremonies. The peak of the movement apparently came during the winter of 1892–93, when dances were held at both Sheep Tank and Black Tank.[46]

It was at this moment, as the Ghost Dance movement was reaching its high-water mark with the Havasupai, that the tribe found itself confronted by what would prove to be its greatest challenge since the army's efforts to place them on a reservation in 1881: an executive order issued on February 20, 1893, by President Benjamin Harrison, setting aside the Grand Cañon Forest Reserve. This newly created reserve—a rectangular block straddling both sides of the Colorado River and containing some 1,850,000 acres—took in not only the Havasupais' hunting and grazing lands on the plateau but all the territory for miles in every direction from the tribe's reservation, leaving the village in Havasu Canyon a solitary island in a sea of conservation land. Although the Havasupai did not realize it at the time, their struggles for their foraging sites and water holes on the plateau to the south of the Grand Canyon had been thrust into a new context, one in which their opponent was not the scattered ranchers and tourist-camp owners along the south rim but their nominal protector: the federal government.[47]

The forest reserve that Harrison established at the Grand Canyon in 1893 was one of seven forest reserves that the president created that year alone. All were part of a dramatic expansion in federal conservation policy that took place following the passage of what has come to be known as the Forest Reserve Act of 1891. Motivated largely by the example of the Adirondack Forest Preserve and George Perkins Marsh's predictions about the negative impact of forest destruction on water flow, Congress attached to a general revision of the land law a provision authorizing the president to withdraw from settlement any tract of public land "wholly or in part covered with timber or undergrowth" as a permanent forest reservation. As befitted its status as the birthplace of federal conservation policy, the first place where this new law was applied was Yellowstone: on March 30, 1891, President Harrison created the Yellowstone Park Timberland Reserve, embracing 1,239,040 acres on the park's southern and eastern edges and taking in the headwaters of the Yellowstone and Snake Rivers that before then had remained outside the park. This was followed in quick succession by the establishment of reserves in other locations where the local forests appeared vital to protecting water supplies. By 1902, a decade after the passage of the initial law allowing for their creation, there were fifty-four forest reserves in all, enclosing some 60 million acres; over the next decade, the system more than tripled, reaching 190 million acres by 1911. Although there would later be national forests in Puerto Rico and eastern states such as New Hampshire, Arkansas, Florida, and North Carolina, the first forest reserves clustered west of the Mississippi, where the federal government's continued possession of large expanses of timbered territory facilitated the setting aside of extensive forestlands. The arid southwest, where protecting water for irrigation projects was viewed as vital for the region's development, was a favorite target of forestry planners. By the early 1900s, Arizona could claim not only the Grand Cañon Forest Reserve but seven other reserves as well, with an aggregate of 6,740,000 acres—about 9.2 percent of Arizona's total land surface. Neighboring California and New Mexico possessed another eleven reserves, which contained more than 12 million acres combined.[48] (See Map 4.)

Like their predecessors in the Adirondacks, the administrators of the federal forest reserve system invoked conservation's degradation discourse to predict that rural folk would irredeemably damage the environment if left unchecked by government regulations. At times, this discourse focused on Native Americans, with some conservationists echoing John Wesley Powell's warnings about the need to control Indians' use of fire.[49] As an agent for the General Land Office asserted in an early study of the Grand Canyon, "Indians should be rigidly excluded from the Cañon country...being reckless of fire, they destroy large bodies of timber and slaughter game by the wholesale."[50] But when groups such as the American Forestry Association began the campaign for federally protected woodlands in the 1880s, their chief concern was

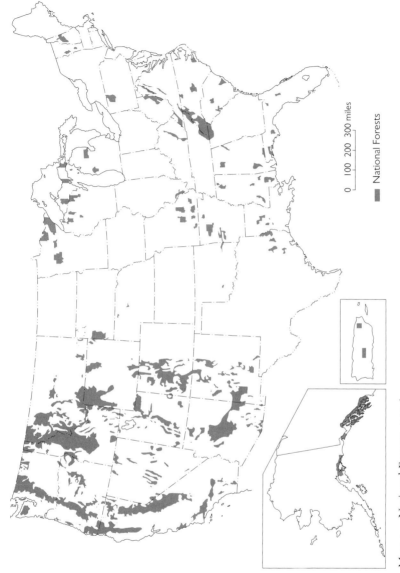

0 100 200 300 miles

■ National Forests

Map 4.   National Forests, 1936

not Indians but the white settlers supplanting native peoples throughout much of the American countryside. The writings of Franklin Hough—who served on the 1872 committee that recommended the creation of a park in the Adirondacks, before becoming the first federal Forest Commissioner in 1876—provide a vivid illustration of such early conservationist thinking. In a passage anticipating Frederick Jackson Turner's taxonomy of shifting frontier types, Hough expressed particular concern about the "unstable and transient class" of farmers, hunters, and trappers who were often "the earliest of the pioneers." "The history of settlements everywhere," he argued, "begins with a class of pioneers who frequently prove unthrifty, are often poor, and generally exposed to privations and inconveniences."[51] As they "have little to lose," such people often acted in what Hough and other conservationists considered to be an environmentally destructive manner: "They are accustomed to regard the world around them as open for their use...in matters of pasturage for their stock, as well as forest products for their own supply.... They often appropriate wherever it is most convenient. It is from this class of our population that we have the most to fear in the way of forest fires. Habitually careless and improvident, they do not hesitate, where there is a motive and an opportunity, to apply fires to lands not their own, for the purpose of improving and extending the range for their cattle, or to clear lands for cultivation, and sometimes to destroy the evidence of their own trespass and depredations."[52] For Hough and others like him, the foremost example of the dangers such "squatters" presented could be found in the ongoing "trespass and depredations" on the public lands, where each year thousands of trees were cut in violation of federal law. "Depredations upon public timber are universal, flagrant, and limitless," complained William A. Sparks, the commissioner of the General Land Office in 1885, who would report 1,219 cases of timber poaching from federal lands the following year.[53]

To Hough, Sparks, and other early conservationists, such appropriations were not only illegal, they nurtured a worrisome set of values. In the absence of governmental oversight, many rural Americans had, it seemed, formulated their own, deviant interpretation of property rights. "Depredations [upon the public lands] have been going on through a long period of years..., until the practice has gained from long indulgence the semblance of a right," warned a special investigating committee of the American Association for the Advancement of Science in 1882. "Criminal practice" had become "sanctioned by custom." *Garden and Forest* took a similar stance: "The frontiersman has become so

accustomed to preying upon timber of the Government as if it was his
own, that any check upon this unrestricted privilege is looked upon as
an infringement of his personal rights." Forest Commissioner Hough
was even more alarmist: "A demoralizing effect has been wrought in the
minds of a certain class, who, seeing government property openly taken
…have come to regard this class of property as common, and com-
munistic principles of most dangerous tendencies have been encouraged." Framed in such a manner, the need for federal conservation became all the more urgent. To remain inactive in the face of widespread
timber poaching from public lands was, according to such logic, not
only to risk ecological disaster but to encourage movements that might
question the prevailing conceptions of law and of property. Conversely,
to stabilize environmental relations via conservation was also to ensure
that social relations maintained their proper course.[54]

The "unstable and transient" lower classes were not the only group
to find their environmental practices under assault at this time. Conservationists also focused their ire on the threat from above—the "unscrupulous companies, composed of men of wealth and influence…, [that]
seek by every means known to such combinations to thwart the efforts
of the Government." Along with other Progressive Era reformers, conservationists stressed the need to rein in reckless monopolies and eliminate unethical business practices. The ultimate goal of conservation,
however, remained not the elimination of industrial capitalism but its
reformation. "The first principle of conservation," emphasized Gifford
Pinchot in 1910, "is development.…[Conservation] proposes to secure
a continuous and abundant supply of the necessaries of life, which
means a reasonable cost of living and business stability." Industry often
welcomed the coming of conservation for these very reasons. From the
perspective of many large businesses, conservation meant predictability.
The movement regularized the supply of materials and maintained conditions such as water flow that were vital to downstream navigation,
mills, and irrigation projects. Many corporations discovered that their
goals meshed well with those of government planners, for both shared
a concern with limiting inefficient uses of the environment.[55]

At the Grand Canyon, this close relationship between forestry
officials and business interests began to take shape not long after the forest reserve's creation in 1893. By the early twentieth century, the canyon's new federal managers had reached a series of accommodations
with the local mining, railroad, and lumber companies that allowed
these businesses access to the reserve's natural resources. In 1901, for ex-

ample, the canyon's regional superintendent supported plans by "a large
cattle man, Mr. Wm. Donaldson of Williams, Arizona," to build a reservoir for his cattle within the reserve. The following year, officials permitted the "Cañon Copper Company" to cut timber for free on the reserve.[56] Once Gifford Pinchot's Forest Service assumed control of the
canyon in 1907, such ties increased further. The service established the
nation's first forestry experiment station on the south rim of the Grand
Canyon, where it undertook studies designed to maximize the yield of
turpentine, rosin, and other supplies from the region's yellow pines. The
Forest Service also expanded grazing at the canyon and initiated a program that permitted corporations such as Arizona Lumber and Timber
Company, the Flagstaff Lumber and Manufacturing Company, and the
Saginaw and Manistee Lumber Company of Michigan to cut millions of
board feet a year from the forests bordering the Grand Canyon's south
rim.[57]

Left outside of the Forest Service's plans were groups such as the Havasupai, whose uses of the environment seldom met conservationists'
definitions of productive or efficient. Indeed, to administrators attempting to institute a system of governmental controls over the Grand Canyon landscape, the presence of a group of transient Indians like the Havasupai was at best a reminder of a vanishing era and at worst an
ongoing menace to official efforts to manage the canyon in a rational
manner. The Havasupai, of course, did not view matters in quite the
same light. Having managed to preserve a presence on the plateau to the
south of the Grand Canyon despite the encroachments of ranchers, tourist-camp operators, and the Bureau of Indian Affairs, tribe members regarded this territory as still rightfully theirs. The Havasupai were not
about to abandon their lands on the canyon's rim simply to accommodate the new vision of nature put forth by conservationists.

CHAPTER 8

Farewell Song

History does not record how or when the Havasupai became aware of the existence of a forest reserve at the Grand Canyon. Perhaps they first learned of the reserve's creation in April of 1894, when federal administrators, upset by the numerous attempts that had been made "to secure right of entrance, occupancy and use of tracts of public land embraced in forest reservations," posted signs printed on linen cloth at reserves throughout the West, detailing the new reserves' prohibitions against the setting of fires, the cutting of trees, and the grazing of livestock. Any violators of these rules, the signs cautioned, would be "prosecuted for trespass, and will be held responsible pecuniarily, for any waste or damage, whether done intentionally or caused by neglect."[1] At many reserves, irate locals tore down these newly erected signs (a gesture that officials deemed "indicative of the spirit of lawlessness prevailing among those depredating upon these lands"), but whether the Havasupai acted in such a manner is uncertain. Most likely, given the fact that most of the Havasupai could not read English at the time, these signs did not mean much to them, although the sudden posting of linen squares on trees throughout the plateau to the south of the canyon must have signaled to tribe members that something peculiar was afoot.[2]

What exactly this something was, however, may have remained unclear to the Havasupai for some time. During the forest reserves' early years, posting warnings was about all that the reserves' nominal manager—the General Land Office (GLO), the branch of the Department of the Interior responsible for handling public lands—was able to do. The 1891 law allowing for the creation of forest reserves had sidestepped the issue of administration, leaving the GLO to rely on its preexisting force of twenty-odd special agents—already scattered nationwide to investigate fraudulent entries and other violations of the public land laws—to enforce the new reserve's regulations. Since the number of agents, as the GLO's commissioner aptly put it, was "infinitesimal, considering the magnitude of the work and the territory to be covered," the government had little success in apprehending violators during the forest reserves' early years. Each season brought reports of "continued trespassing and depredating within the reserves" by locals living nearby. "As it now stands," complained one conservation journal, "these...millions of acres have nothing but the President's proclamation to protect them from sheep-herders or timber-thieves, and it is well known that any one can plunder or burn them with little fear of punishment."[3]

As a solution, outraged conservationists and federal administrators proposed that the militarized conservation already enacted at Yellowstone and the other national parks be expanded to the forest reserves. "Unless the reservations are protected by detachments from the army, as has been done in the Yellowstone Park[,]...there is no way to save them from the depredations of thieves or the still more sweeping desolation by fire," asserted *Garden and Forest,* perhaps the era's leading advocate of enlarging the military role in conservation.[4] The viability of the forest reserves, according to the magazine, could be ensured only by "the presence of the visible power of the Federal Government": "These forests would be safer under the control of the army than under any other administration. As matters now stand, the army is the only force that will be likely to represent with any firmness the dignity of the nation against local interest, and against the right which herders and lumbermen, and, in fact, settlers of all kinds, feel they have acquired by long usage, to cut or pasture or burn over the woods on the public lands as it may seem for their profit or pleasure to do so."[5] These themes were echoed by Robert Underwood Johnson, the editor of *Century* magazine and an early associate of Muir and Pinchot. In a series of influential editorials, Johnson linked the defense of the forest reserves with the defense of the nation itself: "There is in time of peace no other work of national defense or protection so valuable as this which the army can perform, and...the national forests cannot be adequately guarded and protected by any other means."[6] But even after the assistant commissioner of the GLO, Edward Bowers, made a formal appeal to the secretary of war for troops to police the forest reserves, the army's leadership showed little enthusiasm for such a venture. Apparently concerned that its policing of the American environment was absorbing increasingly large quantities of its monies and manpower, the top brass resisted any expansion of the army's role in conservation.[7]

As a result, the forest reserves languished in an administrative vacuum during their early years. As the commissioner of the GLO observed in his annual report of 1896, "Forest reservations have been made which are such in name only. For lack of means they are no more protected by reason of reservation than other public lands." Capitalizing upon their knowledge of the rural landscape, many locals found it a simple matter to hide their activities from the GLO's special agents during the agents' rare trips to their jurisdictions. At other times, such guile may not even have been necessary. The Havasupai, for example, did not learn for several years that their annual trips to the plateau involved any violation of reserve regulations: the tribe's use of the lands within the reserve occurred primarily in the winter, when the GLO's agents, because of the region's heavy snows and the difficulties of transportation, were seldom present. Thus, the same year that the Grand Cañon Forest Reserve was created, the BIA's instructional farmer at the reservation, John Gaddis, could report that his charges were making much the same use of the lands within the reserve as they always had: "There was [sic] very few Indians that spent the winter in the Cañon. They most all went on a hunt." This pattern held in later years as well. Despite the fact that their activities on the plateau to the south of the Grand Canyon were illegal according to the GLO's regulations, the Havasupai went untroubled by federal officials for several winters. Nor were the Havasupai the only rule breakers within the Grand Canyon reserve during this period. On the mesas to the south and north of the canyon, both white ranchers and Navajo Indians could be found hunting, grazing livestock, and kindling fires.[8]

As ineffective as the early forest reserves often were, their creation nonetheless reconfigured property rights throughout much of the American countryside. In accordance with conservation's logic of placing natural resources under scientific management, the Forest Reserve Act stripped away any competing local claims to the lands within the reserves. Only those individuals who had already filed a homestead entry on property enclosed within a forest reservation would be allowed to remain within the reserve. Explained the GLO's commissioner in 1893, "Persons who established residence on land within the reserve prior to the date of the President's proclamation, with intention of acquiring homes under the U.S. land laws, will be protected by reason of prior settlement; but no one will be allowed to settle within the reservation after the date of said proclamation." Furthermore, added the commissioner, "a mere squatter, with no intention of acquiring title, is a trespasser, and has no rights that the government is bound to respect."[9]

In theory, such policies were race blind. In actual practice, however, they posed a special barrier for the Havasupai, who, like many other Indian peoples, were unfamiliar with English and the United States legal code and based their land claims on tribal custom rather than American law. Under such conditions, the establishment of a forest reserve at the Grand Canyon reinforced the Havasupais' displacement from their traditional hunting and gathering areas on the south rim. Previously, the Havasupais' use of the lands along the canyon's edge had been problematic only when it conflicted with the undertakings of ranchers and tourist-camp operators. Now tribe members had become "squatters" whose very presence on the plateau was being called into question. Initially, of course, this change existed solely on paper, for the federal government lacked the ability to turn its vision for the forest reserves into a reality. But the stage had been set for a confrontation pitting conservationists and the Havasupai against one another. All that was needed was for the federal government to attempt to enforce its newly created conservation policy.[10]

The first step in this direction came in 1897. After years of pleading, the GLO finally obtained—via Congress's passage of the Forest Management Act—the funding necessary "to inaugurate a practical scheme of administration" for the forest reservations. The agency quickly set about creating a corps of forest rangers, whose primary duty, following the pattern established by the army at Yellowstone, was "to patrol the reserves, to prevent forest fires and trespasses from all sources." Other tasks allotted to the rangers included marking the reserves' boundaries, cutting firebreaks, and, to speed official travel through the forests, building trails. To oversee these activities, the GLO installed several layers of managers. Rangers reported to forest supervisors, each of whom had a specific reserve under his care. Supervisors, in turn, reported to regional superintendents, who were responsible for a number of forest reserves, often across several states. These forces expanded rapidly, so that by 1900 the GLO had 445 rangers, 39 supervisors, and 9 superintendents working in forest reserves nationwide.[11]

The first force of rangers at the Grand Canyon arrived in August 1898, when the newly appointed forest supervisor, W. P. Hermann, hired five men "to reside in forests at danger points to prevent fires and trespass." These rangers were to make regular patrols of the Grand Cañon Forest Reserve and "report upon all squatters, or other parties occupying or using lands therein without right or title," so that the reserve could "be cleared of all parties intruding thereon unlawfully."[12] In the course of fulfilling their duties, the rangers stumbled across the Havasupai, triggering the first of many complaints about the tribe's behavior within the forest reserve. The initial confrontation came in the fall as the Havasupai began to leave their village in Havasu Canyon and move out onto the plateau to gather plants and hunt wild game as they had for generations. In November 1898, Supervisor Hermann informed his superiors that bands of "Supai Indians" were pursuing "the very few beautiful and agile antelope and deer, yet proudly roaming in the Coconino forest." Not only were these Indians violating Arizona's game law (which in 1897 barred all Indians from hunting off their reservation), in Hermann's eyes, they were acting in a wasteful, deliberately provocative manner: "It is principally to obtain the hides for the tanning of buckskin, that the Indians kill these noble animals, and then trade the buckskin to the Moqui and Navajo Indians for blankets &c., and to the town Merchants for clothing &c. The Indians boast and threaten to kill the deer and antelope, so long as the 'Government does not supply them with cow meat.'" Moreover, Hermann asserted, the Havasupai disturbed the scenic beauty that the forest reserve sought to protect: "The Grand Cañon of the Colorado River is becoming so renowned for its wonderful and extensive natural gorge scenery and for its open clean pine woods, that it should be preserved for the everlasting pleasure and instruction of our intelligent citizens as well as those of foreign countries. Henceforth, I deem it just and necessary to keep the wild and unappreciable Indian from off the Reserve and protect the game."[13]

To achieve these aims, Hermann instituted a ban against not only the Havasupais' winter hunting and gathering expeditions but also any travel by tribe members through the forest for whatever purpose, "even ...to get from his little reservation in the cañon to the railroad or anywhere else." Since the forest reserve completely surrounded the Havasupai Indian Reservation, this edict in effect made it illegal for tribe members to set foot off their reservation. As a committee investigating conditions among the tribe concluded in 1902, "The authorities in charge of the Grand Cañon Forest Reserve seek to deprive the Indians of the privilege of crossing the Forest Reserve, and have notified the official in charge of the Havasupai Indians that they should not be allowed to trespass upon or roam over said reserve. If this rule is enforced, these Indians will be prisoners within the cañon walls.... Two hundred and fifty souls are deprived by law of all contact with the outside world."[14]

While Hermann's policies may seem extreme, they were in no way unique. The ban on Indians at the Grand Canyon was paralleled at many other forest reserves—from Washington State, where administrators complained that the Yakima and Klickitat Indians "roam about [Ranier Forest Reserve] with large bands of horses, setting fires for amusement"; to Oregon, where GLO agents were attempting to keep Indians from the Warm Spring Agency off the Cascade Forest Reserve; to New Mexico, where officials grumbled that hunters and herders from the Navajo and White Mountain Apache agencies were "slaughtering game and causing fires" in the Gila River Forest Reserve.[15] As the administrators at these and other reserves discovered, it was a simple enough matter to order "the wild and unappreciable Indian...off the Reserve." But enforcing this policy upon a group of people with powerful incentives to act otherwise—and often with a much more thorough knowledge of the reserves than the officials involved—was much harder. Administrators were further hindered by the fact that, despite the seemingly impressive set of state agencies arrayed against Indian peoples, these agencies were often fractured among themselves, each lacking the power to act independently. The responsibility for dealing with the Havasupai at the Grand Canyon, for instance, was spread across several offices. While the GLO (and later the Forest and Park Services) had authority over the Grand Canyon and other forest reserves, jurisdiction over Indian peoples rested in another office, the BIA. Moreover, the game law that prevailed at the Grand Canyon for much of the late nineteenth and early twentieth centuries was not a federal statute at all, but a measure passed by the Arizona legislature, which the territory's game wardens were supposed to enforce. There were attempts to coordinate efforts between these various groups—the GLO, for example, regularly communicated with state game agencies and distributed maps of the various forest reserves, along with pamphlets detailing its forestry regulations, to all Indian agents—but bureaucratic divisions remained, which the Havasupai and other tribes often exploited to their benefit.[16]

Many Indians realized that the figure most susceptible to their pressure was the Indian agent, who occupied a rather ambivalent position as both the defender of his or her Native American wards and the enforcer of governmental programs designed to extirpate native customs. Since the agents' chief concerns typically involved enrolling their charges in schools and other training programs, they often felt little inclination to squander their energies on a rigorous enforcement of the GLO's unpopular rules against off-reservation travel and hunting. In addition, one measure of success for agents was their ability to keep the distribution of food rations to a minimum—a goal that competed with the efforts of the GLO to end Indian taking of game. As a result of such tensions, a number of agents appear to have been willing to tolerate a certain level of violations of conservation laws, so long as their charges were not blatant in their lawbreaking. Flora Gregg Iliff, the superintendent on the Havasupai reservation in the early 1900s, for instance, refused to report the Indians she encountered hauling home deer poached in the forest reserve—a stance which earned her the scorn of the rangers at the Grand Canyon, who informed her, "You permit the Indians to kill deer out of season."[17] The Havasupais' agent during the 1890s, Henry P. Ewing, also took few steps to prevent the tribe's annual winter journey to the plateau. Just months after receiving orders to "prevent, as far as possible, Indians under your charge from causing forest fires and unlawfully killing game upon the various forest reservations in the neighborhood of your agency," Ewing admitted that "during January the Supais have been out of their cañon home, upon the mesas, hunting nuts, fruits, and other means of subsistence."[18] Unamused forest reserve managers responded with a chorus of angry letters to the BIA: "Forest Superintendent Isaac B. Hanna...reports that the Grand Cañon Forest Reserve in Arizona is overrun with Suppai Indians who kill game and start forest fires"; "a great many of the Suppai Indians have entered the said reserve with their horses....they are slaughtering the deer, killing not only the bucks but the does"; "The Indian claims the deer as his 'cows' and his property and not the property of the white man." To prevent such developments from spiraling out of control, forestry officials demanded that the BIA's orders "that certain Indians be prevented from entering the Grand Cañon Forest Reserve" be strictly enforced.[19]

As similar complaints flowed into the Bureau of Indian Affairs from forest reserves throughout the West, the BIA did indeed take an increasingly hard line against off-reservation Indian activities—even in cases where the group involved had a treaty right to forage or "hunt on any unoccupied lands contiguous to their reservation." As the agency's commissioner admitted in 1902, "It has been the policy of this office, even where such rights have been granted to Indians, to restrict them from hunting on lands outside of the limits of their reserve where they would be likely to come into contact with the whites, and to wantonly slaughter game."[20] Although there was nothing in the Forest Reserve Act itself that denied Indian peoples the right to travel across reserves or to hunt in them during the open season, the BIA took such a position with both the Havasupai and the Navajo (whose seasonal range extended into the northern and eastern portions of the Grand Cañon Forest Reserve). In the case of the Havasupai, the BIA notified Ewing that "the wishes of this office [are] that they give up visiting the forest reserves for any purpose whatsoever.... The Indians under your charge are not to be granted passes to visit the forest reserves; and ... your efforts are to be directed with the view to keeping them out of the same."[21] As the BIA's commissioner noted in a later letter, he realized that this policy clashed with Havasupai tribal custom but the exigencies of conservation demanded it: "This office fully realizes the difficulty with which you have to contend in this matter of preventing the Indians under your charge from trespassing and committing depredations on the said forest reserve—especially as the Suppai reservation is situated entirely within the Grand Cañon Forest Reserve which has been for generations their hunting and camping ground—yet it is desired that so far as possible they be kept out of this reserve." Both the GLO and the BIA were now in agreement: the Havasupai and other Indian peoples were to be prevented from entering the Grand Cañon Forest Reserve.[22]

Yet neither agency had much success in making the Indians perform in accordance with this agreed-on script. Ewing stopped issuing passes to the Havasupai for travel off the reservation and endeavored to make regular counts of his charges in an effort to make sure that none had slipped away, but the tribe still persisted in making its annual winter journey to the forest reserve. As J. S. Perkins, Ewing's replacement as Indian agent, acknowledged in 1904, "The Havasupais hunt in the winter and get a great deal of deer meat in that way."[23] A BIA employee sent to investigate conditions on the reservation the following year issued a similar report. Tribe members, the inspector declared, were continuing to go into the "forest reserve, hunting and visiting," despite the protests of officials at the canyon: "Mr. Fenton, the forest ranger, tells me they [the Havasupai] killed by far too many deer, more for their hides than for meat, and that he has instructions to stop it and that he will have to make arrests and perhaps cause much trouble if the forestry law is not more closely observed this coming winter."[24]

As it became increasingly apparent that simply ordering the Havasupai off the forest reserve was having little effect, several administrators decided there might be an easier solution: recognizing the Havasupais' presence while at the same time placing limits on its extent. The Indian agents at the Havasupai reservation, for example, arranged for an unusual two-month school vacation during the winter, timed so as to coincide with the tribe's journey to the plateau. Observed the BIA's inspector in 1905, "It has heretofore been the custom to discontinue the school for two months in the fall and winter season and thus permitting all...to leave the canyon and go where they chose over and through the vast forest reserve." After assuming control of the reserve in 1907, the Forest Service set aside some 75,000 acres on the south rim for the Havasupai, located near the trail leading down to their summer village in Havasu Canyon. Technically, this area, known among the rangers as Indian Pasture, was to be a grazing area for the tribe's livestock, but it became a de facto winter camping ground, within which forestry officials tolerated the Havasupais' constructing of hoganlike shelters out of logs and dirt, cutting of trees for firewood, and setting of fires for cooking and warmth.[25]

Such an arrangement could be interpreted as evidence that the Havasupai had finally won a victory in their battle against conservation. But the situation at Indian Pasture represented not so much a triumph as a temporary truce—one in which the tribe agreed to become short-term renters with "no right[s] excepting some grazing permits" on lands that had once been theirs.[26] Under these conditions, the Havasupais' position on the plateau was virtually identical to that of the non-Indian ranchers whom the Forest Service, in a break with the GLO's previous policies, allowed to graze a specified number of animals within the forest reserve. Moreover, as the Forest Service's grazing permits were good for only twelve months, the Havasupai had to renegotiate their rights to Indian Pasture every year. Access to this grazing area could, as one of the tribe's later permits read, "be terminated at any time at the discretion of the Director," making it unclear, in the words of one BIA official, "how permanent the present arrangement as to this land is."[27] In fact, the Forest Service did upon occasion open up the Havasupais' area to other groups. Several times in the second decade of the twentieth century, for example, non-Indians were allowed to cut the drift fence that the Havasupai had erected around their tribal plot and to graze their animals in Indian Pasture and water their animals at the tanks that tribe members had constructed in the area—actions that underscored for the Havasupai the fragility of their hold upon the plateau lands.[28]

The decision by the Havasupai to graze livestock on the plateau marked an important shift in tribal subsistence for other reasons as well. Although the Havasupai had been exposed to European livestock for generations, even as late as the 1880s and 1890s, tribe members had kept horses and burros almost exclusively. "Those years they don't have no cattle; just one or two horses each family," remembered one Havasupai, Big Jim. Beginning sometime in the early 1900s, however, a few of the tribe members who had found temporary wage work on nearby ranches brought back cattle with them to the reservation. Together with "a pretty scrubby lot" of cows that other tribe members "traded for and purchased from the Navajos," these animals became the nucleus of a Havasupai cattle herd, which by 1918 numbered about eighty head. This incipient herd represented what was, in essence, an effort by the Havasupai to privatize the animal supply upon the plateau. Cattle were a key element of this strategy, for in contrast with deer and other wild animals, whose ownership under U.S. law was established only once someone killed them, steer belonged to specific individuals. By adopting domestic livestock, then, the Havasupai were in essence repopulating the plateau with grazing animals—but, this time, with animals to which they would have clear rights of ownership. It is possible that tribe members once thought about the deer, antelope, mountain sheep, and other creatures that roamed the south plateau in similarly proprietary terms (such a belief might help explain the complaints of GLO administrators that "the Indian claims the deer as his 'cows'"). But this sense of ownership had meant little to forestry officials, who persisted in viewing Havasupai hunting as poaching. Such misunderstandings were less likely to occur if tribe members substituted domestic cattle into the niche once occupied by wild game.[29]

Yet as ingenious a solution as cattle raising was to some of the limits that conservation had placed on the Havasupai, it nonetheless possessed certain drawbacks. Most immediately, cattle were more environmentally destructive than deer, for they ate several of the plants from which female tribe members had traditionally gathered seeds.[30] Thus, by stocking the plateau with cattle, the Havasupai were increasing their access to meat and hides, but at the cost of undermining other aspects of their previous mode of production. In addition, not every member of the tribe could trade for or purchase livestock—even by 1930, only twenty out of the fifty-two families on the reservation owned cattle—so the turn toward ranching introduced a number of class schisms into the community, which the Havasupais' traditions of redistribution could only partially bridge.[31]

For such reasons, cattle raising represented an incomplete solution to the challenges confronting the Havasupai, one that did not totally replace other, preestablished ways of interacting with the environment. Even as the Grand Canyon went through a flurry of administrative changes—it became a federal game reserve in 1906, was declared a national monument in 1908, and, in 1919, was made a national park and placed under the management of the newly created Park Service—the Havasupai clung to their customary uses of the plateau to the south of the canyon. Tribe members, for instance, gathered piñon nuts—one of the few foodstuffs unaffected by the expansion of cattle raising—well into the 1920s. Reported the agent to the Havasupai in 1921, "All the Indians are now on the flats, some being away from the reservation as far as Flagstaff, Arizona, which is 80 to 100 miles from this village. All of those Indians are picking piñons." Although the supply of these nuts varied from year to year, in good years, rangers observed large numbers of Havasupai "squaws" in Grand Canyon National Park, each gathering several hundred pounds of piñon nuts, which they stored in cast-off flour sacks. During this time, tribe members also continued to harvest the agave cactus, which they would prepare by roasting for several hours in a deep, rock-lined pit.[32]

While rangers seem to have tolerated the tribe's gathering of wild plants, they were much less accommodating of other aspects of Havasupai subsistence, particularly male tribe members' persistent hunting of deer, which conflicted with official plans to turn the Grand Canyon into a game preserve. By 1908 "hunting, trapping, killing, or capturing of game animals" within the forest reserve had become a crime punishable by a fine of one thousand dollars or a year in prison.[33] Nevertheless, the Havasupai, declared the tribe's agent, "pay no heed to the existing Game Law and go on continually killing all those animals which the Government is trying so hard to protect. Since being stationed here 3 cases of deer killing upon the mesa has [sic] come under my observation. Those deer were either killed in the Park forest or adjacent to the same and out of season. After the killing the Indian or Indians bring the dead animal on the reservation, with the thought that they are free from local or state arrest."[34] Aware that such activities were going on, rangers from the Park Service tried to make regular checks of the Havasupais' winter camps on the plateau. During the 1920s, almost every winter season was marked by "patrols...to Indian camps in woods on South Rim."[35] Reported the park's superintendent in 1922, "Patrol duties have been increased somewhat lately, by the presence of approximately 15 families of Havasupai Indians, encamped in this section.... They are inclined to kill deer at any opportunity and require more or less watching in any event." This surveillance of the Havasupai continued in following years, as records from 1923 indicate: "Ranger Peck at Rowe Well Station reports evidence of game returning to the Park, as well as the fact that certain Havasupai Indians are 'dogging' the trails. He picked up several of them on patrol, took them into their Camp, but found no evidences of poaching." A few years later, in February 1926, the park superintendent noted that "it was suspected that Indians were killing deer in the Park early in the month, and a very close watch was kept in sections where their camps are located."[36]

To elude such surveillance, the Havasupai relied upon their encyclopedic knowledge of their home territory—its topography and vegetation, its game trails and hiding places—acquired through generations of inhabiting the area. They may have also reworked certain traditions to fit the tribe's altered circumstances. Male tribe members, for instance, likely revived several hunting techniques that predated the tribe's adoption of firearms, since traditional devices such as snares and clubs enabled the Havasupai to kill rabbits, birds, and other small game without making the noise that would have attracted the unwanted attention of rangers. On other occasions, the tribe adopted new practices designed to hide all evidence of wrongdoing from prying rangers. Hunters never kept wild game or buckskins in camp, for example, but instead secreted such goods in a secluded location nearby. Once the winter snows arrived, tribe members often placed hides or meat under the snow, then wiped away any tracks leading to the spot; any bones or other remains from the butchering process that the Havasupais' dogs did not eat were quickly buried as well.[37]

The Havasupais' efforts at eluding the park's rangers were facilitated by the highly stratified form that conservation assumed at the canyon. Unlike either the Adirondacks or Yellowstone, where conservation officials found their most effective enforcers to be local people hired as wardens or scouts, administrators at the Grand Canyon never sought to use the people who knew the area best, the Havasupai, to patrol the park. (The BIA did have an Indian policeman on the Havasupai reservation during this time, but he was apparently never used against poachers.) As a result of the ensuing racial and cultural divides that existed at the Grand Canyon between the enforcers of conservation and the local population, one finds little of the slipping back and forth between categories that occurred in the Adirondacks or at Yellowstone, where a sympathetic game warden or soldier might, under certain circumstances, turn a blind eye to poaching, or local inhabitants might inform authorities of lawbreaking by their neighbors. Instead, conservation at the Grand Canyon more closely resembled the colonial conservation regimes that the British and other European powers were imposing in Africa and Asia at this time—a unilateral assertion of state authority over a politically disempowered indigenous population.

With few go-betweens to mediate conservation's impact, the Havasupai found their environmental practices subjected to an especially radical program of state simplification at the turn of the century. The new regulations at the canyon wreaked havoc on several facets of Havasupai subsistence. Firewood, for instance, had long been scarce in Havasu Canyon. Many of the trees that grew in the canyon's moister climate, such as the willow and the cottonwood, while suitable for making baskets or fence poles, burned poorly. The Coconino Forest on the plateau above, however, abounded with piñon, ponderosa pine, and juniper, all of which burned well. For this reason, the Havasupai had traditionally located their winter camps in thick stands of these trees, which provided both firewood and protection against the wind. Since bringing an entire season's supply of fuel down the steep, fourteen-mile trail from the mesa to Havasu Canyon was impractical—if not impossible—the Havasupai, even after the coming of conservation, tried to spend part of each winter on the plateau above their reservation. As one tribe member, Billy Burro, explained, "They are up here because there is a shortage of wood in Supai.... In the summertime when wood is not needed very much they would drift back into Supai and do their gardening."[38]

Like firewood, meat was another subsistence item whose supply was disrupted by the creation of the Grand Cañon Forest Reserve. If records from 1896 (the last year it was legal for tribe members to hunt) are any indication, the Havasupai typically killed more than three hundred deer on the plateau each winter. Although male tribe members continued to hunt game after 1896, the secrecy poaching demanded meant that the number of deer that the Havasupai killed in the forest reserve never came close to equaling the quantity taken prior to the game law's implementation. The result, several observers noted, was a sharp change in the tribe's dietary habits. "The setting aside of the forest reserves and preventing their [the Havasupais'] killing game in the great Coconino forest has reduced them entirely to a vegetable diet," reported Henry Ewing in 1900.[39] A decade and a half later, an inspector for the BIA made much the same observation: "The Havasupai eat very little meat." On those rare occasions when the Havasupai justified their poaching to outsiders, they often did so in terms that stressed their natural right to sustenance. In his letter to the Commissioner of Indian Affairs, for instance, Captain Jim spoke of the fact that "the women and children all like deer meat very much," while in a similar missive to the secretary of the interior, a Havasupai named Watahomigie declared, "We get pretty hungry for meat sometimes." Chickapanyegi, a tribe member caught bringing an illegally killed deer onto the reservation in the early 1900s, was even blunter: "We got no meat. My family hungry."[40]

To this defense, Chickapanyegi appended a few revealing lines: "Indians, deer, here first. White man no here. Now white man make law."[41] This issue of prior right doubtless underlay much of the Havasupais' critique of federal conservation policy. From the tribe members' perspective, there was something capricious about the establishment of the Grand Cañon Forest Reserve and the ensuing conversion of long-standing tribal customs into crimes. Moreover, the rationale that conservationists put forth for implementing this stringent new set of rules over the landscape must have appeared misguided to the Havasupai. After all, it was not the region's Indian peoples who caused the collapse of the wildlife population during the 1890s. Nor was it Indian peoples who brought about the environmentally devastating overpopulation of deer on the Kaibab Plateau north of the Grand Canyon in the 1920s, which took place after the Forest Service forbade Indians to hunt and exterminated the wolves and cougars that had been the deer's natural predators.[42] Yet Native American groups bore the brunt of the state's new environmental regulations. Many of Arizona's game laws, for instance, were targeted specifically at Indians' hunting. Similarly, the GLO had taken special efforts to limit travel by Native Americans through the forest reserves.[43]

To the Havasupai, the message behind such measures was simple: conservationists believed them to be irresponsible and immature. As one tribe member exclaimed bitterly in the early 1900s, "We are no longer men, but are little children who must *ask* when we go out or come in." This antipathy of Havasupai to the limits that the forest reserve placed on their actions also surfaced in the report filed by Carl Moore, an inspector for the Indian Service: "Just as I was leaving the reservation an old Indian spoke to me in a more or less complaining attitude regarding alleged restrictions placed on their movements. I was not able with the interpreter at hand to get clearly his point but in a general way this was the substance of his statements." According to D. Clinton West, the tribe's agent in the early 1900s, the Havasupai felt that their prior, proper use of the environment ought to exempt them from the new conservation laws. "These Indians hunted long before the white man came to this part of the state," West wrote, "and they have hunted some every year since the game laws went into effect....The Indian does not believe that the white man has any business in the matter of hunting." The Havasupai, concluded the agent, "think that the White man's law in regard to hunting...is very wrong indeed."[44]

The issue of prior right may have animated Havasupai lawbreaking in the forest reserve for another reason as well. For the Havasupai, property rights depended on the use of the goods one claimed. Thus, had the Havasupai failed to return to their traditional wintering places on the plateau or to hunt the local mule deer, they would have considered themselves to be relinquishing their title to these items. On the other hand, by continuing to use the plateau, the Havasupai saw themselves as strengthening their claim to the south rim's water tanks and hunting grounds.[45]

The Havasupais' opposition to conservation, however, extended beyond these material bases. To the Havasupai, their environmental practices were fundamental to the structure of their culture. An activity such as hunting, for example, was embedded in a number of rites essential to one's journey to manhood. A Havasupai father with an infant son would run early every morning for a month so that his child might grow up to be a swift and tireless hunter. Once the boy was a few years older, male elders would teach him that to be successful in the chase he needed to exercise every morning and to keep himself clean. Explained a Havasupai named Sinyella, "When you wash, your sight will be sharp, then you can see the game—rabbits lying under the bushes, or deer visible only through an opening in the trees. If you do not wash every morning, you will miss seeing a deer, even though he stands close to you; he will scare you when he bounds off." The killing of a boy's first deer marked his entry into manhood. The animal would be left lying where it fell until the boy could summon his grandfather or other tribal elder, who would skin the deer and eat its liver. Once fully grown, a man needed to engage in several days of sexual abstinence and to eat a special diet of corn and mescal (but no meat) to have success on the hunt. Any game killed was typically distributed through the community, helping to solidify the ties of kinship and obligation.[46]

To hunt was also to bring the natural and the supernatural into proper alignment with one another. The Havasupai had a number of game shamans whose task it was the night before a hunting expedition to sing special songs to quiet the deer and to express the hunters' sorrow for having to kill the animals. The typical song was described by one Havasupai as follows: "So this man, when he's ready to go, this is just like praying, he sing this, then go out and kill deer. If he don't kill deer in four days, he'll sing it again, then go out and get meat for relatives.... Someplace in the song he talking to the deer—not *just* the deer; the trees, rocks, air, everything—he tell them not to turn the deer wild. Just stand still, lay down so he could come close, shoot the deer, kill him with bow and arrow."[47] Other songs asked the sun, who was thought to be the source of deer and other game, permission to kill some of his animals: "Sun, my relative / look at us / that is why I am here / you should give us / your domestic animals / let us see them quickly / we want to kill some." Besides such songs, a hunter's success also depended on a number of rites, such as the burning of deer droppings and marking one's face with the ashes, as well as on the visions that occasionally came in dreams.[48]

In much the same manner, Havasupai women took great pride in their vast knowledge of the local plant ecology. These skills allowed them to gather the foodstuffs and medicinal plants on which their families depended, and mothers seem to have taken special care to pass their expertise on to their children. "My mother told me a lot of sweet things to find to eat that grow around here," explained Mark Hanna. "She told me where to find them. I learned a lot about where things grow from my mother."[49]

Given this context, to insist that the Havasupai stop their hunting, gathering, and other subsistence activities in the Coconino Forest was, in essence, to insist that the tribe abandon many of the cultural forms that composed the backbone of daily existence. Much of an individual's identity—as male, as female, as a member of the Havasupai tribe—was linked to how they interacted with the landscape around them. And so, from the perspective of the Havasupai and other groups like them, conservation represented an assault not only on the material underpinnings of their existence, but also on many of the less tangible, but no less real, spiritual and moral understandings that gave their lives meaning.

Of all the many changes that conservation brought in the opening decades of the twentieth century, the most significant for the Havasupai was the creation of the Grand Canyon National Park in 1919. The Park Service's arrival at the canyon signaled a marked shift in the Havasupais' ability to hunt and gather within the reserve. If never able to completely halt such illegal activities, the Park Service, with the expanded force of rangers at its disposal, did make the Havasupais' covert uses of the plateau more difficult to pursue than before.[50] Just as important, the establishment of a park at the Grand Canyon marked the onset of a determined federal effort to open the region to large-scale tourism. Park officials drew up plans for a village to be built on the south rim, surrounding the El Tovar, the fashionable hotel that the Atchison, Topeka, and Santa Fe Railroad had constructed near the canyon's edge in 1905. According to the plans, a network of well-groomed trails would radiate outward from the village, leading tourists to a series of scenic overlooks—many given exotic Indian names such as Yavapai Walk, Papago Point, and, ironically, Supai Formation—where they would find seats and shelters to accommodate them, and unimpeded views of the canyon beyond, created by clearing away the trees and bushes along the rim.[51]

Making the canyon more accessible in this way, however, required the Park Service to embark on a rash of construction projects, from erecting ranger stations, warehouses, mess halls, and administration buildings to paving roads and building trails along the rim itself. With labor scarce because of the canyon's remote location, administrators often found themselves casting about for workers. "About the middle of the month," reported the park's superintendent in 1919, "the labor force was almost entirely depleted and work for a few days almost at a standstill." Struggling to secure enough laborers for their various undertakings, the Park Service eventually fastened upon the Havasupai, who in past years had found temporary wage work along the south rim, washing dishes or doing other odd jobs for the Fred Harvey Company and other tourist businesses that had developed in the area. Concluding that "for ordinary labor such as digging ditches, mucking, etc., Supai Indians are at least equal to any labor," park administrators soon began to hire large numbers of male Havasupais during the summer and fall months when work on the construction projects at the Grand Canyon was at its peak.[52] Recalled tribe member Mark Hanna, "I heard there were some jobs at Grand Canyon....I went up there. They told us they wanted some stones and tar to build a walk for the tourists by the canyon. [Various Havasupai were up there] and we built that walk. When we got done we dug some places."[53] In 1925, thirty-eight Havasupais—most of the able-bodied adult male population of the tribe—were employed for several months, digging ditches for the sewage plant that the Park Service was erecting to cope with the increase in tourist traffic to the canyon. Three years later, forty-two male Havasupai were hired for the construction of a suspension bridge across the Colorado River designed to aid tourists hiking from one rim of the Grand Canyon to the other.[54]

Even when there were no such ambitious projects going on, the number of Havasupai laborers at the south rim could be quite large. "Our Indians are employed here at the park a good deal," observed the tribe's agent. "I expect...as many as 20 and 30 at a time." While most of the labor available to the Havasupai was unskilled "road work, pick and shovel" paying three dollars a day, with time a few tribe members moved into more skilled and slightly better paying positions. By the late 1920s the Park Service payroll included a Havasupai named Jim Crook, who worked as a powder man responsible for setting the dynamite blasts used to clear pathways along the canyon's rock walls; another Havasupai who worked as an air-compressor operator; and a third who was a truck driver. During this period, the Atchison, Topeka and Santa Fe Railroad also employed several Havasupais, including one who ran the company's garbage incinerator and can-mashing machine.[55]

As dirty and dangerous as the jobs available to them frequently were, such wage labor had by the early twentieth century become an inescapable fact of life for Havasupai men. As early as the 1890s, male tribe members had experimented with temporary wage labor as a way to supplement a subsistence cycle diminished by the loss of game and the tribe's increasingly unstable trading situation. In subsequent years, the Havasupais' need for the cash and supplies that wage labor brought had only increased. By 1914, the tribe's agent, D. Clinton West, could report that "every able-bodied man must leave the reservation and his family (if he has a family) and procure work in railroad camps or with white men in order to earn the means of support that cannot be produced upon his little farm." The necessity of finding outside sources of income reached an even more acute level in the 1920s, as what remained of the

Havasupais' subsistence cycle eroded further. The grazing of cattle within the forest reserve (both by the Havasupai and by non-Indian ranchers) had rendered the gathering of wild plant stuffs increasingly unviable, while the Park Service's heightened surveillance of the Havasupais' winter camps made the hunting of deer and other wild game a riskier activity.[56]

Although tribe members continued to return to the plateau after the establishment of the park in 1919, the locus of their activities gradually shifted eastward, away from the grazing area at the head of Havasu Canyon, to Grand Canyon Village itself. Here, using lumber, cardboard, and other materials salvaged from the village's dump, tribe members built themselves a collection of "ramshackle huts." From their base in this improvised settlement, many Havasupai males passed a large portion of each year in Grand Canyon Village, where they could find frequent day labor. Declared the tribe's agent in 1926, "Most of the male, able-bodied Indians [are] employed in the vicinity of Grand Canyon with the Park Service and the Fred Harvey System, for which they receive $3 per day. These Indians remain at Grand Canyon with their families about nine months of the year." Under these circumstances, Supai, as the tribe's summer village in Havasu Canyon came to be known, remained a touchstone for communal life, but only on certain ceremonial occasions did the entire tribe come together there. During much of the rest of the year, the Havasupai community was segmented along the lines of age and gender, with those living in the camp on the south rim tending to be younger and male, and those residing in Supai older and female. It was this latter group that now had the responsibility for minding the tribe's fields during much of the spring and summer season. "The farming activities," noted an investigator for the Indian Service in 1926, "are mostly carried on by the men unable to go outside to work, and the women." Tribe members "cultivat[ed] just enough land to supply the older members of the tribe (those who are unable to go outside and work) with such products as corn, beans, pumpkins and a few melons." To supplement these crops, the men working in the Grand Canyon Village would "send in provisions, such as flour, sugar, and coffee, to their families, and whatever clothing they may need."[57]

One might expect that the presence of an "impoverished and unauthorized camp built by the Indians" only a few miles from park headquarters would draw official criticism. And at times this was the case. "The Indians now living in the Colony," charged one administrator, "apparently, have simply 'moved in' and, by constructing shacks of all descriptions and conditions are, in reality, violating park regulations by residing in the park without written permission from the Superintendent." But for the first decade or so of the camp's existence, the park's supervisors did little to hinder its development. Indeed, throughout the 1920s, the Park Service encouraged the shift by the Havasupai to wage labor in the Grand Canyon Village, even seeking to give tribe members "preferential employment status...for unskilled work." As P. P. Patraw, the Grand Canyon's acting superintendent, admitted in 1930, "For some time past it has been the policy of this park to make fullest possible use of available Indian labor. The policy has developed to the point where the local Supai Indians are employed in preference to outside white labor." Patraw's replacement, M. R. Tillotson, put it more bluntly: "We plan on taking care of these boys first." In addition to using Havasupai laborers on many of its construction projects, Tillotson explained, it was Park Service policy to "always recommend the Supais to the contractors."[58]

An implicit bargain underlay such practices. In exchange for the Havasupais abandoning their subsistence uses of the lands within the reserve, the Park Service was, in essence, offering to make tribe members the favored casual laborers at the park. On one level, this pact reflected the arrangement that eventually took hold at the Grand Canyon, for the Havasupai did end up performing much of the off-stage labor necessary to make the park more accessible to tourists. But this unspoken agreement never functioned as elegantly in practice as it did in theory. Tribe members remained unwilling to surrender their ties to Supai, and to their traditions of hunting and gathering on the plateau, and transform themselves into the disciplined workforce that the Park Service sought. The park's managers, for their part, rarely had enough work on hand to employ all the male tribe members needing wage labor. The result was a situation rife with friction. While park authorities tried to limit the inhabitants of the Indian camp to the people actually employed at the canyon, the Havasupai, considering the camp a tribal enclave, used it as a general camping spot, a place where any tribe member or their guests might stay and, to the dismay of the park's managers, bring along their dogs or horses. Inevitable confrontations followed, with the Park Service even razing the camp in the late 1930s during the tribe members' absence in an attempt to force the Havasupai into park-controlled housing.[59]

Although such skirmishes would have important consequences for the Havasupai, they did little to alter the fundamental conditions that the arrival of conservation had created for the tribe. The institution of government controls over the environment that accompanied conservation had solidified the Havasupais' transition from a community that supported itself through farming and hunting to one dependent on outside wage labor in order to survive. This shift affected not only the tribe's mode of production but, ultimately, how individual members related to the natural world around them. By the 1920s, the plateau lands above the Havasupais' reservation, which for the tribe had once been an intimate geography of family camping grounds, of hunting areas, and of places for gathering wild stuffs, had instead become a symbol of their diminished status as wageworkers in a touristic "wilderness." This sense of loss pervaded the tribe's "Farewell Song," a composition that, it was said, often brought tears to the eyes of its listeners:

> Dripping Spring
> Land I used to roam,
> That place,
> Listen to what I say,
> Don't mourn for me,
> I thought I would be alive forever
> I thought I would roam forever,
> I can't continue on,
> Now I am too weak.[60]

There was much more going on in such a song, of course, than a mere critique of conservation. "Farewell Song" gains much of its power from the sense of lost youth and of human mortality that runs through it, and from the links that it draws between these interior emotions and the exterior landscape. Yet this intimate subject matter intersected in significant ways with the history of conservation. The "Dripping Spring" referred to in the song was located in the tribe's former territory on the plateau—"land I used to roam"—terrain which had been lost to the forest reserve and subsequent national park. The nostalgia and sense of loss that pervade the song can therefore be read as referring not only to the singer but to the tribe as a whole. Set in this context, "Farewell Song" becomes a composition about the Havasupais' journey into a new and confusing era—one in which the practices of the past were forbidden and the future appeared uncertain.[61]

Landscapes of Memory and Myth

Once an event takes place, it lingers on in "the present of things past": memories preserved in the human consciousness. Memory, however, is rarely an impartial record keeper. Details can fade over time. Understandings can shift as individuals reimagine the past in light of current concerns. The powerful can attempt to advance their own visions of the past, dismissing those whose recollections they find threatening or inconvenient. In the case of American conservation, memory formation and policy making evolved in tandem with one another, for in justifying their programs, many of the movement's leading proponents found it useful to offer a vision of the past to which conservation emerged as the only logical response. With rural folk seldom possessing the same means by which to disseminate their own versions of events, the accounts put forth by Marsh, Fernow, Pinchot, and other early conservationists have come to occupy a prominent place in American popular memory. Even today, they shape our understanding of conservation, supporting a number of myths about the movement's early years that deserve closer historical scrutiny.[1]

The first of these myths is perhaps the most pervasive: the belief that prior to the advent of conservation, rural folk, in keeping with the supposed rugged individualism of the American frontier, did as they pleased with the natural world. In Gifford Pinchot's words, "The American people had no understanding either of what Forestry was or of the bitter need for it.... To waste timber was a virtue and not a crime." In fact, as we have seen, country people fashioned a variety of arrangements designed to safeguard the ecological base of their way of life. In the

Adirondacks, for instance, there existed several closely guarded use areas—some, such as the territory held by each guides' club, defined at the level of the community; others, such as traplines and fish weirs, considered to belong to a particular individual or family. Although the area surrounding Yellowstone was considerably more unstable because of its rapid transformation from an Indian to non-Indian landscape, even here, in the efforts by local community members to rein in shepherds and poachers such as the "gang" at Henry's Lake, we can witness attempts to establish a set of norms governing the use of the environment. For their part, the Havasupai provide an example of the array of strategies that native communities used to regulate their use of the natural world: exclusion of non–tribe members, family ownership of farmlands and hunting and gathering areas, ceremonial practices relating to the hunt, a strong ethos of sharing of resources within the tribe.[2]

It is important not to sentimentalize these local, extralegal systems. They functioned best only under particular circumstances—when participants had inhabited an area for an extended period of time, had come to understand the local ecology, and expected to remain in the vicinity, which gave them an interest in stewarding local resources—conditions that were often the opposite of what one found among the disrupted and transitory communities of the American frontier. In addition, most systems of local control hinged on exclusion as much as on inclusion, be it of non–village members in the Adirondacks, of Indians and migratory shepherds in the villages near Yellowstone, or of non-Havasupais in the Grand Canyon. Indeed, to protect local resources from potential intruders, most communities relied on the frequent exercise of physical violence against outsiders, a tendency that was sometimes turned inward to restrain those seen as wayward community members. In sum, as E. P. Thompson has observed, there was no "generous and universalistic communist spirit" underlying the concept of customary use rights. Instead, such rights were "parochial and exclusive," connected to a "bounded, circular, jealously possessive consciousness." Moreover, since customary rights regimes were not static but rather existed in a constant state of flux, as issues such as insider/outsider status or environmentally appropriate behavior were renegotiated in light of changing circumstances, a certain level of conflict was likely endemic to any system of local control, making the American countryside in the preconservation era a surprisingly violent place.[3]

Still, the existence of this patchwork of local controls serves as an important reminder that rural folk were not ignorant of their impact on the natural world. Conservation did not, as its nineteenth-century supporters often maintained, bring order to a chaotic, unstructured situation. Rather, it replaced a local, informal set of rules and customs relating to the natural world with a formal code of law, created and administered by the bureaucratic state. Seen from this perspective, conservation is consistent with the broader array of regulatory shifts posited by the political theorists William Novak and Stephen Skowronek, who argue that during the latter half of the nineteenth century in the United States, local, self-governed communities gave way to a mode of governance based on the centralized authority of the state and federal governments.[4]

The implications of this shift for the inhabitants of the American countryside proved to be complex and contradictory. On the one hand, the imposition of law as the dominant mode of determining rights to natural resources may well have curbed the violence between rural folk that had been so much a part of the previous, decentralized system.[5] Even though early regulations were often designed to benefit sports hunters and other outsiders, by establishing a legal framework governing struggles over natural resources, conservation opened up a space where the principles governing the use of the environment could be publicly debated.[6] Such actions could be both indirect (as when those arrested for violations of the new conservation code escaped prosecution by appealing to the sympathies of local juries) or direct (as when individuals, such as Oliver Lamora or the Bannock chief Racehorse, used the legal system to challenge what they considered to be the inequities of conservation). At the same time, however, the substitution of law for custom by no means relegated all struggles over the environment to the courtroom. If the coming of conservation reduced the violence between rural folk that had been so integral to the earlier pattern of resource control, the movement also created new conflicts as conservation authorities and the inhabitants of the American countryside battled over access to the resources contained within the newly protected areas. Conservation thus did not so much eliminate violence as redefine it, with the legitimate exercise of violence becoming the sole prerogative of the state, and rural folk resorting to violence as a potent but illegal way of resisting or reshaping the new conservation order taking place in their midst.[7]

The second myth associated with conservation was that it acted upon a pure, self-regulating nature, one that existed wholly apart from human institutions. The origins of this particular myth can be traced to the very birth of the conservation movement and George Perkins Marsh's depiction in *Man and Nature* of a sharp divide between humanity and the rest of the natural world. "Of all organic beings," wrote Marsh, "man alone is to be regarded as essentially a destructive power....though living in

physical nature, he is not of her." To Marsh and his fellow early conservationists, the existence of such a division justified their dismissal of local
use rights, which posed an unwanted interference to their proposals for
state management of nature. "Even now the notion of a common right of
property in the woods still lingers, if not as an opinion at least as a sentiment," observed Marsh in 1874. "Under such circumstances it has been
difficult to protect the forest, whether it belongs to the State or to individuals." Franklin Hough adopted a similar stance in his dual roles as an
early spokesperson for the Adirondack Forest Reserve and as the first federal forest commissioner. "We may at least congratulate ourselves that
rights of common are quite unknown among us, as regards the woodlands
of our country, and dismiss them from further notice." Because nature in
the United States existed independent of human beings, Hough and others
argued, the state was free to refashion woodlands and other areas as it
saw fit—a decided advantage over conditions in Europe, Africa, or India,
where customary rights regimes often circumscribed the conservation policies taking shape in these areas. "The difficulties in our way," explained
Hough in 1882, "are...much less than in some of these new and forming
administrations of the forest service[,]...where a dense native population
have, from time immemorial, enjoyed rights of usage in cultivation and
pasturage wholly inconsistent with successful forest culture."[8]

In a certain sense, Marsh's and Hough's observations were entirely
correct. In contrast with many other countries, the United States did not
possess a legally recognized tradition of usufruct rights. Yet such a state
of affairs did not necessarily mean that the doctrine held no appeal for
rural folk in the United States. Left to their own designs, country people
often spun a web of local use rights that held the natural world in a tight
embrace. As evidence from the Adirondacks, Yellowstone, and the
Grand Canyon reveals, even at the turn of the century large numbers of
rural Americans regarded usufructure as a valid ideology, especially in
those cases where natural resources were appropriated for purposes of
basic subsistence: food, firewood, building supplies, and the like. Claiming access to such staples as a natural right, rural folk launched persistent efforts to impose a common rights doctrine from below. And from
time to time, there were brief moments when local pressure did bring
something close to such a regime into existence: in the Adirondacks during the early 1880s, when much of the region was controlled by community-based guides' clubs; in Yellowstone during the 1880s and 1890s,
when the area's inhabitants were allowed to pasture livestock and gather
dead wood in the park; at the Grand Canyon in the early 1900s, when
the Havasupai managed to obtain from the Forest Service a grazing and

camping territory on the plateau. But such arrangements never achieved the status of enforceable rights. Lacking any legal basis, these informal accords were frequently short-lived, often falling apart when conservation authorities were able to strengthen their position and force local inhabitants to accept state management of the landscape.

The third myth associated with conservation concerned the landscapes that the movement created. Drawing on a vocabulary of protection and preservation, conservationists consistently portrayed the areas affected by their policies as uniquely natural spaces. In its most extreme form, this vision expressed itself through the trope of wilderness—primordial, undisturbed nature. "The dominant idea" of Yellowstone National Park, contended the secretary of the interior in 1886, is "the preservation of the wilderness of forests, geysers, mountains, &c ...common to that region in as nearly the condition of nature as possible." "[In] a great park like the Adirondack, or the Yellowstone," agreed Robert Underwood Johnson in 1892, "the essential quality is that of a solitude, a wilderness, a place of undisturbed communion with nature in all her primitive beauty."[9] In the Adirondacks, the language of wilderness even inscribed itself into New York's 1894 constitution, which proclaimed that "the lands of the State...constituting the forest preserve...shall be forever kept as wild forest lands."[10] While conservationists did not always employ the trope of wilderness when describing their policies, the very term *conservation*, with its etymological links to *conservative* and its connotations of guarding and preserving, summoned up many of the same images: the protection of an unchanged, unchanging natural landscape.[11]

In reality, however, the movement played a powerful role in transforming the American countryside. The rise of conservation involved a number of unprecedented state interventions into the rural periphery: the passage of new laws governing the setting of fires, the taking of game, the cutting of timber, the grazing of animals, and other longstanding practices; and the deployment of a veritable army of wardens, foresters, rangers, scouts, and soldiers to ensure compliance with these measures. Such actions rewove the existing web of social and environmental relationships in much of the rural United States. Plant and animal populations, for instance, underwent significant shifts as officials took steps to prevent poaching and predation, while new regulations undermined the subsistence patterns of rural folk, pushing them farther into the market economy, particularly the market for wage labor.

The arrival of conservation thus marks a crucial divide in the history of rural America. Amid the swirl of regulation and resistance that surrounded the movement's birth, we can glimpse the modern American countryside taking shape—a place where market relationships and wage labor predominated, where law took precedence over custom, and where the state played a powerful managerial role, standardizing and simplifying what had been a dense thicket of particularistic, local approaches toward the natural world. Set within this context, wilderness reveals itself to be not some primeval character of nature but rather an artifact of modernity, a concept employed by conservationists to naturalize the transformations taking place in rural America during the late nineteenth and early twentieth centuries.

Conservation's final myth involved the relationship between the movement and the people it most directly affected. Ever since Marsh's *Man and Nature,* a key component of conservation's degradation discourse has been the need to use science and the state to protect nature from the recklessness of rural folk. If Marsh's work prefigured any sustained governmental effort to manage the environment, the dissatisfaction that country people manifested with early projects such as the Adirondack Park only confirmed conservationists' initial suspicions of them. As Ernest Bruncken, a member of the Wisconsin State Forestry Commission, asserted at the turn of the century, "The backwoodsman, to be sure, derive[s] his sustenance from the woods, but he d[oes] so by destroying them.... The latter-day backwoodsman has the poverty, the ignorance, the lack of civilized ways which we found in his predecessor, to an exaggerated degree." Perceiving rural folk to be stubborn obstacles rather than potential allies, conservationists made little effort to build on the local systems of environmental control already existing in the areas they targeted (although, ironically, conservationists did find local knowledge invaluable when it came to matters such as finding foresters or scouts to enforce their new regulations).[12]

By adopting what can only be termed an authoritarian stance toward environmental problems, early conservationists were able to formulate quick responses to some of the nation's more pressing ecological concerns. Yet these actions also left behind a troubling legacy. As conservation's hidden history reveals, Americans have often pursued environmental quality at the expense of social justice. One would like to imagine that the two goals are complementary and that the only way to achieve a healthy environment is through a truly democratic society. But for now, these two objectives remain separate guiding stars in a dark night sky, and we can only wonder if they will lead us to the same hoped-for destination.

Chronology of American Conservation

1864   George Perkins Marsh publishes *Man and Nature*.

1869   William H.H. Murray releases *Adventures in the Wilderness; or, Camp-Life in the Adirondacks*. The book quickly becomes a best-seller, attracting extensive public attention to the Adirondacks region.

1872   The New York State Legislature establishes a State Park Commission (members include Franklin Hough and Verplanck Colvin) to explore the viability of a forest preserve in the Adirondacks counties.

   The U.S. Congress creates Yellowstone National Park.

1873   *Forest and Stream* commences publication.

   Franklin Hough gives a speech, "On the Duty of Governments in the Preservation of Forests," at the annual meeting of the American Association for the Advancement of Science. The association subsequently submits a memorial on forest preservation to Congress.

   Congress passes the Timber Culture Act, granting settlers 160-acre plots if they will cultivate trees on one-fourth of the land for four years.

1875   The American Forestry Association is founded.

1876   Franklin Hough becomes the first federal forestry agent.

1878   John Wesley Powell publishes *Report on the Lands of the Arid Region of the United States*.

1880   George Bird Grinnell assumes editorship of *Forest and Stream*.

1881   The Division of Forestry is established in the Department of Agriculture. Franklin Hough is named the division's first chief.

1882   Franklin Hough, Bernhard Fernow, and John Warder found the American Forestry Congress.

1883   New York discontinues the selling of state-owned land in the Adirondacks.

1884   The New York State Legislature appoints a commission chaired by Charles Sargent, professor of arboriculture at Harvard and head of the Arnold Arboretum, to "investigate and report a system of forest preservation" on state lands.

        Charles Sargent publishes *Report on the Forests of North America* as part of the tenth federal census.

1885   New York State establishes the Adirondack Forest Preserve, to be "forever kept as wild forest lands" and to be overseen by a Forest Commission.

1886   Bernhard E. Fernow is named chief of the Division of Forestry.

        The U.S. Army assumes control of Yellowstone National Park.

        George Bird Grinnell founds the nation's first chapter of the Audubon Society.

1887   Theodore Roosevelt and George Bird Grinnell found the Boone and Crockett Club.

        Charles Sargent commences publication of *Garden and Forest.*

1889   Robert Underwood Johnson publishes the first of several editorials in *Century* magazine calling for federal forest conservation.

1890   Congress establishes Sequoia National Park (California), Yosemite National Park (California), and General Grant National Park (California).

        The Census Bureau announces the "closing" of the frontier.

1891   Congress repeals the Timber Culture Act of 1873 and passes the Forest Reserve Act, authorizing the president to create forest reserves (later national forests) on public land.

        President Benjamin Harrison establishes the Yellowstone Park Timberland Reserve, the nation's first forest reserve.

1892   New York State creates the Adirondack Park. The park's "blue line" encloses some 2,800,000 acres, including Forest Preserve lands as well as private holdings.

        The Sierra Club is founded in San Francisco. John Muir serves as the club's first president.

1893   Grand Cañon Forest Reserve (Arizona) is created. By the end of the year, fifteen forest reserves with a total area of some 16.7 million acres are established in the western United States.

Gifford Pinchot, the nation's first "consulting forester," opens an office in New York City.

1894   The New York State Constitutional Convention passes a constitutional amendment stating that the lands of the Forest Preserve "shall be forever kept as wild forest lands" and that the preserve's timber shall not be sold, leased, or otherwise harvested.

Congress passes "An Act to Protect the Birds and Animals in Yellowstone National Park" (also known as the National Park Protective Act) clarifying and reinforcing the parks' role as wildlife preserves.

1895   New York combines the previously separate Fisheries and Forest Commissions into the Fisheries, Game, and Forest Commission.

1897   Congress passes the Forest Management Act, placing the forest reserves under the management of the General Land Office and authorizing it to oversee the reserves for purposes of lumbering, grazing, and mining. The Forest Management Act defines the character of the national forests for the next sixty years, being superseded only when Congress passes the Multiple Use-Sustained Yield Act in 1960.

1898   Gifford Pinchot succeeds Bernhard E. Fernow as chief of the Forestry Division.

Carl Schenk opens Biltmore Forest School, the nation's first forestry school. One month later, Bernhard Fernow establishes a forestry school at Cornell University.

1900   Gifford Pinchot helps to found the Yale School of Forestry.

New York reorganizes the Fisheries, Game, and Forest Commission into the Forest, Fish and Game Commission.

Congress passes the Lacey Act, prohibiting the interstate shipment of wildlife killed in violation of state game laws.

1901   Theodore Roosevelt becomes president.

The city of San Francisco applies for a permit to build a reservoir in Yosemite's Hetch Hetchy Valley, igniting a twelve-year fight between the "utilitarian" and "preservationist" wings of the conservation movement.

1902   Bernhard Fernow begins publication of *Forestry Quarterly*.

1905   Under the terms of the Transfer Act of 1905, control of the forest reserves passes from the General Land Office to the Bureau of Forestry, which is thereafter known as the Forest Service.

1906   Congress passes the American Antiquities Act, authorizing the president to establish national monuments. Devil's Tower (Wyoming) and the Petrified Forest (Arizona) are proclaimed the nation's first two national monuments.

1908   The Governors' Conference on the Conservation of Natural Resources, organized by Gifford Pinchot, is held at the White House. The meeting leads to creation of the National Conservation Commission.

        Grand Canyon National Monument is created.

1909   Theodore Roosevelt presides over the North American Conservation Conference, which attracts delegates from the United States, Canada, and Mexico.

1910   Gifford Pinchot is dismissed from the Forest Service. He becomes president of the National Conservation Association (founded the previous year) and publishes *The Fight for Conservation*.

1911   New York reorganizes the Forest, Fish and Game Commission into the Conservation Commission.

1913   Congress passes the Migratory Bird Act, proclaiming all migratory and insectivorous birds to be subject to federal oversight.

        Congress passes the Raker Bill, permitting San Francisco to convert Yosemite's Hetch Hetchy Valley into a reservoir.

1916   The National Park Service is established within the Department of the Interior. Stephen Mather is named the service's first director.

1918   The National Park Service assumes control of Yellowstone National Park from the U.S. Army.

1919   Congress elevates the Grand Canyon to the status of national park.

Notes

PREFACE

1. See, for example, the contrast between South African and American parks that William Beinart and Peter Coates draw in *Environment and History: The Taming of Nature in the USA and South Africa* (New York: Routledge, 1995), 85.

2. Hal Barron, *Those Who Stayed Behind: Rural Society in Nineteenth-Century New England* (New York: Cambridge University Press, 1984), xi.

3. I attempt to develop my critique of environmental history's neglect of social power in greater depth in "Class and Environmental History: Lessons from the 'War in the Adirondacks,'" *Environmental History* 2 (July 1997): 324–42. A thoughtful recent treatment of this topic can be found in Alan Taylor, "Unnatural Inequalities: Social and Environmental Histories," *Environmental History* 1 (October 1996): 6–19.

4. See, for instance, New York Fisheries Commission, *Sixteenth Annual Report, 1887* (Albany: Troy Press, 1888), 163.

INTRODUCTION

1. Richard H. Grove, *Green Imperialism: Colonial Expansion, Tropical Island Edens, and the Origins of Environmentalism, 1600–1860* (New York: Cambridge University Press, 1995), 2. There is a long list of scholarly studies that seek to understand the natural world by focusing on a few well-placed figures. Among the most prominent of such works are Roderick Nash, *Wilderness and the American Mind,* 3rd ed. (New Haven: Yale University Press, 1982); Barbara Novak,

Nature and Culture: American Landscape and Painting, 1825–1875 (New York: Oxford University Press, 1980); Max Oelschlaeger, *The Idea of Wilderness: From Prehistory to the Age of Ecology* (New Haven: Yale University Press, 1991); Patricia Nelson Limerick, *Desert Passages: Encounters with the American Deserts* (Albuquerque: University of New Mexico Press, 1985); Leo Marx, *The Machine in the Garden: Technology and the Pastoral Ideal in America* (New York: Oxford University Press, 1964); John F. Reiger, *American Sportsmen and the Origins of Conservation,* rev. ed. (Norman: University of Oklahoma Press, 1986); and Donald Worster, *Nature's Economy: A History of Ecological Ideas,* 2nd ed. (New York: Cambridge University Press, 1994).

2. Having begun this study with the sense that I was voyaging alone into uncharted territory, I have been pleased to encounter several fellow explorers of conservation's hidden history along the way. Louis Warren studies poaching in *The Hunter's Game: Poachers and Conservationists in Twentieth-Century America* (New Haven: Yale University Press, 1997); Mark Spence focuses on the impact that the park movement had on American Indians in *Dispossessing the Wilderness: The Preservationist Ideal, Indian Removal, and National Parks* (New York: Oxford University Press, 1999); Richard Judd attempts to place rural New Englanders at the forefront of the conservation movement in *Common Lands, Common People: The Origins of Conservation in Northern New England* (Cambridge: Harvard University Press, 1997); and Ben Johnson explores the effect of conservation on working-class immigrants in "Conservation, Subsistence, and Class at the Birth of Superior National Forest," *Environmental History* 4 (January 1999): 80–99.

3. One of the clearest proofs of this shift is the fact that by the turn of the century it was possible for the first time to find thick manuals of forest law. See, for instance, George W. Woodruff, *Federal and State Forest Laws,* Bureau of Forestry Bulletin No. 57 (Washington, D.C.: GPO, 1904); and J.P. Kinney, *The Development of Forest Law in America* (New York: John Wiley and Sons, 1917). For an example from British India at much the same time, see B.H. Baden-Powell, *Forest Law: A Course of Lectures on the Principles of Civil and Criminal Law and on the Law of the Forest* (London: Bradbury, Agnew, and Co., 1893).

4. The term "environmental bandits" is derived, of course, from the "social bandits" that Eric Hobsbawm first described in his work *Primitive Rebels: Studies in Archaic Forms of Social Movement in the Nineteenth and Twentieth Century* (New York: W.W. Norton, 1959); he developed his concept further in *Bandits,* rev. ed. (New York: Pantheon, 1981). Hobsbawm's work has spawned a huge literature, too vast to note here. One useful recent review essay, however, is Gilbert Joseph, "On the Trail of Latin American Bandits: A Reexamination of Peasant Resistance," *Latin American Research Review* 25 (1990): 7–53.

5. Although such language was widespread in early conservation literature, these particular quotes come from the commission in charge of the Adirondack Park. New York Forest, Fish and Game Commission, *Eighth and Ninth Annual Reports, 1902–1903* (Albany: James B. Lyon, 1904), 107–8.

6. Roderick Nash, "The Value of Wilderness," *Environmental Review* 3 (1977): 14–25. For a discussion of the development of environmental history as a distinct discipline and Nash's place in the field, see Richard White, "American

Environmental History: The Development of a New Historical Field," *Pacific Historical Review* 54 (August 1985): 297–335.

7. As Stephen Fox contends in his history of conservation, "Politics seldom lends itself to such simple morality plays. But environmental issues have usually come down to a stark alignment of white hats and black hats." Stephen Fox, *John Muir and His Legacy: The American Conservation Movement* (Boston: Little, Brown, 1981), 103. Among those works that adopt a similarly heroic stance toward conservation history are Frank Graham Jr., *Man's Dominion: The Story of Conservation in America* (New York: M. Evans, 1971); Frank E. Smith, *The Politics of Conservation* (New York: Pantheon, 1966); Douglas H. Strong, *Dreamers and Defenders: American Conservationists* (Lincoln: University of Nebraska Press, 1988); Richard Stroud, ed., *National Leaders of American Conservation* (Washington, D.C.: Smithsonian Institution Press, 1985); and Peter Wild, *Pioneer Conservationists of Western America* (Missoula, Mont.: Mountain Press, 1979), and *Pioneer Conservationists of Eastern America* (Missoula, Mont.: Mountain Press, 1986).

8. See E. P. Thompson, "The Moral Economy of the English Crowd in the Eighteenth Century," and "The Moral Economy Reviewed," in *Customs in Common: Studies in Traditional Popular Culture* (New York: New Press, 1993), 185–258, 259–351. There is also a growing body of work that focuses on matters of political ecology—that is, on the "political sources, conditions, and ramifications of environmental change." Raymond L. Bryant, "Political Ecology: An Emerging Research Agenda in Third-World Studies," *Political Geography* 11 (January 1992): 13; see also Leslie Anderson, *The Political Ecology of the Modern Peasant: Calculation and Community* (Baltimore: Johns Hopkins University Press, 1994); and Adrian Atkinson, *Principles of Political Ecology* (London: Belhaven Press, 1991).

9. For examples of illiteracy or near-illiteracy in the Adirondacks, see the testimony of Joseph Lahey and Joseph Mitchell in New York State Assembly, *Report and Testimony of the Special Committee Appointed to Investigate the Depredations of Timber in the Forest Preserve,* New York State Assembly Document No. 67, 1895 (Albany: Wynkoop, Hallenbeck, Crawford, 1896), 253, 314. (Hereafter referred to as *Report, 1895.*) The following chapters on Yellowstone also reveal numerous examples of people whose command of written English was quite limited.

10. A fascinating case study of how scholarly sleuthing can occasionally unearth the popular folklore that surrounded the rise of conservation can be found in Edward D. Ives, *George Magoon and the Down East Game War: History, Folklore, and the Law* (Urbana: University of Illinois Press, 1988).

11. This emphasis on rereading elite documents to understand peasant consciousness has been central to the subaltern school of Indian studies. See Ranajit Guha, *Elementary Aspects of Peasant Insurgency in Colonial India* (Delhi: Oxford University Press, 1983), 14–17; and Ranajit Guha and Gayatri Chakravortry Spivak, eds., *Selected Subaltern Studies* (New York: Oxford University Press, 1988). The term *hidden transcript* comes from the work of James Scott on the discourse of resistance. Scott, *Domination and the Arts of Resistance: Hidden Transcripts* (New Haven: Yale University Press, 1990).

12. Information on the European roots of American forestry can be found in Nancy Peluso, *Rich Forests, Poor People: Resource Control and Resistance in Java* (Berkeley and Los Angeles: University of California Press, 1992), 7–8.

13. Bernhard E. Fernow, "Report of the Forestry Division," in U.S. Department of Agriculture, *Annual Report of the Commissioner of Agriculture, 1887* (Washington, D.C.: GPO, 1888), 605–6. Fernow was scarcely alone in pointing to the example of Europe. In his first official report as federal forest commissioner, Franklin B. Hough included a detailed discussion of environmental legislation in Prussia, along with a description of the course of study at the German Royal Forest Academy. Hough, *Report upon Forestry, 1877* (Washington, D.C.: GPO, 1878), 360–65, 613–15.

14. E. P. Thompson, *Whigs and Hunters: The Origins of the Black Act* (New York: Pantheon, 1975); John Broad, "Whigs and Deer-Stealers in Other Guises: A Return to the Origins of the Black Act," *Past and Present* 119 (May 1988): 56–72; and Peter Sahlins, *Forest Rites: The War of the Demoiselles in Nineteenth-Century France* (Cambridge: Harvard University Press, 1994). Although the Captain Swing riots also focused on concerns about the mechanization of rural labor, many of the rioters came from the Forest of Dean, where they acted in defiance of state controls over the forest. See Richard H. Grove, "Colonial Conservation, Ecological Hegemony, and Popular Resistance: Towards a Global Synthesis," in *Imperialism and the Natural World*, ed. John M. MacKenzie (Manchester, U.K.: Manchester University Press, 1990), 46, n. 58. More general treatments of poaching in Great Britain can be found in Harry Hopkins, *The Long Affray: The Poaching Wars, 1760–1914* (London: Secker and Warburg, 1985); E. G. Walsh, ed., *The Poacher's Companion* (Suffolk, U.K.: Boydell Press, 1982); and the classic article by Douglas Hay, "Poaching and the Game Laws on Cannock Chase," in *Albion's Fatal Tree: Crime and Society in Eighteenth-Century England*, ed. Douglas Hay, Peter Linebaugh, John Rule, E. P. Thompson, and Cal Winslow (New York: Pantheon, 1975).

15. James Scott, *Weapons of the Weak: Everyday Forms of Peasant Resistance* (New Haven: Yale University Press, 1985), 35; see also Peluso, *Rich Forests, Poor People*, 14. For more on the poaching of game in Germany, see Regina Schulte, *The Village in Court: Arson, Infanticide, and Poaching in the Court Records of Upper Bavaria, 1848–1910*, trans. Barrie Selman (New York: Cambridge University Press, 1994).

16. Peter Linebaugh, "Karl Marx, the Theft of Wood, and Working Class Composition: A Contribution to the Current Debate," *Crime and Social Justice* 6 (fall-winter 1976): 5–16.

17. Grove, "Colonial Conservation," passim; David Anderson and Richard Grove, eds., *Conservation in Africa: People, Policies, and Practice* (Cambridge: Cambridge University Press, 1987). The literature on conservation in India is particularly well developed. See, for example, Ramachandra Guha, *The Unquiet Woods: Ecological Change and Peasant Resistance in the Himalaya* (Berkeley and Los Angeles: University of California Press, 1990); Madhav Gadgil and Ramachandra Guha, *This Fissured Land: An Ecological History of India* (Delhi: Oxford University Press, 1992); Mahesh Rangarajan, *Fencing the Forest: Conservation and Ecological Change in India's Central Provinces,*

1860–1914 (Delhi: Oxford University Press, 1996); David Arnold and Rama-chandra Guha, eds., *Nature, Culture, Imperialism: Essays on the Environmental History of South Asia* (Delhi: Oxford University Press, 1996); K. Sivara-makrishnan, "Colonialism and Forestry in India: Imagining the Past in Present Politics," *Comparative Studies in Society and History* 37 (January 1995): 3–40; and K. Sivaramakrishnan, "The Politics of Fire and Forest Regeneration in Co-lonial Bengal," *Environment and History* 2 (1996): 145–94.

18. Samuel P. Hays, *Conservation and the Gospel of Efficiency: The Progressive Conservation Movement, 1890–1920* (Cambridge: Harvard University Press, 1959), 2–4; Robert H. Weibe, *The Search for Order, 1877–1920* (New York: Hill and Wang, 1967), xiii–xiv, 185–86. As Andrew Ross has observed, "Ideas that draw upon the authority of nature nearly always have their origin in ideas about society." Andrew Ross, *The Chicago Gangster Theory of Life: Nature's Debt to Society* (New York: Verso, 1994), 15.

19. For those wishing more background information on the rise of conser-vation, a chronology of major events has been provided following the text.

CHAPTER 1. THE RE-CREATION OF NATURE

1. Joel T. Headley, *The Adirondack; or, Life in the Woods* (New York: Baker and Scribner, 1849), 13, 167–68. For more on Headley, see Philip G. Terrie, *Contested Terrain: A New History of Nature and People in the Adirondacks* (Blue Mountain Lake, N.Y.: Adirondack Museum and Syracuse University Press, 1997), 45–60.

2. *The Opening of the Adirondacks* (New York: Hurd and Houghton, 1865), 30; A. Judd Northrup, *Camps and Tramps in the Adirondacks, and Grayling Fishing in Northern Michigan: A Record of Summer Vacations in the Wilderness* (Syracuse: Davis, Bardeen, 1880), 27; Nathaniel Bartlett Sylvester, *Historical Sketches of Northern New York and the Adirondack Wilderness* (Troy, N.Y.: William H. Young, 1877), 41–42.

3. David Arnold, *The Problem of Nature: Environment, Culture, and Euro-pean Expansion* (Oxford: Blackwell, 1996), 19. For the American reception of some of the era's multiple ideas of nature, see Richard Hofstadter, *Social Darwinism in American Thought,* rev. ed. (New York: George Braziller, 1959); G. J. Cady, "The Early American Reaction to the Theory of Malthus," in *Thomas Malthus: Critical Assessments,* ed. John Cunningham Wood (London: Croom Helm, 1986), 4:18–42; Linda Gordon, "Birth Control, Socialism, and Fem-inism in the United States," in *Malthus Past and Present,* ed. J. Dupaquier, A. Fauve-Chamoux, and E. Grebenik (London: Academic Press, 1983), 313–27; Frank Forester [Henry William Herbert], *Complete Manual for Young Sports-men* (New York: W. A. Townsend, 1866); and Thomas R. Dunlap, *Saving America's Wildlife* (Princeton: Princeton University Press, 1988), 9.

4. George Perkins Marsh, *Man and Nature,* ed. David Lowenthal (1864; re-print, Cambridge: Harvard University Press, 1965), 42. The quote on Marsh's contribution to land management comes from Worster, *Nature's Economy,* 268. Useful summaries of Marsh's views can be found in David Lowenthal, *George Perkins Marsh: Versatile Vermonter* (New York: Columbia University Press,

1958); Donald J. Pisani, "Forests and Conservation," *Journal of American History* 72 (September 1985): 340–59; and William Cronon, "Forests and Civilization," *Yale Review* 80 (October 1992): 79–84. For a discussion of Marsh's import to conservation and ecology, see Daniel Botkin, *Discordant Harmonies: A New Ecology for the Twenty-first Century* (New York: Oxford University Press, 1990), 8–9, 54; and Peter Coates, *Nature: Western Attitudes since Ancient Times* (Berkeley and Los Angeles: University of California Press, 1998), 21–25.

5. Marsh, *Man and Nature,* 43.

6. Ibid., 204.

7. Ibid., 204, 258.

8. Ibid., 189, 233, 257, 260, 274. Robert L. Dorman analyzes the relation between Marsh's Whig politics and his approach to conservation in *A Word for Nature: Four Pioneering Environmental Advocates, 1845–1913* (Chapel Hill: University of North Carolina Press, 1998), 12–16.

9. Marsh, *Man and Nature,* xxiii–xxiv, 29–30, 36. For a critique of the climax community model, first popularized by Frederic Clements, see the essays by William Cronon, "In Search of Nature," and Michael G. Barbour, "Ecological Fragmentation in the Fifties," in *Uncommon Ground: Rethinking the Human Place in Nature,* ed. William Cronon (New York: W. W. Norton, 1995), 24–25, 233–55; and Donald Worster, "The Shaky Ground of Sustainable Development," in *The Wealth of Nature: Environmental History and the Ecological Imagination* (New York: Oxford University Press, 1993), 144–51.

10. Lewis Mumford, *The Brown Decades: A Study of the Arts in America, 1865–1895* (New York: Dover, 1955), 78. Among those conservationists to acknowledge their debt to Marsh are Fernow, who wrote of "George P. Marsh's classical book," in *Our Forestry Problem* (n.p., 1887), 3; and Andrew Fuller, *Practical Forestry* (New York: Orange Judd, 1900), 14. I have borrowed the term "degradation discourse" from James Fairhead and Melissa Leach, *Misreading the African Landscape: Society and Ecology in a Forest-Savanna Mosaic* (New York: Cambridge University Press, 1996), 292–93. James C. McCann employs a similar term—"degradation narratives"—in "The Plow and the Forest: Narratives of Deforestation in Ethiopia, 1840–1992," *Environmental History* 2 (April 1997): 138–59, while Vasant K. Saberwal has recently traced the rise of a "desiccationist discourse" in Anglo-American conservation. Saberwal, "Science and the Desiccationist Discourse of the Twentieth Century," *Environment and History* 4 (October 1998): 309–43. Fairhead and Leach revisit their argument in *Reframing Deforestation: Global Analyses and Local Realities: Studies in West Africa* (New York: Routledge, 1998).

11. New York Commissioners of State Parks, *First Annual Report, 1872* (Albany: Argus, 1873), 5, 13–14, 20–21. The link between Marsh and the Adirondacks was drawn even more explicitly in a later report, in which the New York Forest Commission quoted at length from *Man and Nature.* New York Forest Commission, *Second Annual Report, 1886* (Albany: Argus, 1887), 85–86. Other sections of this passage emphasize hunting and fishing as producing better businessmen and soldiers, an argument derived in large part from the writings of Frank Forester. See Forester, *Complete Manual for Young Sportsmen,* 27–33.

12. As Louise Halper has observed, "Proponents of the wilderness aesthetic were among the most avid exploiters of natural resources in their business dealings." Halper, "'A Rich Man's Paradise': Constitutional Preservation of New York State's Adirondack Forest, A Centenary Consideration," *Ecology Law Quarterly* 19 (1992): 230. T. J. Jackson Lears has argued convincingly that the rise of antimodernism ultimately helped many American elites accommodate themselves to the jarring transitions of the late nineteenth century. Lears, *No Place of Grace: Antimodernism and the Transformation of American Culture, 1880–1920* (New York: Pantheon, 1981). The connection between modernism and antimodernism can be seen in one of the very first articles to support the idea of a park in the Adirondacks, an unsigned editorial that appeared in the *New York Times* in 1864, which spoke in almost the same breath about preserving the region for its watershed and for its natural beauty. *New York Times,* August 9, 1864. Because of such similarities, I, unlike some scholars, have not found it useful to categorize turn-of-the-century environmental reformers as either "preservationists" or "conservationists." An extended discussion of some of the similarities between "preservationists" and "technocratic utilitarians" can be found in Christopher McGrory Klyza, *Who Controls Public Lands? Mining, Forestry, and Grazing Policies, 1870–1990* (Chapel Hill: University of North Carolina Press, 1996), 21–26.

13. Material on early Forest Preserve legislation can be found in Norman J. Van Valkenburgh, *Land Acquisition for New York State: An Historical Perspective* (Arkville, N.Y.: Catskill Center for Conservation and Development, 1985), 12–51; Hays, *Conservation and the Gospel of Efficiency,* 191; Seneca Ray Stoddard, *The Adirondacks: Illustrated,* 19th ed. (Glen Falls, N.Y.: 1889), 218; Philip Terrie, "'One Grand Unbroken Domain': Ambiguities and Lessons in the Origins of the Adirondack Park," *Hudson Valley Regional Review* 6 (March 1989): 10–17; and the Fish and Game Law file at the Adirondack Museum Archives.

14. Hough, later the first head of the federal government's Division of Forestry, was a member of the 1872 committee that recommended the creation of a park in the Adirondacks. See F. B. Hough, *Report upon Forestry, 1877,* 436–37. For examples of Pinchot's and Fernow's work in the Adirondacks, see Gifford Pinchot, *The Adirondack Spruce: A Study of the Forest in Ne-Ha-Sa-Ne Park* (New York: Critic Co., 1898); and Fernow's plan for the Adirondack League Club, published in the U.S. Department of Agriculture, *Annual Report of the Division of Forestry, 1890* (Washington, D.C.: GPO, 1891), 214–23.

15. U.S. Department of Agriculture, *Annual Report of the Division of Forestry, 1887* (Washington, D.C.: GPO, 1888), 106. See also American Forestry Congress, *Proceedings, 1885* (Washington, D.C.: Judd and Detweiler, 1886), 16; U.S. Department of Agriculture, *Annual Report of the Division of Forestry, 1886* (Washington, D.C.: GPO, 1887), 173; *Forestry Bulletin* (May 1884), 1, 8–9; and Arnold Hague's references to the Adirondacks in "The Yellowstone Park as a Forest Reservation," *The Nation* 46 (January 5, 1888): 9–10.

16. A useful discussion of parallels between the forest reserves and the Adirondacks can be found in William Cronon, "Landscapes of Abundance and Scarcity," in *The Oxford History of the American West,* ed. Clyde A. Milner II,

Carol A. O'Connor, and Martha A. Sandweiss (New York: Oxford University Press, 1994), 607–9. Other writers to mention the links between the Adirondacks and the forest reserves include Harold K. Steen, *The Beginning of the National Forest System* (Washington, D.C.: GPO, 1991), 15; and A. B. Recknagel, *The Forests of New York State* (New York: Macmillan, 1923), 50.

17. Bernhard E. Fernow, *A Brief History of Forestry* (Toronto: University Press, 1911), 493. Fernow played a pivotal role in exporting the Adirondacks model to the rest of the American landscape. Not only did he write the plan for forest administration that New York instituted in the Adirondacks in 1885 (soon followed by forestry plans for various private parks in the Adirondacks), but he also helped draft the Forest Reserve Act of 1891. Bernhard E. Fernow, "Report of the Forestry Division," in U.S. Department of Agriculture, *Annual Report of the Commissioner of Agriculture, 1886* (Washington, D.C.: GPO, 1887), 166, 173; and Bernhard E. Fernow, *Report upon the Forestry Investigations of the U.S. Department of Agriculture, 1877–1898* (Washington, D.C.: GPO, 1899), 172–74. See also William G. Robbins, *American Forestry: A History of National, State, and Private Cooperation* (Lincoln: University of Nebraska Press, 1985), 7; and Andrew Denny Rodgers III, *Bernhard Eduard Fernow: A Story of North American Forestry* (1951; reprint, Durham, N.C.: Forest History Society, 1991), 98.

18. Accurate population figures for the Adirondacks are surprisingly hard to come by. A figure of 15,832 (which does not include tourists or transient employees of lumber camps) is given in New York Fisheries, Game, and Forest Commission, *Third Annual Report, 1897* (Albany: Wynkoop, Hallenbeck, Crawford, 1898), 270. An earlier report by the Forest Commission, however, places the number at 6,167. But this seems low: according to the 1880 federal census, there were some 3,923 people living in Hamilton County alone (Hamilton being the only county completely within the confines of the Adirondack park). See New York Forest Commission, *Annual Report, 1893* (Albany: James B. Lyon, 1894), 1:9. If one does a rough count by township using the 1880 summaries of census data, it is possible to get a population total closer to 30,000. But because many townships extend outside the park limits, and population density outside the park was typically much higher than inside it, this number seems too large.

19. New York Forest Commission, *Preliminary Report, 1885,* New York State Assembly Document No. 36, 1885, 5–6.

20. Ted Aber and Stella King, *The History of Hamilton County* (Lake Pleasant, N.Y.: Great Wilderness Books, 1965), 37, 75; New York Forest Commission, *First Annual Report, 1885* (Albany: Argus, 1886), 40. Depopulation was not a phenomenon unique to the Adirondacks. Out-migration is a recurring, if little-noted, theme in the history of the American countryside, a counternarrative to the often naive optimism of the frontier paradigm.

21. New York Commissioners of State Parks, *First Annual Report, 1872,* 22. This prediction by the commissioners would seem to presage present-day efforts to encourage "eco-tourism" in environmentally sensitive areas.

22. New York Forest Commission, *First Annual Report, 1885,* 87–88, 96–97, 99. Although one might argue that these supportive responses came

about because of the intimidating presence of a special agent from the Forest Commission, some of those interviewed made clear their opposition to the plan (92, 97).

23. New York Fisheries Commission, *Twenty-second Annual Report, 1893* (Albany: James B. Lyon, 1894), 177; New York Fisheries Commission, *Eighteenth Annual Report, 1889* (Albany: James B. Lyon, 1890), 219; *New York Times,* September 25, October 2, October 4, and October 16, 1889.

24. Headley, *Adirondack,* 204–5; William Murray, *Adventures in the Wilderness; or, Camp-Life in the Adirondacks* (Boston: Fields, Osgood, 1869), 37–38; [J. P. Lundy,] *The Saranac Exiles; or, a Winter's Tale of the Adirondacks* (Philadelphia: privately printed, 1880), 118–19, 169; Elizabeth Seelye, "Abandoned Farms Again," *Century* 48 (1894): 792; "A Word about Hoodlums," *Forest and Stream* 38 (February 25, 1892): 176–77. This rise of the hillbilly as a southern stereotype is discussed in John Gaventa, *Power and Powerlessness: Quiescence and Rebellion in an Appalachian Valley* (Urbana: University of Illinois Press, 1980), 65–66. Useful studies of nineteenth-century rural life include John Mack Faragher, *Sugar Creek: Life on the Illinois Prairie* (New Haven: Yale University Press, 1986); Steven Hahn, *The Roots of Southern Populism: Yeoman Farmers and the Transformation of the Georgia Upcountry, 1850–1890* (New York: Oxford University Press, 1983); Altina Waller, *Feud: Hatfields, McCoys, and Social Change in Appalachia, 1860–1900* (Chapel Hill: University of North Carolina Press, 1988); and Thomas Summerhill, "The Farmers' Republic: Agrarian Protest and the Capitalist Transformation of Upstate New York" (Ph.D. diss., University of California at San Diego, 1993).

25. At times, the Huron and the Iroquois periodically initiated truces to permit members of both groups to pursue the game animals of the region. Most truces, however, were short-lived; once the number of animals began to decline with widespread hunting, hostilities were often renewed. Bruce Trigger, *The Children of Aataentsic: A History of the Huron People to 1660* (Montreal: McGill-Queen's University Press, 1976), 345, 488, 618. For more on buffer zones, see Richard White, *The Roots of Dependency: Subsistence, Environment, and Social Change among the Choctaws, Pawnees, and Navajos* (Lincoln: University of Nebraska Press, 1983), 9; and Elliot West, *The Way to the West: Essays on the Central Plains* (Albuquerque: University of New Mexico Press, 1995), 61–62.

26. Alfred B. Street, *Woods and Waters; or, the Saranacs and Racket Lake* (New York: M. Doolady, 1860), 210. (The odd spelling in this quotation is a result of Street's efforts to set down Moody's distinctive Adirondacks dialect.) Dean R. Snow, "Eastern Abenaki," and Gordon M. Day, "Western Abenaki," in *The Handbook of North American Indians: Northeast,* ed. William Sturtevant, vol. 15 (Washington, D.C.: Smithsonian, 1978), 137–47, 148–59; and Aber and King, *History of Hamilton County,* 19. See also Hilda Robtoy, Dee Brightstar, Tom Obomsawin, and John Moody, "The Abenaki and the Northern Forest," in *The Future of the Northern Forest,* ed. Christopher McGrory Klyza and Stephen C. Trombulak (Hanover, N.H.: University Press of New England, 1994), 27–35.

27. For some rather gory tales of fights over hunting grounds, see Samuel Hammond, *Hills, Lakes, and Forest Streams; or, a Tramp in the Chateaugay Woods* (New York: J. C. Derby, 1854), 71–77. Another often-told story in this regard is that of Nat Foster, who allegedly killed the Indian Peter Woods in 1832. Although often taken as evidence of the antipathy existing between whites and Indians in the Adirondacks, it is worth noting that Foster and Woods were neighbors, part of a larger mixed settlement made up of both white and Indian families. Alfred L. Donaldson, *A History of the Adirondacks* (New York: Century, 1921), 1:118–19.

28. 1880 Population Census, Manuscript Schedules, Hamilton County, Roll 837, T9, Records of the Bureau of the Census, RG 29, National Archives. It is possible there were more Indians dwelling in the area than such records indicate, for many census takers neglected to record Native Americans out of a belief that they were not citizens. See Aber and King, *History of Hamilton County,* 21–22.

29. The quote about the cost of shipping crops to market can be found in Joel T. Headley, *The Adirondack; or, Life in the Woods,* rev. ed. (New York: Scribner, Armstrong, 1875), 411–12. See also *Heartwood: The Adirondack Homestead Life of W. Donald Burnap, as told to Marylee Armour* (Baldwinsville, N.Y.: Brown Newspapers, 1988), 50; and New York Forest Commission, *First Annual Report, 1885,* 40. The quote about fish and potatoes is from David Shepard Merrill, "The Education of a Young Pioneer in the Northern Adirondacks in Franklin and Clinton Counties after the Civil War," *New York History* 39 (July 1958): 240. A discussion of letting livestock roam loose in the woods can be found in Henry Conklin, *Through "Poverty's Vale": A Hardscrabble Boyhood in Upstate New York, 1832–1862* (Syracuse: Syracuse University Press, 1974), 111. For a useful overview of Euro-American settlement in upstate New York, consult Alan Taylor, "The Great Change Begins: Settling the Forest of Central New York," *New York History* 76 (July 1995): 265–90.

30. Much of this information on foraging is from Conklin, *Through "Poverty's Vale,"* 34–35, 48, 51–52, 107–8. Bill Smith tells of his mother killing deer for the family. Smith, *Tales from the Featherbed: Adirondack Stories and Songs* (Greenfield Center, N.Y.: Bowman Books, 1994), 18–19. For a discussion of the use of shanties, see New York Forest Commission, *Annual Report, 1892* (Albany: James B. Lyon, 1893), 30. References to the gathering of spruce gum (used in the manufacture of chewing gum) and ginseng can be found in Ira Gray, *My Memories, 1886–1977* (N.p., n.d.), 59; "Bill Rasbeck's Diary," in *Cranberry Lake from Wilderness to Adirondack Park,* ed. Albert Fowler (Syracuse: Syracuse University Press, 1968), 39–40; and New York Forest Commission, *First Annual Report, 1885,* 91–92; see also Mary Hufford, "American Ginseng and the Idea of the Commons," *Folklife Center News* 19 (winter-spring 1997): 3–18. Estimates of the lengths of traplines in the Adirondacks vary from sixteen to fifty miles; it sometimes took residents over a week to check all their traps. See Seneca Ray Stoddard, *Old Times in the Adirondacks: The Narrative of a Trip into the Wilderness in 1873* (Burlington, Vt.: George Little Press, 1971), 124–25; Street, *Woods and Waters,* 43; and the testimony of Charles Blanchard in *The People of the State of New York v. Jennie H. Ladew and Joseph H.*

Ladew (Supreme Court of New York, Appellate Division, Third Department), 273. (A copy of this last document can be found at the Adirondack Museum Archives, where it is filed as Manuscript 65–26, Box 6.) A useful survey of Adirondacks plant life is included in Michael Kudish, *Adirondack Upland Flora: An Ecological Perspective* (Saranac, N.Y.: Chauncy Press, 1992).

31. New York Forest Commission, *First Annual Report, 1885,* 21; *Report, 1895,* 106. For discussions of common rights ideology in the United States, see Steven Hahn, "Hunting, Fishing, and Foraging: Common Rights and Class Relations in the Postbellum South," *Radical History Review* 26 (1982): 37–64; Stephen Aron, *How the West Was Lost: The Transformation of Kentucky from Daniel Boone to Henry Clay* (Baltimore: Johns Hopkins University Press, 1996), 102–23, and "Pigs and Hunters: 'Rights in the Woods' on the Trans-Appalachian Frontier," in *Contact Points: American Frontiers from the Mohawk Valley to the Mississippi, 1750–1830,* ed. Andrew Cayton and Frederika Teute (Chapel Hill: University of North Carolina Press, 1998), 175–204; Lloyd C. Irland, *Wildlands and Woodlots: The Story of New England's Forests* (Hanover, N.H.: University Press of New England, 1982), 72; and Judd, *Common Lands, Common People,* 40–47. A useful glimpse of this ideology at work in the Adirondacks can be found in Lloyd Blankman, "Burt Conklin, the Greatest Trapper," *New York Folklore Quarterly* 22 (December 1966): 274–97, which discusses the setting of traplines and the erection of shelters on private and state-owned lands.

32. Kenneth Durant, *The Adirondack Guide-Boat* (Camden, Maine: International Marine Publishing, 1980), 44. Blankman, "Burt Conklin, the Greatest Trapper," 281–82, 289. The most famous feud in the Adirondacks is the one between Alvah Dunning and Ned Buntline. See Harold Hochschild, *Township 34: A History* (N.p., 1952), 154; Stoddard, *Old Times in the Adirondacks,* 110–11.

33. Merrill, "Education of a Young Pioneer," 246; Charles Brumley, *Guides of the Adirondacks: A History* (Utica, N.Y.: North Country Books, 1994), 128. Such practices would seem to fit well with the recent scholarship by legal theorists on social norms. According to such research, many everyday interactions among closely knit groups are governed by informal norms that help people achieve order without law. See Robert C. Ellickson, *Order without Law: How Neighbors Settle Disputes* (Cambridge: Harvard University Press, 1991).

34. For more on the killing of dogs, see *Boonville (New York) Herald,* November 11, 1897; Rodney West, "Restoring Hounding," *Forest and Stream* 66 (January 6, 1906): 18; and Ira Gray, *Follow My Moccasin's Tracks* (Schuylerville, N.Y.: Napaul Publishers, 1975), 106–7. Accounts from elsewhere in the rural Northeast at this time tell of frequent ambushes arising out of disagreements over trapping and hunting. Edward Ives, ed., "Wilbur Day: Hunter, Guide, and Poacher: An Autobiography," *Northeast Folklore* 26 (1985): 50. For stories of running off intruders on local lands, see Hochschild, *Township 34,* 157; and Hammond, *Hills, Lakes, and Forest Streams,* 71–77.

35. William F. Fox, *A History of the Lumber Industry in the State of New York.* Bureau of Forestry Bulletin No. 34 (Washington, D.C.: GPO, 1902); Terrie, *Contested Terrain,* 35–38. Even today, large timber companies in Maine

and New York allow public access on their lands for hunting and camping. Ireland, *Wildlands and Woodlots,* 71–72.

36. New York Forest Commission, *Annual Report, 1891* (Albany: James B. Lyon, 1892), 6.

37. New York Fisheries, Game, and Forest Commission, *Second Annual Report, 1896* (Albany: Wynkoop, Hallenbeck, Crawford, 1897), 92.

38. The most thorough study of the Adirondacks forest at the time of the Forest Preserve's creation has been done by Barbara McMartin, who asserts that "as late as 1885, no more than fifteen to thirty percent of the forest cover had been taken from little more than a third of the original park." Barbara McMartin, *The Great Forest of the Adirondacks* (Utica, N.Y.: North Country Books, 1994), 68–69, 93.

39. A technical discussion of the parasitic links between deer and moose can be found in Thomas Nudds, "Retroductive Logic in Retrospect: The Ecological Effects of Meningeal Worms," *Journal of Wildlife Management* 54 (July 1990): 396–402; and Frederick Gilbert, "Retroductive Logic and the Effects of Meningeal Worms: A Comment," *Journal of Wildlife Management* 56 (July 1992): 614–16. For a broader discussion of moose in the Adirondacks and of the edge effect, see Philip Terrie, *Wildlife and Wilderness: A History of Adirondack Mammals* (Fleischmanns, N.Y.: Purple Mountain Press, 1993), 77–80; and William Cronon, *Changes in the Land: Indians, Colonists, and the Ecology of New England* (New York: Hill and Wang, 1983), 51.

40. Aber and King, *History of Hamilton County,* 148; Seneca Ray Stoddard, *The Adirondacks: Illustrated* (Albany: Weed, Parsons, 1874), 95, 113.

41. Donaldson, *History of the Adirondacks,* 1:320–29; Frank Graham Jr., *The Adirondack Park: A Political History* (New York: Alfred A. Knopf, 1978), 33–35; Northrup, *Camps and Tramps,* 111; "Theodore Roosevelt: Founder of the Boone and Crockett Club," in *American Big Game in Its Haunts,* ed. George Bird Grinnell (New York: Harper and Brothers, 1904), 16; Martin L. Fausold, *Gifford Pinchot: Bull Moose Progressive* (Syracuse: Syracuse University Press, 1961), 8; and "The Changed Adirondacks," *Forest and Stream* 51 (November 26, 1898): 431. Smith's quotation is from Brenda Parnes, "Trespass: A History of Land-Use Policy in the Adirondack Forest Region of Northern New York State" (Ph.D. diss., New York University, 1989), 122.

42. Testimony of William Helms from *The People of the State of New York v. Jennie H. Ladew and Joseph H. Ladew,* 413; Pierce is quoted in Craig Gilborn, *Adirondack Furniture and the Rustic Tradition* (New York: Harry N. Abrams, 1987), 59. The debate over the degree of market orientation of rural folk during the eighteenth and nineteenth centuries has been ongoing since the early 1900s. Useful recent contributions to the discussion include Steven Hahn, *Roots of Southern Populism;* Allan Kulikoff, *The Agrarian Origins of American Capitalism* (Charlottesville: University Press of Virginia, 1992); Christopher Clark, *The Roots of Rural Capitalism: Western Massachusetts, 1780–1860* (Ithaca: Cornell University Press, 1990); and Winifred Barr Rothenberg, *From Market-Places to a Market Economy: The Transformation of Rural Massachusetts, 1750–1850* (Chicago: University of Chicago Press, 1992).

CHAPTER 2. PUBLIC PROPERTY AND PRIVATE PARKS

1. New York Forest Commission, *First Annual Report, 1885,* 82. In 1895, the Forest Commission was merged with several other preexisting departments and renamed the Fisheries, Game, and Forest Commission. In 1900, this organization was retitled the Forest, Fish and Game Commission, before becoming in 1911 the Conservation Commission. For simplicity's sake, I have utilized the original and less-cumbersome term Forest Commission throughout these chapters. For an overview of these administrative changes, see Association for the Protection of the Adirondacks, *Twelfth Annual Report of the President* (n.p., 1913), 4; and Association for the Protection of the Adirondacks, *Eighteenth Annual Report of the President* (n.p., 1919), 28–34.

For statistics on the acreage of the Adirondack Park, see New York Fisheries, Game, and Forest Commission, *Third Annual Report, 1897,* 269. Even today, the Adirondack Park is the largest park in the contiguous United States, exceeded in size only by the Alaska National Park created by the Alaska lands bill of 1980.

2. James Scott, *Seeing Like a State: How Certain Schemes to Improve the Human Condition Have Failed* (New Haven: Yale University Press, 1998).

3. New York Forest Commission, *First Annual Report, 1885,* 207–356; New York Forest, Fish and Game Commission, *List of Lands in the Forest Preserve* (Albany: James B. Lyon, 1901), 3.

4. New York Forest, Fish and Game Commission, *List of Lands in the Forest Preserve,* 165–66, 196.

5. Verplanck Colvin, *Report on the Progress of the Adirondack State Land Survey to the Year 1886* (Albany: Weed, Parsons, 1886), 7; *New York Tribune,* January 28, 1895; New York Fisheries, Game, and Forest Commission, *Second Annual Report, 1896,* 126.

6. New York Forest Commission, *Annual Report, 1890* (Albany: James B. Lyon, 1891), 163. See also Bernhard Fernow, "Adirondack Forestry Problems," *The Forester* 6 (October 1900): 231, in which Fernow asserts, "The first step... towards a technical management of the State's forest property must be a forest survey." The best overview of the mapping of the Adirondacks is Paul G. Bourcier, *History in the Mapping: Four Centuries of Adirondack Cartography* (Blue Mountain Lake, N.Y.: Adirondack Museum, 1986), 41–43.

7. *Report, 1895,* 28–29. For accounts of the destruction of property markers, see ibid., 28–29, 87; the change in the legal code can be found in New York Forest Commission, *Annual Report, 1888* (Albany: Troy Press, 1889), 16. My insights on the cartographic process come from Raymond B. Craib III, "Power and Cartography in Early Modern Spain and Early Colonial New Spain" (Seminar paper, Yale University, 1997); Scott, *Seeing Like a State,* 44–52; and Matthew Edney, *Mapping an Empire: The Geographical Construction of British India, 1765–1843* (Chicago: University of Chicago Press, 1997).

8. New York Forest Commission, *Second Annual Report, 1886,* 10; New York Forest Commission, *Annual Report, 1890,* 52.

9. For a detailed discussion of squatting and the "homestead ethic," see Stephen Aron, "Pioneers and Profiteers: Land Speculation and the Homestead Ethic in Frontier Kentucky," *Western Historical Quarterly* 23 (May 1992): 179–98.

10. New York State Assembly, *Reports of the Majority and Minority of the Committee on Public Lands and Forestry Relative to the Administration of the Laws in Relation to the Forest Preserve by the Forest Commission*, New York Assembly Document No. 81, 1891, 250. (Hereafter referred to as *Reports, 1891*.)

11. New York Fisheries, Game, and Forest Commission, *Second Annual Report, 1896*, 129, 334; Ted Aber, *Adirondack Folks* (Prospect, N.Y.: Prospect Books, 1980), 216. Additional tallies of the number of squatters can be found in Association for the Protection of the Adirondacks, *Fifteenth Annual Report of the President* (n.p., 1916), 23; Association for the Protection of the Adirondacks, *Sixteenth Annual Report of the President,*(n.p., 1917), 17; and Gurth Whipple, *Fifty Years of Conservation in New York State, 1885–1935* (Albany: James B. Lyon, 1935), 74. For an example of the complexities that could arise when local squatters sold lands to outsiders, see *The People of the State of New York v. Jennie H. Ladew and Joseph H. Ladew.*

12. New York Fisheries, Game, and Forest Commission, *Second Annual Report, 1896,* 334, 341; *Forest and Stream,* 61 (September 19, 1903): 213. See also *St. Regis (N.Y.) Adirondack News,* August 8, 1903; and *New York Times,* August 1, 1903, and October 5, 1910.

13. "The Commissioners have determined that, whatever may be done as regards to the present occupants of State lands, no further occupancies shall occur if they can prevent it." New York Fisheries, Game, and Forest Commission, *Second Annual Report, 1896,* 340; *New York Times,* August 1, 1903; "Squatters to be Fired," *Field and Stream* 10 (February 1906): 1059. A complete file of contested holdings can be found in: New York Forest Commission, Records of Occupancy, Bureau of Real Property, New York State Department of Environmental Conservation.

14. New York Forest, Fish and Game Commission, *Sixth Annual Report, 1900* (Albany: James B. Lyon, 1901), 63; "New York's New Protectors," *Forest and Stream* 58 (June 21, 1902): 481; "Adirondack Game Wardens," *Forest and Stream* 23 (October 2, 1884): 181; New York Forest Commission, *First Annual Report, 1885,* 13; Henry Chase, *Game Protection and Propagation in America: A Handbook of Practical Information for Officials and Others Interested in the Cause of Conservation of Wildlife* (Philadelphia: J.B. Lippincott, 1913), 126. An insightful examination of the foresters' European counterpart, the English gamekeeper, can be found in P.B. Munsche, "The Gamekeeper and English Rural Society, 1660–1830," *Journal of British Studies* 20 (spring 1981): 82–105. An illuminating account of the game warden's role in the twentieth-century American countryside can be found in David H. Swendsen, *Badge in the Wilderness: My Thirty Dangerous Years Combating Wildlife Violators* (Harrisburg, Penn.: Stackpole Books, 1985).

15. New York Forest Commission, *Second Annual Report, 1886,* 18; Whipple, *Fifty Years of Conservation in New York State,* 111–12; "The Adirondack Reservation," *Garden and Forest* 7 (March 7, 1894): 91; "The Need for More

Wardens," *Forest and Stream* 76 (April 8, 1911): 536; and "Conditions in the Adirondacks," *Forest and Stream* 76 (April 29, 1911): 658.

16. New York Fisheries Commission, *Twenty-third Annual Report, 1894* (Albany: James B. Lyon, 1895), 109, 155; A.P. Williams, "The Adirondacks in Summer," *Field and Stream* 13 (February, 1909): 883; "Conditions in the Adirondacks," *Forest and Stream* 76 (April 29, 1911): 658.

17. "Deer in the Adirondacks," *Forest and Stream* 25 (September 17, 1885): 147.

18. "Adirondack Deer Hounding," *Forest and Stream* 53 (October 28, 1899): 345.

19. Gray, *My Memories*, 17. (Gray concluded his tale by asserting that the local never again poached deer.) Interviews with Clarence Petty and Fred Fountain in Brumley, *Guides of the Adirondacks*, 206, 247.

20. "The Essex County Protector," *Forest and Stream* 53 (November 11, 1899), 387; *New York Tribune*, August 10, 1902; New York Forest, Fish and Game Commission, *Annual Reports for 1907, 1908, and 1909* (Albany: James B. Lyon, 1910), 367. As Henry Chase observed in 1913, if wardens "do their duty and cause a prosecution they become unpopular with their neighbors." Chase, *Game Protection and Propagation in America*, 106–7; see also Ted Aber and Stella King, *Tales from an Adirondack County* (Prospect, N.Y.: Prospect Books, 1961), 88.

21. Smith, *Tales from the Featherbed*, 21; *New York Tribune*, August 10, 1902; J.H. Woodward, "Protection of Deer in the Adirondacks," *Forest and Stream* 52 (February 4, 1899): 86.

22. New York Fisheries Commission, *Fifteenth Annual Report, 1886* (Albany: Argus, 1887), 102; *Reports, 1891*, 174; New York Forest, Fish and Game Commission, *Sixth Annual Report, 1900*, 63; New York Forest, Fish and Game Commission, *Annual Reports for 1907, 1908, 1909*, 359.

23. Corruption among foresters was a reoccurring problem in the force. For examples, see *New York Times*, September 11, 1894; *New York Herald*, September 11 and September 14, 1894; "Adirondack Timber Stealing," *Forest and Stream* 70 (February 8, 1908): 219; "Adirondack Timber Thefts," *Forest and Stream* 70 (April 4, 1908): 538; *New York Herald*, August 25, 1910.

24. "The State grants exemption from taxes provided the landowner will agree to restrict all timber cutting to certain species and to a minimum diameter of twelve inches." New York Forest Commission, *Annual Report, 1893*, 1:10, 153, 2:40–47.

25. "Preserves in the Adirondack Park," *Forest and Stream* 43 (December 22, 1894): 552; New York Forest Commission, *Annual Report, 1893*, 1:9–10; Edward Comstock and Mark C. Webster, eds., *The Adirondack League Club, 1890–1990* (Old Forge, N.Y.: Adirondack League Club, 1990), 12; "An Ideal Game Preserve," *Recreation* 14 (April 1901): 263–65; and Seneca Ray Stoddard, *The Adirondacks: Illustrated*, 23rd ed. (Glen Falls, N.Y.: 1898), 219b. A survey of Adirondacks private parks can be found in H.L. Ives, "Some Adirondack Preserves," *Forest and Stream* 50 (May 21, 1898): 406.

26. *Lelia E. Marsh and George W. Ostrander v. Ne-Ha-Sa-Ne Park Association* (Supreme Court of Hamilton County, March 1897, Civil Case #352,

Hamilton County Court House), 33–34. It bears noting that during this time, the state's force of foresters for the entire Adirondacks was scarcely much larger than the number of men Webb had employed to protect his park. For more on the creation of Ne-Ha-Sa-Ne, see the *New York Times,* June 29, 1891. The figure for Ne-Ha-Sa-Ne's acreage comes from New York Forest Commission, *Annual Report, 1893,* 1:154.

27. *Lelia E. Marsh and George W. Ostrander v. Ne-Ha-Sa-Ne Park Association,* 12. The 1,580 signs around William Rockefeller's park in the Adirondacks read: "NOTICE! PRIVATE PARK. All persons are hereby warned not to hunt, fish, camp or in any manner trespass upon the following described premises or any stream or body of water within their boundaries, or disturb or interfere in any way with the fish or wild birds or wild animals upon said premises, under strict penalty of the law, as the premises described now constitute a private park for the protection, preservation and propagation of fish, birds and wild animals." *William Rockefeller v. Oliver Lamora* (New York Supreme Court, Cases and Briefs, 4004, Appellate Division, 1896–1911, New York State Library), Case on Appeal, 26–28.

28. Adirondack League Club. *Adirondack League Club Hand-Book for 1894* (n.p., n.d.), 17–18; Comstock and Webster, *Adirondack League Club,* 12, 58. For information on poaching and the dispute over wages, see Adirondack League Club, *Annual Report, 1911* (n.p., n.d.), 12–13; and Brumley, *Guides of the Adirondacks,* 47–48. One wonders whether, having lost the dispute over wages, guides decided to give themselves an informal "raise" by taking game from the ALC's lands.

29. New York State Assembly, *Report of the Special Committee Appointed to Investigate as to What Additional Lands Shall Be Acquired within the Forest Preserve,* Document No. 43, 1899, 9.

30. *Albany Argus,* September 28 and October 12, 1903; *New York World,* September 22, 1903; *New York Herald,* September 29 and October 11, 1903; *New York Times,* August 26, 1910; Neal S. Burdick, "Who Killed Orrando P. Dexter?" *Adirondack Life* (May-June 1982): 23–49. For more on Dexter, see *A Biographical Sketch of Orrando Perry Dexter* (n.p., n.d. [1903?]), located in the New York Public Library.

31. *Malone (N.Y.) Palladium,* January 21, 1904. For instances of arson and tearing down of signs at the Adirondack League Club, see Adirondack League Club, *Annual Report, 1899* (n.p., n.d.), 24; and Adirondack League Club, *Annual Report, 1904* (n.p., n.d.), 15.

32. *New York Times,* November 23, 1904. See also *New York Herald,* November 25, 1904.

33. Adirondack League Club, *Annual Report, 1898* (n.p., n.d.), 33.

34. Samuel Hopkins Adams, "William Rockefeller, Maker of Wilderness," *Collier's* 35 (April 22, 1905): 15. For more on Rockefeller's park in the Adirondacks, see Neil Suprenant, *Brandon: Boomtown to Nature Preserve* (Paul Smith's, N.Y.: St. Regis Press, 1982).

35. *William Rockefeller v. Oliver Lamora,* Case on Appeal, 65; Adams, "William Rockefeller, Maker of Wilderness," 18. Lamora's pension was eight dollars a month. *Utica (N.Y.) Herald-Dispatch,* September 29, 1903.

36. *William Rockefeller v. Oliver Lamora*, Case on Appeal, 65; Statement under Rule 41, 40–41.

37. *New York Times*, December 28, 1904; Raymond Spears, "Some Legal Aspects of the Case of Rockefeller vs. Lamora," *Forest and Stream* 65 (October 21, 1905): 335–36. See also the *New York Times*, June 29, 1902, December 17, 1903, and December 28, 1904. Lamora's penalty of 18¢ worked out to 6¢ per supposed trespass. Adams, "William Rockefeller, Maker of Wilderness," 18.

38. *New York Times*, July 3 and September 27, 1903.

39. *William Rockefeller v. Oliver Lamora*, Statement under Rule 41, 63, Respondent's Brief and Points, 8; Aber, *Adirondack Folks*, 135; Spears, "Some Legal Aspects," 355. For more on McNeil, see his testimony in *William Rockefeller v. Oliver Lamora*, Case on Appeal, 137–38.

40. "The Passing of the Adirondack Guide," *Forest and Stream* 43 (December 22, 1894): 529; *Albany Press-Knickerbocker*, September 20, 1903; and Peter Flint, "Private Parks Do Not Protect Game," *Forest and Stream* (December 13, 1913): 757–58.

41. Hochschild, *Township 34*, 314.

42. New York Fisheries, Game, and Forest Commission, *Third Annual Report, 1897*, 140; New York Forest, Fish and Game Commission, *Seventh Annual Report, 1901* (Albany: James B. Lyon, 1902), 20–23; New York Forest, Fish and Game Commission, *Eighth and Ninth Annual Reports, 1902–1903*, 43; and John Ise, *The United States Forest Policy* (New Haven: Yale University Press, 1920), 144. For a summary of the increases in state-owned lands within the forest reserve, see the Association for the Protection of the Adirondacks, *Eighteenth Annual Report of the President*, 7.

43. In 1970, for instance, thirty-two individual or corporate owners held title to about 30 percent of all Adirondack Park land. See Halper, "A Rich Man's Paradise," 194–99, especially 194, n. 5; *New York World*, September 28, 1903.

CHAPTER 3. WORKING-CLASS WILDERNESS

1. "Report of the New York Forest Commission," *Garden and Forest* 4 (October 14, 1891): 481; *New York Times*, October 6, 1889. See also *Garden and Forest* 2 (October 16, 1889): 493.

2. New York State Assembly, *Report of the Committee Appointed to Investigate as to What Additional Lands Shall be Acquired within the Forest Preserve*, 4. See also the account written by one of the committee members, Martin Van Buren Ives, *Through the Adirondacks in Eighteen Days* (New York: Wynkoop, Hallenbeck, Crawford, 1899), 38.

3. Both of Cronon's pathbreaking works position capitalism—specifically, the market—as the main engine of environmental destruction. See Cronon, *Changes in the Land*, and *Nature's Metropolis: Chicago and the Great West* (New York: W. W. Norton, 1991). Donald Worster's most eloquent critique of the "capitalistic ethos" can be found in *Dust Bowl: The Southern Plains in the 1930's* (New York: Oxford University Press, 1979), 6. For other environmental historians who have incorporated capitalism (albeit far less systematically) into their analyses, see Reiger, *American Sportsmen and the Origins of Conserva-*

tion, 60; Dunlap, *Saving America's Wildlife,* 5; and Nash, *Wilderness and the American Mind,* 8–43, 238, 388.

4. "The Forest," *Garden and Forest* 3 (September 10, 1890): 445–46. This critique of rural folk was echoed in many other conservationist writings at this time. See, for example, Ernest Bruncken, *North American Forests and Forestry: Their Relations to the National Life of the American People* (New York: G. P. Putnam's Sons, 1900), 54–56; and P. P. Schotzka, *American Forests* (Minneapolis, 1887), 11.

5. For a work that attempts to explore Euro-American noncapitalistic traditions of resource management in relation to the famous example of "the fisherman's problem," see Sean Cadigan, "The Moral Economy of the Commons: Ecology and Equity in the Newfoundland Cod Fishery, 1815–1855," *Labour/Le Travail* 43 (spring 1999): 9–42. The classic environmental history of American fisheries remains Arthur McEvoy, *The Fisherman's Problem: Ecology and the Law in the California Fisheries, 1850–1980* (New York: Cambridge University Press, 1986).

6. *Reports, 1891,* 161–63. Basselin's position as both Forest Commissioner and lumberman would eventually lead to charges of conflict of interest. See McMartin, *Great Forest of the Adirondacks,* 93–96, 198.

7. New York Forest Commission, *First Annual Report, 1885,* 120–21; New York Forest Commission, *Annual Report, 1888,* xi.

8. *Reports, 1891,* 363.

9. *Report, 1895,* 5.

10. Ibid., 760–61. For a similar statement, see the testimony of John Burke, *Reports, 1891,* 372.

11. All trespasses during the Forest Preserve's early years were entered into a single comprehensive ledger. See New York Forest Commission, Records of Trespass, Ledger, Bureau of Real Property, Department of Environmental Conservation, 23, 30, 239. (Hereafter *Ledger.*)

12. *Reports, 1891,* 372; New York Forest, Fish and Game Commission, *Annual Reports for 1907, 1908, 1909,* 168; *Ledger,* 236; New York Forest Commission, *Annual Report, 1890,* 50.

13. New York Fisheries, Game, and Forest Commission, *Preliminary Report to the Fifth Annual Report, 1899* (Albany: James B. Lyon, 1900), 59–60; New York Fisheries, Game, and Forest Commission, *Third Annual Report, 1897,* 274; New York Forest, Fish and Game Commission, *Annual Reports for 1904, 1905, 1906* (Albany: James B. Lyon, 1907), 60, 110; New York Forest, Fish and Game Commission, *Sixteenth Annual Report, 1910* (Albany: James B. Lyon, 1911), 67.

14. *Report, 1895,* 31, 785; New York Fisheries, Game, and Forest Commission, *Preliminary Report to the Fifth Annual Report, 1899,* 59–60.

15. *Ledger,* 221, 236; *Report, 1895,* 505; *Reports, 1891,* 278, 372.

16. New York Forest Commission, *Annual Report, 1890,* 51; New York Forest, Fish and Game Commission, *Sixth Annual Report, 1900,* 35–36; Nelson Courtlandt Brown, *Forest Products: Their Manufacture and Use* (New York: John Wiley and Sons, 1919), 351. A highly experienced shingle maker

could shave 400 to 500 shingles a day. For a description of shingle making in Herkimer County, see Conklin, *Through "Poverty's Vale,"* 102–3, 156.

17. Accounts of the scale of timber theft by lumber companies can be found in New York Forest Commission, *First Annual Report, 1885,* 28–29; McMartin, *Great Forest of the Adirondacks,* 3–4, 92–96; *New York Times,* September 18, 1889; and *Report, 1895,* 30–32. For a reference to oral contracts to cut wood, see *Report, 1895,* 149.

18. For a discussion of the rise of pulp mills in the Adirondacks, see Eleanor Amigo and Mark Neuffer, *Beyond the Adirondacks: The Story of the St. Regis Paper Company* (Westport, Conn.: Greenwood Press, 1980), 8–10; and "The Lumber Industry in New York," *Forestry and Irrigation* 8 (September 1902): 381–85. My figures on timber production come from Barbara McMartin's analysis of Adirondacks forest composition. McMartin, *Great Forest of the Adirondacks,* 3, 117–22.

19. Letter of D. F. Sperry, *Woods and Waters* 5 (summer 1902): 17. See also the resolution against lumbering on state lands in "Brown's Tract Guides," *Forest and Stream* 60 (January 24, 1903): 71. Pond's testimony can be found in *Orrando P. Dexter v. Warren Joseph Alfred,* (Supreme Court of Franklin County, 1891, Cases on Appeal: Box 7, Folder 1, Position 2, Franklin County Courthouse), 60–61. The editorial appears in the *St. Regis (N.Y.) Adirondack News,* February 7, 1891. See also the case of arson against a paper company reported in the *St. Regis (N.Y.) Adirondack News,* May 23, 1903; and the complaints of several guides about lumbering operations in Herbert F. Keith, *Man of the Woods* (Syracuse: Syracuse University Press, 1972), 32, 75.

20. *Report, 1895,* 571; New York Forest Commission, *First Annual Report, 1885,* 28, 120–21; *Reports, 1891,* 282. Such findings would seem to fit with the arguments advanced by some of the critics of Hobsbawm's model of social banditry, who have asserted that many bandits, rather than taking the side of fellow community members, often sought to form alliances with or gain entry into the upper classes. The leading proponent of this position is Anton Blok in "The Peasant and the Brigand: Social Banditry Reconsidered," *Comparative Studies in Society and History* 14 (September 1972): 494–503; a useful recent collection in this vein is Richard W. Slatta, ed., *Bandidos: The Varieties of Latin American Banditry* (New York: Greenwood, 1987).

21. New York Forest, Fish and Game Commission, *Sixth Annual Report, 1900,* 35–36. For accounts of collusion between forestry officials and the lumber industry, see *New York Tribune,* September 11, 1894; *New York Herald,* September 11, 1894, August 25, 1910; *New York Times,* September 11 and September 14, 1894, August 30, 1910; *Albany Times-Union,* August 23, August 29, and August 30, 1910; Association for the Protection of the Adirondacks, *Tenth Annual Report of the President* (n.p., 1911), 25–26; and McMartin, *Great Forest of the Adirondacks,* 97, 109.

22. New York Fisheries, Game, and Forest Commission, *Third Annual Report, 1897,* 274; New York Forest Commission, *Annual Report, 1890,* 51; *Reports, 1891,* 288. See also *Report, 1895,* 500. For accounts of timber theft in the twentieth century, see New York Forest, Fish and Game Commission, *An-*

nual Reports for 1904, 1905, 1906, 110; and New York Forest, Fish and Game Commission, *Sixteenth Annual Report, 1910,* 67.

23. Quotations are from the 1890 prospectus of the Adirondack League Club, reprinted in Comstock and Webster, *Adirondack League Club,* 10. For more on the British roots of American sports hunting, see Samuel Truett, "A Wilderness of One's Own: Sports Hunting and Manliness in Nineteenth-Century America" (seminar paper, Yale University, 1992). As Thomas Altherr and John Reiger have recently noted, the historical scholarship on hunting in the United States is still quite thin. Altherr and Reiger, "Academic Historians and Hunting: A Call for More and Better Scholarship," *Environmental History Review* 19 (fall 1995): 39–56. One exception to this trend is Stuart A. Marks, *Southern Hunting in Black and White: Nature, History, and Ritual in a Carolina Community* (Princeton: Princeton University Press, 1991). By contrast, the material on hunting in British culture is far richer. See, for example, John M. MacKenzie, *The Empire of Nature: Hunting, Conservation, and British Imperialism* (Manchester, U.K.: Manchester University Press, 1988).

24. *New York Tribune,* October 16, 1893. For a survey of different sport-hunting techniques in the Adirondacks, see Clinton Hart Merriam, *The Mammals of the Adirondack Region* (New York: Henry Holt, 1886), 124–35.

25. "Deer Slaughter in the Adirondacks," *Forest and Stream* 3 (November 26, 1874): 249; J.H. Woodward, "Protection of Deer in the Adirondacks," *Forest and Stream* 52 (February 4, 1899): 86. See also C. Fenton, "Adirondack Slaughter," *Forest and Stream* 4 (March 18, 1875), 91; and New York Fisheries, Game, and Forest Commission, *First Annual Report, 1895* (Albany: Wynkoop, Hallenbeck, Crawford, 1896), 206. The arguments of many American sports hunters echo the English claim that the elite possessed a "gentleman's right" to hunt.

26. Bill Smith, "Songs and Stories from the 'Featherbed,'" (Voorheesville, NY: Front Hall Enterprises, 1987), sound recording. See also the testimony of Paul Blanchard, who admitted, "We hunted in and out of season." Paul Blanchard, "Reminiscing the Old Guide Days" (August 10, 1986, Tape C-46, Adirondack Museum Archives), sound recording.

27. "The Adirondack Deer Law," *Forest and Stream* 51 (November 12, 1898): 391; New York Fisheries, Game, and Forest Commission, *First Annual Report, 1895,* 212.

28. *Boonville (N.Y.) Herald,* April 15, 1897. This article is an interview with Dunning, in which the writer tried to render Dunning's distinctive Adirondacks dialect. Dunning was arrested for poaching a deer in 1894. For the record of his arrest, see New York Fisheries Commission, *Twenty-third Annual Report, 1894* (Albany: James B. Lyon, 1895), 128.

29. Charles Fenno Hoffman, *Wild Scenes in the Forest and Prairie* (New York: William H. Colyer, 1843), 69. See also Cheney's lament about having to kill "beautiful" deer "with their bright eyes, graceful necks, and sinewy legs.... I wish I could get my living without killing this beautiful animal!—But I must live, and I suppose they were made to die. The cry of the deer, when in the agonies of death, is the awfulest sound I ever heard." Quoted in Brumley, *Guides of the Adirondacks,* 108.

30. Merrill, "The Education of a Young Pioneer," 251–52. As one observer noted in a similar vein, "Their [the Adirondackers'] reason for hunting...is to obtain meat, and they do not believe in killing for the mere pleasure of the sport." J.B. Burnham, "Adirondack Deer Law," *Forest and Stream* 41 (July 29, 1893): 75.

31. Edward Rawson, "An Adirondack Elegy," *Forest and Stream* 46 (February 8, 1896): 116. Rawson notes that this poem was delivered orally; it was written down only when he expressed interest in having it published in *Forest and Stream*. For a similar example of Adirondackers protecting a favored local deer, see the *Boonville (N.Y.) Herald,* March 5, 1903.

32. Terrie, *Contested Terrain,* 132; *Boonville (N.Y.) Herald,* November 9, 1882.

33. Headley, *Adirondack,* rev. ed., 331; *Boonville (N.Y.) Herald,* January 25, 1883; X [pseud.], "June Deer Floating," *Forest and Stream* 26 (July 8, 1886): 469; and "The Boycott in the Woods," *Forest and Stream* 27 (July 29, 1886).

34. New York Fisheries Commission, *Twenty-third Annual Report, 1894,* 158. J. Warren Pond described a similar shift in his district in New York Fisheries Commission, *Nineteenth Annual Report, 1890* (Albany: James B. Lyon, 1891), 201.

35. Norman J. Van Valkenburgh, *The Adirondack Forest Preserve: A Narrative of the Evolution of the Adirondack Forest Preserve of New York State* (Blue Mountain Lake, N.Y.: Adirondack Museum, 1979), 72; Aber, *Adirondack Folks,* 135–36; *St. Regis (N.Y.) Adirondack News,* November 28, 1903; *New York Tribune,* May 11, 1906; and "A Hounding Prosecution Threatened," *Forest and Stream* 66 (April 7, 1906): 547.

36. *American Angler* 3 (May 5, 1883): 276; *New York Tribune,* July 3, 1903.

37. "Current Literature and Reviews," *Forestry Quarterly* 1 (October 1902): 27; New York Fisheries Commission, *Sixteenth Annual Report, 1887,* 161; and New York Fisheries Commission, *Twenty-third Annual Report, 1894,* 128, 155.

38. *Boonville (N.Y.) Herald,* April 15, 1897. Further references to the supposedly "un-American" aspects of the game law in the Adirondacks can be found in T.S. Palmer, *Private Game Preserves and Their Future in the United States,* United States Bureau of Biological Survey, Circular No. 72 (Washington, D.C.: GPO, 1910), 7; and New York State Assembly, *Report of the Committee Appointed to Investigate as to What Additional Lands Shall be Acquired within the Forest Preserve,* 4. For thoughtful studies of the relationship between republicanism and the right to game, see Harry L. Watson, "'The Common Rights of Mankind': Subsistence, Shad, and Commerce in the Early Republican South," *Journal of American History* (June 1996): 13–43; James A. Tober, *Who Owns the Wildlife? The Political Economy of Conservation in Nineteenth-Century America* (Westport, Conn.: Greenwood Press, 1981), 18–20; and Alan Taylor, "The Unadilla Hunt Club: Nature, Class, and Power in Rural New York during the Early Republic" (manuscript, July 1996).

39. Hammond, *Hills, Lakes, and Forest Streams,* 118 (the odd spelling is a result of Hammond's effort to record the Adirondacks dialect); quoted in Terrie, *Wildlife and Wilderness,* 70; Gray, *My Memories,* 17. Other local statements about the Adirondacks being outside of the reach of Albany lawmakers can be found in George H. Worden, "Not Guilty; or, the Farce of Adirondack Game Protection," *Outing Magazine* 14 (April 1889): 69; and "The Changed Adirondacks," *Forest and Stream* 51 (November 26, 1898): 431. For an attack on this natural rights argument, see "Essentially a Thief," *Forest and Stream* 51 (August 13, 1898): 121. Deer meat was often called "mountain mutton," in apparent reference to its importance to the local diet.

40. Conklin, *Through "Poverty's Vale,"* 107–8; New York Fisheries, Game, and Forest Commission, *First Annual Report, 1895,* 205, 209; *Boonville (N.Y.) Herald,* October 22, October 27, and December 3, 1885. See also *Boonville (N.Y.) Herald,* February 3, 1898. Even today, Adirondackers draw a distinction between "outlaws" (people illegally killing deer for trophies) and "woods bandits" (people who are out of work and need wild game to survive). See Felicia Romano McMahon, "Wilderness and Tradition: Power, Politics, and Play in the Adirondacks" (Ph.D. diss., University of Pennsylvania, 1992), 186.

41. Deposition of George B. Howland, November 10, 1914. Lake Pleasant Town Records, Hamilton County, New York.

42. *Hamilton County (N.Y.) Record,* February 1, 1895. See also the fierce debate in "The Anti-Hounding Law," *Recreation* 14 (June 1901): 445–46. For accounts of accidental shootings of guides, see *Malone (N.Y.) Palladium,* September 11, 1902; *Malone (N.Y.) Palladium,* September 17, 1903; *Boonville (N.Y.) Herald,* January 10, 1901; and "The Adirondack Man Killings," *Forest and Stream* 59 (November 1, 1902): 350.

43. *New York Times,* September 17, 1889. In the 1890s and 1900s, many Adirondacks towns and counties voted to tighten restrictions on the taking of local game. In 1894, for instance, the board of supervisors of Franklin County passed rules closing several rivers to fishing for a period of three years. That same year, the board of supervisors of Herkimer County voted in similar measures for several creeks in the county. New York Fisheries Commission, *Twenty-second Annual Report, 1893,* 423–24. Further examples can be found in Aber and King, *History of Hamilton County,* 212, 218, 415, 573; and *Boonville (N.Y.) Herald,* January 18, 1912.

44. "Adirondack Guides' Association," *Forest and Stream* 46 (May 2, 1896): 354. For accounts of the impact of new environmental controls elsewhere, see E.P. Thompson, *Customs in Common;* Steven Hahn, "Hunting, Fishing, and Foraging," 43–51; and Rangarajan, *Fencing the Forest,* 109.

45. Piseco [pseud.], "The Adirondack Guide System," *Forest and Stream* 20 (May 3, 1883): 262–63. See also the article "Guides and Tourists" in the same issue.

46. *New York Times,* July 14, 1895.

47. "The Adirondack Guide System," 262–64. See also Brumley, *Guides of the Adirondacks,* 20, 167.

48. A copy of the 1897 broadside is available in the Adirondack Guides' Association file at the Adirondack Museum. A journal article from the same time

period reported that the AGA consisted of 250 guides and 100 honorary members. Seaver A. Miller, "The Adirondacks as a Resort for Sportsmen," *Recreation* 7 (August 1897): 128.

49. New York Forest Commission, *Annual Report, 1893,* 350; Seaver A. Miller, "The Adirondack Guides' Association," *Sportsman's Magazine* 2 (March 1898): 129–32; "Adirondack Guides' Association," *Forest and Stream* 38 (March 24, 1892): 274; "Adirondack Guides' Association, Season of 1897," Adirondack Museum Archives, broadside. Such associations were not unique to the Adirondacks; there was also a long tradition of guides' unions in the Swiss Alps. *Malone (N.Y.) Palladium,* November 20, 1902. For a broader discussion of working-class hierarchies, see the essays "Debating the Labour Aristocracy," "The Aristocracy of Labour Reconsidered," and "Artisans and Labour Aristocrats," in Eric Hobsbawm, *Workers: Worlds of Labor* (New York: Pantheon, 1984).

50. "Adirondack Guides' Association," *Forest and Stream* 48 (February 6, 1897), 108; "Address of Verplanck Colvin at the First Annual Meeting of the Adirondack Guides' Association," Adirondack Guides' Association file, Adirondack Museum; "Adirondack Guides' Association," *Forest and Stream* 50 (February 5, 1898), 105; and *Boonville (N.Y.) Herald,* February 10, 1898. A number of scholars, such as E. Anthony Rotundo in his study *American Manhood,* have suggested that the ideals of masculinity were generated by an urban, northern middle class. But the history of the AGA hints at another model, one in which the ideals of manliness were exported from the rural periphery to the metropolitan core. E. Anthony Rotundo, *American Manhood: Transformations in Masculinity from the Revolution to the Modern Era* (New York: Basic Books, 1993). For a discussion of manliness in the late nineteenth century that recognizes its cross-class dimensions, see Elliott Gorn, *The Manly Art: Bare-Knuckle Prize Fighting in America* (Ithaca: Cornell University Press, 1986).

51. Consider, for instance, E. P. Thompson's emphasis on the importance of consciousness to the formation of class in *The Making of the English Working Class* (New York: Pantheon, 1963).

52. Miller, "The Adirondack Guides' Association," 132. The records of one meeting, for example, tell of "substantial cash contributions" from several associate members. *Boonville (N.Y.) Herald,* January 10, 1901.

53. *Boonville (N.Y.) Herald,* March 6, 1902.

54. *Albany Argus,* September 22, 1903.

55. "Adirondack Guides' Convention," *Forest and Stream* 44 (March 16, 1895): 207.

56. The AGA favored the continuation of hounding, while the BTGA wanted to outlaw all hounding. "The Adirondack Deer Law," *Forest and Stream* 51 (November 12, 1898): 391; *Boonville (N.Y.) Herald,* January 15, 1903; *St. Regis (N.Y.) Adirondack News,* January 23, 1904; Brumley, *Guides of the Adirondacks,* 30–31.

57. "New York Game Protectors," *Forest and Stream* 53 (December 9, 1899): 469. The invited members, it should be noted, were regular guides and not the associate members.

58. *Boonville (N.Y.) Herald,* January 8, 1903; "The Adirondack Guides' Association," *Recreation* 2 (May 1895): 383; "Adirondack Guides' Association,"

Forest and Stream 48 (February 6, 1897): 108. For similar statements of the guides' perspective on their profession, see *Recreation* 6 (June 1897): 462; *Boonville (N.Y.) Herald,* February 22, 1900, and January 15, 1903.

59. Consider, for example, this excerpt from the BTGA's account of its founding: "With the invasion of railroads and facilities which made the woods easy of access, came a large number of unscrupulous sportsmen, who had little regard for the laws, and the guides felt the necessity of uniting for the protection of the game and preservation of the forests." *Boonville (N.Y.) Herald,* March 10, 1898.

60. Harry Radford, "History of the Adirondack Beaver," in New York Forest, Fish and Game Commission, *Annual Reports for 1904, 1905, 1906,* 405–18; "Adirondack Beaver," *Forest and Stream* 66 (April 28, 1906): 671; Brumley, *Guides of the Adirondacks,* 32–33; and Terrie, *Wildlife and Wilderness,* 128–30.

61. *Boonville (N.Y.) Herald,* January 10, 1901; see also the letter of Martin Moody in *Woods and Waters* 2 (winter 1899): 7.

62. *Boonville (N.Y.) Herald,* January 15, 1903.

63. "Brown's Tract Guides," *Forest and Stream* 60 (January 24, 1903): 70.

64. *Boonville (N.Y.) Herald,* January 14, 1904. See also "The Adirondack Elk," *Forest and Stream* 61 (September 19, 1903): 213; and the *Albany Times-Union,* September 21, 1903. For a similar incident surrounding a later elk stocking, see New York Forest, Fish and Game Commission, *Thirteenth Annual Report, 1907* (Albany: James B. Lyon, 1908), 201. One example of local frustration with the introduction of elk to the region can be found in the *New York Tribune,* June 7, 1904.

65. Terrie, *Wildlife and Wilderness,* 121–22. See also "Elk and Moose to the Slaughter," *Recreation* 19 (November, 1903): 400; *Forest and Stream* 61 (October 10, 1903): 273; and *Albany Argus,* September 22, 1903.

66. New York Forest, Fish and Game Commission, *Eighth and Ninth Annual Reports, 1902–1903,* 107–8.

67. For a detailed discussion of the damage caused by arson, see H. M. Suter, *Forest Fires in the Adirondacks in 1903,* Bureau of Forestry Circular No. 26. (Washington, D.C.: GPO, 1904). Additional discussions of arson in the Adirondacks can be found in the *New York Times,* July 18, 1903, and May 1, 1904; "June Forest Fires," *Forestry and Irrigation* 9 (July 1903): 363; Ralph Chipman Hawley and Austin Foster Hawes, *Manual of Forestry for the Northeastern United States,* 2nd ed. (New York: John Wiley and Sons, 1918), 143.

68. Guha, *Unquiet Woods,* 55–58, emphasis in the original; Eugen Weber, *Peasants into Frenchmen: The Modernization of Rural France* (Stanford: Stanford University Press, 1976), 59–60. Further accounts of arson against national parks in India can be found in Madhav Gadgil and Ramachandra Guha, *Ecology and Equity: The Use and Abuse of Nature in Contemporary India* (New York: Routledge, 1995), 92. For other studies of the social causes of arson, see the chapter on "Arson and the Rural Community" in David Jones, *Crime, Protest, Community and Police in Nineteenth-Century Britain* (London: Routledge and Kegan Paul, 1982), 33–61; Martin J. Murray, " 'Burning the Wheat Stacks': Land Clearances and Agrarian Unrest along the Northern Middelburg Frontier,

c. 1918–1926," *Journal of Southern African Studies* 15 (October 1988): 74–95; and André Abbiateci, "Arsonists in Eighteenth-Century France: An Essay in the Typology of Crime," in *Deviants and the Abandoned in French Society: Selections from the Annales,* ed. Robert Forster and Orest Ranum, trans. Elborg Forster and Patricia Ranum (Baltimore: Johns Hopkins University Press, 1978), 157–79.

69. Quoted in Anthony D'Elia, *The Adirondack Rebellion* (Onchiota, N.Y.: Onchiota Books, 1979), 20. D'Elia, who during the 1970s was active in local opposition to state control in the Adirondacks, notes that when he interviewed his informant in the 1970s, the man was over eighty years old, which would have made him a direct observer of the large forest fires at the turn of the century.

70. The quoted sections come from Aber, *Adirondack Folks,* 169; the *New York Times,* August 24, 1910; and E. T. Stokes to Thomas Benedict, January 1, 1886 (emphasis in the original), Letters from Agents Appointed to Serve Notice on Illegal Occupants of State Lands (BO942), Records of the New York Department of Taxation and Finance, New York State Archives. See also *New York Herald,* August 24, 1910.

71. *Reports, 1891,* 163.

72. New York Forest Commission, *First Annual Report, 1885,* 21; New York Forest, Fish and Game Commission, *Eighth and Ninth Annual Reports, 1902–1903,* 128. In 1903, more than forty thousand acres on the Rockefeller estate were burned by suspicious fires, along with another twelve thousand acres on the Ne-Ha-Sa-Ne preserve. See Stewart Holbrook, *Burning an Empire: The Story of American Forest Fires* (New York: Macmillan, 1943), 160–61; and "Rockefeller's Fight with the Woodsmen," *Angler and Hunter* 2 (October, 1910): 514. For a case of arson on Orrando Dexter's estate, see *Horace Gilman v. Orrando P. Dexter* (Supreme Court of Franklin County, 1900; Judgments: Box 73, Folder 2, Position 3, Franklin County Courthouse).

73. *New York Herald,* June 8, 1903; Raymond Spears, "Adirondack Notes," *Forest and Stream* 60 (June 20, 1903): 483. See also Bill Smith, "Stories and Songs from the 'Featherbed.'" In the introduction to this collection of folk tales, Smith describes how, during the Great Depression, Adirondackers sometimes set parts of the forest on fire so they could get employment on firefighting crews. Both employment and revenge appear to be the motivations for two of the leading arson prosecutions to come out of the 1903 fires: *The People v. Alvin Pasco* (Supreme Court of Warren County, June 1903; Minutes of the Supreme Court, 1901–21, D/7 Box 3, Warren County Courthouse); and *The People v. Alvin Pasco and Harry Wood* (Supreme Court of Warren County, June 1903; Minutes of the Supreme Court, 1901–21, D/8 Box 4, Warren County Courthouse). Jack Temple Kirby records incidents of locals setting the forest on fire to gain fire-fighting wages during the early twentieth century in the American South. Kirby, *The Countercultural South* (Athens: University of Georgia Press, 1995), 52.

74. Fernow, *Report upon the Forestry Investigations of the U.S. Department of Agriculture, 1877–1898,* 25; Bernhard Fernow, *Economics of Forestry* (New York: Thomas Y. Crowell, 1902), 387, 390; New York State Assembly,

Report of the Adirondack Committee, Assembly of 1902, New York State Assembly Document No. 46. 1903 (Albany: Argus, 1903), 16; Stoddard, *The Adirondacks: Illustrated,* 19ᵗʰ ed., 218; and Clifford R. Pettis, "The New York Forest Fire Law," *Forestry Quarterly* 1 (July 1903): 134–39. See also the pamphlet the state produced after the fires of 1903: New York Forest, Fish and Game Commission, *Fire! Fire! Fire!: An Appeal to the Citizens of the Adirondack and Catskill Regions* (Albany: Evening Union Company, 1904).

75. William G. Howard, *Forest Fires,* New York Conservation Commission Bulletin No. 10 (Albany: James B. Lyon, 1914), 8, 14; New York Forest, Fish and Game Commission, *Eight and Ninth Annual Reports of the Forest, Fish and Game Commission, 1902–1903,* 125; New York Forest Commission, *Annual Report, 1890,* 7; New York Forest Commission, *Annual Report, 1892,* 65; and *Reports, 1891,* 187–89. In 1903, New York fined sixty-four persons for "burning their fallows during the closed season." New York Forest, Fish and Game Commission, *Thirteenth Annual Report, 1907,* 29.

76. New York Forest Commission, *Annual Report, 1890,* 10.

77. New York Forest Commission, *Annual Report, 1891,* 47–48; Recknagel, *Forests of New York State,* 63; "The Adirondack Park: The New Fire Extinguishing System," in American Scenic and Historic Preservation Society, *Annual Report, 1910* (Albany: James B. Lyon, 1910), 81–82; New York Forest, Fish and Game Commission, *Annual Reports for 1907, 1908, 1909,* 179; New York Conservation Commission, *Circular of Information Relating to Lands and Forests* (Albany: James B. Lyon, 1918), 27–28; and New York Conservation Commission, *Fourth Annual Report, 1914* (Albany: James B. Lyon, 1915), 12–15.

CHAPTER 4. NATURE AND NATION

1. Frank D. Carpenter, "The Wonders of Geyser Land," in *Adventures in Geyserland,* ed. Heister Dean Guie and Lucullus Virgil McWhorter (Caldwell, Idaho: Caxton Printers, 1935), 25. For a useful overview of Yellowstone's topography and ecology, see Dennis H. Knight, *Mountains and Plains: The Ecology of Wyoming Landscapes* (New Haven: Yale University Press, 1994), 215–32; and Don G. Despain, *Yellowstone Vegetation: Consequences of Environment and History in a Natural Setting* (Boulder, Colo.: Roberts Rinehart, 1990). A discussion of the origins of the nickname "Wonderland" can be found in Aubrey L. Haines, *The Yellowstone Story: A History of Our First National Park* (Niwot, Colo.: University Press of Colorado, 1977), 1:354, n. 55. Lee Whittlesey discusses early touristic images of Yellowstone in " 'Everyone Can Understand a Picture': Photographers and the Promotion of Early Yellowstone," *Montana* 49 (summer 1999): 2–13.

2. Carpenter, "The Wonders of Geyser Land," 91–98. A useful summary of the Nez Perce "war" can be found in Robert M. Utley, *The Indian Frontier of the American West, 1846–1890* (Albuquerque: University of New Mexico Press, 1984), 189–193; and Haines, *The Yellowstone Story,* 1:216–239. While Carpenter and his sisters survived their encounter with the Nez Perce, the Indians killed two tourists in skirmishes in Yellowstone.

3. The American Association for the Advancement of Science, for instance, took an active interest in conditions at the park, petitioning the federal government in 1877 to expand its protective efforts at Yellowstone before "irreparable injury to natural accumulations of the highest value in scientific investigation" occurred. See U.S. Congress, House, *Protection of Yellowstone National Park,* 45th Cong., 2nd sess., 1877–78, House Ex. Doc. 75 (Serial Set 1809), 5. For other examples of some of the scientific papers produced, see "The National Park in 1889," *Forest and Stream* 33 (November 21, 1889): 341. The reference to Yellowstone as a "laboratory" comes from Nash, *Wilderness and the American Mind,* 113.

Yellowstone's significance as a symbolic national landscape was such that Congress purchased a rendition of it, *The Grand Canyon of the Yellowstone,* from the famed landscape painter Thomas Moran in 1872. The seven-by-twelve-foot canvas hung in a prominent position in the Senate lobby for years afterward. Alfred Runte, *National Parks: The American Experience,* 2nd ed. (Lincoln: University of Nebraska Press, 1987), 39. One cannot help wondering if, as a young country whose very existence the Civil War had called into question, the United States found Yellowstone's evocation of primeval nature a useful way to convey what Benedict Anderson has termed "that image of antiquity so central to the subjective idea of the nation." See Benedict Anderson, *Imagined Communities: Reflections on the Origin and Spread of Nationalism,* rev. ed. (New York: Verso, 1991), 44.

4. The quote on "greatest wonders of Nature" comes from Nathaniel Pitt Langford, *The Discovery of Yellowstone Park: Journal of the Washburn Expedition to the Yellowstone and Firehole Rivers in the Year 1870* (1905; reprint, Lincoln: University of Nebraska Press, 1972), 97. For a useful study of the debate surrounding Yellowstone's creation, see Katherine E. Early, *"For the Benefit and Enjoyment of the People": Cultural Attitudes and the Establishment of Yellowstone National Park* (Washington, D.C.: Georgetown University Press, 1984).

5. U.S. Congress, House, *Boundaries of Yellowstone National Park,* 53rd Cong., 3rd sess., 1894–95, H. Rept. 1763 (Serial Set 3346).

6. For a discussion of Yellowstone's role in shaping federal policy making, see Louis C. Cramton, *Early History of Yellowstone National Park and Its Relation to National Park Policies* (Washington, D.C.: GPO, 1932).

7. Joel Janetski, *The Indians of Yellowstone Park* (Salt Lake City: University of Utah Press, 1987), 57. Although Euro-American settlers called this route the "Bannock Trail," it was actually used by many Indian groups.

8. Alston Chase, *Playing God in Yellowstone: The Destruction of America's First National Park* (Boston: Atlantic Monthly Press, 1986), 98. Obsidian from Yellowstone was a common trade item among local Indians and was traded from group to group for long distances; indeed, it has been found as far away as Ohio. Janetski, *Indians of Yellowstone Park,* 6, 22; Hiram Chittenden, *The Yellowstone National Park: Historical and Descriptive* (Cincinnati: Robert Clarke, 1895), 11. On page ten of this work, Chittenden provides a map of some of the more notable early Indian trails.

9. Julian H. Steward, *Basin-Plateau Aboriginal Sociopolitical Groups* (1938; reprint, Salt Lake City: University of Utah Press, 1970), 192–93, 207–9; and Frederick E. Hoxie, *Parading through History: The Making of the Crow Nation in America, 1805–1935* (New York: Cambridge University Press, 1995), 47–53. An excellent survey of the uses that Indian peoples made of Yellowstone can be found in Spence, *Dispossessing the Wilderness*, 41–53. See also Robert F. Murphy and Yolanda Murphy, "Northern Shoshone and Bannock," in *Handbook of North American Indians: Great Basin*, ed. Warren L. D'Azevedo (Washington, D.C.: Smithsonian Institution Press, 1986), 285–86, 307–10; and Ake Hultkrantz, "The Indians of Yellowstone Park," *Annals of Wyoming* 29 (October 1957): 125–49.

10. U.S. Department of the Interior, *Annual Report of the Superintendent of Yellowstone National Park, 1880*, by Philetus W. Norris (Washington, D.C.: GPO, 1881), 605; U.S. Department of the Interior, *Annual Report of the Superintendent of Yellowstone National Park, 1879*, by Philetus W. Norris (Washington, D.C.: GPO, 1880), 11; Langford, *Discovery of Yellowstone Park*, 92; Gustavus Doane, *Yellowstone Expedition of 1870*, 41st Cong., 3rd sess., Senate Ex. Doc. 51 (Serial Set 1440), 26.

11. Aubrey Haines, *Yellowstone National Park: Its Exploration and Establishment* (Washington, D.C.: GPO, 1974), 48; Doane, *Yellowstone Expedition of 1870*, 5; W. H. Jackson, *Descriptive Catalogue of Photographs of North American Indians* (Washington, D.C.: GPO, 1877), 70–71. For accounts of the Bannock and Shoshone as guides and horse thieves, see William A. Jones, *Report upon the Reconnaissance of Northwestern Wyoming, including Yellowstone National Park* (Washington, D.C.: GPO), 16; and George Francis Brimlow, *The Bannock Indian War of 1878* (Caldwell, Idaho: Caxton Printers, 1938), 222–23. For more on Hayden, see Mike Foster, *Strange Genius: The Life of Ferdinand Vandeveer Hayden* (Niwot, Colo.: Roberts Rinehart, 1994).

12. Doane, *Yellowstone Expedition of 1870*, 19, 26; Walter Trumbull, "The Washburn Yellowstone Expedition," *Overland Monthly* 6 (May 1871): 436. The quote from Carpenter's sister can be found in Mrs. George Cowan, "Reminiscences of Pioneer Life," in *Adventures in Geyserland*, ed. Heister Dean Guie and Lucullus Virgil McWhorter (Caldwell, Idaho: Caxton Printers, 1935), 286. Such pronouncements also filtered down into the tourist literature. As one guidebook confidently stated in 1884, "Indians avoided it [Yellowstone] as a place inhabited by evil spirits." William Hardman, *A Trip to America* (London: T. Vickers Wood, 1884), 154.

13. Carpenter, "The Wonders of Geyser Land," 127–28; A. Chase, *Playing God in Yellowstone*, 109; Willard Parsons, *Middle Rockies and Yellowstone* (Dubuque, Iowa: Kendall-Hunt, 1978), 48–53; T. Scott Bryan, *The Geysers of Yellowstone*, rev. ed. (Boulder: Colorado Associated University Press, 1986), 17.

14. Such modes of thought have deep antecedents. William Cronon describes a nearly identical situation more than a century earlier in colonial New England. Cronon, *Changes in the Land*, 54–57.

15. John J. Craighead, "Yellowstone in Transition," in *The Greater Yellowstone Ecosystem: Redefining America's Wilderness Heritage*, ed. Robert B. Keiter and Mark S. Boyce (New Haven: Yale University Press, 1991), 27; Dale

L. Taylor, "Forest Fires in Yellowstone National Park," *Journal of Forest History* 18 (July 1974): 69; Nancy Langston, *Forest Dreams, Forest Nightmares: The Paradox of Old Growth in the Inland West* (Seattle: University of Washington Press, 1995), 26–27; and Cronon, *Changes in the Land,* 52.

16. Doane, *Yellowstone Expedition of 1870,* 5–6; Philip Sheridan, *Expedition through the Big Horn Mountains, Yellowstone Park, Etc.* (Washington, D.C.: GPO, 1882), 8–9. For accounts of the ecological effects of native use of fire, see Langston, *Forest Dreams, Forest Nightmares,* 259–60; and Knight, *Mountains and Plains,* 227. Even in 1898, a visitor to the region could observe that "there is very little commercial timber within this area[,] owing to the fact that it has been in the past persistently burned by the Indians." Walcott to Secretary of the Interior, September 16, 1898, Records of the Department of the Interior, Patents and Miscellaneous, Entry 168 (Records Relating to Forest Reserves), Box 1, RG 48, National Archives.

17. John Wesley Powell, *Report on the Lands of the Arid Region of the United States* (1878; reprint, Cambridge: Harvard University Press, 1962), 27–28. Unlike most of his contemporaries, Powell later revised his opinion of Indian fire-setting. A similar effort to control forest fire took place at much the same time in colonial India, where, as K. Sivaramakrishnan has noted, "By attempting to banish fire from the landscape, European forestry distinguished modern forest management from the primitive techniques it claimed to supersede." Sivaramakrishnan, "Politics of Fire and Forest Regeneration," 145.

18. Mann to Superintendent of Indian Affairs, September 28, 1865. Reprinted in Dale Morgan, "Washakie and the Shoshoni: A Selection of Documents from the Records of the Utah Superintendency of Indian Affairs," *Annals of Wyoming* 29 (October 1957): 215.

19. For a discussion of American ideas of wilderness and their impact on Native Americans, see William Cronon, "The Trouble with Wilderness; or, Getting Back to the Wrong Nature," in *Uncommon Ground,* ed. Cronon, 79. The linkage between the rise of national parks and Indian reservations is explored in detail in Spence, *Dispossessing the Wilderness,* 27–39. The specifics of treaty making in the Yellowstone region are as follows: a series of treaties in 1855, 1866, and 1868 confined the Blackfeet to a reservation in northern Montana. An 1867 executive order by President Andrew Johnson placed some bands of the Bannocks and Shoshones on the Fort Hall reservation in Idaho. The second Treaty of Fort Laramie in 1868 located the Crow on a reservation in southern Montana, while the Treaty of Fort Bridger, also in 1868, established the Wind River Reservation in Wyoming for other Bannock and Shoshone bands. An 1875 executive order assigned the remaining Bannocks and Shoshones to the Lemhi Reservation in Idaho. See Dale K. McGinnis and Floyd W. Sharrock, *The Crow People* (Phoenix: Indian Tribal Series, 1972), 41; Hultkrantz, "Indians of Yellowstone Park," 145; U.S. Bureau of Indian Affairs, *Annual Report of the Commissioner of Indian Affairs, 1881* (Washington, D.C.: GPO, 1881), 263–71.

20. The phrase "landscape of enclaves" comes from Sarah Deutsch's essay, "Landscape of Enclaves: Race Relations in the West, 1865–1990," in *Under an Open Sky: Rethinking America's Western Past,* ed. William Cronon, George Miles, and Jay Gitlin (New York: W. W. Norton, 1992), 110–31.

21. U.S. Bureau of Indian Affairs, *Annual Report of the Commissioner of Indian Affairs, 1882* (Washington, D.C.: GPO, 1882), 499; U.S. Bureau of Indian Affairs, *Annual Report of the Commissioner of Indian Affairs, 1883* (Washington, D.C.: GPO, 1883), 313–14. For a description of the shortage of rations on the Crow reservation to the north of the park, see Hoxie, *Parading through History,* 114–15.

22. U.S. Bureau of Indian Affairs, *Annual Report of the Commissioner of Indian Affairs, 1895* (Washington, D.C.: GPO, 1896), 65–66; "Indian Hunting Rights," *Forest and Stream* 46 (May 30, 1896): 429.

23. "A Case for Prompt Action," *Forest and Stream* 32 (April 11, 1889): 233. The figures for early tourists to Yellowstone are from Haines, *Yellowstone Story,* 2:478.

24. U.S. Department of the Interior, *Annual Report of the Acting Superintendent of Yellowstone National Park, 1889,* by Moses Harris (Washington, D.C.: GPO, 1889), 15; U.S. Department of the Interior, *Annual Report of the Superintendent of Yellowstone National Park, 1886,* by David W. Wear (Washington, D.C.: GPO, 1886), 7; U.S. Department of the Interior, *Annual Report of the Superintendent of Yellowstone National Park, 1877,* by Philetus W. Norris (Washington, D.C.: GPO, 1878), 837.

25. U.S. Department of the Interior, *Annual Report of the Acting Superintendent of Yellowstone National Park, 1889,* 15–16; "A Case for Prompt Action," *Forest and Stream,* 233–34. The quote about "game-butchery" comes from "Protect the National Park," *Frank Leslie's Illustrated Newspaper* 68 (April 27, 1889): 182.

26. U.S. Department of the Interior, *Annual Report of the Acting Superintendent of Yellowstone National Park, 1889,* 16; see also "A Case for Prompt Action," *Forest and Stream,* 234.

27. See the scouts' reports reprinted in U.S. Department of the Interior, *Annual Report of the Acting Superintendent of Yellowstone National Park, 1889,* 16–17.

28. See, for example, Harris to Muldrow, August 24, 1888, "Letters Sent, March 17, 1887-August 18, 1889," Bound Volume II, Item 214, Yellowstone National Park Archives. (Hereafter YNPA.)

29. "A Case for Prompt Action," *Forest and Stream,* 234.

30. U.S. Department of the Interior, *Annual Report of the Superintendent of Yellowstone National Park, 1878,* by Philetus W. Norris (Washington, D.C.: GPO, 1879), 9.

31. U.S. Department of the Interior, *Annual Report of the Superintendent of Yellowstone National Park, 1880,* 3. For copies of the treaties signed with the Crow, Shoshone, and Bannock, see U.S. Bureau of Indian Affairs, *Annual Report of the Commissioner of Indian Affairs, 1880* (Washington, D.C.: GPO, 1880), 277–78. Despite Norris's urgings that the members of these tribes not enter the Yellowstone park, nothing in these treaties placed such limits on Indian mobility.

32. U.S. Department of the Interior, *Annual Report of the Acting Superintendent of Yellowstone National Park, 1889,* 13.

33. "A Case for Prompt Action," *Forest and Stream,* 235.

34. U.S. Bureau of Indian Affairs, *Annual Report of the Commissioner of Indian Affairs, 1888* (Washington, D.C.: GPO, 1888), 244–45; Woodbridge to Commissioner of Indian Affairs, August 24, 1886 (1886: Letter 23,077) Letters Received, Records of the Bureau of Indian Affairs, RG 75, National Archives. (Hereafter LR/BIA.)

35. Wingate's turn of phrase seems particularly poorly chosen, given that several of the best-known inhabitants of the Adirondacks were, in fact, Native Americans. For accounts of the Indian incursions into Yellowstone in 1886–87, see Wear to Muldrow, June 1, 1886 (1886: Letter 14,893) LR/BIA; Harris to Muldrow, August 22, 1887 (1887: Letter 22,870) LR/BIA; Woodbridge to Atkins, September 15, 1886 (1886: Letter 25,659) LR/BIA; and George W. Wingate, *Through the Yellowstone Park on Horseback* (New York: Orange Judd, 1886), 140. Later Indian hunting expeditions and fire setting are discussed in Cooper to Warren, May 5, 1891 (1891: Letter 17,211) LR/BIA; Hermann to Secretary of the Interior, November 5, 1898 (1898: Letter 50,866) LR/BIA.

36. U.S. Congress, House, *Report of the Committee on Expenditures for Indians and Yellowstone Park,* 49th Cong., 1st sess., 1885–86, H. Rept. 1076 (Serial Set 2438), LIII, 265.

37. "Our National Parks," *Forest and Stream* 37 (December 3, 1891): 385.

38. U.S. Department of the Interior, *Annual Report of the Superintendent of Yellowstone National Park, 1886,* 7.

39. See William L. Simpson, "The Game Question in Jackson's Hole," *Forest and Stream* 51 (December 10, 1898): 468; S. T. Davis, "Game in Jackson's Hole," *Forest and Stream* 52 (January 21, 1899): 47; as well as the reference to encountering a "man, once white" in Mary B. Richards, *Camping Out in the Yellowstone* (Salem, Mass.: Newcomb and Gauss, 1910), 15.

This fear that whites might revert to an Indian-like savagery was not unique to Yellowstone. As early as 1782, Crèvecoeur was complaining of "new made Indians": Euro-Americans who "have degenerated altogether into the hunting state." Similarly, Richard Slotkin has demonstrated "the metaphorical equation of Indians and [white] strikers" as "savages" and "murderous reds" that took place in the urban press during the late nineteenth century. J. Hector St. John de Crèvecoeur, *Letters from an American Farmer* (1782; reprint, New York: E. P. Dutton, 1957), 49; Richard Slotkin, *The Fatal Environment: The Myth of the Frontier in the Age of Industrialization, 1800–1890* (New York: Atheneum, 1985), 480–84.

40. For a discussion of the "ignorance" of Indians concerning game and fire laws, see "Their Right to Roam," *Forest and Stream* 32 (April 18, 1889): 253.

41. "The Indian and the Big Game," *Forest and Stream* 41 (August 19, 1893): 137.

42. "Snap Shots," *Forest and Stream* 50 (January 22, 1898): 61.

43. U.S. Department of the Interior, *Annual Report of the Superintendent of Yellowstone National Park, 1879,* 21; U.S. Department of the Interior, *Annual Report of the Superintendent of Yellowstone National Park, 1880,* 39; W. E. Strong, *A Trip to the Yellowstone National Park* (Washington, D.C., 1876), 28, 92–93; see also the illustrations in the *Daily Graphic,* July 11, 1878.

44. W. E. Strong, *Trip to the Yellowstone National Park,* 92–93.

45. H. Duane Hampton, *How the U.S. Cavalry Saved Our National Parks* (Bloomington: Indiana University Press, 1971), 33–34; Haines, *Yellowstone Story,* 1:213–14.

46. W. Scott Smith to Teller, October 15, 1883, in U.S. Congress, Senate, *Correspondence on Yellowstone National Park,* 48ᵗʰ Cong., 1ˢᵗ sess., Senate Ex. Doc. 47 (Serial Set 2162), 17. Background information on the assistant superintendents can be found in Haines, *Yellowstone Story,* 1:292–93.

47. Wear to Secretary of the Interior, September 7, 1885, Records of the Department of the Interior, Yellowstone National Park, 1872–1886: Concerning Superintendents, 1872–1886, Roll 4, (M62) RG 48, National Archives.

48. Conger to Secretary of the Interior, November 27, 1883; U.S. Congress, Senate, *Correspondence on Yellowstone National Park,* 25.

49. U.S. Department of the Interior, *Annual Report of the Superintendent of Yellowstone National Park, 1886,* 6, 11. See also U.S. Department of the Interior, *Annual Report of the Superintendent of Yellowstone National Park, 1882,* by P. H. Conger (Washington, D.C.: GPO, 1883), 6.

50. Trevanion Hall to C. W. Stewart, August 19, 1885. Records of the Wyoming State Auditor, Correspondence, July 1885–October 1885, Wyoming State Archives. All misspellings reflect the original letter. The passage about squatters in the park comes from a letter written to the secretary of the interior quoted in Richard A. Bartlett, *Yellowstone: A Wilderness Besieged* (Tucson: University of Arizona Press, 1985), 119. See also U.S. Department of the Interior, *Annual Report of the Secretary of the Interior, 1885* (Washington, D.C.: GPO, 1885), 71–72; and U.S. Department of the Interior, *Annual Report of the Secretary of the Interior, 1889* (Washington, D.C.: GPO, 1890), CI–CIII. For more on the ejection of squatters, see *Livingston (Mont.) Enterprise,* December 13 and December 20, 1884; and Records of the Wyoming State Auditor, Financial, December 1884, Yellowstone National Park Justice of the Peace, Wyoming State Archives.

51. Haines, *Yellowstone Story,* 1:195; U.S. Congress, House, *Report of the Committee on Expenditures for Indians and Yellowstone Park,* L; U.S. Congress, House, *Inquiry into the Management and Control of the Yellowstone National Park,* 52ⁿᵈ Cong., 1ˢᵗ sess., 1891–92, H. Rept. 1956 (Serial Set 3051), 214–16; Bill Whithorn and Doris Whithorn, *Photohistory of Gardiner, Jardine, Crevasse* (Livingston, Mont.: Park County News, 1972), 1.

52. U.S. Department of the Interior, *Annual Report of the Acting Superintendent of Yellowstone National Park, 1887,* by Moses Harris (Washington, D.C.: GPO, 1887), 11, 25–26.

53. William T. Hornaday, *Our Vanishing Wildlife: Its Extermination and Preservation* (New York: New York Zoological Society, 1913), 337.

54. Haines, *Yellowstone Story,* 1:312–13, 322–23.

55. Quoted in Hampton, *How the U.S. Cavalry Saved Our National Parks,* 41.

56. Ibid., 42, 51; P. Sheridan, *Expedition,* 9. See also U.S. Congress, Senate, *Agreement with Certain Parties for Privileges in Yellowstone National Park,* 47ᵗʰ Cong., 2ⁿᵈ sess., 1882–83, S. Rept. 911 (Serial Set 2087), 5.

57. "Can the Nation Defend Its Forests?" *Garden and Forest* 2 (April 3, 1889): 157. A more extensive account of the use of the army to maintain internal security can be found in Joan M. Jensen, *Army Surveillance in America, 1775–1980* (New Haven: Yale University Press, 1991).

58. Quoted in Hampton, *How the U.S. Cavalry Saved Our National Parks,* 79. See also U.S. Department of the Interior, *Annual Report of the Secretary of the Interior, 1886* (Washington, D.C.: GPO, 1886), 75.

59. U.S. Department of the Interior, *Annual Report of the Superintendent of Yellowstone National Park, 1889,* 10–11.

60. For a discussion of the role played by the army in the emergence of the modern American state, see Stephen Skowronek, *Building a New American State: The Expansion of National Administrative Capacities, 1877–1920* (New York: Cambridge University Press, 1982), 85–120, 212–47. The army's influence on its ultimate successor, the National Park Service, is obvious in several regards. When the newly formed Park Service reestablished civilian control of Yellowstone in 1918, it adopted much of its uniform from the army dress of the day. Moreover, the first rangers at the park were all soldiers whom the army had specially discharged so that they could then be hired by the Park Service. See Haines, *Yellowstone Story,* 2:289; and "Uniforms of Forest Officers," *Forestry and Irrigation* (August 1908): 446.

CHAPTER 5. FORT YELLOWSTONE

1. John Muir, *Our National Parks* (Boston: Houghton Mifflin, 1901), 40, 188.

2. Charles Dudley Warner, "Editor's Study," *Harper's* 94 (January 1897): 323–24.

3. "The Army and the Forests," *Garden and Forest* 3 (September 10, 1890): 437.

4. "National Forest-Reservations," *Garden and Forest* (December 3, 1890): 581.

5. References to the proposed militarization of conservation can be found in a large number of sources. See "The Forestry Movement in the United States," *Garden and Forest* 5 (January 20, 1892): 34; *Garden and Forest* 5 (February 24, 1892): 86; "Our National Parks and Forest Reservations," *Garden and Forest* 5 (December 28, 1892): 613–14; "National Forest-Reservations," *Garden and Forest* 3 (December 3, 1890): 581; Charles E. Whitehead, "Game Laws," in *Hunting in Many Lands: The Book of the Boone and Crockett Club,* ed. Theodore Roosevelt and George Bird Grinnell (New York: Forest and Stream, 1895), 370; Ise, *Forest Policy,* 121; "Troops for the Forests," *Forest and Stream* 42 (March 3, 1894): 177; *Report of the Committee Appointed by the National Academy of Sciences upon the Inauguration of a Forest Policy for the Forested Lands of the United States to the Secretary of the Interior* (Washington, D.C.: GPO, 1897), 18, 25. For a discussion of the military's role in conservation in present-day Africa, see Nicholas Gordon, *Ivory Knights: Man, Magic, and Elephants* (London: Chapmans, 1991).

6. *Livingston (Mont.) Enterprise,* December 11, 1897, January 1, 1898, February 19, 1898.

7. *Livingston (Mont.) Post,* October 24, 1889, and July 12, 1894.

8. See, for example, "Captain Anderson and the Park," *Forest and Stream* 48 (April 17, 1897): 301; "Death of General Anderson," *Forest and Stream* 84 (April 1915): 234–35; and "The Yellowstone Park Report," *Forest and Stream* 39 (October 13, 1892): 309.

9. *Livingston (Mont.) Post,* April 19, 1894. See also the poem printed in the *Livingston (Mont.) Enterprise,* February 18, 1893.

10. For a fuller description of local customs surrounding the use of public lands elsewhere in the West, see Faragher, *Sugar Creek,* 73, 132–36, 184.

11. Yellowstone's early regulations are reprinted in U.S. Congress, House, *Report of the Committee on Expenditures for Indians and Yellowstone Park,* 270; Conger to Secretary of the Interior, November 14, 1883, in U.S. Congress, Senate, *Correspondence on Yellowstone National Park,* 24.

12. Terry to Conger, April 29, 1884, Document 1566, "Employees, etc., January 1, 1882-December 31, 1897," Item 9, YNPA; Terry to Conger, December 11, 1883, Document 1570, "Employees, etc. January 1, 1882-December 31, 1897," Item 9, YNPA.

13. Maginnis to Secretary of the Interior, June 15, 1884, Records of the Department of the Interior, Yellowstone National Park, 1872–1886: Letters Received, 1883–1884, Roll 2 (M62) RG 48, National Archives.

14. Chambers to Conger, November 22, 1883, Document 1345, "Employees, etc., January 1, 1882-December 31, 1897," Item 9, YNPA.

15. Duret to Anderson, December 6, 1893, Document 819, "A-E, January 1, 1882-December 31, 1894," Item 4, YNPA; Randall to Sands, November 3, 1891, Document 1273, "L-R, January 1, 1882-December 31, 1895," Item 6, YNPA; Gassert to Goode, March 21, 1901, Document 3988, "F-K, January 1, 1900-December 31, 1903," Item 17, YNPA; Duret to Anderson, January 22, 1892, "A-E, January 1, 1882-December 31, 1894," Item 4, YNPA.

16. Anderson to Scott, April 14, 1891, Bound Volume III, "Letters Sent, August 18, 1889-June 25, 1892," Item 215, YNPA. Emphasis in the original.

17. *Livingston (Mont.) Enterprise,* January 1, 1898.

18. For evidence of continued taking of timber, see George Whittaker, Diary 32, December 4, 1898, Scout Diaries, Manuscript 92–42, YNPA; and U.S. Department of the Interior, *Annual Report of the Acting Superintendent of Yellowstone National Park, 1908,* by Samuel B.M. Young (Washington, D.C.: GPO, 1908), 12.

19. For more information on the early treatment of the lodgepole pine, see Langston, *Forest Dreams, Forest Nightmares,* 150.

20. *Livingston (Mont.) Enterprise,* January 1, 1898.

21. *Livingston (Mont.) Enterprise,* January 13, 1900.

22. U.S. Department of the Interior, *Annual Report of the Acting Superintendent of Yellowstone National Park, 1903,* by John Pitcher (Washington, D.C.: GPO, 1903), 3; U.S. Department of the Interior, *Annual Report of the Acting Superintendent of the Yellowstone National Park, 1914,* by Lloyd M. Brett (Washington, D.C.: GPO, 1914), 17. Information on earlier livestock pol-

icies can be found in Goode to Secretary of the Interior, August 30, 1900, Bound Volume IX, "Letters Sent, October 2, 1899-September 9, 1900," Item 221, YNPA; and U.S. Department of the Interior, *Annual Report of the Acting Superintendent of Yellowstone National Park, 1908*, 18.

23. U.S. Department of the Interior, *Annual Report of the Superintendent of Yellowstone National Park, 1878*, 9; U.S. Department of the Interior, *Annual Report of the Acting Superintendent of Yellowstone National Park, 1887*, 11.

24. U.S. Department of the Interior, *Annual Report of the Acting Superintendent of Yellowstone National Park, 1900*, by George Goode (Washington, D.C.: GPO, 1900), 8; U.S. Department of the Interior, *Annual Report of the Acting Superintendent of the Yellowstone National Park, 1903*, 5; U.S. Department of the Interior, *Annual Report of the Acting Superintendent of the Yellowstone National Park, 1904*, by John Pitcher (Washington, D.C.: GPO, 1904), 3–4; *Gardiner (Mont.) Wonderland*, February 13, 1904.

25. Henry T. Finck, *The Pacific Coast Scenic Tour* (London: Sampson Low, Marston, Searle and Rivington, 1891), 282; U.S. Department of the Interior, *Annual Report of the Acting Superintendent of the Yellowstone National Park, 1898*, by James Erwin (Washington, D.C.: GPO, 1898), 6; U.S. Department of the Interior, *Annual Report of the Acting Superintendent of the Yellowstone National Park, 1907*, by Samuel B. M. Young (Washington, D.C.: GPO, 1907), 23–24.

26. U.S. Department of the Interior, *Annual Report of the Acting Superintendent of Yellowstone National Park, 1897*, by Samuel B. M. Young (Washington, D.C.: GPO, 1897), 29. Also see: Orders, July 12, 1910, Document 7114, "Employees, January 1, 1904-December 31, 1908," Item 27, YNPA; and U.S. Army, *Rules, Regulations, and Instructions for the Information and Guidance of Officers and Enlisted Men of the United States Army, and of the Scouts Doing Duty in the Yellowstone National Park* (Washington, D.C.: GPO, 1907), 13.

27. U.S. Department of the Interior, *Annual Report of the Acting Superintendent of Yellowstone National Park, 1898*, 17–18. For an example of an arrest being made for lacking the proper permit, see Scout Diary 32 (George Whittaker), September 23, 1898, Manuscript 92–42, YNPA.

28. U.S. Department of the Interior, *Annual Report of the Acting Superintendent of Yellowstone National Park, 1907*, 24.

29. Gardner Stilson Turrill, *A Tale of the Yellowstone; or, in a Wagon through Western Wyoming and Wonderland* (Jefferson, Iowa: G. S. Turrill Publishing, 1901), 56, 64. See also T. J. Patterson, "Rambling in Wyoming," *Forest and Stream* 42 (May 5, 1894): 378.

30. Haines, *Yellowstone Story,* 2:174; U.S. Congress, House, *Report of the Committee on Expenditures for Indians and Yellowstone Park,* 248; Report of Peter Holte (Scout), Document No. 7095, "Employees, January 1, 1904-December 31, 1908," Item 27, YNPA; U.S. Department of the Interior, *Annual Report of the Acting Superintendent of Yellowstone National Park, 1907*, 23–24.

31. Frank Calkins, *Jackson Hole* (New York: Alfred A. Knopf, 1973), 135; Conger to Secretary of the Interior, March 28, 1884, and April 13, 1884, in U.S. Congress, Senate, *Management of Yellowstone National Park*, 48th Cong., 1st

sess., 1883–84, Senate Ex. Doc. 207 (SS 2168), 11–12. See also Haines, *Yellowstone Story,* 2:24–25; Elmer Lindsey, "A Winter Trip through the Yellowstone Park," *Harper's Weekly* 42 (January 19, 1898): 107. For a fuller description of poachers' cabins, see Verba Lawrence, "The Elk Tuskers' Cabin," Tusk Hunters File, Jackson Hole Historical Society. Lawrence reported that many of the poachers' cabins were located at ten-mile intervals from one another.

32. U.S. Department of the Interior, *Annual Report of the Acting Superintendent of Yellowstone National Park, 1891,* by George S. Anderson, (Washington, D.C.: GPO, 1891), 9; U.S. Department of the Interior, *Annual Report of the Acting Superintendent of Yellowstone National Park, 1907,* 25–26. Even as late as 1918, the inexperience and lack of enthusiasm of many soldiers for their duty at Yellowstone drew complaints from their superiors: "The soldiers formerly controlling the park were never sent there for a long tour of duty, and, consequently, never became thoroughly acquainted with the park or intensely interested in the performance of their duties." U.S. National Park Service, *Annual Report of the Director of the National Park Service, 1918* (Washington, D.C.: GPO, 1918), 39, 126, 129.

33. Report of Elmer Lindsley, January 16, 1898, Document 4881, "Employees, January 1, 1898–December 31, 1903," Item 20, YNPA; U.S. Department of the Interior, *Annual Report of the Acting Superintendent of Yellowstone National Park, 1907,* 26; Young to Secretary of the Interior, August 1, 1897, "Letters Sent, July 24, 1896–October 1, 1897," Item 218, Bound Volume VI, YNPA.

34. Pitcher to Secretary of the Interior, February 8, 1902, "Letters Sent, September 27, 1901–July 14, 1902," Item 223, Bound Volume XI, YNPA. In 1907, three more soldiers were charged with violating park rules. U.S. Department of the Interior, *Annual Report of the Acting Superintendent of Yellowstone National Park, 1907,* 24. In 1915, a soldier pleaded guilty to killing an elk in the park, for which he was dishonorably discharged from the army and sentenced to one and a half years hard labor at Alcatraz. U.S. Department of the Interior, *Annual Report of the Acting Superintendent of Yellowstone National Park, 1915,* by Lloyd M. Brett (Washington, D.C.: GPO, 1915), 23.

35. Romey to Pitcher, April 12, 1902, Document No. 4932, and Romey to Pitcher, March 10, 1902, Document No. 4934, "Employees, January 1, 1898–December 31, 1903," Item 20, YNPA. According to Haines, Romey took a local poacher, Ed Hunter, nicknamed the "King of the Forest," with him on several of his patrols "in order to keep track of him." Haines, *Yellowstone Story,* 2:447.

36. D. W. Spaulding to Pitcher, February 5, 1902, Document No. 4579, "Letters Received, S–Z, January 1, 1900–December 31, 1902," Item 19, YNPA. Additional accounts of corruption can be found in Document No. 4307, "Letters Received, F–K, January 1, 1900–December 31, 1900," Item 17, YNPA. Similar forms of corruption among army forces are common in Africa today; see N. Gordon, *Ivory Knights,* 40–41.

37. R. A. Wagner, a Yellowstone scout, related one such account of a dutiful soldier at the park. According to Wagner, two men from Bozeman offered an enlisted man twenty dollars if he would let them hunt in the park. Even though

the soldier was making only thirteen dollars a month, he refused the bribe. R. A. Wagner to Pitcher, December 29, 1903, Document No. 5001, "Employees, January 1, 1898–December 31, 1903," Item 20, YNPA.

38. *Livingston (Mont.) Post,* December 11, 1902. For further attacks on corruption at Yellowstone, see the *Livingston (Mont.) Enterprise,* February 12, 1898, and *Gardiner (Mont.) Wonderland,* February 5, 1903.

39. "Actual Interviews on Segregation," *Forest and Stream* 42 (May 19, 1894): 420.

40. Frederic Remington, *Pony Tracks* (1895; reprint, Norman: University of Oklahoma Press, 1961), 119. Unimpressed, local poachers regularly broke into these cabins, both to steal the supplies cached within and to disrupt the plans of passing patrols. Hitchcock to Pitcher, n.d., Document No. 4938, "Employees, January 1, 1898–December 31, 1903," Item 20, YNPA; Romey to Pitcher, September 12, 1904, Document No. 7199, "Employees, January 1, 1904–December 31, 1908," Item 27, YNPA. See also U.S. Department of the Interior, *Annual Report of the Acting Superintendent of Yellowstone National Park, 1907,* 23.

41. U.S. Department of the Interior, *Annual Report of the Acting Superintendent of Yellowstone National Park, 1899,* by Oscar Brown (Washington, D.C.: GPO, 1899), 3–4. The "snowshoe cabins" were typically located ten miles apart, ten miles being what the army considered a decent day's journey during Yellowstone's harsh winter months. U.S. Department of the Interior, *Annual Report of the Acting Superintendent of Yellowstone National Park, 1900,* 4; Paul Schullery, *Yellowstone's Ski Pioneers: Peril and Heroism on the Winter Trail* (Worland, Wyo.: High Plains Publishing, 1995), 78–79.

42. See, for example, "The Yellowstone Park" and "Snapshots," *Forest and Stream* 36 (January 22, 1891): 1.

43. "Scouts for Park Poachers," *Forest and Stream* 42 (June 30, 1894): 551. My understanding of army tactics in the late nineteenth-century Indian wars is derived largely from Robert M. Utley, *Frontier Regulars: The United States Army and the Indian, 1866–1891* (New York: Macmillan, 1973), 44–56; and Thomas W. Dunlay, *Wolves for the Blue Soldiers: Indian Scouts and Auxiliaries with the United States Army, 1860–90* (Lincoln: University of Nebraska Press, 1982).

44. Anderson to Secretary of the Interior, December 16, 1895, "Letters Sent, March 17, 1894–July 23, 1896," Bound Volume V, Item 217, YNPA. See also Anderson to Secretary of the Interior, September 16, 1893, "Letters Sent, June 25, 1892–March 17, 1894," Bound Volume IV, Item 216, YNPA.

45. Young to Secretary of the Interior, August 1, 1897, "Letters Sent, July 24, 1896–October 1, 1897," Bound Volume VI, Item 218, YNPA; U.S. Department of the Interior, *Annual Report of the Acting Superintendent of Yellowstone National Park, 1898,* 12.

46. *Livingston (Mont.) Enterprise,* January 1, 1898; G. L. Scott to Anderson, February 21, 1896, Document No. 1497, "Employees, etc., January 1, 1882-December 31, 1897," Item 9, YNPA. Yellowstone officials' use of private spies echoes the tactics of the famous Pinkerton Detective Agency, which rose to prominence during this era. An extended and illuminating discussion of the Pinkertons can be found in J. Anthony Lukas, *Big Trouble: A Murder in a Small*

Western Town Sets Off a Struggle for the Soul of America (New York: Simon and Schuster, 1997), 74–87, 171–95.

47. Romey to Pitcher, January 18, 1903, Document No. 4925, "Employees, January 1, 1898-December 31, 1903," Item 20, YNPA. All misspellings reflect the original letter.

48. Erwin to Young, February 14, 1898, "Letters Sent, October 1, 1897–November 9, 1898," Bound Volume VII, Item 219, YNPA.

49. *Gardiner (Mont.) Wonderland,* February 5, 1903; *Livingston (Mont.) Enterprise,* January 1, 1898. The archival evidence of corruption among the scouts is quite slim. Yellowstone's records indicate only one instance of a scout arrested for poaching: Tom Newcomb, who, after being dismissed because his work was not "wholly satisfactory," was later found guilty of killing an elk in the park and fined fifty dollars. But the temptation for scouts to break some of the park's regulations or to turn a blind eye to illegal acts must have been constant. The scout Ed Romey reported one such case in 1904: three trappers who lived along Yellowstone's southern edge offered to split their earnings with Romey if he would only overlook their trapping in the park for a few months. Anderson to Elihu Root, June 8, 1896, "Letters Sent, March 17, 1894–July 23, 1896," Bound Volume V, Item 217, YNPA; Document No. 7199, YNPA. See also Haines, *Yellowstone Story,* 2:447.

50. M.P. Dunham to Anderson, July 7, 1893, Document No. 821, "A–E, January 1, 1882–December 31, 1894," Item 4, YNPA. All misspellings reflect the original letter. No doubt some would-be scouts found the potential wages of seventy-five dollars a month to be an inducement as well. For information on the scouts' salaries, see Anderson to Secretary of the Interior, November 5, 1894, "Letters Sent, March 17, 1894–July 23, 1896," Bound Volume V, Item 217, YNPA.

51. White to Anderson, October 26, 1892; November 29, 1892, Documents No. 571 and 572, "S–Z, January 1, 1882–December 31, 1893," Item 3, YNPA.

52. Morrison's diary is reprinted in U.S. Department of the Interior, *Annual Report of the Acting Superintendent of Yellowstone National Park, 1898,* 30.

53. Sheffield to Brett, November 1, 1912, "Poaching, Reports of and Inquiries, 1909–1913," in "Protection, 1908–1914," Item 105, YNPA. All misspellings reflect the original letter.

54. George Whittaker, November 13 and November 14, 1898, "Scout Diaries," Manuscript 92-42, YNPA.

55. Quoted in Schullery, *Yellowstone's Ski Pioneers,* 84.

56. George Whittaker, November 13 and November 14, 1898, "Scout Diaries," Manuscript 92-42, YNPA.

57. George Whittaker, November 11, 1898, Diary 32, "Scout Diaries," Manuscript 92-42, YNPA.

58. U.S. Department of the Interior, *Annual Report of the Acting Superintendent of Yellowstone National Park, 1898,* 39, 41.

59. Remington, *Pony Tracks,* 119.

60. George Whittaker, November 24, 1898, Diary 38, "Scout Diaries," Manuscript 92-42, YNPA. All misspellings reflect the original manuscript.

61. Interview with Jim McBride, in Dorr G. Yeager, "Some Old Timers of the Yellowstone" (manuscript, 1929), YNPA.

62. These findings are summarized in Olof C. Wallmo, ed., *Mule and Black-Tailed Deer of North America* (Lincoln: University of Nebraska Press, 1981), 312; see also Michael Milstein, "The Quiet Kill," *National Parks* 63 (May-June 1989): 21. A number of studies indicate that not only are poachers rarely caught, but their activities are seldom reported to law enforcement officials by members of the public.

63. U.S. Department of the Interior, *Annual Report of the Acting Superintendent of Yellowstone National Park, 1908,* 34; Erwin to Young, February 5, 1898, "Letters Sent, October 1, 1897–November 9, 1898," Bound Volume VII, Item 219, YNPA.

64. U.S. Department of the Interior, *Annual Report of the Acting Superintendent of Yellowstone National Park, 1908,* 37; Erwin to Young, January 14, 1898, "Letters Sent, October 1, 1897–November 9, 1898," Bound Volume VII, Item 219, YNPA.

65. *Livingston (Mont.) Enterprise,* February 19, 1898.

66. E. Hough, "Yellowstone Park Poachers," *Forest and Stream* 51 (July 16, 1898): 45; Remington, *Pony Tracks,* 119. For those unfamiliar with the army terminology of the time, a troop usually had one hundred men.

67. U.S. Bureau of Indian Affairs, *Annual Report of the Commissioner of Indian Affairs, 1894* (Washington, D.C.: GPO, 1895), 66.

68. U.S. Bureau of Indian Affairs, *Annual Report of the Commissioner of Indian Affairs, 1895,* 63–68; "Two Official Opinions" and "As to the Jackson Hole Outrage," *The Indian's Friend* 8 (October 1895): 6, 9–10. An account of an earlier confrontation can be found in S.N. Leek, "Indians in Jackson's Hole," *Recreation* 3 (August 1895): 90.

69. Minnesota, for example, quickly followed Wyoming's lead in curtailing Indian hunting rights. "Indians are Amenable to Game Laws," *Recreation* 7 (July 1897): 45. See also Brian Czech, "Ward vs Racehorse—Supreme Court as Obviator?" *Journal of the West* 35 (July 1996): 61–69. Even after the Racehorse case, members of the Bannock and Shoshone occasionally made hunting forays into the Yellowstone area in later years. Hermann to Commissioner of Indian Affairs, November 5, 1898 (1898: Letter 50,866) LR/BIA.

70. U.S. Department of the Interior, *Annual Report of the Acting Superintendent of Yellowstone National Park, 1886,* 7. See also Stephen J. Pyne, *Fire in America: A Cultural History of Wildland and Rural Fire* (Princeton: Princeton University Press, 1982), 228.

71. U.S. Department of the Interior, *Annual Report of the Superintendent of Yellowstone National Park, 1892,* by George S. Anderson (Washington, D.C.: GPO, 1892), 4; Pyne, *Fire in America,* 228–29; and George S. Anderson, "Protection of the Yellowstone National Park," in *Hunting in Many Lands: The Book of the Boone and Crockett Club,* ed. Theodore Roosevelt and George Bird Grinnell (New York: Forest and Stream, 1895), 392.

72. During the famous fires of 1988, 720,000 acres burned within the park. William H. Romme and Don G. Despain, "The Yellowstone Fires," *Scientific*

American 261 (November 1989): 37–46. For more general descriptions of the role of fire in shaping the Yellowstone ecosystem, see A. Chase, *Playing God in Yellowstone,* 105–15; Langston, *Forest Dreams, Forest Nightmares,* 26–27; D. L. Taylor, "Forest Fires in Yellowstone National Park," 68–77; and the essays in *The Greater Yellowstone Ecosystem: Redefining America's Wilderness Heritage,* ed. Robert B. Keiter and Mark S. Boyce (New Haven: Yale University Press, 1991), 87–179.

73. Edward A. Preble, *Report on the Condition of Elk in Jackson Hole, Wyoming, in 1911,* U.S. Biological Survey Bulletin No. 40 (Washington, D.C.: GPO, 1911), 7; U.S. Department of the Interior, *Annual Report of the Acting Superintendent of Yellowstone National Park, 1904,* 8; Haines, *Yellowstone Story,* 2:80–83; and Vernon Bailey, *Animal Life of Yellowstone National Park* (Springfield, Ill.: Charles C. Thomas, 1930), 129–41.

74. U.S. Department of the Interior, *Annual Report of the Acting Superintendent of Yellowstone National Park, 1895,* by George S. Anderson, (Washington, D.C.: GPO, 1895), 13; W. M. Rush, *Northern Yellowstone Elk Study* ([Helena?]: Montana Fish and Game Commission, 1933), 20–21; and Douglas B. Houston, *The Northern Yellowstone Elk: Ecology and Management* (New York: Macmillan, 1982), 12–13, 25.

75. Steve W. Chadde and Charles E. Kay, "Tall-Willow Communities on Yellowstone's Northern Range: A Test of the 'Natural-Regulation' Paradigm," in *The Greater Yellowstone Ecosystem: Redefining America's Wilderness Heritage,* ed. Robert B. Keiter and Mark S. Boyce (New Haven: Yale University Press, 1991), 231–62; A. Chase, *Playing God in Yellowstone,* 11–13, 61–70. For an examination of a similar scenario in Rocky Mountain National Park, see Karl Hess Jr., *Rocky Times in Rocky Mountain National Park: An Unnatural History* (Niwot, Colo.: University Press of Colorado, 1993), 42–49.

76. James Scott discusses the ecological dangers of state simplification in *Seeing Like a State,* 11–22. Examples of martial imagery in conservation can be found in "The Army and the Forests," *Garden and Forest* 3 (September 10, 1890): 437; "The Nation's Forests," *Garden and Forest* 2 (October 30, 1889): 517–18; and "More Forest-Reservations," *Garden and Forest* 5 (January 20, 1892): 25–26. Stephen Pyne comments on the inappropriateness of the military metaphor for forest fires (and, by implication, for conservation in general) in "Flame and Fortune," 8–10, and *America's Fires: Management on Wildlands and Forests* (Durham, N.C.: Forest History Society, 1997), 16–23.

CHAPTER 6. MODES OF POACHING AND PRODUCTION

1. U.S. Department of the Interior, *Annual Report of the Acting Superintendent of Yellowstone National Park, 1892,* by George S. Anderson (Washington, D.C.: GPO, 1892), 3, 5, 9; U.S. Department of the Interior, *Annual Report of the Acting Superintendent of Yellowstone National Park, 1895,* 12. Anderson's comments were echoed by *Garden and Forest* magazine, which observed in 1892 that "poachers have settled all around it [Yellowstone] so that the game has no adequate protection." "Our National Parks and Forest Reservation," *Garden and Forest* 5 (December 28, 1892): 613–14.

2. U.S. Department of the Interior, *Annual Report of the Superintendent of Yellowstone National Park, 1886,* 7.

3. William Hornaday, *Wildlife Conservation in Theory and Practice: Lectures Delivered before the Forest School of Yale University* (New Haven: Yale University Press, 1914), 189–90. See also Hornaday, *The Extermination of the American Bison, with a Sketch of Its Discovery and Life History* (Washington, D.C.: U.S. National Museum, 1889), 520.

4. Hornaday, *Our Vanishing Wildlife,* 335.

5. Letter to the editor, *Recreation* 3 (September 1895): 141. See also "West's Vanishing Big Game," *Recreation* 25 (October 1906): 368–69. For an account of local residents using wild game, see Mildred Albert Martin, *The Martins of Gunbarrel* (Caldwell, Idaho: Caxton, 1959), 16, 86.

6. Eric Van Young issued a provocative call for historians to move beyond structural models of causation, in "To See Someone Not Seeing: Historical Studies of Peasants and Politics in Mexico," *Mexican Studies/Estudios Mexicanos* 6 (1990): 133–59.

7. Haines, *Yellowstone Story,* 2:62; *Chicago Tribune,* December 23, 1894.

8. Chittenden, *Yellowstone National Park,* 143–44; "The Capture of Howell," *Forest and Stream* 42 (March 31, 1894): 270; U.S. Department of the Interior, *Annual Report of the Acting Superintendent of Yellowstone National Park, 1894,* by George S. Anderson (Washington, D.C.: GPO, 1894), 9–10; *Livingston (Mont.) Enterprise,* March 31, 1894.

9. "The Yellowstone National Park Protection Act," in *Hunting in Many Lands: The Book of the Boone and Crockett Club,* ed. Theodore Roosevelt and George Bird Grinnell (New York: Forest and Stream, 1895), 414; *Livingston (Mont.) Post,* April 12, 1894.

10. Grinnell's efforts were not limited to the pages of *Forest and Stream.* See, for instance, "The Yellowstone National Park," *Garden and Forest* 7 (April 4, 1894): 131.

11. "A Premium on Crime," *Forest and Stream* 42 (March 24, 1894): 243. In a similar vein *Garden and Forest* remarked, "The fact that Yellowstone Park and the adjacent reservation has been set aside for the use and enjoyment of the people forever is really no protection to its forests or its game, but rather an advertisement to every outlaw that he can steal the timber, or set the woods on fire, or slaughter the big game, without fear of punishment." "The Yellowstone National Park," *Garden and Forest* 7 (April 4, 1894): 131.

12. *Livingston (Mont.) Post,* March 22, 1894.

13. Anderson to Secretary of the Interior, May 14, 1897, "Letters Sent, July 24, 1896-October 1, 1897," Bound Volume VI, Item 218, YNPA; Anderson to Secretary of the Interior, April 8 and June 27, 1891, "Letters Sent, August 18, 1889-June 25, 1892," Bound Volume III, Item 215, YNPA. Emphasis in the original. The 1900 census records forty-nine people living in Cooke City. 1900 Population Census, Manuscript Schedules, Park County, Montana, Roll 913, T623, Records of the Bureau of the Census, RG 29, National Archives.

14. Anderson to Secretary of the Interior, January 20, 1893, and January 7, 1894, "Letters Sent, June 25, 1892–March 17, 1894," Bound Volume IV, Item 216, YNPA; Anderson to Blaine, December 26, 1896, "Letters Sent, July 24,

1896-October 1, 1897," Bound Volume VI, Item 218, YNPA. See also U.S. Department of the Interior, *Annual Report of the Acting Superintendent of Yellowstone National Park, 1889*, CII.

15. *Chicago Tribune*, December 23, 1894; U.S. Department of the Interior, *Annual Report of the Acting Superintendent of Yellowstone Park, 1894*, 9–10. A discussion of the role played by both the Boone and Crockett Club and *Forest and Stream* in passing the Park Protection Act can be found in George Bird Grinnell, *Brief History of the Boone and Crockett Club* (New York: Forest and Stream Publishing, 1910), 18–20.

16. *Livingston (Mont.) Post*, March 29, 1894.

17. *Livingston (Mont.) Enterprise*, March 31, 1894.

18. Anonymous, n.d., Document No. 696, "A-E, January 1, 1882-December 31, 1894," Item 4, YNPA; Anonymous, n.d., Document No. 2553, "F-K, January 1, 1895-December 31, 1899," Item 11, YNPA.

19. Doyle to Pitcher, July 7, 1901, Document No. 3759, "Letters Received, A-E, January 1, 1900-December 31, 1902," Item 15, YNPA; *Livingston (Mont.) Enterprise*, January 1, 1898.

20. *Livingston (Mont.) Post*, April 12 and August 2, 1894.

21. "Park Poachers and Their Ways," *Forest and Stream* 42 (May 26, 1894): 444.

22. Sheffield to Anderson, November 19, 1895, Document No. 1621, "S-Z, January 1, 1894-December 31, 1895," Item 7, YNPA; Anonymous ["Quill"] to Wear, August 14, 1885, Document 679, "A-E, January 1, 1882-December 31, 1894," Item No. 4, YNPA. *United States v. William Binkley, Charles Purdy, and Oscar Adams* (United States District Court, Ninth Circuit, Southern District of California, 1906, Yellowstone National Park Archives), 228. A transcript of this trial is located in "U.S. Commissioner Meldrum—Trial Records," Item 82, YNPA. For more on the linkage between saloons and manliness, see Michael Kaplan, "New York City Tavern Violence and the Creation of a Working-Class Male Identity," *Journal of the Early Republic* 15 (winter 1995): 591–617; and Gorn, *Manly Art,* 133–34.

23. In his study of poaching in England, for example, Roger B. Manning argues that poaching often served as a "symbolic substitute for war": "For those young men whose families did not possess hunting privileges, the act of hunting outside the law, at night, with weapons, and in the face of gamekeepers, must have further satisfied their compulsive need to prove their masculinity and martial valor." Manning, *Hunters and Poachers: A Social and Cultural History of Unlawful Hunting in England, 1485–1640* (Oxford: Clarendon Press, 1993), 8, 35–56. A more general survey of risk and daring as masculine attributes can be found in David Gilmore, *Manhood in the Making: Cultural Concepts of Masculinity* (New Haven: Yale University Press, 1990), 56–77. Gunther Peck offers a provocative discussion of risk-taking in the American West in "Manly Gambles: The Politics of Risk on the Comstock Lode, 1860–1880," *Journal of Social History* 26 (summer 1993): 701–23.

24. "The Account of Howell's Capture," *Forest and Stream,* 377–78.

25. Hofer to Hill, February 5, 1927, Manuscript 91-188, YNPA.

26. Howell to Young, September 24, 1897, Document No. 1504, "Employees, etc., January 1, 1882-December 31, 1897," Item 9, YNPA. On Howell's reward, see Haines, *Yellowstone Story,* 2:205–7. Oddly enough, the money had to be sent to the Philippines, where Howell was working in a restaurant.

27. For these very reasons, conservationists in Africa often hire former poachers as informers or park rangers. N. Gordon, *Ivory Knights,* 137–38.

28. U.S. Department of the Interior, *Annual Report of the Acting Superintendent of Yellowstone National Park, 1895,* 12. The 1900 census records ninety-eight people, comprising thirty-four families, dwelling in Henry's Lake. 1900 Population Census, Manuscript Schedules, Henry's Lake, Fremont County, Idaho, Roll 232, T623, Records of the Bureau of the Census, RG 29, National Archives.

29. Elmer Lindsley, "A Winter Trip through Yellowstone Park," *Harper's Weekly* 42 (January 19, 1898): 106.

30. Emerson Hough, "Yellowstone Park Poachers," *Forest and Stream* 51 (July 16, 1898): 45; U.S. Department of the Interior, *Annual Report of the Acting Superintendent of Yellowstone National Park, 1896,* by George S. Anderson (Washington, D.C.: GPO, 1896), 11.

31. John E. Archer, *By a Flash and a Scare: Incendiarism, Animal Maiming, and Poaching in East Anglia, 1815–1870* (Oxford: Clarendon Press, 1990), 235–37. See also the studies of "poaching fraternities" in Roger Manning, "Unlawful Hunting in England, 1500–1640," *Forest and Conservation History* 38 (January 1994): 20; and in Michael Carter, *Peasants and Poachers in Norfolk: A Study in Rural Disorder in Norfolk* (Suffolk: Boydell Press, 1980), 48–59. Discussions of poaching organizations in the African context can be found in Peter T. Dalleo, "The Somali Role in Organized Poaching in Northeastern Kenya, 1909–1939," *International Journal of African Historical Studies* 12 (1979): 472–82; and Michael L. Stone, "Organized Poaching in Kitui District: A Failure in District Authority," *International Journal of African Historical Studies* 5 (1972): 436–52.

32. U.S. Department of the Interior, *Annual Report of the Acting Superintendent of Yellowstone National Park, 1896,* 11; Roland Whitman, interview by author, March 5, 1996; 1900 Population Census, Manuscript Schedules, Fremont County, Idaho, Roll 232, T623, Records of the Bureau of the Census, RG 29, National Archives.

33. John Whitman, interview by author, October 26, 1994; Trude to Goode, September 12, 1900, Document No. 4620, "Letters Received, S-Z, January 1, 1900-December 31, 1902," Item 19, YNPA; "Killing Park Buffalo," *Forest and Stream* 45 (December 7, 1895): 494; Anderson to Secretary of the Interior, December 16, 1895, "Letters Sent, March 17, 1894–July 23, 1896," Bound Volume V, Item 217, YNPA. See also U.S. Department of the Interior, *Annual Report of the Acting Superintendent of Yellowstone National Park, 1896,* 11.

34. Leigh to Lindsley, December 1 and December 11, 1897, "Leigh, Richard (aka 'Beaver Dick')," Manuscript 91-120, YNPA; McDermott to Anderson, n.d., Document No. 1142, "F–K, January 1, 1881-December 31, 1894," Item 5, YNPA; Manuscript 91-198, YNPA; U.S. Department of the Interior, *Annual*

Report of the Acting Superintendent of Yellowstone National Park, 1891, 10; John Whitman, interview by author.

35. "Veritas" to Anderson, September 18, 1895, Document No. 1699, "S–Z, January 1, 1894-December 31, 1895," Item 7, YNPA.

36. Anonymous, January 24, 1909, "Poaching, Reports of and Inquiries," in "Protection, 1908–1914," Item 105, YNPA. All misspellings reflect the original letter.

37. Anonymous to Anderson, n.d., Document No. 2069, Anonymous to Anderson, n.d., Document 2070, "A–E, January 1, 1895–December 31, 1899," Item 10, YNPA. All misspellings reflect the original letter.

38. In addition to the two letters in the paragraph above, examples of using "citizen" as a pen name include Anonymous to Pitcher, November 17, 1906, Document No. 5818, "A–E, January 1, 1903–December 31, 1906," Item 24, YNPA; Pratt to Erwin, January 4, 1898, Document No. 2852, "L–R, January 1, 1896–December 31, 1899," Item 12, YNPA; Anonymous to Anderson, September 20, 1895, Document No. 2068, "A–E, January 1, 1895–December 31, 1899," Item 10, YNPA.

39. Hague to Pitcher, n.d., Document No. 4042, "F-K, January 1, 1900–December 31, 1903," Item 17, YNPA; Cummins to Anderson, May 18, 1892, Document No. 779, "A–E, January 1, 1882–December 31, 1894," Item 4, YNPA; Lindsley to Young, January 11, 1898, Document No. 1458, "Employees, etc., January 1, 1882–December 31, 1897," Item 9, YNPA; Marshall to Anderson, August 27, 1895. Document No. 1157, "L–R, January 1, 1882–December 31, 1895," Item 6, YNPA. All misspellings reflect the original letters.

40. Leigh to Lindsley, February 20, 1898, Manuscript 91-210, YNPA. All misspellings reflect the original letter.

41. Report of Elmer Lindsley, January 16, 1898, Document No. 4881, "Employees, January 1, 1898–December 31, 1903," Item 20, YNPA; Dean H. Green, *History of Island Park* (Ashton, Idaho: Island Park–Gateway Publishing, 1990), 115.

42. "The Courtenay Buffalo Case," *Forest and Stream* 46 (February 1, 1896): 95; "Snap Shots," *Forest and Stream* 48 (May 8, 1897): 361; "Protect Idaho Buffalo," *Forest and Stream* 45 (July 13, 1895): 23; *Transcript of Trial of James Courtenay, December 26, 1895,* "Undesirables in Park," Item 78, YNPA.

43. "Record of Violations of Rules and Regulations," Item 145, YNPA, 3–9; Nolie Mumey, *Rocky Mountain Dick: Stories of His Adventures in Capturing Wild Animals* (Denver: Range Press, 1953), 65–66, 73; "Yellowstone Park Poachers," *Forest and Stream* 51 (December 31, 1898): 527.

44. "Elk Slaughter in Wyoming," *Forest and Stream* 52 (March 4, 1899): 167; "Slaughtering Elk for Their Teeth," *Forest and Stream* 58 (January 11, 1902): 30.

45. Josephine Paterek, *Encyclopedia of American Indian Costume* (New York: W. W. Norton, 1994), 95, 101, 108–9, 137, 193; "Extinction of the Elks," *Forest and Stream* 59 (September 13, 1902): 205; James Fullerton, *Autobiography of Roosevelt's Adversary* (Boston: Roxburgh Publishing, 1912), 123–24; Calkins, *Jackson Hole,* 133; Elizabeth Wied Hayden, "Driving Out the Tusk Hunters," *Teton Magazine* (winter-spring 1971): 22.

46. Robert B. Betts, *Along the Ramparts of the Tetons: The Saga of Jackson Hole, Wyoming* (Boulder, Colo.: Colorado Associated University Press, 1978), 181. Occasionally, if the animal were frozen solid, one might have to cut off the jaw and boil it to free the canine teeth. See Report of Lt. Ware, November 24, 1903, Document No. 4944, "Employees, January 1, 1898–December 31, 1903," Item 20, YNPA.

47. U.S. Department of the Interior, *Annual Report of the Superintendent of National Parks, 1916* (Washington, D.C.: GPO, 1916), 37; Palmer to Pitcher, April 9, 1907, "U.S. Commissioner Meldrum—Trial Records, Miscellaneous Correspondence," Item 83, YNPA; *U.S. v. Binkley,* 30–31. See also "The Wyoming Game Situation," *Forest and Stream* 52 (June 17, 1899): 466; and the Tusk Hunters file and Binkley file of the Jackson Hole Historical Society.

48. Elinore Pruitt Stewart, *Letters on an Elk Hunt: By a Woman Homesteader* (Boston: Houghton Mifflin, 1915), 127–28; Preble, *Report on the Condition of Elk,* 21. A general recollection of tusking in Jackson Hole can be found in Sam Hicks, "Ivory Dollars," *High Country* 3 (winter 1967): 40–45. A fictional portrait of tusking at this time can be found in Joe Back, *The Sucker's Teeth* (Denver: Sage Books, 1965).

49. *U.S. v. Binkley,* 69; 1900 Population Census, Manuscript Schedules, Records of the Bureau of the Census, RG 29, Election District 13, Uinta County, Wyoming, Roll 1827, T623, National Archives.

50. David Saylor, *Jackson Hole, Wyoming* (Norman: University of Oklahoma Press, 1970), 142; *U.S. v. Binkley,* 292; Stewart, *Letters on an Elk Hunt,* 127.

51. *U.S. v. Binkley,* 99, 291. Other poachers attached elk hooves to the soles of their boots to achieve a similar effect. Calkins, *Jackson Hole,* 135.

52. *U.S. v. Binkley,* 230.

53. Palmer to Pitcher, April 9, 1907, "U.S. Commissioner Meldrum—Trial Records, Miscellaneous Correspondence," Item 83, YNPA.

54. Richard White has suggested that, through such labor, rural folk acquired "a bodily knowledge of the natural world" that has often been overlooked by modern-day environmentalists. See White, "'Are You an Environmentalist or Do You Work for a Living?': Work and Nature," in *Uncommon Ground: Rethinking the Human Place in Nature,* ed. William Cronon (New York: W. W. Norton, 1995), 172; and White, *The Organic Machine* (New York: Hill and Wang, 1995).

55. For an extended discussion of American views on wage work and dependency at this time, see Daniel T. Rodgers, *The Work Ethic in Industrial America, 1850–1920* (Chicago: University of Chicago Press, 1978), 30–40.

56. Sheffield to Brett, November 1, 1912, "Poaching, Reports of and Inquiries, 1909–1913," in "Protection, 1908–1914," Item 105, YNPA. See also the letter to the editor in *Recreation* 6 (May 1897): 368, complaining about "coal diggers" from Aldridge, Montana, poaching Yellowstone's elk. Census information from 1900 indicates that many of the inhabitants of Horr, Aldridge, and Jardine, Montana, were coal or quartz miners. 1900 Population Census, Manuscript Schedules, Park County, Montana, Roll 913, T623, Records of the Bureau of the Census, RG 29, National Archives.

57. D. Jones, *Crime, Protest, Community,* 69. Similarly, West Virginia coal miners often found gardens, livestock, and hunting to be "a highly important economic safety valve in an industry plagued with irregular employment and periodic depressions." David Alan Corbin, *Life, Work, and Rebellion in the Coal Fields: The Southern West Virginia Miners, 1880–1922* (Urbana: University of Illinois Press, 1981), 33–35.

58. "Record of Violations of Rules and Regulations, 1887–1921," Item 145, YNPA; see also U.S. Department of the Interior, *Annual Report of the Acting Superintendent of Yellowstone National Park, 1908,* 12. Although it could be that this increase in arrests came as a result of heightened vigilance by the army, there were no changes in the park's administration until mid-May 1908, when Major H.C. Benson was appointed new acting superintendent and the number of troops at Yellowstone was increased to three hundred.

59. Sacket to Lindsay, January 23, 1914, "Poaching, Reports of and Inquiries, 1909–1913," in "Protection, 1908–1914," Item 105, YNPA; U.S. Department of the Interior, *Annual Report of the Acting Superintendent of Yellowstone National Park, 1912,* by Lloyd M. Brett (Washington, D.C.: GPO, 1912), 11.

60. Letter to the editor, *Recreation* 6 (May 1897): 368; *Livingston (Mont.) Enterprise,* January 22, 1898.

61. William Simpson, "The Game Question in Jackson Hole," *Forest and Stream* 51 (December 10, 1898): 468. Similar discussions of poaching as a questionable alternative to wage labor can be found in Preble, *Report on the Condition of Elk,* 21; Judd, *Common Lands, Common People,* 160, 183–88; and the description of the poacher E.E. Van Dyke in Arnold to Anderson, September 15, 1893, Document No. 670, "A-E, January 1, 1882-December 31, 1894," Item 4, YNPA.

62. W.L. Simpson, "The Jackson Hole's Situation," *Forest and Stream* 51 (December 17, 1898): 485; Romey to Pitcher, May 16, 1902, Document No. 4931, "Employees, January 1, 1898-December 31, 1903," Item 20, YNPA.

63. Quoted in R.B. Betts, *Along the Ramparts of the Tetons,* 184. See also Hayden, "Driving Out the Tusk Hunters," 36. Binkley and his wife took the added precaution of hiding their stash of elk teeth by sewing them into their children's garments, as they "didn't think that the wardens would search the children while they would search those people that came out, grown people." *U.S. v. Binkley,* 289.

64. *U.S. v. Binkley,* 220. For accounts of other Jackson Holers poaching, see R.B. Betts, *Along the Ramparts of the Tetons,* 181. For the story of Binkley's arrest and fine, see Hayden, "Driving Out the Tusk Hunters," 23.

65. Newspaper accounts record Binkley as having anywhere from 227 to 275 elk tusks in his possession. *Pocatello (Idaho) Tribune,* April 26 and April 30, 1907. A similar desire to protect important local resources evinced itself in other communities' attacks on poachers drawn from their own ranks. See, for instance, the account of driving out a rapacious moose poacher in New Hampshire, discussed in Judd, *Common Lands, Common People,* 49.

66. Sign quoted in R.B. Betts, *Along the Ramparts of the Tetons,* 176.

67. "Poaching in the Yellowstone Park," 255; U.S. Department of the Interior, *Annual Report of the Acting Superintendent of Yellowstone National Park, 1907*, 24; and "The Elk Cases," *Forest and Stream* 67 (December 22, 1906): 975. Although authorities tried to get Purdy and Binkley to reveal the whereabouts of their fellow gang members, Adams and Isabel were never caught. Popular legend has it that Binkley killed the two soldiers assigned to guard him and threw their bodies into one of Yellowstone's geysers. *Salt Lake Tribune*, March 13, 1955.

68. U.S. Department of the Interior, *Annual Report of the Acting Superintendent of Yellowstone National Park, 1908*, 12–14; Haines, *Yellowstone Story*, 2:149–53.

69. U.S. Department of the Interior, *Annual Report of the Acting Superintendent of Yellowstone National Park, 1915*, 23; Brett to Nelson, February 5, 1915, "Protection, 1908–1914," Item 105, YNPA.

70. *Livingston (Mont.) Enterprise*, February 9, 1915.

71. "Notes of the Yellowstone Park," *Forest and Stream* 69 (December 28, 1907): 1020; U.S. Department of the Interior, *Annual Report of the Acting Superintendent of Yellowstone National Park, 1909*, by Harry C. Benson (Washington, D.C.: GPO, 1909), 9.

72. U.S. Department of the Interior, *Annual Report of the Acting Superintendent of Yellowstone National Park, 1911*, by Lloyd M. Brett (Washington, D.C.: GPO, 1911), 9; U.S. Department of the Interior, *Annual Report of the Acting Superintendent of Yellowstone National Park, 1912*, 9; U.S. Department of the Interior, *Annual Report of the Acting Superintendent of Yellowstone National Park, 1913*, by Lloyd M. Brett (Washington, D.C.: GPO, 1913), 10.

73. Haines, *Yellowstone Story*, 2:68–72; "Notes from the National Park," *Forest and Stream* 43 (August 11, 1894): 119; U.S. Department of the Interior, *Annual Report of the Superintendent of National Parks, 1916*, 36.

74. Benson to Secretary of the Interior, April 12, 1909, "Undesirables in Park, 1909–1913," Item 78, YNPA; Erwin to Bussear, November 25, 1897, "Letters Sent, October 1, 1897-November 9, 1898," Bound Volume VII, Item 219, YNPA; U.S. Department of the Interior, *Annual Report of the Acting Superintendent of Yellowstone National Park, 1897*, 27–28.

75. *Livingston (Mont.) Enterprise*, December 11, 1897, and February 19, 1898. The parenthetical question mark occurs in the original.

76. "Record of Violations of Rules and Regulations, 1887–1921," 21, 27, Item 145, YNPA.

77. U.S. Department of the Interior, *Annual Report of the Acting Superintendent of Yellowstone National Park, 1915*, 23.

78. In present-day Kenya, Masai warriors have engaged in similar protest behavior, spearing elephants and rhinoceroses in protected parks and then leaving the animals to rot. Tribe members, as one Masai explains, were "turning against wild animals because now they have been brought up to realize that the main cause of their sufferings is wild animals." Quoted in James Hunter, *On the Other Side of Sorrow: Nature and People in the Scottish Highlands* (Edinburgh:

Mainstream Publishing, 1995), 160–61. See also W.K. Lindsay, "Integrating Parks and Pastoralists: Some Lessons from Amboseli," in *Conservation in Africa: People, Policies, and Practice,* ed. David Anderson and Richard Grove (New York: Cambridge University Press, 1987), 159–60.

79. Archer, *By a Flash and a Scare,* 198–221. For a more extensive discussion of the symbology of animal killing, see Robert Darnton, *The Great Cat Massacre and Other Episodes in French Cultural History* (New York: Vintage, 1984), 75–104. Park authorities reported that less than five pounds of meat was taken from the dead elk. Furthermore, the elk killed were two cows and three "spikes" (juvenile animals), all of whose tusks had little or no value. *Livingston (Mont.) Enterprise,* February 9 and February 13, 1915.

80. *Gardiner (Mont.) Wonderland,* May 17, 1902. My insights on revenge killing come from Archer, *By a Flash and a Scare,* 220.

81. *Livingston (Mont.) Enterprise,* February 9 and February 13, 1915.

82. Anderson's comments may be found in U.S. Congress, House, *Inquiry into the Management and Control of the Yellowstone National Park,* 213.

CHAPTER 7. THE HAVASUPAI PROBLEM

1. Captain Jim to Commissioner of Indian Affairs, September 25, 1915, File 115, Havasupai Agency, Central Classified Files, 1907–39, Records of the Bureau of Indian Affairs, RG 75, National Archives. (Hereafter CCF/BIA.) Since Captain Jim could not write, he dictated his letter to D. Clinton West, the Havasupais' Indian agent. The names by which native peoples are referred to in non-Indian documents are often problematic. It is likely, for instance, that "Captain Jim" was a nickname applied by outsiders to someone who was called something quite different by members of his own tribe. Thus, whenever the Indian name is known, I have used this instead of the individual's non-Indian nickname.

2. A number of recent studies have begun to analyze the links between conservation and Indian peoples. See Mark Spence, "Dispossessing the Wilderness: Yosemite Indians and the National Park Ideal, 1864–1930," *Pacific Historical Review* 65 (February 1996): 27–59, and "Crown of the Continent, Backbone of the World: The American Wilderness Ideal and Blackfeet Exclusion from Glacier National Park," *Environmental History* 1 (July 1996): 29–49; Warren, *Hunter's Game,* 71–105, 126–71; and Robert H. Keller and Michael F. Turek, *American Indians and National Parks* (Tucson: University of Arizona Press, 1998). For preliminary sketches of the impact of the national forests on Indian peoples, see Richard White, "Indian Land Use and the National Forests," in Harold K. Steen, *Origins of the National Forests: A Centennial Symposium* (Durham, N.C.: Forest History Society, 1992), 173–80; and Andrew H. Fisher, "The 1932 Handshake Agreement: Yakama Indian Treaty Rights and Forest Service Policy in the Pacific Northwest," *Western Historical Quarterly* 28 (summer 1997): 187–217.

3. Petition of Lac du Flambeau Indians, September 7, 1897 (1897: Letter 37,648) LR/BIA; Bailey to Commissioner of Indian Affairs, May 20, 1903 (1903: Letter 32,694) LR/BIA (although his exact tribal affiliation is hard to determine, Bailey was likely a member of either the Chippewa or Ottawa nations);

Rodwell to Scott, April 21, 1902 (1902: Letter 25,016) LR/BIA. Further evidence of Indian responses to game laws can be found in Campbell to Scott, April 15, 1897 (1897: Letter 15,173) LR/BIA; Mondell to Commissioner of Indian Affairs, August 20, 1904 (1904: Letter 59,861) LR/BIA; Baker to Secretary of the Interior, August 27, 1906 (1906: Letter 91,172) LR/BIA; *Arizona Daily Citizen* (Tucson), October 26 and October 29, 1897; and David Rich Lewis, *Neither Wolf nor Dog: American Indians, Environment, and Agrarian Change* (New York: Oxford University Press, 1994), 50.

4. For a discussion of Indian disempowerment during this time, see Richard White, *"It's Your Misfortune and None of My Own": A History of the American West* (Norman: University of Oklahoma Press, 1991), 439.

5. A memo from J. V. Lloyd to Superintendent Tillotson, November 29, 1937, refers, for example, to the "local Supai problem." See also Tillotson's "The Problem of the Havasupai Camp near Grand Canyon Village," June 18, 1936. Both are from Havasupai Indian Collection, File A9431, Grand Canyon National Park Museum Collection. (Hereafter GCNPMC.)

6. Frank Hamilton Cushing recorded this myth when he visited the Havasupai in 1881. See Frank H. Cushing, *The Nation of the Willows* (Flagstaff, Ariz.: Northland Press, 1965), 73. (This book is a reprint of two articles that Cushing wrote for the *Atlantic Monthly* in 1882.) Other Havasupai myths can be found in Carma Lee Smithson and Robert C. Euler, *Havasupai Legends: Religion and Mythology of the Havasupai Indians of the Grand Canyon* (Salt Lake: University of Utah Press, 1994); and Juan Sinyella, "Havasupai Traditions," ed. J. Donald Hughes, *Southwest Folklore* 1 (spring 1977): 35–52.

7. Useful discussions of Havasupai farming and land use practices can be found in Elman Service, "Recent Observations on Havasupai Land Tenure," *Southwestern Journal of Anthropology* 3 (winter 1947): 360–66; and John F. Martin, "A Reconsideration of Havasupai Land Tenure," *Ethnology* 7 (October 1968): 450–60.

8. Since the Walapai and the Havasupai spoke the same dialect of the Yuman language and often intermarried, some scholars consider the two groups branches of the same tribe that became distinct from one another only as a result of federal policies. Robert A. Manners, *An Ethnological Report on the Hualapai (Walapai) Indians of Arizona* (New York: Garland, 1974), 14–17, 37–39. For more on the relations between the Havasupai and their neighbors, see Steven A. Weber and P. David Seaman, eds., *Havasupai Habitat: A. F. Whiting's Ethnography of a Traditional Indian Culture* (Tucson: University of Arizona Press, 1985), 11; and Thomas A. Sheridan, *Arizona: A History* (Tucson: University of Arizona Press, 1995), 74–75.

9. Mark Hanna, *Autobiography of Mark Hanna, as told to Richard Emerick*, ed. Jon Reyhner (Billings, Mont.: Eastern Montana College, 1988), 19; J. Donald Hughes, *In the House of Stone and Light: A Human History of the Grand Canyon* (Grand Canyon, Ariz.: Grand Canyon Natural History Association, 1978), 12–14; and Leslie Spier, "Havasupai Ethnography," *Anthropological Papers of the American Museum of Natural History* 29 (1928): 244–46.

10. "Depositions of Big Jim, Billy Burro, Supai Mary and Allen Akaba," 7–10, 20, 21, 53, Records of the Indian Claims Commission, Havasupai Tribe,

Docket 91, RG 279, National Archives. (Hereafter "Depositions, 1950.") Big Jim should not be confused with Captain Jim, whose letter opened this chapter.

11. Weber and Seaman, *Havasupai Habitat*, 45–47; "Depositions, 1950," 16. Useful descriptions of the Havasupai seasonal cycle can be found in Douglas W. Schwartz, *On the Edge of Splendor: Exploring Grand Canyon's Human Past* (Santa Fe, N.M.: School of American Research, 1988), 43–45; and Stephen Hirst, *Havsuw 'Baaja: People of the Blue Green Water* (Supai, Ariz.: Havasupai Tribe, 1985), 39–40.

12. Spier, "Havasupai Ethnography," 246–48.

13. The Havasupai apparently had horses as early as 1775. See Francisco Garces, *On the Trail of a Spanish Pioneer: The Diary and Itinerary of Francisco Garces in His Travels through Sonora, Arizona, and California, 1775–1776*, ed. Elliot Coues (New York: Francis P. Harper, 1900), 2:337–39. Garces suspected that many of the Havasupais' animals may have been stolen from settlers in New Mexico, since they sported Spanish brands. One additional advantage of having horses was that the Havasupai could kill and eat them during lean times. See Hanna, *Autobiography of Mark Hanna*, 23; and Weber and Seaman, *Havasupai Habitat*, 28–34.

14. Spier, "Havasupai Ethnography," 362–68; Hirst, *Havsuw 'Baaja,* 45–46; "Depositions, 1950," 35.

15. Hughes, *In the House of Stone and Light*, 47.

16. *Flagstaff, Arizona, Champion*, September 1886 and January 22, 1887. A useful account of early tourism can be found in Frederic Trautmann, trans. and ed., "Germans at the Grand Canyon: The Memoirs of Paul Lindau, 1883," *Journal of Arizona History* 26 (winter 1985): 375–94.

17. Hughes, *In the House of Stone and Light*, 54; and Douglas H. Strong, "The Man Who 'Owned' Grand Canyon," *American West* 6 (September 1969): 33–40. For more on the Hance and Cameron trails, see Thomas E. Way, *Destination: Grand Canyon* (Phoenix: Golden West Publishers, 1990), 83, 85–86, 88–90.

18. Henry F. Dobyns and Robert C. Euler, *The Havasupai People* (Phoenix: Indian Tribal Series, 1971), 34. A glimpse of the Havasupai oral tradition about this population loss can be found in Sinyella, "Havasupai Traditions," 42–43.

19. Cushing, *Nation of the Willows*, 52; and U.S. Bureau of Indian Affairs, *Annual Report of the Commissioner of Indian Affairs, 1892* (Washington, D.C.: GPO, 1892), 650. Mark Hanna recalls searching for old clothing in the Williams dump. Hanna, *Autobiography of Mark Hanna*, 20. During this time, the Walapai also "clothe[d] themselves frequently with garments cast off by the whites." William McConnell to Secretary of the Interior, August 9, 1899, Reports of Inspection of the Field Jurisdictions of the Office of Indian Affairs, 1873–1900, M1070, Roll 20, Records of the Bureau of Indian Affairs, RG 75, National Archives.

20. Earl Henderson, *The Havasupai Indian Agency, Arizona* (Washington, D.C.: GPO, 1928), 8; Frank Hamilton Cushing, "Navajo's Message," July 7, 1881 (1881: Letter 17,434) LR/BIA. This letter was supposedly dictated by Chief Navajo to Cushing.

21. George Wharton James, *Indians of the Painted Desert Region: Hopis, Navahoes, Wallapais, Havasupais* (Boston: Little Brown, 1903), 232–33; Hanna, *Autobiography of Mark Hanna*, 51.

22. Frank E. Casanova, ed., "General Crook Visits the Supais as Reported by John G. Bourke," *Arizona and the West* 10 (autumn 1968): 272–73; *Prescott, Arizona, Journal-Miner*, August 23, 1890; Daniel Dorchester, "Report of Matters Relating to the Supai," March 28, 1892 (1892: Letter 12,588) LR/BIA; Testimony of John Davis, September 14, 1893 (1893: Letter 36,542) LR/BIA.

23. Casanova, "General Crook Visits the Supais," 268; U.S. Bureau of Indian Affairs, *Annual Report of the Commissioner of Indian Affairs, 1892, 650*; Cushing, *Nation of the Willows*, 57; Frank Hamilton Cushing, "Navajo's Message," July 7, 1881 (1881: Letter 17,434) LR/BIA.

24. Symons to Commissioner of Indian Affairs, July 16, 1913, Havasupai Agency, File 307.4, CCF/BIA; Dobyns and Euler, *Havasupai People*, 33.

25. For copies of the original executive order, as well as its subsequent revisions, see the *Phoenix Territorial Expositor*, July 9, 1880; and the U.S. Bureau of Indian Affairs, *Annual Report of the Commissioner of Indian Affairs, 1882* (Washington, D.C.: GPO, 1892), 246–47.

26. Palfrey's report of July 20, 1881, can be found in the Records of the Adjutant General's Office, Letters Received, 1881–1889 (M689), 1528 AGO 1881, RG 94, National Archives. (Hereafter 1528 AGO 1881.)

27. Navajo's supposed recommendations can be found in Report of William Redwood Price, July 1, 1881 (1528 AGO 1881). For the Havasupais' later response to their reservation's monuments, see D. H. Dillon to Secretary of the Interior, January 17, 1891 (1891: Letter 3,266) LR/BIA.

28. Extract from a report of R. K. Evans, February 10, 1881 (1528 AGO 1881). Even in 1930, the chief of the Havasupai could produce documents from the 1880s demonstrating his tribe's right to the lands contained within the reservation. Caring for these documents appears, in fact, to have been a mark of leadership. As the chief Manakaja remarked through an interpreter, "Those letters is from officials; they are official letters.... before he is made a chief one of his relatives had those papers along with him.... He is supposed to keep them as long as this tribe lives." U.S. Congress, Senate, *Survey of Conditions of the Indians in the United States: Part 17: Arizona: Hearings before a Subcommittee of the Committee on Indian Affairs*, 71st Cong., 3rd sess., 1911, 8749.

29. "Examiner's Report on Tribal Claims to Released Railroad Lands in Northwestern Arizona, May 1942," Exhibit DD, Records of the Indian Claim Commission, Havasupai Tribe, Docket 91, RG 279, National Archives.

30. H. S. Welton to Commissioner of Indian Affairs, June 29, 1888 (1888: Letter 16,641) LR/BIA; G. M. Brayton to Assistant Adjutant General, January 26, 1888 (1888: Letter 4,739) LR/BIA; and H. S. Welton to Commissioner of Indian Affairs, June 29, 1888 (1888: Letter 16,641) LR/BIA.

31. W. W. Bass to T. J. Morgan, July 25, 1890 (1890: Letter 23,359) LR/BIA; McGowan to Commissioner of Indian Affairs, September 11, 1890 (1890: Letter 28,941) LR/BIA.

32. W. H. Holabird to Secretary of the Interior, May 26, 1890 (1890: Letter 17,065) LR/BIA.

33. George B. Duncan to Post Adjutant, February 21, 1890 (1890: Letter 20,227) LR/BIA.

34. "Depositions, 1950," 57–58. Supai Mary gives a similar account of dispossession, 46.

35. A similar, if less planned, pattern unfolded in the canyon itself, where feral burros, having escaped from prospectors, competed with the mountain sheep that the tribe normally hunted.

36. Bean to Commissioner of Indian Affairs, December 12, 1885 (Letter 29759:1885) LR/BIA.

37. Bass to Miles, January 28, 1890 (1890: Letter 9,185) LR/BIA.

38. Powell to Belt, February 8, 1892 (1892: Letter 5,117) LR/BIA; W. H. Holabird to Secretary of the Interior, May 26, 1890 (1890: Letter 17,065) LR/BIA. Mark Hanna recollected that during his youth he ate rabbits and rats more often than antelope and mountain sheep. Hanna, *Autobiography of Mark Hanna,* 2.

39. For examples of calls to enlarge the Havasupai reservation, see Brayton to Adjutant General, January 26, 1888 (1888: Letter 4,739) LR/BIA; and Duncan to Post Adjutant, February 21, 1890 (1890: Letter 9,185) LR/BIA. The quotations on BIA efforts to improve Havasupai farming are from the U.S. Bureau of Indian Affairs, *Annual Report of the Commissioner of Indian Affairs, 1892,* 649–50; and Daniel Dorchester, "Report of Matters Relating to the Supai," March 28, 1892 (1892: Letter 12,588) LR/BIA.

40. Gaddis to McCowan, April 30, 1892 (1892: Letter 18,326) LR/BIA; U.S. Bureau of Indian Affairs, *Annual Report of the Commissioner of Indian Affairs, 1893* (Washington, D.C.: GPO, 1893), 402; Gaddis to McCowan, May 6, 1893 (1893: Letter 17,893) LR/BIA.

41. U.S. Bureau of Indian Affairs, *Annual Report of the Commissioner of Indian Affairs, 1899* (Washington, D.C.: GPO, 1899), 156; Weber and Seaman, *Havasupai Habitat,* 44.

42. Putesoy quoted in Hirst, *Havsuw 'Baaja,* 91. The poaching of livestock seems to have been more common among the Havasupais' close relatives, the Walapai, who were forced to such desperate measures because of the meager resources on their reservation. See Henry F. Dobyns and Robert C. Euler, *The Ghost Dance of 1889 among the Pai Indians of Northwestern Arizona* (Prescott, Ariz.: Prescott College Press, 1967), 8; and Ewing to Taggart, April 30, 1899 (1899: Letter 21,339) LR/BIA.

43. U.S. Bureau of Indian Affairs, *Annual Report of the Commissioner of Indian Affairs, 1906* (Washington, D.C.: GPO, 1906), 179; Hanna, *Autobiography of Mark Hanna,* 30, 44–46. Arizona resident A. G. Oliver reported in 1890 that the Havasupai were "industrious and at all times willing to work having had a number of them in my employ, in the mines at several times." Oliver to Russell, February 11, 1890 (1890: Letter 9,185) LR/BIA. For a discussion of the appeals of seasonal wage labor for marginal groups, see Sarah Deutsch, *No Separate Refuge: Culture, Class, and Gender on an Anglo-His-*

panic Frontier in the American Southwest, 1880–1940 (New York: Oxford University Press, 1987), 30–31.

44. Bass to McGowan, March 2, 1891 (1891: Letter 9,602) LR/BIA.

45. This description of the dance, which comes from a Walapai informant, must have closely paralleled the Havasupai understanding of the ceremony. Quoted in Dobyns and Euler, *Ghost Dance,* 20. For a description of the official reaction to the Ghost Dance, see Ewing to Commissioner of Indian Affairs, March 29, 1898 (1898: Letter 15,139) LR/BIA.

46. Dobyns and Euler, *Ghost Dance,* 27; Hirst, *Havsuw 'Baaja,* 56–57; Spier, "Havasupai Ethnography," 261–66. Most scholars, following Spier, have argued that the Ghost Dance movement died out after a year. There is some evidence, however, that certain elements of the dance were integrated into the Havasupais' ongoing ceremonial life. Smithson and Euler, *Havasupai Legends,* 28–30.

47. A copy of the order creating the Grand Cañon Forest Reserve can be found in Records of the Department of the Interior, Patents and Miscellaneous, Entry 168 (Records Relating to Forest Reserves), RG 48, National Archives. See also U.S. General Land Office, *Annual Report of the Commissioner of the General Land Office, 1893* (Washington, D.C.: GPO, 1893), 77–79; and "List of the Western Forest Reserves," *Forest and Stream* 52 (January 28, 1899): 67.

48. Henry S. Graves, *The Principles of Handling Woodlands* (New York: John Wiley and Sons, 1911), v; U.S. General Land Office, *Annual Report of the Commissioner of the General Land Office, 1902* (Washington, D.C.: GPO, 1902), 81–83. References to the import of forest conservation for irrigation can be found in Edward Braniff, "The Reserve Policy in Operation," *Forestry Quarterly* 2 (May 1904): 142; and "Forest Reserves of North America," in *American Big Game in Its Haunts,* ed. George Bird Grinnell (New York: Harper and Brothers, 1904), 455–60. Marsh's arguments are referred to in U.S. General Land Office, *Annual Report of the Commissioner of the General Land Office, 1877* (Washington, D.C.: GPO, 1877), 25. For a discussion of national forests in the East, see William E. Shands, "The Lands Nobody Wanted: The Legacy of the Eastern National Forests," in *Origins of the National Forests: A Centennial Symposium,* ed. Harold K. Steen (Durham, N.C.: Forest History Society, 1992), 19–44.

49. See, for example, the mentions of Indian incendiarism in Franklin B. Hough, *Report upon Forestry, 1877,* 155, *Report upon Forestry, 1878–79* (Washington, D.C.: GPO, 1880), 12, and *Report upon Forestry, 1882* (Washington, D.C.: GPO, 1882), 224; as well as Schotzka, *American Forests,* 11. Even as late as 1901, federal administrators would blame native peoples for setting 124 fires on national forest lands during the previous year. U.S. General Land Office, *Annual Report of the Commissioner of the General Land Office, 1901* (Washington, D.C.: GPO, 1901), 135, 441.

50. Report of Edward Bender, January 31, 1898, Records of the General Land Office, Division R, National Forests, Grand Canyon, Box 59, RG 49, National Archives.

51. F. B. Hough, *Report upon Forestry, 1877*, 26–27.

52. F. B. Hough, *Report upon Forestry, 1882*, 129–30.

53. U.S. General Land Office, *Annual Report of the Commissioner of the General Land Office, 1885* (Washington, D.C.: GPO, 1885), 81–82; U.S. General Land Office, *Annual Report of the Commissioner of the General Land Office, 1886* (Washington, D.C.: GPO, 1886), 101; and Schotzka, *American Forests*, 11.

54. The report of the American Association for the Advancement of Science is reprinted in F. B. Hough, *Report upon Forestry, 1882*, 54; "Recent Forest Legislation," *Garden and Forest* 4 (April 22, 1891): 181; F. B. Hough, *Report upon Forestry, 1877*, 15, n. 1. A concern for morality floated near the surface of much of the late nineteenth-century writing about conservation. Fernow, for example, spoke of "the wide bearing which a proper forestry policy has upon the material and moral development of a country," arguing that it was "the moral aspect of our present condition in regard to our public timber lands" that necessitated the creation of governmentally protected forest preserves. Bernhard E. Fernow, "Report of the Forestry Division," in U.S. Department of Agriculture, *Annual Report of the Commissioner of Agriculture, 1887*, 606. See also Samuel Hays's intriguing discussion of how the term *conservation* was applied to all sorts of crusades during the progressive era, in *Conservation and the Gospel of Efficiency*, 175.

55. The quote about "unscrupulous companies" can be found in U.S. General Land Office, *Annual Report of the Commissioner of the General Land Office, 1886*, 102; see also U.S. General Land Office, *Annual Report of the Commissioner of the General Land Office, 1880* (Washington, D.C.: GPO, 1881), 171; Gifford Pinchot, *The Fight for Conservation* (New York: Doubleday, Page, 1910), 43, 80. The argument that corporations favored conservation has been made most eloquently by Samuel Hays in *Conservation and the Gospel of Efficiency*, 1–2, 50. Other scholars to reach similar conclusions include Gabriel Kolko, *The Triumph of Conservatism: A Reinterpretation of American History, 1900–1916* (New York: Free Press, 1963); and Michael Williams, *Americans and Their Forests: A Historical Geography* (New York: Cambridge University Press, 1989), 407–9.

56. Breen to Commissioner of GLO, May 10, 1902 (1902: Letter 1,583) Records of the Department of the Interior, Lands and Railroad Division, Entry 550, RG 48, National Archives; and Hanna to Commissioner of GLO, March 9, 1901 (Letterbook of Isaac B. Hanna) Records of the Forest Service, Entry 13, RG 95, National Archives.

57. H. S. Betts, *Possibilities of Western Pines as a Source of Naval Stores*. Forest Service Bulletin No. 116 (Washington, D.C.: GPO, 1912); Entry 64 (General Correspondence, Forest Supervision, Region 3), Records of the Forest Service, RG 95, National Archives. See also Hays, *Conservation and the Gospel of Efficiency*, 57–60; Robbins, *American Forestry*, 17; and J. H. Allison, "Silvical Report on the Coconino National Forest," 1906, Box 65, Entry 115 (Forest Research Compilation Files) Records of the Forest Service, RG 95, National Archives; and George W. Kimball, "The Silvicultural and Commercial Future of the Woodland Type in Northern Arizona," 1914, Box 27, Entry 115 (Forest Re-

search Compilation Files), Records of the Forest Service, RG 95, National Archives. Unlike the managers of the Adirondacks, Pinchot, in keeping with his European training, believed that forest resources could be harvested without damaging the water flow that the reserves sought to protect. Pinchot's rather negative assessment of the Adirondack Park's contribution to scientific forestry can be found in *Breaking New Ground* (New York: Harcourt, Brace, Jovanovich, 1947), 26–27, 182–87.

CHAPTER 8. FAREWELL SONG

1. Lamoreux to Secretary of the Interior, April 14, 1894, Records of the Department of the Interior, Patents and Miscellaneous, Entry 168, RG 48, National Archives. This order forbade the driving, feeding, grazing, pasturing, or herding of cattle, sheep, or other livestock in the forest reserves. See also Hays, *Conservation and the Gospel of Efficiency*, 55.

2. Descriptions of the tearing down of signs posted at forest reserves can be found in U.S. General Land Office, *Annual Report of the Commissioner of the General Land Office, 1894* (Washington, D.C.: GPO, 1894), 95; and U.S. General Land Office, *Annual Report of the Commissioner of the General Land Office, 1900* (Washington, D.C.: GPO, 1900), 113.

3. U.S. General Land Office, *Annual Report of the Commissioner of the General Land Office, 1892* (Washington, D.C.: GPO, 1892), 48; U.S. General Land Office, *Annual Report of the Commissioner of the General Land Office, 1897* (Washington, D.C.: GPO, 1897), 85; "Forestry by Proclamation," *Garden and Forest* 7 (December 12, 1894): 491.

4. "Our National Parks and Forest Reservations," *Garden and Forest* 5 (December 28, 1892): 613–14.

5. "The Army and the Forests," *Garden and Forest* 3 and 4 (September 10, 1890): 437, and (January 7, 1891): 2.

6. [Robert Underwood Johnson,] "How to Preserve the Forests," *Century* 38 (June 1889): 312–13. Johnson's editorial drew much of its inspiration from "The Nation's Forests," *Garden and Forest* 2 (January 30, 1889): 49, in which the magazine's editors first proposed using the army to patrol public forestlands.

7. Bowers to Secretary of the Interior, June 23, 1893. The army's response can be found in Grant to Secretary of the Interior, August 28, 1893, Records of the Department of the Interior, Patents and Misc., Entry 168, Box 1, RG 48, National Archives. Further discussions on having the military manage the forest reserves can be found in U.S. General Land Office, *Annual Report of the Commissioner of the General Land Office, 1890* (Washington, D.C.: GPO, 1890), 81–82; U.S. General Land Office, *Annual Report of the Commissioner of the General Land Office, 1894*, 97; U.S. General Land Office, *Annual Report of the Commissioner of the General Land Office, 1896* (Washington, D.C.: GPO, 1896), 71–73; "Extending the National Park," *Forest and Stream* 52 (January 7, 1899): 1; and the *New York Sun*, November 5, 1896.

8. U.S. General Land Office, *Annual Report of the Commissioner of the General Land Office, 1896*, 72; Gaddis to Dorchester, April 2, 1893 (1893: Letter 14,387) LR/BIA. The best study of GLO management during this time

period is James Muhn's, "Early Administration of the Forest Reserve Act: Interior Department and General Land Office Policies, 1891–1897," in *Origins of the National Forests: A Centennial Symposium*, ed. Harold K. Steen (Durham, N.C.: Forest History Society, 1992), 259–75. Muhn argues convincingly that the GLO's administration was as good as could be expected, given "the limited means available to them" at the time.

9. Commissioner of GLO to Stewart, August 5, 1893, Letterbook 12, 168, Records of the General Land Office, Division R, Entry 911, RG 49, National Archives (hereafter LS/GLO); Commissioner of GLO to Tilton, October 21, 1893, Letterbook 12, 456, LS/GLO.

10. In New Mexico, Spanish-speaking Hispanos were to find a similar set of legal barriers barring their use of collective lands enclosed within forest reserves during the late nineteenth and early twentieth centuries.

11. U.S. General Land Office, *Annual Report of the Commissioner of the General Land Office, 1898* (Washington, D.C.: GPO, 1898), 85, 91–92; U.S. General Land Office, *Annual Report of the Commissioner of the General Land Office, 1900*, 96–97. See also Charles D. Walcott, *The United States Forest Reserves* (New York: D. Appleton, 1898), a reprint of an article that appeared in *Appletons' Popular Science Monthly* in February 1898.

12. B. Hermann to W.P. Hermann, August 1, 1898, Letterbook 28, 249, LS/GLO; B. Hermann to Allen, September 28, 1898, Letterbook 30, 1–6, LS/GLO.

13. W.P. Hermann to Commissioner of the GLO, November 9, 1898 (1898: Letter 53,747) LR/BIA. Arizona's game law is discussed in the U.S. Bureau of Indian Affairs, *Annual Report of the Commissioner of Indian Affairs, 1897* (Washington, D.C.: GPO, 1897), 105. The Havasupais' agent worried that tribe members, who continued to hunt off the reservation despite the changes in Arizona's law, might find themselves in the same sort of violent confrontation that had occurred near Yellowstone between the Bannock Indians and white settlers: "I devoutly hope that the 'Jackson Hole' trouble will not be repeated with these Indians as victims."

14. Holland to Commissioner of Indian Affairs, September 14, 1901 (1901: Letter 51,455) LR/BIA; Indian Rights Association, *Nineteenth Annual Report of the Executive Committee of the Indian Rights Association* (Philadelphia: Indian Rights Association, 1902), 22–23. See also Indian Rights Association to Secretary of the Interior, May 21, 1901 (1901: Letter 8,079) Records of the Department of the Interior, Indian Division, Entry 653, RG 48, National Archives; and Ewing's comments in U.S. Bureau of Indian Affairs, *Annual Report of the Commissioner of Indian Affairs, 1901* (Washington, D.C.: GPO, 1901), 527.

15. Richards to Commissioner of Indian Affairs, February 10, 1903 (1903: Letter 9,631) LR/BIA; Kirk to Commissioner of Indian Affairs, April 18, 1901 (1901: Letter 22,004) LR/BIA; Reed to Forester, November 24, 1900 (1906: Letter 107,320) LR/BIA; and Commissioner of General Land Office to Secretary of the Interior, October 18, 1898 (1898: Letter 47,743) LR/BIA. For more on the presence of Navajos and Apaches in the Gila River Forest Reserve,

see Commissioner of Indian Affairs to Hayzlett, December 3, 1900, Letterbook 460 (Land), Letters Sent, Records of the Bureau of Indian Affairs, RG 75, National Archives. (Hereafter LS/BIA.)

16. Big Jim's letter to the Commissioner of Indian Affairs is best read as one effort in this direction—an appeal to one branch of the state, the BIA, to nullify the position taken by another branch, the Arizona Fish and Game Commission and the Forest Service. For examples of interagency cooperation, see Commissioner of GLO to Secretary of the Interior, October 29, 1898 (1898: Letter 49,680) LR/BIA; and Commissioner of GLO to Commissioner of Indian Affairs, October 29, 1898 (1898: Letter 49,346) LR/BIA.

17. Flora Gregg Iliff, *People of the Blue Water: My Adventures among the Walapai and Havasupai Indians* (New York: Harper and Brothers, 1954), 196–97. A similar example comes from the agent at the La Pointe Reservation in Wisconsin, who admitted to his superiors, "I would not report or prosecute an Indian, if I saw him kill a deer for his own use in closed season." Campbell to Commissioner of Indian Affairs, August 23, 1906 (1906: Letter 74,394) LR/BIA.

18. Assistant Commissioner of Indian Affairs to Ewing, December 2, 1898, Letterbook 392 (Land), 385–87, LS/BIA. Ewing to Commissioner of Indian Affairs, February 4, 1899 (1899: Letter 6,835) LR/BIA.

19. Commissioner of Indian Affairs to Secretary of the Interior, December 13, 1900, Letterbook 461 (Land), 147–48, LS/BIA; Hanna to Commissioner of the General Land Office, October 6, 1900 (1900: Letter 53,353) LR/BIA; and Commissioner of the GLO to Secretary of the Interior, February 8, 1900, and Commissioner of Indian Affairs to Secretary of the Interior, February 17, 1900 (1898: Letter 4,437) Records of the Department of the Interior, Lands and Railroads Division, Entry 550, RG 48, National Archives. (These last two letters are included within the same GLO file.)

20. Commissioner of Indian Affairs to Sliker, November 8, 1902, Letterbook 567 (Land), 27–28, LS/BIA. Sliker was Arizona's Fish and Game Commissioner. See also Commissioner of Indian Affairs to Hayzlett, December 3, 1900, Letterbook 460 (Land), 67–69, LS/BIA.

21. Commissioner of Indian Affairs to Ewing, November 3, 1900, Letterbook 457 (Land), 198–99, LS/BIA.

22. Commissioner of Indian Affairs to Ewing, December 13, 1900, Letterbook 461 (Land), 168–70, LS/BIA.

23. Ewing to Commissioner of Indian Affairs, December 18, 1900 (1900: Letter 63,048) LR/BIA; U.S. Bureau of Indian Affairs, *Annual Report of the Commissioner of Indian Affairs, 1904* (Washington, D.C.: GPO, 1904), 154.

24. Taggart to Commissioner of Indian Affairs, June 30, 1905 (1905: Letter 52,472) LR/BIA. Taggart was a Special U.S. Indian Agent, charged with investigating conditions on reservations throughout the West.

25. Ibid.; Iliff, *People of the Blue Water*, 200; Association of American Indian Affairs, *The Havasupai: Prisoners of the Grand Canyon* (N.p.: Association of American Indian Affairs, [1972?]), 8; Barbara J. Morehouse, *A Place Called Grand Canyon: Contested Geographies* (Tucson: University of Arizona Press,

1996), 45–46; Hirst, *Havsuw 'Baaja*, 74. For a discussion of Havasupai build-ing techniques, see Weber and Seaman, *Havasupai Habitat*, 78–82.

26. Report of H. F. Robinson in U.S. Congress, House, *Grand Canyon Na-tional Park*, 65th Cong., 2nd sess., 1917–18, H. Rept. 832 (Serial Set 7308), 4.

27. National Park Service Grazing Permit, 1923. Records of the National Park Service, File 901, Central Classified File, 1907–32: Grand Canyon, RG 79, National Archives. (Hereafter CCF/NPS.) Inspection report of S. A. M. Young, May 8, 1916, File 150, Havasupai Agency, CCF/BIA.

28. Lovenskiold to Commissioner of Indian Affairs, July 8, 1924, and Gens-ler to Commissioner of Indian Affairs, September 4, 1919; both are in File 916, Havasupai Agency, CCF/BIA; Lovenskiold to Commissioner of Indian Affairs, January 8, 1926, File 100, Havasupai Agency, CCF/BIA.

29. "Depositions, 1950," 15; U.S. Bureau of Indian Affairs, *Annual Report of the Commissioner of Indian Affairs, 1906, 179*; Taylor to Commissioner of Indian Affairs, May 11, 1914, File 255, Havasupai Agency, CCF/BIA. The adoption of cattle raising did not completely prevent all conflicts over own-ership: non-Indian ranchers occasionally accused the Havasupai of poaching their cattle. One such misunderstanding led to the death of Wa luthma (Supai Charley), who died in the Flagstaff jail of pneumonia after being arrested for killing a cow that he asserted belonged to him but which ranchers claimed as their own. See File 175, Havasupai Agency, CCF/BIA; and Hirst, *Havsuw 'Baaja*, 80–82. A useful analysis of the legal history of rights to wild game can be found in Arthur McEvoy, "Toward an Interactive Theory of Nature and Cul-ture: Ecology, Production, and Cognition in the California Fishing Industry," in *The Ends of the Earth: Perspectives on Modern Environmental History*, ed. Donald Worster (New York: Cambridge University Press, 1988), 211–29.

30. By 1941, the impact of cattle grazing was such that "the Havasupai often found it difficult to locate even an isolated specimen of many of the old staple wild food plants." Weber and Seaman, *Havasupai Habitat*, 45–47.

31. U.S. Congress, Senate, *Survey of Conditions of the Indians in the United States: Part 17: Arizona*, 8739, 8746. In his ethnography of the Havasupai, Whiting asserted that by 1941 "the feeling of obligation to share with everyone was decreasing," with more and more meat being traded or sold for cash in-stead of being given away. See Weber and Seaman, *Havasupai Habitat*, 42–43.

32. Laben to Commissioner of Indian Affairs, December 8, 1921, File 916, Havasupai Agency, CCF/BIA; *News Bulletin*, October 4, 1927, File 501, Grand Canyon, CCF/NPS; Glen Sturdevant, "Mescal," *Grand Canyon Nature Notes* 1 (June 26, 1926): 4–5.

33. "Grand Canyon National Forest Made Game Preserve," *Forestry and Irrigation* 14 (August 1908): 453.

34. Laben to Commissioner of Indian Affairs, April 26, 1921, File 112, Ha-vasupai Agency, CCF/BIA.

35. W. H. Peters, Report for December 1919, Reports Superintendent, PI 166, Entry 7, Central Files, 1907–39, Records of the National Park Service, RG 79, National Archives. (Hereafter RS/NPS.)

36. W. W. Crosby, Report for December 1922, RS/NPS; George Bolton, Report for February 1923, RS/NPS; J. R. Eakin, Report for February, 1926, RS/NPS.

37. A discussion of the Havasupais' use of snares, clubs, and hunting sticks can be found in Weber and Seaman, *Havasupai Habitat,* 37–39; for other hunting tactics used at this time, see Hirst, *Havsuw 'Baaja,* 127–28. The Havasupais' intimacy with their local surroundings did not go unnoticed by contemporary observers. In 1912, the naturalist Charles Sheldon hired a Havasupai named Sinyala "to show me the country up the east canyon." "It is interesting to go with him [Sinyala]," observed Sheldon. "He knows every foot of the country." Sheldon, *The Wilderness of the Southwest: Charles Sheldon's Quest for Desert Bighorn Sheep and Adventures with the Havasupai and Seri Indians,* ed. Neil B. Carmony and David E. Brown (1979; reprint, Salt Lake City: University of Utah Press, 1993), 12.

38. Weber and Seaman, *Havasupai Habitat,* 77–78; U.S. Department of the Interior, *Annual Report of the Board of Indian Commissioners, 1929* (Washington, D.C.: GPO, 1929), 28–29; Spier, "Havasupai Ethnography," 144–45; and "Depositions, 1950," 34. See also Symons to Commissioner of Indian Affairs, January 1, 1913, File 205, Havasupai Agency, CCF/BIA; and White to Commissioner of Indian Affairs, May 23, 1918, File 151, Havasupai Agency, CCF/BIA.

39. U.S. Bureau of Indian Affairs, *Annual Report of the Commissioner of Indian Affairs, 1897,* 105; U.S. Bureau of Indian Affairs, *Annual Report of the Commissioner of Indian Affairs, 1900* (Washington, D.C.: GPO, 1900), 203. See also U.S. Bureau of Indian Affairs, *Annual Report of the Commissioner of Indian Affairs, 1898* (Washington, D.C.: GPO, 1898), 122; and Indian Rights Association, *Nineteenth Annual Report of the Executive Committee of the Indian Rights Association,* 25.

40. Inspection report of S. A. M. Young, May 8, 1916, File 150, Havasupai Agency, CCF/BIA; Watahomigie to Secretary of the Interior, March 21, 1914, File 307.4, Havasupai Agency, CCF/BIA; Iliff, *People of the Blue Water,* 196–97. A further account of the Havasupais' reduced access to meat can be found in Symons to Commissioner of Indian Affairs, July 16, 1913, File 307.4, Havasupai Agency, CCF/BIA.

41. Iliff, *People of the Blue Water,* 196–97. (One cannot help wondering whether Chickapanyegi actually spoke in such a stilted manner or if Iliff felt the need to render his speech into "authentic" Indian fragments.) The travel-book writer George Wharton James alluded to much the same argument in his turn-of-the-century discussion of Havasupai poaching of mountain sheep in the canyon: "This they do regardless of a territorial law, which forbids even an Indian killing mountain sheep at any time. The Indian regards his as a prior right, existing long before there was any territorial legislature, and he acts accordingly." James, *Indians of the Painted Desert Region,* 244.

42. Walter G. Mann and S. B. Locke, *The Kaibab Deer: A Brief History and Recent Developments* (Washington, D.C.: GPO, 1931); and *Report of Kaibab Investigative Committee* (n.p., 1931). (This second pamphlet is located in Yale's forestry collection). See also Dennis Tresidder, "History of Game Management, Part II," *Arizona Wildlife Views* (April 1995): 6–7.

43. Indian Rights Association, *Nineteenth Annual Report of the Executive Committee of the Indian Rights Association,* 26. In addition, Navajo Indians

caught poaching in the Grand Cañon Forest Reserve reported that "the game wardens and their friends hunted and killed deer in the closed season, and...the Indians cannot understand why they cannot do likewise in a section that has always been their hunting ground." Hermann to Hanna, April 11, 1901, Letterbook 62, 394, LS/GLO.

44. Iliff, *People of the Blue Water,* 198, 204; Inspection report of Carl Moore, May 18, 1929, File 150, Havasupai Agency, CCF/BIA; West to Commissioner of Indian Affairs, September 26, 1915, File 115, Havasupai Agency, CCF/BIA; West to Commissioner of Indian Affairs, September 1, 1915, File 115, Havasupai Agency, CCF/BIA.

45. See Service, "Recent Observations on Havasupai Land Tenure," 365; and John Hough, "The Grand Canyon National Park and the Havasupai People: Cooperation and Conflict" (manuscript, n.d.), 6.

46. Weber and Seaman, *Havasupai Habitat,* 41–43, 109; Spier, "Havasupai Ethnography," 323–24. A. F. Whiting was told that Havasupai boys were not allowed to smoke until they had killed their first coyote. Weber and Seaman, *Havasupai Habitat,* 113.

47. Leanne Hinton, *Havasupai Songs: A Linguistic Perspective* (Tübingen: Gunter Narr Verlag, 1984), 265.

48. This song was recorded by Spier in 1918–19. Spier, "Havasupai Ethnography," 110. Cushing recorded a similar song in the 1880s. See Cushing, *Nation of the Willows,* 71–72. Other hunting rituals can be found in Weber and Seaman, *Havasupai Habitat,* 41, 200–1; Spier, "Havasupai Ethnography," 109; and Smithson and Euler, *Havasupai Legends,* 12–13.

49. Hanna, *Autobiography of Mark Hanna,* 16.

50. "Not until after 1919 did the government have either the intent or the personnel required to drive the Havasupai back to Havasu Canyon year-round." Secretary of the Interior and Bureau of Indian Affairs, in consultation with the Havasupai Tribe, *Secretarial Land Use Plan for Addition to Havasupai Indian Reservation: Section 10, Public Law 93–620, Grand Canyon National Park Enlargement Act* (Washington, DC: GPO, 1982), 3.

51. Frank A. Waugh, *Plan for the Development of the Village of Grand Canyon* (Washington, D.C.: GPO, 1918), 12–14. In 1919, the director of the newly created Park Service asserted that "Grand Canyon National Park is in need of broad development." U.S. Department of the Interior, *Annual Report of the Secretary of the Interior, 1919* (Washington, D.C.: GPO, 1919), 1010. See also Gordon Chappell, "Railroad at the Rim: The Origin and Growth of Grand Canyon Village," *Journal of Arizona History* 17 (spring 1976): 89–107; and Marta Weigle, "From Desert to Disney World: The Santa Fe Railway and the Fred Harvey Company Display the Indian Southwest," *Journal of Anthropological Research* 45 (spring 1989): 115–37. Linda Flint McClelland, *Building the National Parks: Historic Landscape Design and Construction* (Baltimore: Johns Hopkins University Press, 1998), provides a useful survey of the Park Service's building and landscaping efforts, including a discussion of Grand Canyon Village, 164–65.

52. Hughes, *In the House of Stone and Light,* 87; W.H. Peters, Report for November 1919, RS/NPS; Patraw to Director of National Park Service, Oc-

tober 16, 1930, Havasupai Indian Collection, File 32096, Folder 1, GCNPMC. See also U.S. Department of the Interior, *Annual Report of the Board of Indian Commissioners, 1929*, 29; and John Hough, "The Grand Canyon National Park and the Havasupai People: Cooperation and Conflict," in *Resident Peoples and National Parks: Social Dilemmas and Strategies in International Conservation*, ed. Patrick C. West and Steven R. Brechin (Tucson: University of Arizona Press, 1991), 218.

53. Hanna, *Autobiography of Mark Hanna,* 71. By "we dug some places," Hanna may be referring to the installation of the sewage system at Grand Canyon Village.

54. J. R. Eakin, Report for December 1925, RS/NPS; Hughes, *In the House of Stone and Light,* 88.

55. U.S. Congress, Senate, *Survey of Conditions of the Indians in the United States: Part 17: Arizona,* 8737; Patraw to Director of National Park Service, October 16, 1930, Havasupai Indian Collection, File 32096, Folder 1, GCNPMC.

56. D. Clinton West to Commissioner of Indian Affairs, December 17, 1914, File 307.4, Havasupai Agency, CCF/BIA. As Martha Knack and Alice Littlefield have argued, the "commitment to wage employment can serve as an index of the extent to which Indians had lost control over the land on which they could practice their traditional subsistence activities of hunting, farming, gathering, and intertribal trading." "Native American Labor: Retrieving History, Rethinking Theory," in Knack and Littlefield, eds., *Native Americans and Wage Labor: Ethnohistorical Approaches* (Norman: University of Oklahoma Press, 1996), 14.

57. Memoranda of September 8, 1938, and May 1, 1939, Havasupai Indians, File A9431, GCNPMC; Hamley to Commissioner of Indian Affairs, October 2, 1926, File 100, Havasupai Agency, CCF/BIA; Henderson, 18; Memorandum of Charles Bender, December 7, 1926, File 100, Havasupai Agency, CCF/BIA; Lovenskiold to Commissioner of Indian Affairs, January 8, 1926, File 100, Havasupai Agency, CCF/BIA. The decline of Havasupai farming is discussed in John F. Martin, "The Organization of Land and Labor in a Marginal Economy," *Human Organization* 32 (summer 1973): 153–61. An excellent example of how other communities in the Southwest became segmented along lines of age and gender following the rise of wage labor can be found in Deutsch, *No Separate Refuge,* 35–40.

58. Demaray to Collier, August 22, 1938, Havasupai Indians, File A9431, GCNPMC; Memorandum of March 17, 1939, Havasupai Indians, File A9431, GCNPMC; Bryant to Shaffer, April 14, 1939, Havasupai Indians, File A9431, GCNPMC; Patraw to Director of National Park Service, October 16, 1930, Havasupai Indian Collection, File 32096, Folder 1, GCNPMC; U.S. Congress, Senate, *Survey of Conditions of the Indians in the United States, Part 17: Arizona,* 8738.

59. Memorandum for the Director, May 2, 1939, and September 8, 1938; McLaughlin, Memorandum, June 4, 1956; Coffin, Memorandum, April 4, 1956: all are in File A9431, Havasupai Indians, GCNPMC. Hirst, *Havsuw 'Baaja,* 151, gives a vivid account of the destruction of the Havasupais' camp.

60. Leanne Hinton, *Havasupai Songs,* 273–75.

61. For an illuminating study of Indian storytelling and its relation to the understanding of landscape, see Keith H. Basso, *Wisdom Sits in Places: Landscape and Language among the Western Apache* (Albuquerque: University of New Mexico Press, 1996).

EPILOGUE

1. By *myth* I mean a narrative that provides its listeners with a way of finding order and meaning in the world. A myth is not necessarily false (in fact, it needs a clear connection to reality to be compelling), but it can contain distortions or simplifications. For more on the relationship between myth and history (and, more particularly, between myth and western and environmental history), see Henry Nash Smith, *Virgin Land: The American West as Symbol and Myth* (Cambridge: Harvard University Press, 1950); Marx, *The Machine in the Garden;* White, *It's Your Misfortune and None of My Own,* 613–31; Simon Schama, *Landscape and Memory* (New York: Vintage, 1995), 14–9; and Mark Fiege, *Irrigated Eden: The Making of an Agricultural Landscape in the American West* (Seattle: University of Washington Press, 1999), 211 n. 1, 269 n. 1.

2. Pinchot, *Breaking New Ground,* 27. See also Gifford Pinchot, "The Fight for Conservation," in *American Environmentalism: The Formative Period, 1860–1915,* ed. Donald Worster (New York: John Wiley and Sons, 1973), 84–90; and Hays, *Conservation and the Gospel of Efficiency,* 5–6, 122–23.

3. Thompson, "Custom Law and Common Right," in *Customs in Common,* 179. Scholars of Europe and Africa have recently argued that in the premodern countryside of these regions, physical force was the most common form of settling disputes over resources. See Eric A. Johnson and Eric H. Monkkonen, eds., *The Civilization of Crime: Violence in Town and Country since the Middle Ages* (Urbana: University of Illinois Press, 1996); and Robert Harms, *Games against Nature: An Eco-Cultural History of the Nunu of Equatorial Africa* (New York: Cambridge University Press, 1987), 128–56. An extended essay on these themes can be found in Lawrence Keeley, *War before Civilization: The Myth of the Peaceful Savage* (New York: Oxford University Press, 1996).

4. William Novak, *The People's Welfare: Law and Regulation in Nineteenth-Century America* (Chapel Hill: University of North Carolina Press, 1996), 17–18; Skowronek, *Building a New American State,* 1–10.

5. Robert Harms makes a similar argument in his discussion of environmental control in Africa. According to Harms, the imposition of European colonialism checked the warfare that had often been endemic to the Nunu of equatorial Africa. Harms, *Games against Nature,* 177–79.

6. This emphasis on the value of the rule of law is also that of E. P. Thompson in the remarkable conclusion to *Whigs and Hunters,* 258–69.

7. As E. P. Thompson once observed, "Stability...may have its own kind of terror." Ibid., 258.

8. Marsh, *Man and Nature,* 36–37; George Perkins Marsh, *The Earth as Modified by Human Action: A New Edition of Man and Nature,* rev. ed. (New

York: Charles Scribner's Sons, 1874), 326; *Address of Dr. Franklin B. Hough on State Forest Management before the Committee on the Preservation of the Adirondack Forests of the Chamber of Commerce of the State of New York* (New York: Press of the Chamber of Commerce, 1884), 4; F. B. Hough, *Report upon Forestry, 1882,* 7; see also F. B. Hough, *Report upon Forestry, 1877,* 8.

9. [Robert Underwood Johnson], "Attacks upon Public Parks," *Century Magazine* 43 (January 1892): 473; and U.S. Department of the Interior, *Annual Report of the Secretary of the Interior, 1886,* 77.

10. For accounts of the passage of the 1894 amendment to New York's constitution, see Terrie, *Contested Terrain,* 102; and Donaldson, *History of the Adirondacks,* 2:183–96. This vision of the Adirondacks' "wildness" also comes through in the 1883 comments of Verplanck Colvin, the head of the Adirondack Survey, who frequently spoke of the "Adirondack wilderness," which he defined as "wild timbered lands which were seldom visited except by sportsmen and explorers." *New York Times,* December 18, 1883.

11. The fullest description of the etymology of *conservation* is, of course, to be found in *The Oxford English Dictionary,* 2ⁿᵈ ed. (Oxford: Oxford University Press, 1989), 3:764–65. But see also Keith Thomas, *Man and the Natural World: Changing Attitudes in England, 1500–1800* (New York: Oxford University Press, 1983), 276.

12. Bruncken, *North American Forests and Forestry,* 54–56. For a recent study of the Adirondacks that reveals present-day resentments on the part of the region's residents at what they still see as their exclusion from the environmental decision-making process, see Catherine Henshaw Knott, *Living with the Adirondack Forest: Local Perspectives on Land Use Conflicts* (Ithaca: Cornell University Press, 1998).

Bibliography

MANUSCRIPT COLLECTIONS

Adirondack Museum Archives
    Adirondack Guides' Association files
    Fish and Game Law files

Franklin County Courthouse, Malone, New York
    Records

Grand Canyon National Park Museum Collection
    Havasupai Indian Collection, File 32906 and File A9431

Hamilton County Courthouse, Lake Pleasant, New York
    Records

Jackson Hole Historical Society
    Binkley files
    Tusk Hunters files

Lake Pleasant Township, Hamilton County, New York
    Records

National Archives
    Records of the Adjutant General's Office, Letters Received, 1991–1889 (M689), Record Group 94
    Records of the Bureau of Indian Affairs, Record Group 75
    Records of the Bureau of the Census, Manuscript Schedules, Record Group 29
    Records of the Department of the Interior, Record Group 48

Records of the Forest Service, Record Group 95
Records of the General Land Office, Record Group 49
Records of the Indian Claims Commission, Havasupai Tribe, Docket 91, Record Group 279
Records of the National Park Service, Record Group 79
New York State Archives
Records of the New York Department of Taxation and Finance
New York State Department of Environmental Conservation
Records of the New York Forest Commission, Bureau of Real Property
Warren County Courthouse, Queensbury, New York
Records
Wyoming State Archives
Records of the Wyoming State Auditor
Yellowstone National Park Archives
Records of Yellowstone National Park

COURT CASES

Horace Gilman v. Orrando P. Dexter. Supreme Court of Franklin County. 1900. Judgments: Box 73, Folder 2, Position 3. Franklin County Courthouse.
Lelia E. Marsh and George W. Ostrander v. Ne-Ha-Sa-Ne Park Association. Supreme Court of Hamilton County. March 1897. Civil Case #352. Hamilton County Court House.
Orrando P. Dexter v. Warren Joseph Alfred. Supreme Court of Franklin County. 1891. Cases on Appeal: Box 7, Folder 1, Position 2. Franklin County Courthouse.
The People v. Alvin Pasco. Supreme Court of Warren County. June 1903. Minutes of the Supreme Court, 1901–21, D/7 Box 3. Warren County Courthouse.
The People v. Alvin Pasco and Harry Wood. Supreme Court of Warren County. June 1903. Minutes of the Supreme Court, 1901–21, D/8 Box 4. Warren County Courthouse.
The People v. Jennie H. Ladew and Joseph H. Ladew. Supreme Court of New York, Appellate Division, Third Department. Manuscript 65–26, Box 6. Adirondack Museum Archives.
Transcript of Trial of James Courtenay, December 26, 1895. "Undesirables in Park," Item 78. Yellowstone National Park Archives.
United States v. William Binkley, Charles Purdy, and Oscar Adams. United States District Court, Ninth Circuit, Southern District of California. 1906. Yellowstone National Park Archives.
William Rockefeller v. Oliver Lamora. New York Supreme Court. Cases and Briefs, 4004, Appellate Division. 1896–1911. New York State Library.

INTERVIEWS

Blanchard, Paul. "Reminiscing the Old Guide Days." Sound recording. August 10, 1986. Tape C-46. Adirondack Museum Archives.

Smith, Bill. "Songs and Stories from the 'Featherbed.'" Sound recording. Voor-
    heesville, N.Y.: Front Hall Enterprises, 1987.
Whitman, John. Interview by author. October 26, 1994.
Whitman, Roland. Interview by author. March 5, 1996.

STATE GOVERNMENT PUBLICATIONS

Colvin, Verplanck. *Report on the Progress of the Adirondack State Land Sur-
    vey to the Year 1886.* Albany: Weed, Parsons, 1886.
Howard, William G. *Forest Fires.* New York Conservation Commission Bul-
    letin No. 10. Albany: James B. Lyon, 1914.
New York Commissioners of State Parks. *First Annual Report, 1872.* Albany:
    Argus, 1873.
New York Conservation Commission. *Circular of Information Relating to
    Lands and Forests.* Albany: James B. Lyon, 1918.
————. *Fourth Annual Report, 1914.* Albany: James B. Lyon, 1915.
New York Fisheries Commission. *Eighteenth Annual Report, 1889.* Albany:
    James B. Lyon, 1890.
————. *Fifteenth Annual Report, 1886.* Albany: Argus, 1887.
————. *Nineteenth Annual Report, 1890.* Albany: James B. Lyon, 1891.
————. *Sixteenth Annual Report, 1887.* Albany: Troy Press, 1888.
————. *Twenty-second Annual Report, 1893.* Albany: James B. Lyon, 1894.
————. *Twenty-third Annual Report, 1894.* Albany: James B. Lyon, 1895.
New York Fisheries, Game, and Forest Commission. *First Annual Report,
    1895.* Albany: Wynkoop, Hallenbeck, Crawford, 1896.
————. *Preliminary Report to the Fifth Annual Report, 1899.* Albany: James B.
    Lyon, 1900.
————. *Second Annual Report, 1896.* Albany: Wynkoop, Hallenbeck, Craw-
    ford, 1897.
————. *Third Annual Report, 1897.* Albany: Wynkoop, Hallenbeck, Craw-
    ford, 1898.
New York Forest Commission. *Annual Report, 1888.* Albany: Troy Press,
    1889.
————. *Annual Report, 1890.* Albany: James B. Lyon, 1891.
————. *Annual Report, 1891.* Albany: James B. Lyon, 1892.
————. *Annual Report, 1892.* Albany: James B. Lyon, 1893.
————. *Annual Report, 1893.* Albany: James B. Lyon, 1894.
————. *First Annual Report, 1885.* Albany: Argus, 1886.
————. *Preliminary Report, 1885.* New York State Assembly Document
    No. 36. 1885.
————. *Second Annual Report, 1886.* Albany: Argus, 1887.
New York Forest, Fish and Game Commission. *Annual Reports for 1904,
    1905, 1906.* Albany: James B. Lyon, 1907.
————. *Annual Reports for 1907, 1908, and 1909.* Albany: James B. Lyon,
    1910.
————. *Eighth and Ninth Annual Reports, 1902–1903.* Albany: James B. Lyon,
    1904.

———. *Fire! Fire! Fire! An Appeal to the Citizens of the Adirondack and Catskill Regions.* Albany: Evening Union Company, 1904.

———. *List of Lands in the Forest Preserve.* Albany: James B. Lyon, 1901.

———. *Seventh Annual Report, 1901.* Albany: James B. Lyon, 1902.

———. *Sixteenth Annual Report, 1910.* Albany: James B. Lyon, 1911.

———. *Sixth Annual Report, 1900.* Albany: James B. Lyon, 1901.

———. *Thirteenth Annual Report, 1907.* Albany: James B. Lyon, 1908.

New York State Assembly. *Report and Testimony of the Special Committee Appointed to Investigate the Depredations of Timber in the Forest Preserve.* New York State Assembly Document No. 67. 1895. Albany: Wynkoop, Hallenbeck, Crawford, 1896.

———. *Report of the Adirondack Committee, Assembly of 1902.* New York State Assembly Document No. 46. 1903. Albany: Argus, 1903.

———. *Report of the Committee Appointed to Investigate as to What Additional Lands Shall Be Acquired within the Forest Preserve.* New York State Assembly Document No. 43. 1899.

———. *Reports of the Majority and Minority of the Committee on Public Lands and Forestry Relative to the Administration of the Laws in Relation to the Forest Preserve by the Forest Commission,* New York State Assembly Document No. 81. 1891.

Ohio Fish Commission. *Sixth Annual Report, 1881.*

Rush, W.M. *Northern Yellowstone Elk Study.* [Helena?]: Montana Fish and Game Commission, 1933.

FEDERAL PUBLICATIONS

Betts, H.S. *Possibilities of Western Pines as a Source of Naval Stores.* Forest Service Bulletin No. 116. Washington, D.C.: GPO, 1912.

Cramton, Louis C. *Early History of Yellowstone National Park and Its Relation to National Park Policies.* Washington, D.C.: GPO, 1932.

Doane, Gustavus. *Yellowstone Expedition of 1870.* 41st Cong., 3rd sess., 1870–71. Senate Ex. Doc. 51.

Fernow, Bernhard E. *Report upon the Forestry Investigations of the U.S. Department of Agriculture, 1877–1898.* Washington, D.C.: GPO, 1899.

Fox, William F. *A History of the Lumber Industry in the State of New York.* Bureau of Forestry Bulletin No. 34. Washington, D.C.: GPO, 1902.

Henderson, Earl. *The Havasupai Indian Agency, Arizona.* Washington, D.C.: GPO, 1928.

Hough, Franklin B. *Report upon Forestry, 1877.* Washington, D.C.: GPO, 1878.

———. *Report upon Forestry, 1878–79.* Washington, D.C.: GPO, 1880.

———. *Report upon Forestry, 1882.* Washington, D.C.: GPO, 1882.

Jackson, W.H. *Descriptive Catalogue of Photographs of North American Indians.* Washington, D.C.: GPO, 1877.

Jones, William A. *Report upon the Reconnaissance of Northwestern Wyoming, including Yellowstone National Park.* Washington, D.C.: GPO, 1875.

Mann, Walter G., and S. B. Locke. *The Kaibab Deer: A Brief History and Recent Developments.* Washington, D.C.: GPO, 1931.

Palmer, T. S. *Private Game Preserves and Their Future in the United States.* United States Bureau of Biological Survey, Circular No. 72. Washington, D.C.: GPO, 1910.

Preble, Edward A. *Report on the Condition of Elk in Jackson Hole, Wyoming, in 1911.* U.S. Bureau of Biological Survey, Bulletin No. 40. Washington, D.C.: GPO, 1911.

Report of the Committee Appointed by the National Academy of Sciences upon the Inauguration of a Forest Policy for the Forested Lands of the United States to the Secretary of the Interior. Washington, D.C.: GPO, 1897.

Secretary of the Interior and Bureau of Indian Affairs, in consultation with the Havasupai Tribe. *Secretarial Land Use Plan for Addition to Havasupai Indian Reservation: Section 10, Public Law 93–620, Grand Canyon National Park Enlargement Act.* Washington, DC: GPO, 1982.

Sheridan, Philip. *Expedition through the Big Horn Mountains, Yellowstone Park, Etc.* Washington, D.C.: GPO, 1882.

Suter, H. M. *Forest Fires in the Adirondacks in 1903.* Bureau of Forestry Circular No. 26. Washington, D.C.: GPO, 1904.

U.S. Army. *Rules, Regulations, and Instructions for the Information and Guidance of Officers and Enlisted Men of the United States Army, and of the Scouts Doing Duty in the Yellowstone National Park.* Washington, D.C.: GPO, 1907.

U.S. Bureau of Indian Affairs. *Annual Report of the Commissioner of Indian Affairs.* Washington, D.C.: GPO, 1880–1906.

U.S. Congress. House. *Boundaries of Yellowstone National Park.* 53rd Cong., 3rd sess., 1894–95. H. Rept. 1763.

——. *Grand Canyon National Park.* 65th Cong., 2d sess., 1917–18. H. Rept. 832.

——. *Inquiry into the Management and Control of the Yellowstone National Park.* 52nd Cong., 1st sess., 1891–92. H. Rept. 1956.

——. *Protection of Yellowstone National Park.* 45th Cong., 2nd sess., 1877–78. House Ex. Doc. 75.

——. *Report of the Committee on Expenditures for Indians and Yellowstone Park.* 49th Cong., 1st sess., 1885–86. H. Rept. 1076.

U.S. Congress. Senate. *Agreement with Certain Parties for Privileges in Yellowstone National Park.* 47th Cong., 2nd sess., 1882–83. S. Rept. 911.

——. *Correspondence on Yellowstone National Park.* 48th Cong., 1st sess., 1883–84. Senate Ex. Doc. 47.

——. *Management of Yellowstone National Park.* 48th Cong., 1st sess., 1883–84. Senate Ex. Doc. 207.

——. *Survey of Conditions of the Indians in the United States: Part 17: Arizona: Hearings before a Subcommittee of the Committee on Indian Affairs.* 71st Cong., 3rd sess. 1931.

U.S. Department of Agriculture. *Annual Report of the Commissioner of Agriculture.* Washington, D.C.: GPO, 1886–87.

———. *Annual Report of the Division of Forestry.* Washington, D.C.: GPO, 1886–1891.

U.S. Department of Agriculture, Division of Forestry. *Report on the Forest Conditions of the Rocky Mountains.* Forestry Division Bulletin No. 2. Washington, D.C.: GPO, 1888.

U.S. Department of the Interior. *Annual Report of the Acting Superintendent of Yellowstone National Park, 1887,* by Moses Harris. Washington, D.C.: GPO, 1887.

———. *Annual Report of the Acting Superintendent of Yellowstone National Park, 1889,* by Moses Harris. Washington, D.C.: GPO, 1889.

———. *Annual Report of the Acting Superintendent of Yellowstone National Park, 1891,* by George S. Anderson. Washington, D.C.: GPO, 1891.

———. *Annual Report of the Acting Superintendent of Yellowstone National Park, 1892,* by George S. Anderson. Washington, D.C.: GPO, 1892.

———. *Annual Report of the Acting Superintendent of Yellowstone National Park, 1894,* by George S. Anderson. Washington, D.C.: GPO, 1894.

———. *Annual Report of the Acting Superintendent of Yellowstone National Park, 1895,* by George S. Anderson. Washington, D.C.: GPO, 1895.

———. *Annual Report of the Acting Superintendent of Yellowstone National Park, 1896,* by George S. Anderson. Washington, D.C.: GPO, 1896.

———. *Annual Report of the Acting Superintendent of Yellowstone National Park, 1897,* by Samuel B. M. Young. Washington, D.C.: GPO, 1897.

———. *Annual Report of the Acting Superintendent of Yellowstone National Park, 1898,* by James Erwin. Washington, D.C.: GPO, 1898.

———. *Annual Report of the Acting Superintendent of Yellowstone National Park, 1899,* by Oscar Brown. Washington, D.C.: GPO, 1899.

———. *Annual Report of the Acting Superintendent of Yellowstone National Park, 1900,* by George Goode. Washington, D.C.: GPO, 1900.

———. *Annual Report of the Acting Superintendent of Yellowstone National Park, 1903,* by John Pitcher. Washington, D.C.: GPO, 1903.

———. *Annual Report of the Acting Superintendent of Yellowstone National Park, 1904,* by John Pitcher. Washington, D.C.: GPO, 1904.

———. *Annual Report of the Acting Superintendent of Yellowstone National Park, 1907,* by Samuel B. M. Young. Washington, D.C.: GPO, 1907.

———. *Annual Report of the Acting Superintendent of Yellowstone National Park, 1908,* by Samuel B. M. Young. Washington, D.C.: GPO, 1908.

———. *Annual Report of the Acting Superintendent of Yellowstone National Park, 1909,* by Harry C. Benson. Washington, D.C.: GPO, 1909.

———. *Annual Report of the Acting Superintendent of Yellowstone National Park, 1911,* by Lloyd M. Brett. Washington, D.C.: GPO, 1911.

———. *Annual Report of the Acting Superintendent of Yellowstone National Park, 1912,* by Lloyd M. Brett. Washington, D.C.: GPO, 1912.

———. *Annual Report of the Acting Superintendent of Yellowstone National Park, 1913,* by Lloyd M. Brett. Washington, D.C.: GPO, 1913.

———. *Annual Report of the Acting Superintendent of Yellowstone National Park, 1914,* by Lloyd M. Brett. Washington, D.C.: GPO, 1914.

————. *Annual Report of the Acting Superintendent of Yellowstone National Park, 1915*, by Lloyd M. Brett. Washington, D.C.: GPO, 1915.

————. *Annual Report of the Board of Indian Commissioners, 1929*. Washington, D.C.: GPO, 1929.

————. *Annual Report of the Secretary of the Interior*. Washington, D.C.: GPO, 1877–80, 1885, 1886, 1890, 1919.

————. *Annual Report of the Superintendent of National Parks, 1916*. Washington, D.C.: GPO, 1916.

————. *Annual Report of the Superintendent of Yellowstone National Park, 1877*, by Philetus W. Norris. Washington, D.C.: GPO, 1878.

————. *Annual Report of the Superintendent of Yellowstone National Park, 1878*, by Philetus W. Norris. Washington, D.C.: GPO, 1879.

————. *Annual Report of the Superintendent of Yellowstone National Park, 1879*, by Philetus W. Norris. Washington, D.C.: GPO, 1880.

————. *Annual Report of the Superintendent of Yellowstone National Park, 1880*, by Philetus W. Norris. Washington, D.C.: GPO, 1881.

————. *Annual Report of the Superintendent of Yellowstone National Park, 1882*, by Patrick H. Conger. Washington, D.C.: GPO, 1883.

————. *Annual Report of the Superintendent of Yellowstone National Park, 1886*, by David W. Wear. Washington, D.C.: GPO, 1886.

U.S. General Land Office. *Annual Report of the Commissioner of the General Land Office*. Washington, D.C.: GPO, 1877–1901.

U.S. National Park Service. *Annual Report of the Director of the National Park Service*. Washington, D.C.: GPO, 1917–18.

Waugh, Frank A. *Plan for the Development of the Village of Grand Canyon*. Washington, D.C.: GPO, 1918.

Woodruff, George W. *Federal and State Forest Laws*. Bureau of Forestry Bulletin No. 57. Washington, D.C.: GPO, 1904.

MAGAZINES

American Angler
American Naturalist
Angler and Hunter
Century
Collier's
Daily Graphic
Field and Stream
Forest and Stream
The Forester
Forestry and Irrigation
Forestry Bulletin
Forestry Quarterly
Frank Leslie's Illustrated Newspaper
Garden and Forest
Grand Canyon Nature Notes

Harper's
Harper's Weekly
The Indian's Friend
The Nation
National Parks
Nature
Outing Magazine
Overland Monthly
Recreation
Sportsman's Magazine
Woods and Waters

NEWSPAPERS

Albany Argus
Albany Press-Knickerbocker
Albany Times-Union
Boonville (N.Y.) Herald
Chicago Tribune
Flagstaff (Ariz.) Champion
Gardiner (Mont.) Wonderland
Hamilton County (N.Y.) Record
Livingston (Mont.) Enterprise
Livingston (Mont.) Post
Malone (N.Y.) Palladium
New York Herald
New York Sun
New York Times
New York Tribune
New York World
Pocatello (Idaho) Tribune
Phoenix Territorial Expositor
Prescott (Ariz.) Journal-Miner
Salt Lake Tribune
St. Regis (N.Y.) Adirondack News
Tucson (Ariz.) Daily Citizen
Utica (N.Y.) Herald-Dispatch

UNPUBLISHED SOURCES

Craib, Raymond B., III. "Power and Cartography in Early Modern Spain and
    Early Colonial New Spain." Seminar paper, Yale University, 1997.
Hough, John. "The Grand Canyon National Park and the Havasupai People:
    Cooperation and Conflict." Manuscript, n.d.
McMahon, Felicia Romano. "Wilderness and Tradition: Power, Politics, and
    Play in the Adirondacks." Ph.D. diss., University of Pennsylvania, 1992.

Parnes, Brenda. "Trespass: A History of Land-Use Policy in the Adirondack Forest Region of Northern New York State." Ph.D. diss., New York University, 1989.

Summerhill, Thomas. "The Farmers' Republic: Agrarian Protest and the Capitalist Transformation of Upstate New York." Ph.D. diss., University of California at San Diego, 1993.

Taylor, Alan. "The Unadilla Hunt Club: Nature, Class, and Power in Rural New York during the Early Republic." Manuscript, July 1996.

Truett, Samuel. "A Wilderness of One's Own: Sports Hunting and Manliness in Nineteenth-Century America." Seminar paper, Yale University, 1992.

BOOKS, ARTICLES, AND PAMPHLETS

Abbiateci, André. "Arsonists in Eighteenth-Century France: An Essay in the Typology of Crime." In *Deviants and the Abandoned in French Society: Selections from the Annales,* ed. Robert Forster and Orest Ranum, trans. Elborg Forster and Patricia M. Ranum. Baltimore: Johns Hopkins University Press, 1978.

Aber, Ted. *Adirondack Folks.* Prospect, N.Y.: Prospect Books, 1980.

Aber, Ted, and Stella King. *The History of Hamilton County.* Lake Pleasant, N.Y.: Great Wilderness Books, 1965.

———. *Tales from an Adirondack County.* Prospect, N.Y.: Prospect Books, 1961.

Address of Dr. Franklin B. Hough on State Forest Management before the Committee on the Preservation of the Adirondack Forests of the Chamber of Commerce of the State of New York. New York: Press of the Chamber of Commerce, 1884.

Adirondack League Club. *Adirondack League Club Hand-Book for 1894.* N.p., n.d.

———. *Annual Report, 1898.* N.p., n.d.

———. *Annual Report, 1899.* N.p., n.d.

———. *Annual Report, 1904.* N.p., n.d.

———. *Annual Report, 1911.* N.p., n.d.

Altherr, Thomas, and John Reiger. "Academic Historians and Hunting: A Call for More and Better Scholarship." *Environmental History Review* 19 (fall 1995): 39–56.

American Forestry Congress, *Proceedings, 1883.* N.p., n.d.

———. *Proceedings, 1885.* Washington, D.C.: Judd and Detweiler, 1886.

American Scenic and Historic Preservation Society. *Annual Report, 1910.* Albany: James B. Lyon, 1910.

Amigo, Eleanor, and Mark Neuffer, *Beyond the Adirondacks: The Story of the St. Regis Paper Company.* Westport, Conn.: Greenwood Press, 1980.

Anderson, Benedict. *Imagined Communities: Reflections on the Origin and Spread of Nationalism.* Rev. ed. New York: Verso, 1991.

Anderson, David, and Richard Grove, eds. *Conservation in Africa: People, Policies, and Practice.* Cambridge: Cambridge University Press, 1987.

Anderson, Leslie. *The Political Ecology of the Modern Peasant: Calculation and Community.* Baltimore: Johns Hopkins University Press, 1994.

Archer, John E. *By a Flash and a Scare: Incendiarism, Animal Maiming, and Poaching in East Anglia, 1815–1870.* Oxford: Clarendon Press, 1990.

Arnold, David. *The Problem of Nature: Environment, Culture and European Expansion.* Oxford: Blackwell, 1996.

Arnold, David, and Ramachandra Guha, eds. *Nature, Culture, Imperialism: Essays on the Environmental History of South Asia.* Delhi: Oxford University Press, 1996.

Aron, Stephen. *How the West Was Lost: The Transformation of Kentucky, from Daniel Boone to Henry Clay.* Baltimore: Johns Hopkins University Press, 1996.

———. "Pigs and Hunters: 'Rights in the Woods' on the Trans-Appalachian Frontier." In *Contact Points: American Frontiers from the Mohawk Valley to the Mississippi, 1750–1830,* ed. Andrew Cayton and Frederika Teute. Chapel Hill: University of North Carolina Press, 1998.

———. "Pioneers and Profiteers: Land Speculation and the Homestead Ethic in Frontier Kentucky." *Western Historical Quarterly* 23 (May 1992): 179–98.

Association for the Protection of the Adirondacks. *Eighteenth Annual Report of the President.* N.p., 1919.

———. *Fifteenth Annual Report of the President.* N.p., 1916.

———. *Sixteenth Annual Report of the President.* N.p., 1917.

———. *Tenth Annual Report of the President.* N.p., 1911.

———. *Twelfth Annual Report of the President.* N.p., 1913.

Association of American Indian Affairs. *The Havasupai: Prisoners of the Grand Canyon.* N.p.: Association of American Indian Affairs, [1972?].

Atkinson, Adrian. *Principles of Political Ecology.* London: Belhaven Press, 1991.

Back, Joe. *The Sucker's Teeth.* Denver: Sage Books, 1965.

Baden-Powell, B.H. *Forest Law: A Course of Lectures on the Principles of Civil and Criminal Law and on the Law of the Forest.* London: Bradbury, Agnew, and Co., 1893.

Bailey, Vernon. *Animal Life of Yellowstone National Park.* Springfield, Ill.: Charles C. Thomas, 1930.

Barron, Hal. *Those Who Stayed Behind: Rural Society in Nineteenth-Century New England.* New York: Cambridge University Press, 1984.

Bartlett, Richard A. *Yellowstone: A Wilderness Besieged.* Tucson: University of Arizona Press, 1985.

Basso, Keith H. *Wisdom Sits in Places: Landscape and Language among the Western Apache.* Albuquerque: University of New Mexico Press, 1996.

Beinart, William, and Peter Coates. *Environment and History: The Taming of Nature in the USA and South Africa.* New York: Routledge, 1995.

Betts, Robert B. *Along the Ramparts of the Tetons: The Saga of Jackson Hole, Wyoming.* Boulder: Colorado Associated University Press, 1978.

A Biographical Sketch of Orrando Perry Dexter. N.p., n.d. [1903?].

Blankman, Lloyd. "Burt Conklin, the Greatest Trapper." *New York Folklore Quarterly* 22 (December 1966): 274–97.

Blok, Anton. "The Peasant and the Brigand: Social Banditry Reconsidered." *Comparative Studies in Society and History* 14 (September 1972): 494–503.

Botkin, Daniel. *Discordant Harmonies: A New Ecology for the Twenty-first Century.* New York: Oxford University Press, 1990.

Bourcier, Paul G. *History in the Mapping: Four Centuries of Adirondack Cartography.* Blue Mountain Lake, N.Y.: Adirondack Museum, 1986.

Brimlow, George Francis. *The Bannock Indian War of 1878.* Caldwell, Idaho: Caxton Printers, 1938.

Broad, John. "Whigs and Deer-Stealers in Other Guises: A Return to the Origins of the Black Act." *Past and Present* 119 (May 1988): 56–72.

Brown, Nelson Courtlandt. *Forest Products: Their Manufacture and Use.* New York: John Wiley and Sons, 1919.

Brumley, Charles. *Guides of the Adirondacks: A History.* Utica, N.Y.: North Country Books, 1994.

Bruncken, Ernest. *North American Forests and Forestry: Their Relations to the National Life of the American People.* New York: G.P. Putnam's Sons, 1900.

Bryan, T. Scott. *The Geysers of Yellowstone.* Rev. ed. Boulder: Colorado Associated University Press, 1986.

Bryant, Raymond L. "Political Ecology: An Emerging Research Agenda in Third-World Studies." *Political Geography* 11 (January 1992): 12–36.

Burdick, Neal S. "Who Killed Orrando P. Dexter?" *Adirondack Life* (May-June 1982): 23–49.

Cadigan, Sean. "The Moral Economy of the Commons: Ecology and Equity in the Newfoundland Cod Fishery, 1815–1855." *Labour/Le Travail* 43 (spring 1999): 9–42.

Cady, G.J. "The Early American Reaction to the Theory of Malthus." In *Thomas Malthus: Critical Assessments,* ed. John Cunningham Wood, 4:18–42. London: Croom Helm, 1986.

Calkins, Frank. *Jackson Hole.* New York: Alfred A. Knopf, 1973.

Carter, Michael J. *Peasants and Poachers: A Study in Rural Disorder in Norfolk.* Suffolk: Boydell Press, 1980.

Casanova, Frank E., ed. "General Crook Visits the Supais, as Reported by John G. Bourke." *Arizona and the West* 10 (autumn 1968): 253–75.

Chappell, Gordon. "Railroad at the Rim: The Origin and Growth of Grand Canyon Village." *Journal of Arizona History* 17 (spring 1976): 89–107.

Chase, Alston. *Playing God in Yellowstone: The Destruction of America's First National Park.* Boston: Atlantic Monthly Press, 1986.

Chase, Henry. *Game Protection and Propagation in America: A Handbook of Practical Information for Officials and Others Interested in the Cause of Conservation of Wildlife.* Philadelphia: J.B. Lippincott, 1913.

Chittenden, Hiram. *The Yellowstone National Park: Historical and Descriptive.* Cincinnati: Robert Clarke, 1895.

Clark, Christopher. *The Roots of Rural Capitalism: Western Massachusetts, 1780–1860.* Ithaca: Cornell University Press, 1990.

Coates, Peter. *Nature: Western Attitudes since Ancient Times.* Berkeley and Los Angeles: University of California Press, 1998.

Comstock, Edward, and Mark C. Webster, eds. *The Adirondack League Club, 1890–1990.* Old Forge, N.Y.: Adirondack League Club, 1990.

Conklin, Henry. *Through "Poverty's Vale": A Hardscrabble Boyhood in Upstate New York, 1832–1862.* Syracuse: Syracuse University Press, 1974.

Corbin, David Alan. *Life, Work, and Rebellion in the Coal Fields: The Southern West Virginia Miners, 1880–1922.* Urbana: University of Illinois Press, 1981.

Crèvecoeur, J. Hector St. John de. *Letters from an American Farmer.* 1782. Reprint, New York: E.P. Dutton, 1957.

Cronon, William. *Changes in the Land: Indians, Colonists, and the Ecology of New England.* New York: Hill and Wang, 1983.

———. "Forests and Civilization." *Yale Review* 80 (October 1992): 79–84.

———. "Landscapes of Abundance and Scarcity." In *The Oxford History of the American West,* ed. Clyde A. Milner II, Carol A. O'Connor, and Martha A. Sandweiss. New York: Oxford University Press, 1994.

———. *Nature's Metropolis: Chicago and the Great West.* New York: W.W. Norton, 1991.

———, ed. *Uncommon Ground: Rethinking the Human Place in Nature.* New York: W.W. Norton, 1995.

Cushing, Frank H. *The Nation of the Willows.* Flagstaff, Ariz.: Northland Press, 1965.

Czech, Brian. "Ward vs Racehorse—Supreme Court as Obviator?" *Journal of the West* 35 (July 1996): 61–69.

Dalleo, Peter T. "The Somali Role in Organized Poaching in Northeastern Kenya, 1909–1939." *International Journal of African Historical Studies* 12 (1979): 472–82.

Darnton, Robert. *The Great Cat Massacre and Other Episodes in French Cultural History.* New York: Vintage, 1984.

Day, Gordon M. "Western Abenaki." In *The Handbook of North American Indians: Northeast,* ed. William Sturtevant. Vol. 15. Washington, D.C.: Smithsonian Institution Press, 1978.

D'Elia, Anthony. *The Adirondack Rebellion.* Onchiota, N.Y.: Onchiota Books, 1979.

Despain, Don G. *Yellowstone Vegetation: Consequences of Environment and History in a Natural Setting.* Boulder, Colo.: Roberts Rinehart, 1990.

Deutsch, Sarah. "Landscape of Enclaves: Race Relations in the West, 1865–1990." In *Under an Open Sky: Rethinking America's Western Past,* ed. William Cronon, George Miles, and Jay Gitlin. New York: W.W. Norton, 1992.

———. *No Separate Refuge: Culture, Class, and Gender on an Anglo-Hispanic Frontier in the American Southwest, 1880–1940.* New York: Oxford University Press, 1987.

Dobyns, Henry F., and Robert C. Euler. *The Ghost Dance of 1889 among the Pai Indians of Northwestern Arizona.* Prescott, Ariz.: Prescott College Press, 1967.

———. *The Havasupai People.* Phoenix: Indian Tribal Series, 1971.

Donaldson, Alfred L. *A History of the Adirondacks*. New York: Century, 1921.

Dorman, Robert L. *A Word for Nature: Four Pioneering Environmental Advocates, 1845–1913*. Chapel Hill: University of North Carolina Press, 1998.

Dunlap, Thomas R. *Saving America's Wildlife*. Princeton: Princeton University Press, 1988.

Dunlay, Thomas W. *Wolves for the Blue Soldiers: Indian Scouts and Auxiliaries with the United States Army, 1860–90*. Lincoln: University of Nebraska Press, 1982.

Durant, Kenneth. *The Adirondack Guide-Boat*. Camden, Maine: International Marine Publishing, 1980.

Early, Katherine E. *"For the Benefit and Enjoyment of the People": Cultural Attitudes and the Establishment of Yellowstone National Park*. Washington, D.C.: Georgetown University Press, 1984.

Edney, Matthew H. *Mapping an Empire: The Geographical Construction of British India, 1765–1843*. Chicago: University of Chicago Press, 1997.

Ellickson, Robert C. *Order without Law: How Neighbors Settle Disputes*. Cambridge: Harvard University Press, 1991.

Fairhead, James, and Melissa Leach. *Misreading the African Landscape: Society and Ecology in a Forest-Savanna Mosaic*. New York: Cambridge University Press, 1996.

———. *Reframing Deforestation: Global Analyses and Local Realities: Studies in West Africa*. New York: Routledge, 1998.

Faragher, John Mack. *Sugar Creek: Life on the Illinois Prairie*. New Haven: Yale University Press, 1986.

Fausold, Martin L. *Gifford Pinchot: Bull Moose Progressive*. Syracuse: Syracuse University Press, 1961.

Fernow, Bernhard. *A Brief History of Forestry*. Toronto: University Press, 1911.

———. *Economics of Forestry*. New York: Thomas Y. Crowell, 1902.

———. *Our Forestry Problem*. N.p., 1887.

Fiege, Mark. *Irrigated Eden: The Making of an Agricultural Landscape in the American West*. Seattle: University of Washington Press, 1999.

Finck, Henry T. *The Pacific Coast Scenic Tour*. London: Sampson, Low, Marston, Searle, and Rivington, 1891.

Fisher, Andrew H. "The 1932 Handshake Agreement: Yakama Indian Treaty Rights and Forest Service Policy in the Pacific Northwest." *Western Historical Quarterly* 28 (summer 1997): 187–217.

Forester, Frank [Henry William Herbert]. *Complete Manual for Young Sportsmen*. New York: W. A. Townsend, 1866.

Foster, Mike. *Strange Genius: The Life of Ferdinand Vandeveer Hayden*. Niwot, Colo.: Roberts Rinehart, 1994.

Fowler, Albert. *Cranberry Lake from Wilderness to Adirondack Park*. Syracuse: Syracuse University Press, 1968.

Fox, Stephen. *John Muir and His Legacy: The American Conservation Movement*. Boston: Little, Brown, 1981.

Fuller, Andrew S. *Practical Forestry*. New York: Orange Judd, 1900.

Fullerton, James. *Autobiography of Roosevelt's Adversary.* Boston: Roxburgh Publishing, 1912.

Gadgil, Madhav, and Ramachandra Guha. *Ecology and Equity: The Use and Abuse of Nature in Contemporary India.* New York: Routledge, 1995.

———. *This Fissured Land: An Ecological History of India.* Delhi: Oxford University Press, 1992.

Garces, Francisco. *On the Trail of a Spanish Pioneer: The Diary and Itinerary of Francisco Garces in His Travels through Sonora, Arizona, and California, 1775–1776.* Ed. Elliott Coues. New York: Francis P. Harper, 1900.

Gaventa, John. *Power and Powerlessness: Quiescence and Rebellion in an Appalachian Valley.* Urbana: University of Illinois Press, 1980.

Gilbert, Frederick. "Retroductive Logic and the Effects of Meningeal Worms: A Comment." *Journal of Wildlife Management* 56 (July 1992): 614–16.

Gilborn, Craig. *Adirondack Furniture and the Rustic Tradition.* New York: Harry N. Abrams, 1987.

Gilmore, David. *Manhood in the Making: Cultural Concepts of Masculinity.* New Haven: Yale University Press, 1990.

Gordon, Linda. "Birth Control, Socialism, and Feminism in the United States." In *Malthus Past and Present,* ed. J. Dupaquier, A. Fauve-Chamoux, and E. Grebenik, 313–27. London: Academic Press, 1983.

Gordon, Nicholas. *Ivory Knights: Man, Magic, and Elephants.* London: Chapmans, 1991.

Gorn, Elliott. *The Manly Art: Bare-Knuckle Prize Fighting in America.* Ithaca: Cornell University Press, 1986.

Graham, Frank, Jr. *The Adirondack Park: A Political History.* New York: Alfred A. Knopf, 1978.

———. *Man's Dominion: The Story of Conservation in America.* New York: M. Evans, 1971.

Graves, Henry S. *The Principles of Handling Woodlands.* New York: John Wiley and Sons, 1911.

Gray, Ira. *Follow My Moccasin's Tracks.* Schuylerville, N.Y.: Napaul Publishers, 1975.

———. *My Memories, 1886–1977.* N.p., n.d.

Green, Dean H. *History of Island Park.* Ashton, Idaho: Island Park–Gateway Publishing, 1990.

Grinnell, George Bird, ed. *American Big Game in Its Haunts.* New York: Harper and Brothers, 1904.

———. *Brief History of the Boone and Crockett Club.* New York: Forest and Stream Publishing, 1910.

Grove, Richard H. "Colonial Conservation, Ecological Hegemony, and Popular Resistance: Towards a Global Synthesis." In *Imperialism and the Natural World,* ed. John M. MacKenzie. Manchester, U.K.: Manchester University Press, 1990.

———. *Green Imperialism: Colonial Expansion, Tropical Island Edens, and the Origins of Environmentalism, 1600–1860.* New York: Cambridge University Press, 1995.

Guha, Ramachandra. *The Unquiet Woods: Ecological Change and Peasant Resistance in the Himalaya.* Berkeley and Los Angeles: University of California Press, 1990.

Guha, Ranajit. *Elementary Aspects of Peasant Insurgency in Colonial India.* Delhi: Oxford University Press, 1983.

Guha, Ranajit, and Gayatri Chakravortry Spivak, eds. *Selected Subaltern Studies.* New York: Oxford University Press, 1988.

Guie, Heister Dean, and Lucullus Virgil McWhorter, eds. *Adventures in Geyserland.* Caldwell, Idaho: Caxton Printers, 1935.

Hahn, Steven. "Hunting, Fishing, and Foraging: Common Rights and Class Relations in the Postbellum South." *Radical History Review* 26 (1982): 37–64.

———. *The Roots of Southern Populism: Yeoman Farmers and the Transformation of the Georgia Upcountry, 1850–1890.* New York: Oxford University Press, 1983.

Haines, Aubrey. *Yellowstone National Park: Its Exploration and Establishment.* Washington, D.C.: GPO, 1974.

———. *The Yellowstone Story: A History of Our First National Park.* Niwot, Colo.: University Press of Colorado, 1977.

Halper, Louise. "'A Rich Man's Paradise': Constitutional Preservation of New York State's Adirondack Forest, A Centenary Consideration." *Ecology Law Journal* 19 (1992): 193–267.

Hammond, Samuel. *Hills, Lakes, and Forest Streams; or, a Tramp in the Chateaugay Woods.* New York: J. C. Derby, 1854.

Hampton, H. Duane. *How the U.S. Cavalry Saved Our National Parks.* Bloomington: Indiana University Press, 1971.

Hanna, Mark. *Autobiography of Mark Hanna, as told to Richard Emerick.* Ed. Jon Reyhner. Billings: Eastern Montana College, 1988.

Hardman, William. *A Trip to America.* London: T. Vickers Wood, 1884.

Harms, Robert. *Games against Nature: An Eco-Cultural History of the Nunu of Equatorial Africa.* New York: Cambridge University Press, 1987.

Hawley, Ralph Chipman, and Austin Foster Hawes. *Manual of Forestry for the Northeastern United States.* 2nd ed. New York: John Wiley and Sons, 1918.

Hay, Douglas. "Poaching and the Game Laws on Cannock Chase." In *Albion's Fatal Tree: Crime and Society in Eighteenth-Century England,* ed. Douglas Hay, Peter Linebaugh, John Rule, E. P. Thompson, and Cal Winslow. New York: Pantheon, 1975.

Hayden, Elizabeth Wied. "Driving Out the Tusk Hunters." *Teton Magazine* (winter-spring 1971): 22–36.

Hays, Samuel P. *Conservation and the Gospel of Efficiency: The Progressive Conservation Movement, 1890–1920.* Cambridge: Harvard University Press, 1959.

Headley, Joel T. *The Adirondack; or, Life in the Woods.* New York: Baker and Scribner, 1849.

———. *The Adirondack; or, Life in the Woods.* Rev. ed. New York: Scribner, Armstrong, 1875.

Heartwood: The Adirondack Homestead Life of W. Donald Burnap, as told to Marylee Armour. Baldwinsville, N.Y.: Brown Newspapers, 1988.

Hess, Karl, Jr. *Rocky Times in Rocky Mountain National Park: An Unnatural History.* Niwot, Colo.: University Press of Colorado, 1993.

Hicks, Sam. "Ivory Dollars." *High Country* 3 (winter 1967): 40–45.

Hinton, Leanne. *Havasupai Songs: A Linguistic Perspective.* Tübingen: Gunter Narr Verlag, 1984.

Hirst, Stephen. *Havsuw 'Baaja: People of the Blue Green Water.* Supai, Ariz.: Havasupai Tribe, 1985.

Hobsbawm, Eric. *Bandits.* Rev. ed. New York: Pantheon, 1981.

———. *Primitive Rebels: Studies in Archaic Forms of Social Movement in the Nineteenth and Twentieth Century.* New York: W. W. Norton, 1959.

———. *Workers: Worlds of Labor.* New York: Pantheon, 1984.

Hochschild, Harold. *Township 34: A History.* N.p., 1952.

Hoffman, Charles Fenno. *Wild Scenes in the Forest and Prairie.* New York: William H. Colyer, 1843.

Hofstadter, Richard. *Social Darwinism in American Thought.* Rev. ed. New York: George Braziller, 1959.

Holbrook, Stewart. *Burning an Empire: The Story of American Forest Fires.* New York: Macmillan, 1943.

Hopkins, Harry. *The Long Affray: The Poaching Wars, 1760–1914.* London: Secker and Warburg, 1985.

Hornaday, William T. *The Extermination of the American Bison, with a Sketch of Its Discovery and Life History.* Washington, D.C.: U.S. National Museum, 1889.

———. *Our Vanishing Wildlife: Its Extermination and Preservation.* New York: New York Zoological Society, 1913.

———. *Wildlife Conservation in Theory and Practice: Lectures Delivered before the Forest School of Yale University.* New Haven: Yale University Press, 1914.

Houston, Douglas B. *The Northern Yellowstone Elk: Ecology and Management.* New York: Macmillan, 1982.

Hoxie, Frederick E. *Parading through History: The Making of the Crow Nation in America, 1805–1935.* New York: Cambridge University Press, 1995.

Hufford, Mary. "American Ginseng and the Idea of the Commons." *Folklife Center News* 19 (winter-spring 1997): 3–18.

Hughes, J. Donald. *In the House of Stone and Light: A Human History of the Grand Canyon.* Grand Canyon, Ariz.: Grand Canyon Natural History Association, 1978.

Hultkrantz, Ake. "The Indians of Yellowstone Park." *Annals of Wyoming* 29 (October 1957): 125–49.

Hunter, James. *On the Other Side of Sorrow: Nature and People in the Scottish Highlands.* Edinburgh: Mainstream Publishing, 1995.

Iliff, Flora Gregg. *People of the Blue Water: My Adventures among the Walapai and Havasupai Indians.* New York: Harper and Brothers, 1954.

Indian Rights Association. *Nineteenth Annual Report of the Executive Committee of the Indian Rights Association.* Philadelphia: Indian Rights Association, 1902.

Irland, Lloyd C. *Wildlands and Woodlots: The Story of New England's Forests.* Hanover, N.H.: University Press of New England, 1982.

Ise, John. *The United States Forest Policy.* New Haven: Yale University Press, 1920.

Ives, Edward D. *George Magoon and the Down East Game War: History, Folklore, and the Law.* Urbana: University of Illinois Press, 1988.

————, ed. "Wilbur Day: Hunter, Guide, and Poacher: An Autobiography." *Northeast Folklore* 26 (1985).

Ives, Martin Van Buren. *Through the Adirondacks in Eighteen Days.* New York: Wynkoop, Hallenbeck, Crawford, 1899.

Jacoby, Karl. "Class and Environmental History: Lessons from the 'War in the Adirondacks.'" *Environmental History* 2 (July 1997): 324–42.

James, George Wharton. *Indians of the Painted Desert Region: Hopis, Navahoes, Wallapais, Havasupais.* Boston: Little Brown, 1903.

Janetski, Joel. *The Indians of Yellowstone Park.* Salt Lake City: University of Utah Press, 1987.

Jensen, Joan M. *Army Surveillance in America, 1775–1980.* New Haven: Yale University Press, 1991.

Johnson, Benjamin Heber. "Conservation, Subsistence, and Class at the Birth of Superior National Forest." *Environmental History* 4 (January 1999): 80–99.

Johnson, Eric A., and Eric H. Monkkonen, eds. *The Civilization of Crime: Violence in Town and Country since the Middle Ages.* Urbana: University of Illinois Press, 1996.

Jones, David. *Crime, Protest, Community, and Police in Nineteenth-Century Britain.* London: Routledge and Keegan Paul, 1982.

Joseph, Gilbert. "On the Trail of Latin American Bandits: A Reexamination of Peasant Resistance." *Latin American Research Review* 25 (1990): 7–53.

Judd, Richard W. *Common Lands, Common People: The Origins of Conservation in Northern New England.* Cambridge: Harvard University Press, 1997.

Kaplan, Michael. "New York City Tavern Violence and the Creation of a Working-Class Male Identity." *Journal of the Early Republic* 15 (winter 1995): 591–617.

Keeley, Lawrence H. *War before Civilization: The Myth of the Peaceful Savage.* New York: Oxford University Press, 1996.

Keiter, Robert B., and Mark S. Boyce, eds. *The Greater Yellowstone Ecosystem: Redefining America's Wilderness Heritage.* New Haven: Yale University Press, 1991.

Keith, Herbert F. *Man of the Woods.* Syracuse: Syracuse University Press, 1972.

Keller, Robert H., and Michael F. Turek. *American Indians and National Parks.* Tucson: University of Arizona Press, 1998.

Kinney, J.P. *The Development of Forest Law in America.* New York: John Wiley and Sons, 1917.

Kirby, Jack Temple. *The Countercultural South.* Athens: University of Georgia Press, 1995.

Klyza, Christopher McGrory. *Who Controls Public Lands? Mining, Forestry, and Grazing Policies, 1870–1990.* Chapel Hill: University of North Carolina Press, 1996.

Knack, Martha, and Alice Littlefield, eds. *Native Americans and Wage Labor: Ethnohistorical Approaches.* Norman: University of Oklahoma Press, 1996.

Knight, Dennis H. *Mountains and Plains: The Ecology of Wyoming Landscapes.* New Haven: Yale University Press, 1994.

Knott, Catherine Henshaw. *Living with the Adirondack Forest: Local Perspectives on Land Use Conflicts.* Ithaca: Cornell University Press, 1998

Kolko, Gabriel. *The Triumph of Conservatism: A Reinterpretation of American History, 1900–1916.* New York: Free Press, 1963.

Kudish, Michael. *Adirondack Upland Flora: An Ecological Perspective.* Saranac, N.Y.: Chauncy Press, 1992.

Kulikoff, Allan. *The Agrarian Origins of American Capitalism.* Charlottesville: University Press of Virginia, 1992.

Langford, Nathaniel Pitt. *The Discovery of Yellowstone Park: Journal of the Washburn Expedition to the Yellowstone and Firehole Rivers in the Year 1870.* 1905. Reprint, Lincoln: University of Nebraska Press, 1972.

Langston, Nancy. *Forest Dreams, Forest Nightmares: The Paradox of Old Growth in the Inland West.* Seattle: University of Washington Press, 1995.

Lears, T.J. Jackson. *No Place of Grace: Antimodernism and the Transformation of American Culture, 1880–1920.* New York: Pantheon, 1981.

Lewis, David Rich. *Neither Wolf nor Dog: American Indians, Environment, and Agrarian Change.* New York: Oxford University Press, 1994.

Limerick, Patricia Nelson. *Desert Passages: Encounters with the American Deserts.* Albuquerque: University of New Mexico Press, 1985.

Linebaugh, Peter. "Karl Marx, the Theft of Wood, and Working Class Composition: A Contribution to the Current Debate." *Crime and Social Justice* 6 (fall-winter 1976): 5–16.

Lowenthal, David. *George Perkins Marsh: Versatile Vermonter.* New York: Columbia University Press, 1958.

Lukas, J. Anthony. *Big Trouble: A Murder in a Small Western Town Sets Off a Struggle for the Soul of America.* New York: Simon and Schuster, 1997.

[Lundy, J.P.] *The Saranac Exiles; or, a Winter's Tale of the Adirondacks.* Philadelphia: n.p., 1880.

MacKenzie, John M. *The Empire of Nature: Hunting, Conservation and British Imperialism.* Manchester, U.K.: Manchester University Press, 1988.

McCann, James C. "The Plow and the Forest: Narratives of Deforestation in Ethiopia, 1840–1992." *Environmental History* 2 (April 1997): 138–59.

McClelland, Linda Flint. *Building the National Parks: Historic Landscape Design and Construction.* Baltimore: Johns Hopkins University Press, 1998.

McEvoy, Arthur F. *The Fisherman's Problem: Ecology and the Law in the California Fisheries, 1850–1980.* New York: Cambridge University Press, 1986.

———. "Toward an Interactive Theory of Nature and Culture: Ecology, Production, and Cognition in the California Fishing Industry." In *The Ends of the Earth: Perspectives on Modern Environmental History,* ed. Donald Worster. New York: Cambridge University Press, 1988.

McGinnis, Dale K., and Floyd W. Sharrock, *The Crow People*. Phoenix: Indian Tribal Series, 1972.

McMartin, Barbara. *The Great Forest of the Adirondacks*. Utica, N.Y.: North Country Books, 1994.

Manners, Robert A. *An Ethnological Report on the Hualapai (Walapai) Indians of Arizona*. New York: Garland, 1974.

Manning, Roger B. *Hunters and Poachers: A Social and Cultural History of Unlawful Hunting in England, 1485–1640*. Oxford: Clarendon Press, 1993.

————. "Unlawful Hunting in England, 1500–1640." *Forest and Conservation History* 38 (January 1994): 16–23.

Marks, Stuart A. *Southern Hunting in Black and White: Nature, History, and Ritual in a Carolina Community*. Princeton: Princeton University Press, 1991.

Marsh, George Perkins. *The Earth as Modified by Human Action: A New Edition of Man and Nature*. Rev. ed. New York: Charles Scribner's Sons, 1874.

————. *Man and Nature*. Ed. David Lowenthal. 1864. Reprint, Cambridge: Harvard University Press, 1965.

Martin, John F. "The Organization of Land and Labor in a Marginal Economy." *Human Organization* 32 (summer 1973): 153–61.

————. "A Reconsideration of Havasupai Land Tenure." *Ethnology* 7 (October 1968): 450–60.

Martin, Mildred Albert. *The Martins of Gunbarrel*. Caldwell, Idaho: Caxton, 1959.

Marx, Leo. *The Machine in the Garden: Technology and the Pastoral Ideal in America*. New York: Oxford University Press, 1964.

Merriam, Clinton Hart. *The Mammals of the Adirondack Region*. New York: Henry Holt, 1886.

Merrill, David Shepard. "The Education of a Young Pioneer in the Northern Adirondacks in Franklin and Clinton Counties after the Civil War." *New York History* 39 (July 1958): 238–54.

Milstein, Michael. "The Quiet Kill." *National Parks* 63 (May-June 1989): 21.

Morehouse, Barbara J. *A Place Called Grand Canyon: Contested Geographies*. Tucson: University of Arizona Press, 1996.

Morgan, Dale L., ed. "Washakie and the Shoshoni: A Selection of Documents from the Records of the Utah Superintendency of Indian Affairs." *Annals of Wyoming* 29 (April 1957) and 29 (October 1957).

Muir, John. *Our National Parks*. Boston: Houghton Mifflin, 1901.

Mumey, Nolie. *Rocky Mountain Dick: Stories of His Adventures in Capturing Wild Animals*. Denver: Range Press, 1953.

Mumford, Lewis. *The Brown Decades: A Study of the Arts in America, 1865–1895*. New York: Dover, 1955.

Munsche, P. B. "The Gamekeeper and English Rural Society, 1660–1830." *Journal of British Studies* 20 (spring 1981): 82–105.

Murphy, Robert F., and Yolanda Murphy. "Northern Shoshone and Bannock." In *Handbook of North American Indians: Great Basin*, ed. Warren L. D'Azevedo. Vol. 11. Washington, D.C.: Smithsonian Institution Press, 1986.

Murray, Martin J. " 'Burning the Wheat Stacks': Land Clearances and Agrarian Unrest along the Northern Middelburg Frontier, c. 1918–1926." *Journal of Southern African Studies* 15 (October 1988): 74–95.

Murray, William. *Adventures in the Wilderness; or, Camp-Life in the Adirondacks.* Boston: Fields, Osgood, 1869.

Nash, Roderick. "The Value of Wilderness." *Environmental Review* 3 (1977): 14–25.

———. *Wilderness and the American Mind.* 3rd ed. New Haven: Yale University Press, 1982.

Northrup, A. Judd. *Camps and Tramps in the Adirondacks, and Grayling Fishing in Northern Michigan: A Record of Summer Vacations in the Wilderness.* Syracuse: Davis, Bardeen, 1880.

Novak, Barbara. *Nature and Culture: American Landscape and Painting, 1825–1875.* New York: Oxford University Press, 1980.

Novak, William. *The People's Welfare: Law and Regulation in Nineteenth-Century America.* Chapel Hill: University of North Carolina Press, 1996.

Nudds, Thomas. "Retroductive Logic in Retrospect: The Ecological Effects of Meningeal Worms." *Journal of Wildlife Management* 54 (July 1990): 396–402.

Oelschlaeger, Max. *The Idea of Wilderness: From Prehistory to the Age of Ecology.* New Haven: Yale University Press, 1991.

The Opening of the Adirondacks. New York: Hurd and Houghton, 1865.

Parsons, Willard. *Middle Rockies and Yellowstone.* Dubuque, Iowa: Kendall-Hunt, 1978.

Paterek, Josephine. *Encyclopedia of American Indian Costume.* New York: W. W. Norton, 1994.

Peck, Gunther. "Manly Gambles: The Politics of Risk on the Comstock Lode, 1860–1880." *Journal of Social History* 26 (summer 1993): 701–23.

Peluso, Nancy. *Rich Forests, Poor People: Resource Control and Resistance in Java.* Berkeley and Los Angeles: University of California Press, 1992.

Pinchot, Gifford. *The Adirondack Spruce: A Study of the Forest in Ne-Ha-Sa-Ne Park.* New York: Critic Co., 1898.

———. *Breaking New Ground.* New York: Harcourt, Brace, Jovanovich, 1947.

———. *The Fight for Conservation.* New York: Doubleday, Page, 1910.

Pisani, Donald J. "Forests and Conservation, 1865–1890." *Journal of American History* 72 (September 1985): 340–59.

Powell, John Wesley. *Report on the Lands of the Arid Region of the United States.* 1878. Reprint, Cambridge: Harvard University Press, 1962.

Pyne, Stephen J. *America's Fires: Management on Wildlands and Forests.* Durham, N.C.: Forest History Society, 1997.

———. *Fire in America: A Cultural History of Wildland and Rural Fire.* Princeton: Princeton University Press, 1982.

———. "Flame and Fortune." *Forest History Today* (1996): 8–10.

Rangarajan, Mahesh. *Fencing the Forest: Conservation and Ecological Change in India's Central Provinces, 1860–1914.* Delhi: Oxford University Press, 1996.

Recknagel, A. B. *The Forests of New York State.* New York: Macmillan, 1923.

Reiger, John F. *American Sportsmen and the Origins of Conservation.* Rev. ed. Norman: University of Oklahoma Press, 1986.

Remington, Frederic. *Pony Tracks.* 1895. Reprint, Norman: University of Oklahoma Press, 1961.

Report of Kaibab Investigative Committee. N.p., 1931.

Richards, Mary B. *Camping Out in the Yellowstone.* Salem, Mass.: Newcomb and Gauss, 1910.

Robbins, William G. *American Forestry: A History of National, State, and Private Cooperation.* Lincoln: University of Nebraska Press, 1985.

Robtoy, Hilda, Dee Brightstar, Tom Obomsawin, and John Moody. "The Abenaki and the Northern Forest." In *The Future of the Northern Forest,* ed. Christopher McGrory Klyza and Stephen C. Trombulak. Hanover, N.H.: University Press of New England, 1994.

Rodgers, Andrew Denny, III. *Bernhard Eduard Fernow: A Story of North American Forestry.* Durham, N.C.: Forest History Society, 1991.

Rodgers, Daniel T. *The Work Ethic in Industrial America, 1850–1920.* Chicago: University of Chicago Press, 1978.

Romme, William H., and Don G. Despain. "The Yellowstone Fires." *Scientific American* 261 (November 1989): 37–46.

Roosevelt, Theodore, and George Bird Grinnell, eds. *Hunting in Many Lands: The Book of the Boone and Crockett Club.* New York: Forest and Stream Publishing, 1895.

Ross, Andrew. *The Chicago Gangster Theory of Life: Nature's Debt to Society.* New York: Verso, 1994.

Rothenberg, Winifred Barr. *From Market-Places to a Market Economy: The Transformation of Rural Massachusetts, 1750–1850.* Chicago: University of Chicago Press, 1992.

Rotundo, E. Anthony. *American Manhood: Transformations in Masculinity from the Revolution to the Modern Era.* New York: Basic Books, 1993.

Runte, Alfred. *National Parks: The American Experience.* 2nd ed. Lincoln: University of Nebraska Press, 1987.

Saberwal, Vasant K. "Science and the Desiccationist Discourse of the Twentieth Century." *Environment and History* 4 (October 1998): 309–43.

Sahlins, Peter. *Forest Rites: The War of the Demoiselles in Nineteenth-Century France.* Cambridge: Harvard University Press, 1994.

Saylor, David. *Jackson Hole, Wyoming.* Norman: University of Oklahoma Press, 1970.

Schama, Simon. *Landscape and Memory.* New York: Vintage, 1995.

Schotzka, P.P. *American Forests.* Minneapolis, 1887.

Schullery, Paul. *Yellowstone's Ski Pioneers: Peril and Heroism on the Winter Trail.* Worland, Wyo.: High Plains Publishing, 1995.

Schulte, Regina. *The Village in Court: Arson, Infanticide, and Poaching in the Court Records of Upper Bavaria, 1848–1910.* Trans. Barrie Selman. New York: Cambridge University Press, 1994.

Schwartz, Douglas W. *On the Edge of Splendor: Exploring Grand Canyon's Human Past.* Santa Fe: School of American Research, 1988.

Scott, James. *Domination and the Arts of Resistance: Hidden Transcripts.* New Haven: Yale University Press, 1990.

———. *Seeing Like a State: How Certain Schemes to Improve the Human Condition Have Failed.* New Haven: Yale University Press, 1998.

———. *Weapons of the Weak: Everyday Forms of Peasant Resistance.* New Haven: Yale University Press, 1985.

Service, Elman. "Recent Observations on Havasupai Land Tenure." *Southwestern Journal of Anthropology* 3 (winter 1947): 360–66.

Sheldon, Charles. *The Wilderness of the Southwest: Charles Sheldon's Quest for Desert Bighorn Sheep and Adventures with the Havasupai and Seri Indians.* Ed. Neil B. Carmony and David E. Brown. 1979. Reprint, Salt Lake City: University of Utah Press, 1993.

Sheridan, Thomas E. *Arizona: A History.* Tucson: University of Arizona Press, 1995.

Sinyella, Juan. "Havasupai Traditions," ed. Donald Hughes. *Southwest Folklore* 1 (spring 1977): 35–52.

Sivaramakrishnan, K. "Colonialism and Forestry in India: Imagining the Past in Present Politics." *Comparative Studies in Society and History* 37 (January 1995): 3–40.

———. "The Politics of Fire and Forest Regeneration in Colonial Bengal." *Environment and History* 2 (1996): 145–94.

Skowronek, Stephen. *Building a New American State: The Expansion of National Administrative Capacities, 1877–1920.* New York: Cambridge University Press, 1982.

Slatta, Richard W., ed. *Bandidos: The Varieties of Latin American Banditry.* New York: Greenwood, 1987.

Slotkin, Richard. *The Fatal Environment: The Myth of the Frontier in the Age of Industrialization, 1800–1890.* New York: Atheneum, 1985.

Smith, Bill. *Tales from the Featherbed: Adirondack Stories and Songs.* Greenfield Center, N.Y.: Bowman Books, 1994.

Smith, Frank E. *The Politics of Conservation.* New York: Pantheon, 1966.

Smith, Henry Nash. *Virgin Land: The American West as Symbol and Myth.* Cambridge: Harvard University Press, 1950.

Smithson, Carma Lee, and Robert C. Euler. *Havasupai Legends: Religion and Mythology of the Havasupai Indians of the Grand Canyon.* Salt Lake: University of Utah Press, 1994.

Snow, Dean R. "Eastern Abenaki." In *The Handbook of North American Indians: Northeast,* ed. William Sturtevant. Vol. 15. Washington, D.C.: Smithsonian Institution Press, 1978.

Spence, Mark. "Crown of the Continent, Backbone of the World: The American Wilderness Ideal and Blackfeet Exclusion from Glacier National Park." *Environmental History* 1 (July 1996): 29–49.

———. *Dispossessing the Wilderness: Indian Removal and the Making of the National Parks.* New York: Oxford University Press, 1999.

———. "Dispossessing the Wilderness: Yosemite Indians and the National Park Ideal, 1864–1930." *Pacific Historical Review* 65 (February 1996): 27–59.

Spier, Leslie. "Havasupai Ethnography." *Anthropological Papers of the American Museum of Natural History* 29 (1928): 87–408.

Steen, Harold K. *The Beginning of the National Forest System.* Washington, D.C.: GPO, 1991.

———. *Origins of the National Forests: A Centennial Symposium.* Durham, N.C.: Forest History Society, 1992.

Steward, Julian H. *Basin-Plateau Aboriginal Sociopolitical Groups.* 1938. Reprint, Salt Lake City: University of Utah Press, 1970.

Stewart, Elinore Pruitt. *Letters on an Elk Hunt: By a Woman Homesteader.* Boston: Houghton Mifflin, 1915.

Stoddard, Seneca Ray. *The Adirondacks: Illustrated.* Albany: Weed, Parsons, 1874.

———. *The Adirondacks: Illustrated.* 19th ed. Glen Falls, N.Y.: n.p., 1889.

———. *The Adirondacks: Illustrated.* 23rd. ed. Glen Falls, N.Y.: n.p., 1898.

———. *Old Times in the Adirondacks: The Narrative of a Trip into the Wilderness in 1873.* Burlington, Vt.: George Little Press, 1971.

Stone, Michael L. "Organized Poaching in Kitui District: A Failure in District Authority, 1900–1960." *International Journal of African Historical Studies* 5 (1972): 436–52.

Street, Alfred B. *Woods and Waters; or, the Saranacs and Racket Lake.* New York: M. Doolady, 1860.

Strong, Douglas H. *Dreamers and Defenders: American Conservationists.* Lincoln: University of Nebraska Press, 1988.

———. "The Man Who 'Owned' Grand Canyon." *American West* 6 (September 1969): 33–40.

Strong, W. E. *A Trip to the Yellowstone National Park.* Washington, D.C.: n.p., 1876.

Stroud, Richard, ed. *National Leaders of American Conservation.* Washington, D.C.: Smithsonian Institution Press, 1985.

Suprenant, Neil. *Brandon: Boomtown to Nature Preserve.* Paul Smith's, N.Y.: St. Regis Press, 1982.

Swendsen, David H. *Badge in the Wilderness: My Thirty Dangerous Years Combating Wildlife Violators.* Harrisburg, Penn.: Stackpole Books, 1985.

Sylvester, Nathaniel Bartlett. *Historical Sketches of Northern New York and the Adirondack Wilderness.* Troy, N.Y.: William H. Young, 1877.

Taylor, Alan. "The Great Change Begins: Settling the Forest of Central New York." *New York History* 76 (July 1995): 265–90.

———. "Unnatural Inequalities: Social and Environmental Histories." *Environmental History* 1 (October 1996): 6–19.

Taylor, Dale L. "Forest Fires in Yellowstone National Park." *Journal of Forest History* 18 (July 1974): 69.

Terrie, Philip. *Contested Terrain: A New History of Nature and People in the Adirondacks.* Blue Mountain Lake, N.Y.: Adirondack Museum and Syracuse University Press, 1997.

———. "'One Grand Unbroken Domain': Ambiguities and Lessons in the Origins of the Adirondack Park." *Hudson Valley Regional Review* 6 (March 1989): 10–17.

——. *Wildlife and Wilderness: A History of Adirondack Mammals.* Fleischmanns, N.Y.: Purple Mountain Press, 1993.

Thomas, Keith. *Man and the Natural World: Changing Attitudes in England, 1500–1800.* New York: Oxford University Press, 1983.

Thompson, E. P. *Customs in Common: Studies in Traditional Popular Culture.* New York: New Press, 1993.

——. *The Making of the English Working Class.* New York: Pantheon, 1963.

——. *Whigs and Hunters: The Origins of the Black Act.* New York: Pantheon, 1975.

Tober, James A. *Who Owns the Wildlife? The Political Economy of Conservation in Nineteenth-Century America.* Westport, Conn.: Greenwood Press, 1981.

Trautmann, Frederic, trans. and ed. "Germans at the Grand Canyon: The Memoirs of Paul Lindau, 1883." *Journal of Arizona History* 26 (winter 1985): 375–94.

Tresidder, Dennis. "History of Game Management, Part II." *Arizona Wildlife Views* (April 1995): 6–7.

Trigger, Bruce. *The Children of Aataentsic: A History of the Huron People to 1660.* Montreal: McGill-Queen's University Press, 1976.

Turrill, Gardner Stilson. *A Tale of the Yellowstone; or, in a Wagon through Western Wyoming and Wonderland.* Jefferson, Iowa: G. S. Turrill Publishing, 1901.

Utley, Robert M. *Frontier Regulars: The United States Army and the Indian, 1866–1891.* New York: Macmillan, 1973.

——. *The Indian Frontier of the American West, 1846–1890.* Albuquerque: University of New Mexico Press, 1984.

Van Valkenburgh, Norman J. *The Adirondack Forest Preserve: A Narrative of the Evolution of the Adirondack Forest Preserve of New York State.* Blue Mountain Lake, N.Y.: Adirondack Museum, 1979.

——. *Land Acquisition for New York State: An Historical Perspective.* Arkville, N.Y.: Catskill Center for Conservation and Development, 1985.

Van Young, Eric. "To See Someone Not Seeing: Historical Studies of Peasants and Politics in Mexico." *Mexican Studies/Estudios Mexicanos* 6 (1990): 133–59.

Walcott, Charles D. *The United States Forest Reserves.* New York: D. Appleton, 1898.

Waller, Altina. *Feud: Hatfields, McCoys, and Social Change in Appalachia, 1860–1900.* Chapel Hill: University of North Carolina Press, 1988.

Wallmo, Olof C. *Mule and Black-Tailed Deer of North America.* Lincoln: University of Nebraska Press, 1981.

Walsh, E. G., ed. *The Poacher's Companion.* Suffolk, U.K.: Boydell Press, 1982.

Warren, Louis. *The Hunter's Game: Poachers and Conservationists in Twentieth-Century America.* New Haven: Yale University Press, 1997.

Watson, Harry L. " 'The Common Rights of Mankind': Subsistence, Shad, and Commerce in the Early Republican South." *Journal of American History* (June 1996): 13–43.

Way, Thomas E. *Destination: Grand Canyon.* Phoenix: Golden West Publishers, 1990.

Weber, Eugen. *Peasants into Frenchmen: The Modernization of Rural France.* Stanford: Stanford University Press, 1976.

Weber, Steven A., and P. David Seaman, eds. *Havasupai Habitat: A. F. Whiting's Ethnography of a Traditional Indian Culture.* Tucson: University of Arizona Press, 1985.

Weibe, Robert H. *The Search for Order, 1877–1920.* New York: Hill and Wang, 1967.

Weigle, Marta. "From Desert to Disney World: The Santa Fe Railway and the Fred Harvey Company Display the Indian Southwest." *Journal of Anthropological Research* 45 (spring 1989): 115–37.

West, Elliot. *The Way to the West: Essays on the Central Plains.* Albuquerque: University of New Mexico Press, 1995.

West, Patrick C., and Steven R. Brechin. *Resident Peoples and National Parks: Social Dilemmas and Strategies in International Conservation.* Tucson: University of Arizona Press, 1991.

Whipple, Gurth. *Fifty Years of Conservation in New York State, 1885–1935.* Albany: James B. Lyon, 1935.

White, Richard. "American Environmental History: The Development of a New Historical Field." *Pacific Historical Review* 54 (August 1985): 297–335.

———. *"It's Your Misfortune and None of My Own": A History of the American West.* Norman: University of Oklahoma Press, 1991.

———. *The Organic Machine.* New York: Hill and Wang, 1995.

———. *The Roots of Dependency: Subsistence, Environment, and Social Change among the Choctaws, Pawnees, and Navajos.* Lincoln: University of Nebraska Press, 1983.

Whithorn, Bill, and Doris Whithorn. *Photohistory of Gardiner, Jardine, Crevasse.* Livingston, Mont.: Park County News, 1972.

Whittlesey, Lee. " 'Everyone Can Understand a Picture': Photographers and the Promotion of Early Yellowstone." *Montana* 49 (summer 1999): 2–13.

Wild, Peter. *Pioneer Conservationists of Eastern America.* Missoula, Mont.: Mountain Press, 1986.

———. *Pioneer Conservationists of Western America.* Missoula, Mont.: Mountain Press, 1979.

Williams, Michael. *Americans and Their Forests: A Historical Geography.* New York: Cambridge University Press, 1989.

Williams, Raymond. *Problems in Materialism and Culture.* London: NLB, 1980.

Wingate, George W. *Through the Yellowstone Park on Horseback.* New York: Orange Judd, 1886.

Worster, Donald, ed. *American Environmentalism: The Formative Period, 1860–1915.* New York: John Wiley and Sons, 1973.

———. *Dust Bowl: The Southern Plains in the 1930's.* New York: Oxford University Press, 1979.

———. *Nature's Economy: A History of Ecological Ideas.* 2nd ed. New York: Cambridge University Press, 1994.

———. *The Wealth of Nature: Environmental History and the Ecological Imagination.* New York: Oxford University Press, 1993.

Index

Abenaki tribe, 20
Adams, Oscar, 136, 249n67
Adirondackers, 17–23; access to resources, 33, 50, 52, 67; arson by, 73, 76, 77; disregard of regulations, 48–49; divisions among, 72; exclusion from decision-making, 265n12; farmers, 14, 21; feuds among, 213n32; foresters, 36; on game laws, 58–66; homesteads of, 33, 66; illiteracy of, 205n9; land use practices of, 47; marriage with Indians, 21; nonmarket ideology of, 53–54; occupations of, 21, 27–28; opposition to private parks, 41–46, 47, 67; opposition to state control, 227n69; protection of deer, 60, 223n31; relations with Forest Commission, 19, 57–58; right to subsistence, 52–53, 64; support for conservation, 47; surveillance of foresters, 37–38; use of natural resources, 50; view of timber cutting, 51–54, 65; violation of forest code, 66, 76–78; violation of game laws, 63–64, 72–73; wage labor by, 27–28, 67; women, 21, 27. *See also* Rural society
Adirondack Game and Fish Protective Association, 63
Adirondack Guides' Association (AGA), 68–71; and game laws, 70–71; on hounding, 225n56; membership of, 69–70, 225n48
Adirondack League Club (ALC), 39, 47, 136, 209n14; court cases against, 42; guides of, 40–41, 218n28; vandalism against, 218n31
Adirondack News: on poaching, 62; on timber industry, 56
Adirondack Park: acreage of, 215n1; creation of, 16–17, 168, 209n14; destruction of property markers, 32, 215n2; environmental regulations in, 30, 224n43, fig. 7; fishing in, 17, 32, 59–60; hounding in, 17; land classification in, 26; local use of, 32; map of, 10; mapping of, 31–32; planning for, 48. *See also* New York Forest Preserve
Adirondacks: arson in, 2, 72–73, 76, 218n31; beaver population of, 71; common rights ideology in, 23–24, 213n31; community solidarity in, 37; conservation program in, 4, 6, 29, 38, 47, 82; crops of, 22–23, 212n29; deer population of, 26, 36–37; deforestation of, 14, 25; depopulation of, 18, 210n20; dialect of, 224n39; early settlers of, 20–21; economic life of, 21; in eighteenth century, 20; elk population of, 72, 226n64; farmers of, 14, 21; feuds in, 213n32; fire towers in,

293

Text: Sabon
Display: Sabon
Composition: Impressions Book and Journal Services, Inc.
Printing and binding: Edwards Brothers, Inc.
Maps: Bill Nelson
Index: Roberta Engleman